Contents

Acknowledgements

Different versions of these materials were tried out with students in five countries. The book is in its present form partly as a result of the useful reports and in many cases the very detailed comments received while the work was being developed. I would like to thank the following:

Brazil	Vera Regina de A Couto and staff	Cultura Inglesa, Rio
	Rosa Lenzuén	
	Louise Towersey	Cultura Inglesa, Curitiba
	Michael Watkins	
Germany	Werner Kieweg	University of Munich
	Norman Lewis	Gymnasium Wildeshausen
	Robert Nowacek	Volkshochschule, Kaufbeuren
Greece	Sandra Klapsis	Homer Association, Athens
	Joanna Malliou	
	George Rigas	The Moraïtis School, Athens
Italy	Paola Giovamma Ottolino	Liceo Linguistico, A. Manzoni, Milano
United Kingdom	Sue Boardman	Bell School, Saffron Walden
	Pat Lodge	
	Alan Fortune	Ealing College of Higher Education
	Mary Stephens	Eurocentre, Bournemouth
	M. Milmo	Eurocentre, Lee Green
	Steve Moore	
	Jennifer Swift	
	Ann Timson	
	Josephine von Waskowski	

I would also like to thank:

- Donald Adamson and Neville Grant for their detailed and stimulating commentaries and particularly Roy Kingsbury for his comprehensive report and notes on exercise-types.

- my personal assistant, Penelope Parfitt, and my wife, Julia, for reading and commenting on the work at every stage of its development.

I am especially grateful to my publishers and their representatives for administering and monitoring the trialling of the manuscript in various locations round the world and for exercising such care and skill to see the work through to publication.

To the student

Why do we learn grammar?

There is no point in learning grammar for the sake of learning grammar. Grammar is the support system of communication and we learn it to communicate better. Grammar explains the *why* and *how* of language. We learn it because we just can't do without it.

Who is this book for and what does it cover?

This book deals entirely with English as a foreign language (EFL). It is for intermediate students who are working with a teacher or working on their own. It covers every important area of the English language. If you look at the Contents pages, you will find sixteen major areas which form the basis of English grammar. This book is based on the *Longman English Grammar* and the grammatical information in it is all drawn from this work. *Longman English Grammar Practice* has been designed to stand on its own. Students who require further grammatical information can refer to the *Longman English Grammar*.

How the material is organized

Longman English Grammar Practice is a practice book. It is intended to support (not replace) the material in language courses and is organized for this purpose:

- The material is laid out on facing pages.
- Each set of facing pages deals with a major point of grammar.
- This major point is divided into small, manageable amounts of information. Clear notes explain the points to be practised, followed by an exercise on just those points.
- The last exercise is in context, usually an entertaining story with a cartoon illustration. It sums up all you have learnt in the exercises you have just done and shows you how the language works. It is a 'reward' for the hard work you have just been doing!

Cross references

If you see e.g. [> 7.3A] in the notes, it means that a similar point is discussed in some other part of the book. Follow up the reference for parallel practice or information if you want to. If you see e.g. [> LEG 4.30] at the top of the notes, it means that the point is dealt with in the *Longman English Grammar*. Follow up the reference if you want 'the whole story'.

How to work

> YOU DON'T HAVE TO WORK THROUGH THIS BOOK FROM START TO FINISH!
> It is not arranged in order of increasing difficulty.
>
> Select a chapter or part of a chapter which you want to study. Do this by referring to the Contents pages or the Index. Usually, this will be a topic you have been dealing with in your language course. Then:
>
> 1 Read the notes carefully (called **Study**). Notes and exercises are marked like this:
>   ⊡ = Elementary   ⊡⊡ = Intermediate (most exercises)   ⊡⊡⊡ = Advanced
>   You will sometimes find that you know some, but not all, of the points in an exercise marked ⊡⊡.
>
> 2 Do the exercises (called **Write**). Always leave the story till last (called **Context**).
>
> 3 Check your answers with your teacher.
>
> 4 If you have made mistakes, study the notes again until you have understood where you went wrong and why.

1 The sentence

1.1 Sentence word order

1.1A The basic word order of an English sentence [> LEG 1.3]

Study:
★

The meaning of an English sentence depends on the word order.

1 We put the subject before the verb and the object after the verb:
The cook | burnt | the dinner.

2 Adverbials (*How?*, *Where?*, *When?*) usually come after the verb or after the object:
He read the note **quickly**. (*How?*) *I waited* **at the corner** (*Where?*) **till 11.30**. (*When?*)

3 The basic word order of a sentence that is not a question or a command is usually:

subject	verb	object	adverbials		
			How?	*Where?*	*When?*
I	*bought*	*a hat*			*yesterday.*
The children	*have gone*			*home.*	
We	*ate*	*our meal*	*in silence.*		

4 We also put the time reference at the beginning: **Yesterday** *I bought a hat.* [> 7.2A]

Write 1:

a Rewrite the sentences that don't make sense.

b Mark all the sentences in the exercise **S V O** to show **S**ubject, **V**erb, **O**bject.

1 Has set John Bailey a new high-jump record. *(S) John Bailey (V) has set (O) a new high-jump recor*

2 The passport examined the passport officer. ....

3 These biscuits don't like the dogs. ....

4 The shop assistant is wrapping the parcel. ....

5 Have seen the visitors the new buildings. ....

6 My father didn't wash the dishes. ....

7 The pipe is going to fix the plumber. ....

8 Will the goalkeeper catch the ball? ....

9 Has the meal enjoyed the guest? ....

10 Can't play John the game. ....

Write 2:

a Arrange these words in the right order. Use a capital letter to begin each sentence.

b Mark each rewritten sentence **S V O M P T** to show:
Subject, **V**erb, **O**bject, **M**anner (*How?*), **P**lace (*Where?*), **T**ime (*When?*).

1 till 11 o'clock this morning | slept | the children *(S) The children (V) slept (T) till 11 o'clock this morni*

2 the papers | into the bin | he threw ....

3 I don't speak | well | English ....

4 hides | Mrs Jones | her money | under the bed ....

5 carefully | this suitcase | you didn't pack ....

6 on this shelf | I left | this morning | some money ....

7 from the bank | a loan | you'll have to get ....

8 the phone | in the middle of the night | woke me up ....

9 in the park | you shouldn't walk | at night ....

10 your food | you should eat | slowly ....

11 my term | begins | in October ....

12 your article | I | quickly | last night | in bed | read ....

1.1B The forms of a sentence [> LEG 1.2]

Study:
★★

1 A sentence can take any one of four forms:
  – **a statement:** *The shops close/don't close at 7 tonight.*
  – **a question:** *Do the shops close at 7 tonight?*
  – **a command:** *Shut the door./Don't shut the door.*
  – **an exclamation:** *What a slow train this is!*

2 When we write a sentence, we must begin with a capital letter and end with a full stop (.), a question mark (?), or an exclamation mark (!).
If there are quotation marks ('...') or ("...") around spoken words in a sentence, we put other punctuation marks 'inside' them:
  'I'm tired,' she said. (Not * *'I'm tired', she said.**) [> 15.1A-B]

Write:
a Arrange these groups of words in the right order. Add (.), (?) or (!).
b Describe each sentence as a statement, question, command or exclamation: S, Q, C or E.

1 the coffee | don't spill ...... *Don't spill the coffee.* .... (*C*)
2 today's papers | have you seen .... (   )
3 to meet you | how nice .... (   )
4 my umbrella | where did you put .... (   )
5 arrived | the train | fifteen minutes late .... (   )
6 on time | the plane | won't arrive .... (   )
7 this electricity bill | I can't pay .... (   )
8 for me | please | open the door .... (   )
9 the nearest hotel | where's | he asked .... (   )
10 the bill | can't pay | I | he cried .... (   )

1.1C Context

Write: Read this story and arrange the words in each sentence in the right order.
Add capital letters and (,), (.), (!) or (?) in the right places.

A QUIET SORT OF PLACE!
1 my car | I parked | in the centre of the village *I parked my car in the centre of the village.*
2 near a bus stop | an old man | I saw ....
3 'beautiful village | what a' | I exclaimed ....
4 'live here | how many people' ....
5 'seventeen people | there are' | the old man said ....
6 'here | have you lived | how long' ....
7 'all my life | I have lived here' ....
8 'isn't it | it's a quiet sort of place' ....
9 'here | a quiet life | we live ....
10 a cinema | we don't have | or a theatre ....
11 our school | five years ago | was closed ....
12 only one shop | we have ....
13 calls | a bus | once a day ....
14 here | in 55 B.C. | came | the Romans ....
15 since then | has happened | nothing' ....

1.2 The simple sentence: verbs with and without objects

1.2A What is a complete sentence? [> LEG 1.2]

Study:
★★

1 When we speak, we often say things like *All right! Good! Want any help?*
These are 'complete units of meaning', but they are not real sentences.

2 **A simple sentence** is a complete unit of meaning which contains a subject and a verb,
followed, if necessary, by other words which make up the meaning. So:
Made in Germany is correct English but it is not a sentence because it doesn't have a subject.
My car was made in Germany. is a complete sentence with a subject and verb.
We can't say e.g. **Is tired** because we need a subject [> 4.1A, 4.3A]: *He is tired.*

3 The subject may be 'hidden': *Open the door.* really means **You** *open the door.* [> 9.10B]

Write: Put a tick (✓) beside real sentences.

1 Made in Germany. __
2 This car was made in Germany. ✓
3 To write a letter. __
4 Standing in the rain. __
5 I want to write a letter. __
6 Is tall. __
7 Do you like? __
8 The train has arrived. __
9 Have finished my work. __
10 You should listen. __

11 Sit down please. __
12 You can't park here. __
13 Don't interrupt. __
14 I understand. __
15 She doesn't like me. __
16 Under the water. __
17 Ate. __
18 A bottle of ink. __
19 He's a doctor. __
20 What happened? __

1.2B Verbs with and without objects [> LEG 1.4, 1.9, 1.10, 1.12, App 1]

Study:
★★

1 We always have to use an object after some verbs: e.g. *beat, contain, enjoy, hit, need.*
We call these **transitive verbs**. We have to say:
Arsenal beat Liverpool. But we can't say **Arsenal beat.**

2 Some verbs never take an object: e.g. *ache, arrive, come, faint, go, sit down, sleep, snow.*
We call these **intransitive verbs**. We have to say:
We arrived at 11. But we can't say **We arrived the station at 11.**

3 Some verbs can be used **transitively** or **intransitively**: e.g. *begin, drop, hurt, open, ring, win.*
We can say: *Arsenal won the match.* (**transitive**) or *Arsenal won.* (**intransitive**)

Write: Put an object (a pronoun or a noun) after these verbs only where possible.

1 The box contains ....*pencils*.............................
2 The train has arrived ....
3 The phone rang ....
4 Someone is ringing ....
5 You need ....
6 We sat down ....
7 Don't hit ....
8 Did you beat .... ?
9 Who opened .... ?

10 The door opened ....
11 This is a game no one can win ....
12 The concert began .... at 7.30.
13 I began ....
14 It's snowing ....
15 Quick! She's fainted ....
16 Did you enjoy .... ?
17 My head aches ....
18 My foot hurts ....

1.2C Sentences with linking verbs like 'be' and 'seem' [> LEG 1.9, 1.11, 10.23-26]

Study:
★★

> 1 Verbs like *be* [> 10.1-3] and *seem* [> 10.4] are 'linking verbs'. They cannot have an object.
> The word we use after *be*, etc. tells us something about the subject. In grammar, we call this a **complement** because it 'completes' the sentence by telling us about the subject.
> In *He is ill. She seems tired.* etc. the words *ill* and *tired* tell us about *he* and *she*.
>
> 2 A complement may be:
> - **an adjective:**   *Frank is **clever.***
> - **a noun:**   *Frank is **an architect.***
> - **an adjective + noun:**   *Frank is **a clever architect.***
> - **a pronoun:**   *This book is **mine.***
> - **an adverb of place or time:**   *The meeting is **here.** The meeting is **at 2.30.***
> - **a prepositional phrase:**   *Alice is **like her father**.*

Write: **a** Complete these sentences using a different complement for each sentence.
         b Say whether you have used a noun, an adjective, an adjective + noun, etc.

1 My neighbour is very ......*tall. (adjective)*...
2 My neighbour is ....
3 This apple tastes ....
4 The children are ....
5 The meeting is ....
6 Whose is this? It's ....
7 John looks ....
8 That music sounds ....
9 Your mother seems ....
10 I want to be .... when I leave school. ....

1.2D Context

Write: Read this story and arrange the words in each sentence in the right order.
Add capital letters and (,), (.), (!) or (?) in the right places [> 1.1B].

SO PLEASE DON'T COMPLAIN!
1 the local school | attends | my son Tim ......*My son Tim attends the local school.*...............
2 to his school | my wife and I went | yesterday ....
3 we | to his teachers | spoke ....
4 Tim's school report | we collected ....
5 very good | wasn't | Tim's report ....
6 in every subject | were | his marks | low ....
7 was waiting anxiously for us | outside | Tim ....
8 'my report | how was' | eagerly | he asked ....
9 'very good | it wasn't' | I said ....
10 'you | harder | must try ....
11 seems | that boy Ogilvy | very clever ....
12 good marks | he got | in all subjects' ....
13 'clever parents | Ogilvy | has' | Tim said ....

5

1.3 The simple sentence: direct and indirect objects

1.3A Subject + verb + indirect object + direct object: 'Show me that photo'
[> LEG 1.13]

Study:
⊡

> **1** We can use two objects after verbs like *give* and *buy*.
> Instead of: **Give** the book **to me**, we can say: **Give me** the book.
> Instead of: **Buy** the book **for me**, we can say: **Buy me** the book.
>
> **2** Some verbs combine with TO: *bring, give, lend, pay, post, sell, send, show, tell, write*:
> *Bring that book* **to me**. → *Bring* **me** *that book*.
>
> **3** Other verbs combine with FOR: *buy, choose, cook, cut, do, fetch, find, get, make, order*:
> *Please order a meal* **for me**. → *Please order* **me** *a meal*.
>
> **4** We can put *it* and *them* after the verb: *Give* ***it*** *to me. Buy* ***them*** *for me. Do* ***it*** *for me.*
> With e.g. *give* and *buy*, we can say: *Give me* ***it***. *Buy me* ***them***. (But not **Do me it**)
> We say: *Give* ***it*** *to John. Buy* ***them*** *for John*. (Not **Give John it* *Buy John them**)

Write: You want people to do things for you. Write suitable polite requests using *it, them* or *one* [> 4.3B].

1 Where are my shoes? (find) Please *...find them for me. / Please find me them...*
2 John needs a new coat. (buy) Please ....
3 I can't reach that cup. (pass) Please ....
4 Ann wants to see our flat. (show) Please ....
5 I can't do the shopping. (do) Please ....
6 I'd like a copy of that book. (order) Please ....

1.3B Verb + object + 'to' + noun or pronoun: 'Explain it to me' [> LEG 1.12.1]

Study:
⊡⊡

> **1** There are some verbs like *explain* which do not behave in exactly the same way as *give*.
> For example, we can say: **Give** the book **to me**, or **Explain** the situation **to me**.
>   **Give me** the book. (but not **Explain me the situation.**)
>
> **2** We cannot use an indirect object (*me*) immediately after *explain*. We can only have:
> **verb + object + 'to'**: He **explained** the situation **to me**.
>   He **confessed** his crime **to the court**.
>
> **3** Other verbs like *explain* and *confess* are: *admit, announce, declare, demonstrate, describe, entrust, introduce, mention, propose, prove, repeat, report, say, suggest*.

Write: Complete these sentences giving the right order of the words in brackets.

1 You must declare (the Customs/this camera) ...*this camera to the Customs*...
2 Aren't you going to introduce (me/your friend)? ....
3 You can say (me/what you like) ....
4 Who suggested (this idea/you)? ....
5 He confessed (his crime/the police) ....
6 I have never admitted (anyone/this) ....
7 Can you describe (me/this man)? ....
8 Please don't mention (this/anyone) ....
9 I'm going to report (this/the headmaster) ....
10 I don't want you to repeat (what I told you/anyone) ....

1.3C The two meanings of 'for' [> LEG 1.13.3]

Study:
★★

> 1 We can use *for* after all verbs which have two objects [> 1.3A].
>
> 2 When we use *for* after verbs normally followed by *to* (*give, post, read, sell, show, tell*, etc.) it can mean 'instead of': *I'll post it for you.* (= to save you the trouble)
>
> 3 When we use *for* after verbs normally followed by *for* (*buy, choose, do, find, keep, order*, etc.) the meaning depends on the context. It can mean 'for someone's benefit':
> *Mother cooked a lovely meal for me.* (= for my benefit, for me to enjoy)
> It can mean 'on someone's behalf/instead of':
> *I'll cook the dinner for you.* (on your behalf/instead of you – to save you the trouble)

Write: Tick (✓) to show whether *for* means 'instead of you/me' or 'for your/my benefit'.

	'instead of'	'for your/my benefit'
1 I've cooked a meal for you and I hope you enjoy it.	__	✓
2 Let me cook the dinner for you this evening. – Thanks!	__	__
3 I've made this cake for you. Do you like it?	__	__
4 I'll post this letter for you, shall I?	__	__
5 I've bought this especially for you.	__	__
6 I've got some change. Let me pay the bill for you.	__	__
7 As you're busy, let me book a room for you.	__	__
8 I've saved some of this pudding for you.	__	__
9 I can't choose a tie myself. Please choose one for me.	__	__
10 My father has bought a wonderful present for me.	__	__

1.3D Context

Write: Put a tick (✓) where you think you can change the word order.

A CURE FOR HYSTERIA

When I was a girl, my parents sent me to a very strict school. They had to *buy an expensive uniform for me* [1] ✓ and *pay school fees for me* [2] __. Our headmistress, Miss Prim, never smiled. She *explained the school rules to us* [3] __ and expected us to obey them. 'I will never *say anything to you* [4] __ twice,' she used to say. We had to *write a letter to our parents* [5] __ once a week and *show it to Miss Prim* [6] __ before we sent it. I can still remember some of the school rules. We were not allowed to *lend anything to anyone* [7] __. We were not allowed to *give each other help* [8] __ with homework. We had to *report unusual situations to the headmistress* [9] __. One morning, during assembly, a girl fainted. The next morning, two more fainted. This continued to happen for several mornings. Mass hysteria had set in! But Miss Prim put an end to it. She *announced a new rule to us* [10] __: 'No girl will faint in College!' And after that, no one did!

No girl will faint in College!

1.4 The compound sentence

1.4A The form of a compound sentence [> LEG 1.17-20]

Study:
★★

1 When we join two or more simple sentences [> 1.2A], we make a **compound sentence**:
Tom phoned. He left a message. → *Tom phoned **and** left a message.*

2 The name we give to 'joining words' is **conjunctions**.
These are the conjunctions we use to make compound sentences:
and, and then, but, for, nor, or, so, yet;
either ... or; neither ... nor ...; not only ... but ... (also/as well/too).

3 We can use conjunctions to show, for example:
– **addition** (*and*):   *He washed the car **and** polished it.*
– **continuation** (*and then*): *He washed the car **and then** polished it.*
– **contrast** (*but, yet*):   *She sold her house, **but/yet** (she) can't help regretting it.*
– **choice** (*or*):   *You can park your car on the drive **or** on the road.*
– **result** (*so*):   *He couldn't find his pen, **so** he wrote in pencil.*
– **reason** (*for*):   *We rarely stay in hotels, **for** we can't afford it.*

4 We do not usually put a comma in front of *and*, but we often use one in front of other
conjunctions: *He washed the car **and** polished it.* (no comma before *and*)
Compare: *He washed the car, **but** didn't polish it.* (comma before *but*)

5 We keep to the basic word order in a compound sentence [> 1.1A, 1.2C]:
subject   verb   object   conjunction   subject   verb   complement
Jimmy   fell off   his bike,   but   (he)   was   unhurt.

6 When the subject is the same in all parts of the sentence, we do not usually repeat it:
same subject: *Tom phoned. He left a message.* → *Tom phoned **and** (he) **left** a message.*
different subjects: *Tom phoned. Frank answered.* → *Tom phoned **and Frank** answered.*

7 We usually repeat the subject after *so*: *He couldn't find his pen, **so he** wrote in pencil.*

8 We always have to repeat the subject after *for. For* is more usual in the written language and we
cannot use it to begin a sentence [compare > 1.9A]:
*We rarely stay at hotels, **for we** can't afford it.*

Write 1: **Compound sentences with the same subject**
Join these simple sentences to make compound sentences. Use the words in brackets.

1 I took the shoes back to the shop. I complained about them. (and)
.... *I took the shoes back to the shop and complained about them* ....

2 Your mother phoned this morning. She didn't leave a message. (but)
....

3 I can leave now. I can stay for another hour. (I can either ... or)
....

4 Jim built his own house. He designed it himself. (Jim not only ... but ... as well)
....

5 I don't know what happened to him. I don't care. (I neither ... nor)
....

6 My new assistant can type very well. He hasn't much experience with computers. (but)
....

Write 2: **Compound sentences with different subjects and with 'so/for'**
Join these simple sentences to make compound sentences. Use the words in brackets.

1 The taxi stopped at the station. Two men got out of it. (and)
The taxi stopped at the station and two men got out of it.

2 You can give me some advice. Your colleague can. (Either you ... or)
....

3 We got ready to get on the train. It didn't stop. (but)
....

4 No one was in when we called. We left a message. (so)
....

5 We didn't want to get home late after the film. We went straight back. (so)
....

6 The old lady was nervous. She wasn't used to strangers calling late at night. (for)
....

7 I've always wanted to live in the country. My parents prefer to live in town. (but)
....

8 The letter has been lost. The postman has delivered it to the wrong address. (or)
....

9 For a moment the top of the mountain was visible. A cloud covered it. (and then)
....

10 Jane was a successful career woman. Her mother wanted her to be a housewife. (yet)
....

1.4B Context

Write: Put a circle round the correct words in brackets.

(NOT SO) MERRY-GO-ROUND!

The customers at the funfair were leaving (¹and/but) the lights were going out. The last two people on dodgem cars paid (²and/so) left. The big wheel stopped (³for/and) the merry-go-round stopped (⁴as well/not only). The stalls closed down (⁵so/and) the stall-owners went home. At 2 a.m. four nightwatchmen walked round the funfair, (⁶but/so) there was no one to be seen. 'I'm fed up walking round,' one of them said, ('⁷yet/and) what can we do?' 'We can (⁸or/either) play cards (⁹either/or) sit and talk.' They were bored, (¹⁰so/for) there was nothing to do on this quiet warm night. 'We can have a ride on the merry-go-round!' one of them cried. 'That'll be fun!' Three of them jumped on merry-go-round horses (¹¹yet/and) the fourth started the motor. Then he jumped on too (¹²and/but) round they went. They were having the time of their lives, (¹³but/so) suddenly realized there was no one to stop the machine. They weren't rescued till morning (¹⁴and/but) by then they felt very sick indeed!

They felt very sick indeed!

1.5 The complex sentence: noun clauses

1.5A Introduction to complex sentences [> LEG 1.21]

Study:

1 We can join two or more simple sentences to make **complex sentences:**
   The alarm was raised. The fire was discovered.
   *The alarm was raised **as soon as** the fire was discovered.*
   *The alarm was raised **when** the fire was discovered.*
   *The alarm was raised **after** the fire was discovered.*

2 We can use many different kinds of 'joining words' (or **conjunctions**) to make complex sentences: *after, as soon as, when, since, that, if, so that, whether*, etc. [> 1.5-10]

3 In a complex sentence there is one 'main' idea and one or more 'subordinate' ideas. We can take the main idea (or **clause**) out of the sentence so that it stands on its own:
   The alarm was raised is a **main clause**: it can stand on its own. ... *as soon as the fire was discovered* cannot stand on its own. It is **subordinate** to the main clause.

Write: Underline the main clauses in these sentences.

1 <u>You can tell me all about the film</u> after I've seen it myself.
2 When you've finished cleaning the car, you can help me with the dishes.
3 You didn't tell me that you were going to invite so many guests.
4 I walk to work every morning so that I can get some exercise.
5 Since no one answered my call, I left a message on the answer-phone.

1.5B Noun clauses derived from statements [> LEG 1.22-23, 15.10-16, Apps 45-46]

Study:

1 **A noun clause** does the work of a noun. It answers the questions *Who?* or *What?*:
   *He told me about **his success**.* (*told me about what?*): *his success* is a 'noun phrase'.
   *He told me **that he had succeeded**.* (*... what?*): *that he had succeeded* is a noun clause.

2 We introduce noun clause statements with *that* after:
   – some adjectives: *It's obvious **that he's going to be late**.*
   – some nouns: *It's a pity **that he's going to be late**.*
   – some verbs: *I know **that he's going to be late**.*

3 We often use noun clauses after 'reporting verbs' like *say, tell (me), think, know* [> 15.2-3]. We can often omit *that*.
   Instead of: *I know **that he's going to be late**,* we can say: *I know **he's going to be late**.*

Write: Complete these sentences with noun clauses.

1 He feels angry. It's not surprising *(that) he feels angry.* ....
2 She has resigned from her job. It's a shame ....
3 You don't trust me. It's annoying ....
4 You are feeling better. I'm glad ....
5 She's upset. I'm sorry ....
6 He didn't get the contract. He told me ....
7 It's a fair price. He believes ....
8 You're leaving. He has guessed ....
9 She's been a fool. She agrees ....

1.5C Noun clauses derived from questions [> LEG 1.24]

Study:
★★

Yes/No questions
1 *Has he signed the contract?* is a direct Yes/No question. [> 13.1]
2 We can introduce a Yes/No question as a **noun clause** after *if* or *whether*. We use 'reporting verbs' like *ask, tell me, want to know* [> 15.4A]:
   *Tell me if **he has signed the contract**.* (*Tell me what?*): *if he has signed the contract.*
   *Ask him **whether he has signed it**.* (*Ask him what?*): *whether he has signed it.*

Question-word questions
1 *When did you sign the contract?* is a question-word question. [> 13.5-8]
2 We can introduce this as a **noun clause** after *Tell me, I want to know*, etc. The word order changes back to subject + verb and we don't use a question mark [> 15.4B]:
   *Tell me **when you signed the contract**.* (Not **Tell me when did you sign**)

Write: Complete these sentences with noun clauses.

 1 Has he passed his exam? I want to know ..*if/whether he has passed his exam.*..
 2 Can you type? You didn't say ....
 3 Will he arrive tomorrow? I wonder ....
 4 Does he like ice-cream? Ask him ....
 5 Was he at home yesterday? I'd like to know ....
 6 Should I phone her? I wonder ....
 7 Is she ready? Ask her ....
 8 When did you meet her? I want to know ....
 9 How will you manage? Tell me ....
10 Why has he left? I wonder ....
11 Where do you live? Tell me ....
12 Which one does she want? Ask her ....
13 Who's at the door? I wonder ....
14 What does he want? I'd like to know ....

1.5D Context

Write: Underline nine noun clauses in this text.

She lifted the car!

YOU DON'T KNOW YOUR OWN STRENGTH!
I suppose <u>you know</u> you can turn into superwoman or superman in an emergency. Mrs Pam Weldon reported that her baby nearly slipped under the wheels of a car. Mrs Weldon weighs only 50 kilos, but she said she lifted the car to save her baby. Dr Murray Watson, a zoologist, wrote that he jumped nearly three metres into the air to grab the lowest branch of a tree when hyenas chased him in Kenya. Perhaps you wonder if you can perform such feats. The chances are that you can. Doctors say that we can find great reserves of strength when we are afraid. It's well-known that adrenalin can turn us into superwomen or supermen!

1.6 The complex sentence: relative pronouns and clauses

1.6A Relative pronouns and clauses [> LEG 1.25-38]

Study:

> **Introduction to relative clauses**
>
> Suppose you want to write a paragraph like this:
>
> *The house we moved into* is absolutely beautiful. *The people who lived* here before us took very great care of it. The garden, *which is quite small*, is lovely. I'm glad we moved. I don't think we'll ever regret *the decision we made*.
>
> If we want to speak or write like this, we have to master **relative clauses**. We introduce relative clauses with these relative pronouns: *who, who(m), which, that* and *whose*.

> **'Who', 'which' and 'that' as subjects of a relative clause** [> LEG 1.27-31]
>
> 1 We use *who* or *that* to refer to people. We use them in place of noun subjects or pronoun subjects (*I, you, he*, etc.) and we cannot omit them.
>   They do not change when they refer to masculine, feminine, singular or plural:
>   *He* is the **man**/*She* is the **woman who/that** lives here. (Not **He is the man who he ...*)
>   *They* are the **men**/the **women who/that** live here. (Not **They are the men who they ...*)
>
> 2 We use *which* or *that* (in place of noun subjects and *it*) to refer to animals and things:
>   *That's the* **cat which/that** *lives next door. Those are the* **cats which/that** *live next door.*
>   *Here's a* **photo which/that** *shows my car. Here are some* **photos which/that** *show my car.*

Write: Join these sentences using *who* or *which*. (All of them will also join with *that*.)

1 He's the accountant. He does my accounts. *He's the accountant who does my accounts.*
2 She's the nurse. She looked after me. ....
3 They're the postcards. They arrived yesterday. ....
4 They're the secretaries. They work in our office. ....
5 That's the magazine. It arrived this morning. ....
6 They're the workmen. They repaired our roof. ....

1.6B 'Who(m)', 'which' and 'that' as objects of a relative clause [> LEG 1.33-34]

Study:

> 1 We use *who(m)* or *that* to refer to people. We use them in place of noun objects or object pronouns (*me, you, him*, etc.). We often say *who* instead of *whom* when we speak.
>   They do not change when they refer to masculine, feminine, singular or plural:
>   *He's the* **man**/*She's the* **woman who(m)/that** *I met.* (Not **He's the man that I met him.*)
>   *They're the* **men/women who(m)/that** *I met.* (Not **They are the men that I met them.*)
>   However, we usually omit *who(m)* and *that*. We say:
>   *He's the man/She's the woman I met. They're the men/They're the women I met.*
>
> 2 We use *which* or *that* (in place of noun objects or *it*) to refer to animals and things:
>   *That's the* **cat which/that** *I photographed. Those are the* **cats which/that** *I photographed.*
>   *That's the* **photo which/that** *I took. Those are the* **photos which/that** *I took.*
>   However, we usually omit *which* and *that*. We say:
>   *That's the cat I photographed. Those are the cats I photographed.*
>   *That's the photo I took. Those are the photos I took.*

Write: Join these sentences with *who(m)*, *which* or nothing. (All of them will join with *that*.)

1 He's the accountant. You recommended him to me. *He's the accountant you recommended...*

2 She's the nurse. I saw her at the hospital. ....

3 They're the postcards. I sent them from Spain. ....

4 They're the secretaries. Mr Pym employed them. ....

5 That's the magazine. I got it for you yesterday. ....

6 They're the workmen. I paid them for the job. ....

7 That's the dog! I saw it at the dog show last week. ....

8 They're the birds. I fed them this morning. ....

1.6C 'Who(m)', 'which' or 'that' as the objects of prepositions [> LEG 1.35-36]

Study:
★★

The position of prepositions in relative clauses is very important. We can say:

1 He is the **person to whom** I wrote. (Never *to who*) (very formal)
*This is the **pan in which** I boiled the milk.* (very formal)

2 He is the **person who(m)** I wrote **to**. This is the **pan which** I boiled the milk **in**.

3 However, we usually prefer to omit the relative and say:
*He is the **person I wrote to**. This is the **pan I boiled the milk in**.*

Write: Join each pair of sentences in three different ways.

1 He's the man. I sent the money to him.
a *He's the man to whom I sent the money.*
b *He's the man who(m) I sent the money to.*
c *He's the man I sent the money to.*

2 She's the nurse. I gave the flowers to her.
a ....
b ....
c ....

3 That's the chair. I sat on it.
a ....
b ....
c ....

4 He's the boy. I bought this toy for him.
a ....
b ....
c ....

5 That's the building. I passed by it.
a ....
b ....
c ....

6 They're the shops. I got these from them.
a ....
b ....
c ....

1.6D Context

Write: Put in the right relative pronouns only where necessary.

... just happened to be passing

A CHANCE IN A MILLION

Cissie, the woman [1] ....*who*.... works in our office, wanted to phone Mr Robinson, but she dialled the wrong number. The number [2] .... she dialled turned out to be the number of a public call box in the street. A man, [3] .... was passing at the time, heard the phone ringing and answered it. 'Is that Mr Robinson?' Cissie asked. 'Speaking,' the man answered. It turned out that the man [4] .... she was speaking to was actually called Robinson and had just happened to be passing the call box when she rang!

1.7 The complex sentence: 'whose'; defining/non-defining clause.

1.7A 'Whose' + noun in relative clauses [> LEG 1.32, 1.37]

Study:
★★

1 We use *whose* in place of possessive adjectives (*my, your, his*, etc.) to refer to people. *Whose* does not change when it refers to masculine, feminine, singular or plural:
He's the **man/She's** the **woman whose car** was stolen. (Not *whose his car was stolen*)
They're the **people whose cars** were stolen. (Not *whose their cars were stolen*)

2 We sometimes use *whose* in place of *its* to refer to things and animals:
*That's the **house whose windows** were broken. (= the windows of which)*

3 We can also use *whose* with prepositions:
*He's the man **from whose house** the pictures were stolen. (formal)*
*He's the man **whose house** the pictures were stolen **from**.*

Write: Join these sentences using *whose*.

1 He is the customer. I lost his address. ...*He's the customer whose address I lost.*...
2 She is the novelist. Her book won first prize. ....
3 They are the children. Their team won the match. ....
4 You are the expert. We want your advice. ....
5 I'm the witness. My evidence led to his arrest. ....
6 She's the woman. The film was made in her house. ....

1.7B Defining and non-defining clauses [> LEG 1.26, 1.29, 1.31-32, 1.34-37]

Study:
★★

1 When we write relative clauses with *who*, *which* or *whose*, we have to decide whether to use commas 'round the clauses' or not.

2 In sentences like:
*I've never met **anyone who** can type as fast as you can.*
*The magazine **which arrived** this morning is five days late.*
the relative clauses tell us which person or thing we mean. They give us essential information which we cannot omit. We call them **defining clauses** because they 'define' the person or thing they refer to. We never use commas in such sentences.
We never use commas with *that* in relative clauses:
*I've just had a phone call from the people (**that**) we met during our holidays.*
*The wallet (**that**) you lost has been found.*

3 In sentences like:
*Our new secretary, **who can type faster than anyone I have ever met**, has completely reorganized our office.*
*Time Magazine, **which is available in every country in the world**, is published every week.*
the relative clauses add 'extra information'. If we take them out of the sentences, we won't seriously change the meaning. We call these **non-defining clauses** (they do not 'define') and we use commas before and after them.

4 Sometimes we have to decide when the information is 'essential' or 'extra' and we may or may not use commas. We must decide this for ourselves:
*He asked lots of questions(,) **which were none of his business**(,) and annoyed everybody.*

Write: Add commas to the following sentences where necessary.

1 My husband, who is on a business trip to Rome all this week, sent me this postcard.
2 The person who told you that story didn't know what he was talking about.
3 Will the driver whose vehicle has the registration number PXB2140 please move it?
4 The author Barbara Branwell whose latest novel has already sold over a million copies will be giving a lecture at the public library tomorrow.
5 The person you got that information from is my cousin.
6 The play *Cowards* which opens at the Globe soon had a successful season on Broadway.
7 *Cowards* is the name of the play which ran for over two years.
8 The thing that pleases me most is that I'll never have to ask for your help again.
9 The manager whom I complained to about the service has refunded part of our bill.
10 Sally West whose work for the deaf made her famous has been killed in a car accident.
11 We found it impossible to cross the river that had flooded after the storm.
12 I have just learned that the engine part which I need is no longer made.

1.7C Sentences with two meanings [> LEG 1.26]

Study:
★★

> The use or omission of commas round relative clauses can sometimes affect the meaning:
> *My wife, who is in Paris, will be returning tomorrow.* Without commas, this could suggest that I have another wife who is (or other wives who are) somewhere else!

Write: Say what these sentences mean a) without commas; b) with commas.

1 The test paper which everyone failed was far too difficult.
....
2 My brother who is in Canada is an architect.
....

1.7D Context

Write: Put in relative pronouns where necessary and commas where necessary.

THIS CHARMING PROPERTY ...
People [1] .....*who*...... tell the truth about the properties they are selling should be given prizes for honesty. A house [2] .... is described as 'spacious' will be found to be too large. Words like 'enchanting', 'delightful', 'convenient', 'attractive' [3] .... are commonly used all mean 'small'. The words 'small' and 'picturesque' [4] .... are not so frequently used both mean 'too small'. A 'picturesque house' is one with a bedroom [5] .... is too small to put a bed in and a kitchen [6] .... is too small to boil an egg in. My prize for honesty goes to someone [7] .... recently described a house [8] .... he was selling in the following way: 'This house [9] .... is situated in a very rough area of London is really in need of repair. The house [10] .... has a terrible lounge and a tiny dining room also has three miserable bedrooms and a bathroom [11] .... is fitted with a leaky shower. The central heating [12] .... is expensive to run is unreliable. There is a handkerchief-sized garden [13] .... is overgrown with weeds. The neighbours [14] .... are generally unfriendly are not likely to welcome you. This property [15] .... is definitely not recommended is ridiculously overpriced at £85,000.'

This charming property ...

1.8 The complex sentence: time, place, manner

1.8A Adverbial clauses of time, place and manner [> LEG 1.44-47]

Study:
★★

> **Introduction to adverbial clauses of time, place and manner**
> Suppose you want to write a paragraph like this:
>
> *When we visited London, we went to the Tower. We saw the spot where so many famous people had lost their heads! We felt as if we had travelled back in time to another world!*
>
> If we want to speak or write like this, we have to master **adverbial clauses of time** (answering *When?*), **place** (answering *Where?*) and **manner** (answering *How?*)

> **Adverbial clauses of time (past reference)** [> LEG 1.45.1]
> To say *when* something happened in the past, we use 'joining words' (or **conjunctions**) like *when, after, as, as soon as, before, by the time (that), once, since, until/till, while*:
> *When we visited London, we went to the Tower.* [compare > 9.6A]

Write: Join these sentences with the conjunctions in brackets.

1 I lost a lot of weight. I was ill. (when)
   I lost a lot of weight when I was ill.

2 I phoned home. I arrived in the airport building. (immediately after)
   ....

3 She had already opened the letter. She realized it wasn't addressed to her. (before)
   ....

4 The building had almost burnt down. The fire brigade arrived. (by the time)
   ....

5 We realized that something had gone wrong. We saw him run towards us. (as soon as)
   ....

1.8B Adverbial clauses of time (future reference) [> LEG 1.45.2]

Study:
★★

> When the time clause refers to the future, we normally use the simple present after: *after, as soon as, before, by the time, directly, immediately, the moment, till, until* and *when*:
> *The Owens will move to a new flat when their baby is born.* (Not **will be born**)

Write: Join these pairs of sentences with the conjunctions in brackets, making necessary changes.

1 I won't know if I have got into university. I will get my exam results. (until)
   I won't know if I have got into university until I get my exam results.

2 I'll give him your message. He will phone. (as soon as)
   ....

3 We should visit the Duty Free Shop. Our flight will be called. (before)
   ....

4 I'll be dead. They will find a cure for the common cold. (by the time)
   ....

5 You'll get a surprise. You will open the door. (the moment)
   ....

1.8C Adverbial clauses of place [> LEG 1.46]

Study:
★★

> To say *where* something happens or happened, we use conjunctions like *where, wherever, anywhere* and *everywhere*: *That dog follows me **wherever** I go.*

Write: Complete the following sentences to say *where*.

1 This is the exact spot where *the accident happened*. ....
2 You're not allowed to park anywhere ....
3 Some television programmes are familiar everywhere ....
4 Please sit wherever ....
5 Let's put the television set in a place where ....

1.8D Adverbial clauses of manner [> LEG 1.47]

Study:
★★

> To say *how* something happens or happened, we use these conjunctions:
> **as**: *Type this again **as** I showed you a moment ago.*
> **(in) the way (that), (in) the same way**: *Type this again **in the way** I showed you.*
> **as if/as though** (especially after *be, seem*, etc.): *I feel **as if/as though** I'm floating on air.*

Write: Complete the following sentences to say *how*.

1 It sounds as if *it's raining*...
2 I think this omelette is exactly as ....
3 When I told her the news she acted as though ....
4 I think you should write the report in the way ....
5 You never do anything the way ....

1.8E Context

Write: Put in the conjunctions *as, as soon as, as if, before, that, the way (that), when, which.*

CAUGHT BY THE HEEL!
Mr Boxell was just shutting his shoe shop at the end of the day
[1].....*when*... a man in a well-cut suit walked in and asked for an
expensive pair of shoes. There was something about [2]................... the
man walked that made Mr Boxell suspicious. He felt [3].................. he had
seen him before somewhere, and then remembered that he had – on
TV! The man was a wanted criminal! The man tried on a few pairs of
shoes [4].................. he bought a pair [5].................. Mr Boxell strongly
recommended. 'They're a bit tight,' the man complained. 'They'll stretch,
sir,' Mr Boxell said. [6].................. Mr Boxell had expected, the man
limped into the shop next day to complain about the shoes. [7]...................
he entered the shop, he was surrounded by police. Mr Boxell had
deliberately sold the man a pair of shoes [8].................. were a size too
small, knowing he would return them the next day!

The man limped into the shop

17

1.9 The complex sentence: reason and contrast

1.9A Adverbial clauses of reason [> LEG 1.48]

Study:
★★

1 **Adverbial clauses of reason** answer the question *Why?* We often give reasons by using 'joining words' (or **conjunctions**) like *because, as, seeing (that)*, and *since*.

2 We often begin sentences with *as* and *since*. [Compare *since* (time) > 1.8A]
As (Since) *it's a public holiday, you won't find many shops open.*

3 We often use *because* in the second half of a sentence:
*Jim's trying to find a place of his own **because** he wants to feel independent.*
We can always use *because* in place of *as, since* and *for* [> 1.4A, Note 8]. We cannot always use *as, since* and *for* in place of *because*.

Write: Join these sentences with the conjunctions to say *why*. More than one order is possible.

1 Service in this hotel ought to improve. There's been a change of management. (because)
Service in this hotel ought to improve because there's been a change of management

2 The Air Traffic Controllers are on strike. We have cancelled our holiday. (as)
....

3 Could you sell your old computer to me? You have no further use for it. (seeing (that))
....

4 She's never in when I phone. I'll have to write to her. (since)
....

5 I've had to have the document translated. I can't read Russian. (since)
....

1.9B Contrast (1) [> LEG 1.50]

Study:
★★

We can introduce **contrast** with conjunctions like *although, considering (that), though, even though, even if, much as, while* and *whereas*:
Though *I've had more than 20 lessons, I'm still not ready to take my driving test.*

Write: Join these sentences using the conjunctions in brackets to introduce *contrast*.
More than one order is possible.

1 I'm going to buy a computer. I haven't got much money. (even though)
I'm going to buy a computer even though I haven't got much money.

2 I intend to go for a walk this morning. It's raining. (even if)
....

3 I'd like to help you. I'm afraid I won't be able to. (much as)
....

4 Your design is excellent. It isn't suitable for our purposes. (while)
....

5 I try hard to play the piano. I don't seem to improve. (although)
....

6 Chinese is so difficult. It's surprising how many people learn it. (considering that)
....

7 The play was wonderful. The film was a commercial failure. (whereas)
....

1.9C Contrast (2) [> LEG 1.50]

Study:
★★★

> We can also introduce contrast with:
>
> – *however* + adjective or adverb: e.g. *however small, however much.*
>   *I intend to buy a CD player* **however much** (or **whatever**) *it costs.*
>
> – *no matter:* e.g. *no matter how much, no matter where, no matter how (slow/slowly).*
>   *They'll find him* **no matter** *where he's hiding.*

Write: Join these sentences using the conjunctions in brackets. Make any necessary changes.

1 It's expensive. He's determined to buy it. (however expensive)
  However expensive it is, he's determined to buy it.

2 I work hard. I still have to take work home with me. (however hard)
  ....

3 You write well. It doesn't mean you will be published. (however well)
  ....

4 She feels sorry. The damage has been done. (no matter how sorry)
  ....

5 How much will they pay us? It will never compensate us. (no matter how much)
  ....

6 It doesn't matter how many cards I send. I always receive more. (no matter how many)
  ....

7 It doesn't matter what he tells you. Don't believe a word he says. (whatever)
  ....

1.9D Context

Write: Put in the conjunctions *as, because, even though, since, though, while.*

A SORT OF HUMANBURGER
[1] *...Even though.....* it's difficult to find work these days, Joe Dobson has just given up his job. They were surprised when he announced this at the Job Centre [2]..........................., after a lot of effort, they had found Joe a job at a Hamburger Bar. [3].......................... Joe wasn't highly-qualified, this hadn't been easy. Yet Joe resigned, [4].......................... the job was easy and quite well-paid. 'What did you have to do for your money?' the young woman at the Job Centre asked. 'Strange [5].......................... it sounds,' Joe said, 'I had to dress up as a hamburger and stand outside the restaurant.' 'A sort of humanburger?' she suggested. 'That's right,' Joe said. 'I had to stand between the two round halves of a bun, [6].......................... I was "disguised" as the hamburger filling, covered in tomato sauce. The uniform was wonderful, [7].......................... I looked good enough to eat. The manager was pleased with me, [8].......................... I attracted a lot of customers.' 'So why did you give up, Joe?' the young woman asked kindly. '[9]...........................,' Joe said, his voice breaking slightly, 'students kept turning me on my side and rolling me down hill!'

A sort of humanburger

1.10 The complex sentence: purpose, result and comparison

1.10A Adverbial clauses of purpose with 'so that' and 'in order that' [> LEG 1.51.2]

Study:
★★★

We can express **purpose** with *so that* and *in order that*:
*I spent a year in Germany **in order that (so that)** I might learn German.*
Note that it's easier to use the *to*-infinitive instead of *so that* and *in order that*:
*I spent a year in Germany **to learn** German.* [> 16.2C]

Write: Rewrite these sentences using *in order that* or *so that* making any necessary changes.

1 I took twenty driving lessons to pass my driving test first time.
I took twenty driving lessons in order that I might pass my driving test first time.

2 I arrived at the cinema early so as not to miss the beginning of the film.
....

3 We stood up in order to get a better view of what was happening.
....

4 Mr Jones bought a second car for his wife to learn to drive.
....

5 I spoke slowly and clearly because I wanted the audience to understand me.
....

1.10B Adverbial clauses of purpose with 'in case' [> LEG 1.51.3]

Study:
★★

In case means 'so as to be on the safe side' and refers to the future. We use the simple present or *should* after *in case*:
Take an umbrella with you. It might rain. →
*Take an umbrella with you **in case** it rains.* (Or ... *in case it should rain*)

Write: Join these sentences with *in case*, making any necessary changes.

1 I'm going to sign the agreement immediately. You might change your mind.
I'm going to sign the agreement immediately in case you change your mind.

2 Take this key with you. You might not be able to get into the house.
....

3 We keep a fire extinguisher in the kitchen. There might be a fire.
....

4 Go by train. There might be a lot of traffic on the roads.
....

5 I'm going to take my passport with me. I might need it.
....

1.10C Adverbial clauses of result with 'so ... (that)' and 'such ... (that)' [> LEG 1.52.1]

Study:
★★

We can describe results with:
1 **so** + adjective (*that*) (= 'as a result'):
We were tired. We went to bed. → *We were **so tired (that)** we went to bed.*

2 **such** + noun (*that*) (= 'as a result'):
He's a fool. He believes anything. → *He's **such a fool (that)** he believes anything.*

Write: Join these sentences with *so ...* (*that*) and *such ...* (*that*).

1 We were late. We missed the first act of the play.
We were so late (that) we missed the first act of the play.

2 I was working hard. I forgot what the time was.

3 There was a delay. We missed our connecting flight.

4 We've had difficulties. We don't think we can stay in business.

1.10D Adverbial clauses of comparison with 'as ... as' [> LEG 1.53]

Study:
★★

We can make comparisons with *as ... as, not so* (or *as*) *... as* and *than*:
We use object pronouns after *as* and *than* [> 4.1B]: *He's as tall as **me**. He's taller than **me**.*
Or we use subject + verb: *He is as tall as **I (am)**. He's taller than **I (am)**.*
We may use *do, does* or *did* to replace a verb in the simple present or simple past:
*He **plays** the piano as well as **I (do)**. He **plays** the piano as well as his sister (**does**).*
*You **didn't finish** the crossword puzzle as quickly as **I (did)**.*

Write: Join or rewrite these sentences using the conjunctions in brackets.

1 John works hard. Susan works hard. (as ... as)
John works as hard as Susan (does).

2 John is less intelligent than Susan. (not so ... as)

3 This computer holds less information than that one. (not ... as much ... as)

4 The film 'Superman 1' is enjoyable. 'Superman 2' is enjoyable, too. (as ... as)

1.10E Context

Write: Put in *as ... as, but, in case, in order that, so ... that, such ... that, when, which*.

'Wysiwyg!'

WYSIWYG /wɪzɪwɪg/
We create new words all the time. We have to do this *in order that* we may express new ideas. Perhaps the strangest word [2].................. has come into the English language recently is 'wysiwyg'. I was [3].................. puzzled by this word .... I kept asking people what it meant, [4].................. no one knew. Last week I found it in a dictionary. It is not [5].................. peculiar .... I had thought. It comes from computers. This is what it means, [6].................. you want to know: '**W**hat **Y**ou **S**ee **I**s **W**hat **Y**ou **G**et'. This means that what you see on your screen is what you get [7].................. you print. Now I discover that everyone knows this word. The other day I was in my favourite restaurant and ordered sausages. They were [8].................. small sausages .... I complained to the waitress. She just smiled at me and whispered, 'Wysiwyg!'

1.11 The complex sentence: present participle constructions

1.11A Joining sentences with present participles ('-ing') [> LEG 1.56-1.58.1]

Study:
★★★

> The **present participle** is the '-ing' form of a verb: *find – finding* [> 16.5].
>
> **1** We can use the present participle in place of *and, so*, etc. to join two simple sentences:
> *I found the front door locked. I went round the back.* (two simple sentences > 1.2A)
> *I found the front door locked **and went** round the back.* [> 1.4A]
> ***Finding** the front door locked, I went round the back.*
>
> **2** To make a negative, we put *not* in front of the *-ing* form:
> ***Not knowing** his phone number, I wasn't able to ring him.* (= I didn't know ...)
>
> **3** Note how we can use *being* in place of *is* or *was*:
> *I **was** short of money. I couldn't afford to buy it.*
> ***Being** short of money, I couldn't afford to buy it.*

Write: Rewrite these sentences using *-ing*, making any necessary changes.

1 She got very worried and thought we had had an accident.
She got very worried, thinking we had had an accident.

2 He went to his room and closed the door behind him.
....

3 I didn't hear what he said and asked him to repeat it.
....

4 You didn't ask me for permission because you knew I would refuse.
....

5 I'm not a lawyer, so I can't give you the advice you are looking for.
....

1.11B The present participle in place of adverbial clauses [> LEG 1.56-60]

Study:
★★★

> We often use the present participle after a 'joining word' (or **conjunction**).
> Instead of: ***Since we arrived** here, we have made many new friends.* [> 1.8A]
> We can say: ***Since arriving** here, we have made many new friends.*

Write: Rewrite these sentences using a joining word + *-ing*.

1 They broke this window when they tried to get into the house.
They broke this window when trying to get into the house

2 Though he refused to eat, he admitted he was very hungry.
....

3 I damaged the car while I was trying to park it.
....

4 While I agree you may be right, I still object to your argument.
....

5 After we looked at the map, we tried to find the right street.
....

6 Don't get into any arguments before you check your facts.
....

1.11C The present participle in place of relative clauses [> LEG 1.58.6]

Study:
★★★

1 We can sometimes omit *who* or *which* + *is/are* when we use the present progressive.
Instead of: **The man who is serving** *at the counter is very helpful.*
We can say: **The man serving** *at the counter is very helpful.*
Instead of: *The new law applies to* **vehicles which are carrying** *heavy loads.*
We can say: *The new law applies to* **vehicles carrying** *heavy loads.*

2 We can sometimes use *-ing* in place of *who* or *which* + simple present:
Instead of: *This job will suit* **students who want** *to work during the holidays.*
We can say: *This job will suit* **students wanting** *to work during the holidays.*

Write: Circle the words you can delete and/or change to use *-ing*.

1 The plane (which is) flying overhead is travelling north.
2 The candidates who are sitting for this examination are all graduates.
3 The woman who is waiting to see you has applied for a job here.
4 What can you do about a dog which is barking all night?
5 Trains which leave from this station take an hour to get to London.
6 Customers who complain about the service should see the manager.
7 Passengers who travel on planes shouldn't smoke.
8 There's a pension scheme for people who work for this company.
9 There's a crime prevention scheme for people who are living in this neighbourhood.
10 There's someone who is knocking at the door.

1.11D Context

Write: Use the *-ing* form of the verbs in brackets and put in *after, as, when* and *who*.

They quickly changed their minds!

THE CASE OF THE POISONED MUSHROOMS
While (*prepare*) [1] *preparing* a meal for her guests, Mrs Grant got
rather worried about some unusual mushrooms which a kind friend had
sent her from the country. (*Feel*) [2] .... suspicious, she gave
a mushroom to her dog. [3] .... the dog ate it with no ill effects,
Mrs Grant decided to cook the mushrooms for her guests. That evening
the guests greatly enjoyed the mushrooms, (*comment*) [4] ....
on their unusual flavour. They quickly changed their minds [5] ....
Mrs Grant's daughter, Jill, burst into the dining-room and announced
that the dog was dead. On (*hear*) [6] .... the news, Mrs Grant,
now in a state of shock, phoned Dr Craig, [7] .... came round
immediately and pumped out the stomachs of all those who had eaten
the mushrooms – a very unpleasant experience for them. [8] ....
Dr Craig asked if he could see the dog, he was led out of the house.
He soon discovered that the dog had been killed by a passing car.
Not (*know*) [9] .... anything of her mother's suspicions about
the mushrooms, Jill hadn't mentioned this important fact when
(*announce*) [10] .... the death of the dog.

1.12 The complex sentence: perfect/past participle constructions

1.12A 'Being' and 'having been' [> LEG 1.60]

Study:
★★★

1 We sometimes use *being* in place of *is, are, was* or *were*, though this is often formal:
Instead of: ***I was lost***, so I had to ask someone the way.
We can say: ***Being lost***, I had to ask someone the way.

2 We sometimes use *having been* in place of *have been* or *had been* (also formal):
Instead of: ***I've been abroad***, so I missed the elections.
We can say: ***Having been abroad***, I missed the elections.

Write: Rewrite these sentences using *being* or *having been*.

1 I am out of work, so I spend a lot of my time at home.
Being out of work, I spend a lot of my time at home.

2 John is a scientist, so he hasn't read a lot of novels.

3 He has been promised a reward, so he hopes he'll get one.

4 I was near a newsagent's, so I went in and got a paper.

5 They had been up all night, so they were in no mood for jokes.

1.12B 'It being' and 'there being' [> LEG 1.60]

Study:
★★★

1 We sometimes use *it being* in place of *it is* or *it was* (formal):
Instead of: ***It was Sunday***, so it was hard to find a garage open.
We can say: ***It being Sunday***, it was hard to find a garage open.

2 We sometimes use *there being* in place of *there is* or *there was* (formal):
Instead of: ***There was*** so much noise, I couldn't hear what was going on.
We can say: ***There being*** so much noise, I couldn't hear what was going on.

3 We can use *it being* and *there being* after *without* (formal):
They often dig up the roads **without it being** necessary. (= it isn't necessary)
She suddenly began shouting **without there being** any reason. (= there was no reason)

Write: Rewrite these sentences using *it being* or *there being*, making any necessary changes.

1 There were no questions so the meeting ended quickly.
There being no questions, the meeting ended quickly.

2 He kept helping himself to money and it wasn't noticed. (without it ...)

3 He kept asking awkward questions and there was no reason for it. (without there ...)

4 It was a holiday, so there were thousands of cars on the roads.

5 There was no one in, so I left a message.

1.12C Agreement between present participle and subject [> LEG 1.61]

Study:
★★★

We have to be very careful to make the participle agree with the subject of both verbs:
Turning the corner, I saw a tile fall off the roof. (= **I** turned ... and **I** saw ...)
If we say or write **Turning the corner, the tile fell off the roof**, this means 'the tile was turning the corner and then fell off the roof'. The sentence is nonsense!

Write: What's wrong with these sentences?

1 Opening the door of the refrigerator, the smell was bad. *It wasn't the smell that was opening the do*
2 Changing gear, the bus had difficulty getting up the hill. ....
3 Burning the rubbish, all my important papers were destroyed. ....

1.12D Past participle constructions [> LEG 1.62]

Study:
★★★

1 The **past participle** is the third part of a verb [> 9.3A-B]:
*play – played – **played*** (regular verbs); *build – built – **built*** (irregular verbs)

2 We sometimes use the past participle instead of the passive:
***Viewed** from a distance, it resembled a cloud.* (When it was viewed ...)
***Although built** years ago, it was in good order.* (Although it was built ...)
***If accepted** for the job, you will be informed soon.* (If you are accepted ...)

3 We can omit *who* and *which*: ***The system used** here is very successful.* (which is used...)

Write: Rewrite these sentences using past participles.

1 The painting was lost for many years. It turned up at an auction.
...*Lost for many years, the painting turned up at an auction*...............

2 Although the meat was cooked for several hours, it was still tough.
....

3 If the picture is seen from this angle, it looks rather good.
....

4 The vegetables which are sold in this shop are grown without chemicals.
....

5 When the poem is read aloud it is very effective.
....

1.12E Context

Write: Put in suitable words (and forms where necessary) in the spaces below.

YAH BOOH!
My cat Blossom is always getting into fights with Ginger, the tomcat next door.
[1]......*When*...... I see Ginger through my window, I shout and wave my arms to frighten him away. [2].................. out of the window yesterday, I saw Ginger near my front door. There [3].................. no one around, I pulled a hideous face, stuck out my tongue, waved my arms over my head and started screaming, 'Yah booh! Yah booh!' [4].................. the front door, I was determined to chase Ginger away.
[5].................. I succeeded admirably, I terrified the postman as well!

25

2 Nouns

2.1 One-word nouns

2.1A Noun endings: people who do things/people who come from places
[> LEG 2.2, App 2]

Study:
★★

> **1** We use some words only as nouns: e.g. *desk, hat, tree*, etc.
>
> **2** However, we often make nouns from other words by adding different endings or **suffixes** and sometimes making other small changes. For example, if we add *-er* to a verb like *play*, we get the noun *player*; if we add *-ity* to the adjective *active*, we get the noun *activity*. There is no easy rule to tell us which endings to use to make nouns.
>
> **3** Typical endings which make nouns:
> **people who do things:** *actor, assistant, beggar, driver, engineer, historian, pianist*.
> **people who come from places:** *Athenian, Berliner, Milanese, Muscovite, Roman*.

Write: Give the nouns which describe people who do things or who come from places.
Use these noun endings: *-an, -ant, -ar, -er, -ian, -ist, -or*. Some are used more than once.

1 He *acts* very well. He's a fine ......*actor*......
2 Don't *beg*. You're not a ....
3 I can't play the *piano*. I'm not a ....
4 She *drives* well. She's a good ....
5 I'm from *Berlin*. I'm a ....

6 She's from *Athens*. She's an ....
7 Manuel *assists* me. He's my ....
8 She always tells *lies*. She's such a ....
9 He's from *Texas*. He's a ....
10 Anna is studying *history*. She's a fine ....

2.1B Nouns formed from verbs, adjectives, other nouns [> LEG 2.2-3, Apps 2, 3.2]

Study:
★★

> **1** Some nouns have the same form as verbs: *act, attempt, blame, book, call, copy, cost, dance, fall, fear, help, joke, kiss, laugh, try, vote, wait, walk, wash, wish*.
>
> **2** Typical endings which make nouns from:
> – **verbs:** *acceptance, agreement, arrival, behaviour, discovery, knowledge, possession*.
> – **adjectives:** *absence, activity, anxiety, constancy, happiness*.
> – **other nouns:** *boyhood, kingdom, lunacy, mouthful, sexism*.
>
> And note *-ing* forms used as nouns: *I've given your shirt an ironing*. [> 2.2A, 16.5]

Write: Give the nouns derived from verbs, adjectives or other nouns. Use these endings: *-age, -hood, -ation, -ion, -ful, -ence, -ency, -ness, -al, -(er)y, -ment, -ety, -ism, -ity, -ing*.

1 I *decided* this. It was my ......*decision*......
2 Don't be so *anxious*. Control your ....
3 Ann's a *socialist*. She believes in ....
4 We all want to be *happy*. We all seek ....
5 We all *agree*. We're all in ....
6 Who *discovered* this? Who made this ....?
7 We'll all *arrive*. We'll be met on ....
8 I was a *child* then. That was in my ....
9 She is *absent*. Can you explain her ....?
10 I'll *post* this. What's the ....?

11 *Try* again. Have another ....
12 Be more *efficient*. Improve your ....
13 Don't be so *curious*. Control your ....
14 *Address* this envelope. I'll give you the ....
15 I *refused* their offer. My .... is final.
16 I *warned* you. I gave you enough ....
17 Put it in your *mouth*. Take one ....
18 Can you *explain* it? Is there an ....?
19 They *tried* him. I was at the ....
20 Don't *argue*. I don't want an ....

26

2.1C Nouns and verbs with the same spelling but different stress

[> LEG 2.3.1, App 3.1]

Study:
⭐⭐

> **1** With some words, when the stress is on the **first syllable**, the word is a **noun**.
> When the stress is on the **second syllable**, it is a **verb**. The meanings are related:
> noun: *We have finished Book 1. We have made good* **'progress**.
> verb: *We are now ready to* **pro'gress** *to Book 2.*
>
> **2** The meanings can also be quite different:
> noun: *My son's* **'conduct** *at school hasn't been very good.*
> verb: *Mahler used to* **con'duct** *the Vienna Philharmonic.*

Write: Underline the syllable that you would stress when speaking.

1 I need a *permit* to work in this country.
2 I can't *permit* you to park here.
3 Will they *increase* my salary next year?
4 I'm looking for an *increase* in salary.
5 Joy *objects* to your proposal.
6 Don't treat me as if I were an *object*.
7 We've had complaints about your *conduct*.
8 I'll *conduct* you to your seat.
9 This is the *entrance* to the building.
10 Gloria will *entrance* you.
11 Do you want to buy this *record*?
12 Let me *record* your voice.

13 I've brought you a *present*.
14 Please *present* my compliments to him.
15 I must *protest* at your proposal.
16 The proposal didn't go without *protest*.
17 I've got an Australian *accent*.
18 Please *accent* every syllable.
19 Our *exports* have increased this year.
20 We *export* everything we make.
21 I'll *escort* you to your new office.
22 You'll need an *escort*.
23 Our *imports* have increased.
24 We *import* too much.

2.1D Context

Write: Refer to the words in brackets and put in the right nouns.

The computer was having a tantrum!

COMPUTER TANTRUMS
A clever computer built at Imperial College, London, often suffers from (*bore*) [1] ....*boredom*.... . The computer was built to find out about human (*communicate*) [2]........................ . The computer acquired a simple vocabulary in the same way as babies do: through (*babble*) [3]........................ . It is common (*know*) [4]........................ that when babies babble, it is a (*prepare*) [5]........................ for speech. When babies make sounds like real words, they are encouraged to remember them. With (*encourage*) [6]........................ from their parents, babies quickly build up their vocabulary. In the same way, the clever computer learnt to use real words. For example, it learnt to identify a black cat. It was then shown a white cat to test how good it was at (*recognize*) [7]........................ . It refused to co-operate because the (*solve*) [8]........................ to the problem was too easy. At first this (*refuse*) [9]........................ puzzled scientists, but then they decided the computer was having a tantrum. 'It just sits there and goes on strike,' a (*science*) [11]........................ said. 'These clever computers must also be taught good (*behave*) [10]........................ .'

27

2.2 Compound nouns

2.2A Nouns formed with gerund ('-ing') + noun: 'dancing-shoes'
[> LEG 2.7, 2.11n.3, 6.3.1, 16.39.3]

Study:
★★

> **1** When a noun has two or more parts (e.g. *classroom*), we call it a **compound noun.**
> We can make compound nouns with the *-ing* form: e.g. *dancing-shoes* [compare > 16.5].
>
> **2** The *-ing* form can sometimes be an **adjective**:
> *Can you see that 'dancing 'couple?* (= couple that is dancing)
> When the *-ing* form is an adjective, we stress both words and never use a hyphen.
>
> **3** The *-ing* form can be the first part of a **compound noun**:
> *I need a pair of 'dancing-shoes.* (= shoes used for dancing; not 'shoes that are dancing')
> When the *-ing* form is a noun, we stress the first word only and a hyphen is optional.

Write: Put a tick if the second word is part of a compound noun.

1 You need a pair of *running shoes.* ✓
2 We sat beside a *running stream.* __
3 Put it in the *frying pan.* __
4 I like the smell of *frying sausages.* __

5 This water is near *boiling point.* __
6 I need some *boiling water.* __
7 Where are my *walking shoes?* __
8 Vera is a *walking dictionary.* __

2.2B Apostrophe s ('s) or compound noun? [> LEG 2.10.1, 2.44, 2.47-48]

Study:
★★★

> **1** We use apostrophe *s* ('s) and *s* apostrophe (s') with people and some living things to show possession: *Gus's car, the girls' shoes, a dog's bark* [> 2.8].
>
> **2** When we want to show possession with things, we can use *of*: *the leg of the table.*
> However, we often prefer to use a compound noun instead of *of*: *the table-leg.*
>
> **3** We can say *the voice of a man* or *a man's voice.* (Not *a man voice*)
> We can say *the leg of a table* or *a table-leg.* (Not *a table's leg*)

Write: Supply a phrase with 's or a compound noun in place of the phrases in italics.

1 Where's *the key of the car?* ...*the car key*...
2 Where's *the surgery of the doctor?* ....
3 It's *the idea of the committee.* ....
4 Don't damage *the nib of the pen.* ....
5 It's *the keyboard of the computer.* ....
6 I've cleaned *the top of the desk.* ....
7 It was in *the reign of King John.* ....
8 Do you like *the poetry of Eliot?* ....
9 It's *the responsibility of no one.* ....
10 Look at *the handle of the suitcase!* ....
11 Polish *the knob of the front door.* ....
12 *The journey of Scott* is historic. ....
13 Who stole *the bicycle of the postman?* ....
14 Put out *the stub of that cigarette.* ....
15 We've got *a new table in the kitchen.* ....
16 Don't pull *the tail of the horse!* ....

17 Please clean *the switches of the lights.* ....
18 I spoke to *the secretary of the boss.* ....
19 This is the new *policy of the party.* ....
20 *The cover of the book* is torn. ....
21 He's *the son of Mr Jones.* ....
22 *The gate of the factory* was shut. ....
23 Please open *the door of the garage.* ....
24 I've lost *the photos of the children.* ....
25 *The phone in the office* is out of order. ....
26 *The critic of the film* was wrong. ....
27 She's a *teacher of dancing.* ....
28 Who's *the mother of the twins?* ....
29 That's *the wife of my brother.* ....
30 I need *a new lamp for reading.* ....
31 *The surface of the road* is slippery. ....
32 He is *the secretary of the President.* ....

2.2C Compound nouns which tell us about materials and substances

[> LEG 2.10.5, 6.13]

Study:
★★

1 Names of materials and substances (*leather, gold*) are like adjectives when we use them to form compound nouns: *a watch made of gold* → *a **gold watch***. (Not **golden**)
These words behave like adjectives in this one way, but they remain nouns because they do not have comparative or superlative forms and we cannot put *very* in front of them.
We stress both words in spoken English: *I can't afford a 'gold 'watch*. [> 6.4B-D]

2 Two important exceptions are *wood* and *wool*, which have adjectival forms:
a table made of wood → *a **wooden** table*; *a dress made of wool* → *a **woollen** dress*.

3 There are adjectival forms for words like *gold*: *glass/glassy, gold/golden, leather/leathery, silver/silvery, silk/silky/silken, steel/steely, stone/stony*.
We use them to mean 'like': *a **golden** sunset* (= a sunset like gold).

Write: Make compound nouns or use adjectival forms.

1 a raincoat made of plastic *a plastic raincoat*
2 a shirt made of silk ....
3 hair like silk ....
4 a table-top made of glass ....
5 eyes like glass ....
6 a wallet made of leather ....
7 a spoon made of stainless steel ....
8 nerves like steel ....
9 a pullover made of wool...............................

10 a blouse made of cotton ....
11 a teapot made of silver ....
12 a voice like silver ....
13 a wall made of stone ....
14 silence like stone ....
15 a tile made of ceramic ....
16 a nailbrush made of nylon ....
17 a tongue like leather ....
18 a spoon made of wood ....

2.2D Context

Write: Refer to the words in brackets and put in the right compounds.

GREEK BIRDMAN
You probably remember the story of Daedalus, who made (*wings of feathers*) [1] *feather wings* for himself and his son, Icarus, to escape Minos, King of Crete. A young Greek, Kanellos Kanellopoulos, recently repeated this journey in (*a machine that flies*) [2]............................. called 'Daedalus'. His (*path of flight*) [3]............................. was from Crete to Santorini, a distance of 119 kilometres. Kanellos, (*a cyclist who is a champion*) [4]............................., didn't use wax and feathers, but (*power from pedals*) [5]............................. to drive his machine. He was in the (*seat of the pilot*) [6]............................. for 3 hours and 5 minutes. His (*machine made of carbon fibre*) [7]............................. weighed 31 kilos and its wings measured 34 metres. Icarus, in the old story, flew too close to the sun. The wax that held his wings melted, so he crashed into the sea. Kanellos, however, kept 3 to 4 metres above the water and had a good (*wind from the south*) [8]............................. . He broke the record for human-powered flight previously set up by Bryan Allen, who 'cycled' 35.8 km across the English Channel.

Daedalus

2.3 Countable and uncountable nouns (1)

2.3A Countable and uncountable nouns compared [> LEG 2.14]

Study:
★★

1 If a noun is **countable**:
  a we can use *a/an* in front of it: *I bought **a book***. (Not **I bought book.**)
  b it has a plural and can be used in questions with *How many?*: *How many **books** ...?*
  c we can use a number in front of it: *one book, two books*.

2 If a noun is **uncountable**:
  a we do not normally use *a/an* in front of it: *I bought **some bread***. (Not **a bread**)
  b it does not normally have a plural and can be used in questions with *How much?*:
    *How much **bread** ...?* (Not **How many breads?**)
  c we cannot normally use a number in front of it. [compare > 2.3C]

3 We need to know whether nouns are countable or uncountable in English to be able to use
  a/an, some, any, much, many, a few, a little, etc. correctly.
  Compare: *It was **a marvellous experience***. (countable = something that happened)
      *We need someone with **experience***. (uncountable = skill and knowledge)

Write: Underline the noun in each sentence and write 'C' or 'U' to show whether the noun is countable or uncountable.

1 This is an excellent painting. *C*
2 I don't like milk. __
3 How many photos did he take? __
4 Add a little more oil. __
5 His drawings really interest me. __

6 Hope keeps me going. __
7 He hasn't a hope. __
8 How much flour did you buy? __
9 Where are my two new shirts? __
10 We've got plenty of coal. __

2.3B Nouns which can be either countable or uncountable: 'an egg/egg'
[> LEG 2.16.1, 2.16.2]

Study:
★★

1 Some nouns are countable when they refer to single items, but they are uncountable when
  they refer to substances:
  countable (a single item)   **uncountable** (substance/material)
  *He ate **a whole chicken**!*   *Would you like **some** chicken?*
  *I had **a boiled egg** for breakfast.*   *There's **egg** on your tie.*

2 Some nouns are uncountable when they refer to a material, but they are countable when
  they refer to an object made from that material:
  countable ('thing')   **uncountable** ('material')
  *I broke **a glass** this morning.*   ***Glass** is made from sand and lime.*
  *I picked up **a stone**.*   *We used **stone** to build our walls.*

Write: Underline the noun in each sentence and write 'C' or 'U' to show whether the noun is being used as a countable or as an uncountable.

1 Add more onion. *U*
2 Would you like some fish? __
3 I eat two eggs every day. __
4 Too much cake isn't good for you. __
5 They've built a new motorway. __

6 Would you like an ice? __
7 I need two clean glasses. __
8 Don't throw stones. __
9 A lot of paper is wasted. __
10 We bought a new iron yesterday. __

2.3C Normally uncountable nouns used as countables (1): 'a coffee/(some) coffee' [> LEG 2.16.3]

Study:
★★

1 Words for drinks like *coffee* are normally uncountable. This means:
   – we use no article: ***Coffee*** is important to the economy of Brazil.
   – or we use *some/any*:   Is there **any coffee**? I'd like **some coffee**, please.

2 However, when we are ordering *coffee*, etc., we normally treat it as countable:
   I'd like **a coffee**, please. **Two coffees**, please. **One coffee** and a glass of milk, please.

Write: Use *I'd like ...*, *please* to ask for drinks in each situation.

1 You have come down to breakfast. There is a choice between tea and coffee.
   I'd like (some) tea, please. I'd like (some) coffee, please.

2 You are ordering drinks. You want coffee for yourself. Your two friends want tea.
   ....

3 You are ordering drinks for three people: beer, lemonade, tomato juice.
   ....

4 You are ordering drinks. Two want coffee. Three want tea. One wants milk.
   ....

2.3D Normally uncountable nouns used as countables (2): 'oil/a light oil'
[> LEG 2.16.3]

Study:
★★★

Words like *oil* and *plastic* for substances and materials are normally uncountable [> 3.5A]:
Oil is produced in the North Sea.
We often use *a/an* with nouns like this when we are describing them with an adjective:
The North Sea produces **a light oil** which is highly prized in the oil industry.

Write: Rewrite these sentences using the nouns as countables.

1 The North Sea produces oil. (light) ....*The North Sea produces a light oil.*....
2 This region produces wine. (excellent) ....
3 This factory produces cloth. (traditional) ....
4 This box is made of wood. (rare) ....

2.3E Context

Write: Put in *a, some,* or '-'.

A terrible tragedy!

OOOPS!
[1]......—...... wine is not cheap and [2].................. good wine can cost a lot of money these days. So spare [3].................. thought for Mr Sokolin, [4].................. New York wine merchant, who recently lost [5].................. bottle of wine worth £305,000 (or about £50,000 [6].................. glass!). It was [7].................. 1784 Chateau Margaux which had once belonged to Thomas Jefferson, the third president of America. Mr Sokolin took the bottle to [8].................. wine tasting and put it on [9].................. table. The bottle was made of [10].................. dark glass and a waiter didn't notice it. He hit it with [11].................. tray, making [12].................. large hole in it. Most of the wine was lost, but Mr Sokolin was able to taste [13].................. of it. He said it was 'not very good', but the loss of the bottle was described as '[14].................. terrible tragedy'.

2.4 Countable and uncountable nouns (2)

2.4A Singular equivalents of uncountable nouns: 'bread/a loaf' [> LEG 2.16.6]

Study:

1 A word like *bread* is uncountable. If we want 'one item', we use a different word:
*I'd like **some bread**, please.* → *I'd like **a loaf** (of bread), please.*

2 Sometimes we have to say exactly what we want. We cannot say **a clothing**, so we ask for *a coat, a shirt*, etc. In the same way, we cannot say **a luggage**, **an accommodation**. We have to say what we want: e.g. *a suitcase, a room*.

Write: Put in any suitable word which means 'one item'.

1 Are you giving away all this clothing/all these clothes? – No, I'm giving away a ......*coat*..........
2 There's a lot of laughter from next door. I just heard a very loud ....
3 My luggage is getting old and worn. I really need a new ....
4 There are a lot of people looking for work. I need a .... myself.
5 I'm looking for accommodation. I'd like a .... for the night.

2.4B Nouns not normally countable in English: 'information'
[> LEG 2.14.1-2, 2.17, 2.30, App 4]

Study:

1 A number of nouns, like *information*, are countable in many languages, but they are uncountable in English. This means we cannot:
– use *a/an* in front of them: *I'd like **some information**, please.* (Not **an information**)
– give them a plural: *I'd like **some information**, please.* (Not **(some) informations**)

Other examples: *advice, clothing, flu, furniture, hair, homework, housework, jewellery, lightning, luggage, meat, money, news, permission, progress, rubbish, scenery, shopping, soap, spaghetti, thunder, toast, traffic, weather.*

2 *News* is plural in form, but takes a singular verb: **The news** is bad. (Not **the news are**)
Hair (that grows on the head) is singular: **My hair is** long. (Not **my hairs are**)
We use *hairs* only for individual strands of *hair*. **There are three hairs** on my nose.

Write 1: Tick the words which normally have plurals in English.

1 *advice* __   4 *answer* __   7 *penny* __   10 *money* __
2 *diamond* ✓   5 *jewellery* __   8 *story* __   11 *news* __
3 *meat* __   6 *carrot* __   9 *scenery* __   12 *shirt* __

Write 2: Put in *some, any, a, the, a lot of* or '-'.

1 I'd like ..*some*.. information, please.
2 The tree was struck by .... lightning.
3 Is there .... toast, please?
4 There's .... slice of toast left.
5 What's .... weather like today?
6 Can I have .... potatoes, please?
7 I need .... new clothing.
8 I'm tired. I've just done .... shopping.
9 I've done .... housework.
10 I've just received .... letter from John.

11 Can you give me .... description of it?
12 I'd like .... tomatoes, please.
13 Would you like .... spaghetti?
14 There was .... traffic this morning.
15 John's gone to bed with .... flu.
16 Have you made .... progress with Chinese?
17 I've got .... permission to park here.
18 Our teacher has given us .... homework.
19 There's .... rubbish in our garden.
20 I'm going to plant .... tree in the garden.

2.4C Partitives: 'a piece of', etc. [> LEG 2.18, App 5]

Study:
★★

1 We use **partitives** to refer to:
– one item: *a loaf of* bread
– a part of a whole: *a slice of* bread
– a collection of items: *a packet of* biscuits

2 The most common partitives are *a piece of* and (in everyday speech) *a bit of*:
*Can I have **a piece of** bread/**a bit of** bread/**two pieces of** bread, please?*

3 There are partitives which go with some words but not with others. So we can say *a slice of bread, a slice of cake, a slice of meat* (but not **a slice of soap**).
Partitives can be 'containers' (*a tin of soup*) or can refer to small amounts (*a drop of rain*).

Write: Match A and B.

A
1 I'd like *some* ice. .....*a cube of ice*..............................
2 Have you got *any* chocolate? ....
3 Can I have *some* bread, please? ....
4 We need *some* paper. ....
5 Buy me *some* soap, please. ....
6 Buy me *some* milk, please. ....
7 We need *some* jam. ....
8 Have you got *any* matches? ....
9 I've made *some* tea. ....
10 Buy *some* toothpaste. ....
11 Add *a little* water. ....
12 Add *a little* salt. ....
13 I've drunk *a little* tea. ....
14 Add *a little* soda. ....
15 I can see *a little* smoke. ....

B
a wisp of ....
a cube of ....
a splash of ....
a box of ....
a sip of ....
a tube of ....
a drop of ....
a bar of ....
a slice of ....
a pinch of ....
a sheet of ....
a jar of ....
a bar of ....
a bottle of ....
a pot of ....

2.4D Context

Write: Put in *a, a lot of* (use once only), *some*, or '-'

JUNK OR ART?
Who became famous for painting [1].......*a*....... tin of soup? The answer is the American pop artist, Andy Warhol. Andy painted everyday objects and he also liked to collect them in large numbers:
[2].................. cookie jars, [3].................. sets of cutlery, [4].................. vases, [5].................. furniture and [6].................. paintings. Andy died in 1987 and his vast collection was sold. Someone paid $23,100 for two cookie jars which had cost a few dollars each. [7].................. pieces of furniture were sold for nearly $300,000. The sale raised [8].................. money for the Andy Warhol Foundation for the Visual Arts, which may now have $100m! So, before you clear out your attic, take another look. What you think is [9].................. rubbish today, might be [10].................. treasure tomorrow. That ugly old vase belonging to Grandma may be more valuable than you think!

2.5 Number (singular and plural) (1)

2.5A Nouns with plurals ending in -s or -es: 'friends', 'matches' [> LEG 2.20, 2.21]

Study:
⭐

1 We add -s to form the plural of most nouns.
We pronounce -s as /s/ after these sounds: /f/ chiefs; /k/ cakes; /p/ taps; /t/ pets; /θ/ months.
We pronounce -s as /z/ after these sounds: /b/ verbs; /d/ friends; /g/ bags; /l/ bells; /m/ names;
/n/ lessons; /ŋ/ songs; vowel (**a, e, i, o, u**) + s: eyes, or vowel sound + r: chairs.

2 We add -es after nouns ending in -**o**: potato – potatoes; -**s**: class – classes;
-**x**: box – boxes; -**ch**: match – matches; -**sh**: dish – dishes.

We do not pronounce e in plurals like: cakes, clothes, tables, names, eyes.
We pronounce the plural as /ɪz/ after these sounds:
/z/: noises; /dʒ/: oranges; /s/: buses; /ʃ/: dishes; /tʃ/: matches; /ks/: boxes.

Write: Write the plurals of these nouns in the columns below to show their pronunciation.
address, beach, bottle, cinema, clock, guitar, hotel, island, lake, light, month, office, park, piece, smile, space, tape, village.

/s/	/z/	/ɪz/
1 clocks	7 bottles	13 addresses
2	8	14
3	9	15
4	10	16
5	11	17
6	12	18

2.5B Nouns with plurals ending in -s or -es: 'countries', 'knives'
[> LEG 2.20, 2.23, 2.36]

Study:
⭐⭐

1 Consonant (**b, c, d**, etc.) + -y becomes -ies: country/countries, strawberry/strawberries.

2 Vowel (**a, e, o** and **u**) + -y adds an -s: days, keys, boys, guys.
Proper nouns (names spelt with a capital letter) ending in -y just add an -s:
Have you met the **Kennedys**? The last four **Januarys** have been very cold.

3 We change the ending -f or -fe into -ves in the plural with the following nouns:
calf/calves, half/halves, knife/knives, leaf/leaves, life/lives, loaf/loaves, self/selves,
sheaf/sheaves, shelf/shelves, thief/thieves, wife/wives and wolf/wolves.

4 We add -s or -ves to: hoof – hoofs/hooves, scarf – scarfs/scarves.

5 We just add -s to: handkerchief/handkerchiefs, roof/roofs.

Write: Rewrite these sentences in the plural making necessary changes.

1 This cherry is very sweet.
These cherries are very sweet.

2 I've lost my key.

3 This knife is blunt.

4 The leaf is turning yellow.

5 The roof has been damaged.

6 We have a Henry in our family.
We have three

2.5C Nouns ending in -o and some irregular plural forms

[> LEG 2.20, 2.25-27, App 49]

Study:
★★

> 1 To nouns ending in -o, we add -es: *hero – heroes, potato – potatoes, tomato – tomatoes.*
> Or we add -es or -s: *cargo – cargoes* or *cargos, volcano – volcanoes* or *volcanos.*
> Or we add only -s: *bamboos, photos, pianos, radios, solos, videos, zoos.*
>
> 2 We change the vowels of some nouns to form the plural: *foot/feet, goose/geese, man/men, mouse/mice, tooth/teeth, woman/women.* And note: *child/children, ox/oxen.*
>
> 3 Some nouns have the same singular and plural forms: *aircraft, deer, salmon, trout, sheep.*
>
> 4 Nationality nouns ending in -ese and -ss have the same singular and plural forms:
> *a Chinese – the Chinese; a Swiss – the Swiss.* [> 3.3C]

Write: Rewrite these sentences in the plural making necessary changes.

1 Which video do you like best?
   Which videos do you like best?

2 Which volcano is erupting?

3 This is John's pet mouse.

4 This tooth is giving me trouble.

5 Can you see that goose?

6 A postman is busy all the time.

7 We're going to sell that sheep.

8 I can see a salmon in the water.

9 Which aircraft has just landed?

10 A Swiss is used to mountains.

2.5D Context

Write: Supply the correct plural forms.

Half a litre of double cream!

WHAT DOES IT COME UNDER?
If you're dieting there are certain (*food*) [1] *foods* you really have to avoid: (*cake*) [2] .... and (*biscuit*) [3] .... are out for a start, but you can't live for ever on (*tomato*) [4] .... and (*orange*) [5] .... There are (*man*) [6] .... and (*woman*) [7] .... who spend their entire (*life*) [8] .... counting the calories they take in each day. Some national (*cuisine*) [9] .... make you fat. The (*Japanese*) [10] .... have a high protein diet, while the (*Swiss*) [11] .... eat a lot of milk (*product*) [12] .... Personally, I'm lucky not to have to diet, but my friend, John, can't eat anything without looking it up in his Calorie Chart. This is carefully organized so that (*strawberry*) [13] .... and (*peach*) [14] .... are under 'Fruit'; (*potato*) [15] .... and (*spaghetti* > 2.4B) [16] .... come under 'Starchy Foods', and so on. I entertained John to a nice low calorie meal yesterday and at the end I offered him some jelly. 'What does "jelly" come under?' he asked looking at his chart. 'Half a litre of double cream,' I said, pouring the stuff over my plate!

2.6 Number (singular and plural) (2)

2.6A Collective nouns followed by singular or plural verbs: 'government'
[> LEG 2.28-29]

Study:
★★

1 Words like *government* and *family* are **collective nouns** because they refer to groups.

2 We can use singular or plural verbs with nouns like *committee, company, family, government* and *jury*: *What will you be doing while **the family is** (or **are**) on holiday?* These words also have regular plurals: *Many **families are** in need of help.*

3 We can use singular or plural verbs with nouns like *the majority, the public* and *the youth of today*: ***The public want** (or **wants**) to know how **they are** (or **it is**) governed.* These words do not have regular plural forms: (Not **the publics**)

4 We use only plural verbs with nouns like *cattle, the military, people, the police* and *vermin*: ***There are** too many **people** in the world.* (Not **There is too many people** **There are too many peoples**) These words do not have normal plural forms, but note that *peoples* means 'national populations': *The **peoples** of the Arab World have a common language.*

Write: Supply *is, are, has* or *have*. Give two forms where possible.

1 The government *is/are* bringing in a new bill.
2 The company .... going to employ six staff.
3 All governments .... trying to control crime.
4 The jury .... trying to decide now.
5 The youth of today .... many advantages.
6 There .... vermin in this restaurant.
7 The military .... occupied the house.
8 The police .... interested in this case.
9 The public .... concerned about it.
10 How many people .... coming tonight?
11 The committee .... meeting now.
12 A lot of people .... signed the petition.

2.6B Nouns with a plural form + singular or plural verbs: 'acoustics' [> LEG 2.31]

Study:
★★★

1 Nouns ending in *-ics*:
 – *athletics, gymnastics, linguistics, mathematics* (*maths*) and *physics* take a singular verb: ***Mathematics is** not the most popular school subject.* (Not **Mathematics are**)
 – *acoustics, economics, phonetics* and *statistics* take a singular verb only when they refer to the academic subject: ***Statistics is** a branch of economics.* (Not **statistics are**) They take a plural verb when the reference is specific: ***Your statistics are** unreliable.*

2 Nouns like *crossroads, headquarters, kennels, series, species* and *works* (= factory) are singular when they refer to one: ***This species** of moth **is** rare.* They are plural when they refer to more than one: ***There are** thousands of **species**.*

Write: Supply *is, are, has* or *have*.

1 The acoustics in this room ...*are*... very good.
2 This crossroads .... dangerous.
3 There .... four crossroads in our village.
4 Acoustics .... a subject I know little about.
5 Our company headquarters .... in London.
6 There .... many series of books on birds.
7 .... there any kennels in this area?
8 The statistics in this report .... inaccurate.
9 .... there any statistics for road accidents?
11 Many species of moth .... disappeared.
11 This species .... green and white spots.
12 Our works .... a good canteen.
13 My maths .... got worse and worse!
14 There .... crossroads every mile.

2.6C Nouns with a plural form + plural verbs: 'trousers' [> LEG 2.32, App 5.8]

Study:
★★

> **1** These nouns have a plural form only and are followed by a plural verb:
> *glasses* (= spectacles), *jeans, pants, pliers, pyjamas, scissors, shorts, tights, trousers*:
> My **trousers are** torn.
> All these nouns can combine with *a pair of*, (*two*) *pairs of*:
> I bought **a pair of shorts** yesterday and **two pairs of trousers**.
>
> **2** These nouns are plural in form and are followed by a plural verb:
> *belongings, brains* (= intellect), *clothes, congratulations, earnings, goods, manners, stairs*:
> **Were** those **clothes** expensive?

Write: Supply the missing words.

1 The goods you ordered ....*have*........... arrived.
2 Where .... the scissors? – .... are in the first drawer on the left.
3 How much .... a good pair of trousers cost these days?
4 How much did you pay for .... trousers? – .... were very expensive!
5 I know he's clever, but .... aren't the only thing in life.
6 I'm so pleased you got into university! .... on your success!
7 If your clothes .... dirty, please put them in the laundry basket.
8 My jeans (not) .... faded much even though I keep washing ....
9 I'm looking for the pliers. – You'll find .... on that shelf.
10 All their belongings .... been destroyed in a fire.
11 My earnings (not) .... high, but at least they .... regular.
12 These shorts .... fit me at all!

2.6D Context

Write: Put in singular or plural verb-forms.

LIES, DAMN LIES?
Statistics (*be*) [1] ....*is*........ a branch of economics, but it is often said that there (*be*) [2] .... lies, damn lies and statistics. Recent statistics of British life (*show*) [3] .... that the family (*be*) [4] .... happier than it used to be. The youth of today (*be*) [5] .... likely to live longer than the previous generation. People (*own*) [6] .... more things than they used to, but more police (*be*) [7] .... employed to fight crime. Mathematics (*be*) [8] .... a subject which is studied more by boys than by girls, as (*be*) [9] .... physics. The earnings of working women (*be*) [10] .... getting higher all the time and many women earn more than their husbands. Good manners (*be*) [11] .... declining. The public (*spend*) [12] .... more on clothes, and clothes (*be*) [13] .... becoming more and more expensive. Glasses (*be*) [14] .... worn by more people, but only a minority (*favour*) [15] .... contact lenses. Statistics (*make*) [16] .... us want to grind our teeth and can probably tell us if we have any teeth left to grind!

Lies, damn lies?   **37**

2.7 Gender

2.7A Male and female word forms: 'waiter/waitress' [> LEG 2.39-40]

Study:
★★

1 In many languages, the names of things such as *book, chair, radio, table* may be grammatically masculine, feminine or neuter. Often gender doesn't relate to sex, so that the word for 'girl' might be neuter and the word for 'chair' might be feminine.

2 There is no grammatical gender for nouns in English. Though there can be exceptions [> 4.1C], we use only *he* and *she* to refer to people and *it* to refer to everything else. It is the pronouns, not the nouns, that tell us whether the reference is to male or female:
He *is the* **person** *you spoke to.* **She** *is the* **person** *you spoke to.*

3 We still have a few male and female word forms (*man/woman*) and a few *-ess* endings that refer to females: *waiter/waitress, lion/lioness*. In the case of people, this *-ess* ending is becoming rare. In the interests of sexual equality, words like *author* and *manager* refer to both sexes, rather than using **authoress** or *manageress* for a woman.

Write: Supply the missing words. Refer to this list as little as possible.

actress, aunt, bachelor, bridegroom, cows, daughter, female, goddess, hens, heroine, heiress, lionesses, mares, nephew, nieces, nuns, prince, queens, ram, saleswoman, sister, sow, spinster, uncle, waitress, widower.

1 John's *brother* is a bank clerk and his ...*sister*... is a nurse.
2 My *aunt* is very nice and my .... has a wonderful sense of humour.
3 My .... is a little boy of four; my *niece* is a little girl of two.
4 My father's *brother* and *sister* have never married. He's still a .... and she's a ....
5 These days, few men become *monks* and few women become ....
6 There is only one *bull* in the field, but there are dozens of ....
7 The *cock* crows at dawn and wakes up all the ....
8 The *stallion* is in a separate stable from the ....
9 We call the *boar* Henry and we call the .... Jemima.
10 The *ewes* look quiet enough, but I don't like the look of that ....
11 Tony is an *actor* and his wife is an ....
12 John and Jane work in a restaurant; he is a *waiter* and she is a ....
13 In fairy tales the handsome .... usually marries the beautiful *princess*.
14 We went to a wildlife park and saw a lot of *lions* and ....
15 In mythology, Mars is the *god* of war; Diana is the .... of hunting.
16 Katerina is the .... to her father's fortune.
17 Why does everyone expect the *hero* of the story to marry the ....?
18 A *widow* can often manage much better on her own than a ....
19 A .... won the award for most sales this month; a *salesman* came second.
20 When you look at fish, it's often difficult to distinguish between *male* and ....
21 Very few people know the names of the *kings* and .... of England.
22 I took a photo of the *bride* and .... at the wedding.
23 The Smiths have a *son* called Robert and a .... called Jill.
24 My *uncle* and .... are over here from Canada.
25 I enjoy being an uncle. I have two .... and three *nephews*.

2.7B Identifying masculine and feminine through pronouns: 'He/She is a student' [> LEG 2.41]

Study:
★★

1 The word forms *man* and *woman* tell us that the reference is to male and female [> 2.7A], but with most nouns that refer to people, we don't know whether the reference is to male or female until we hear the pronoun:
My **neighbour** has just bought a new shed for **his** garden.
My **neighbour** is always telling us about **her** famous son.

2 Other typical nouns like this are:
adult, artist, child, cook, cousin, darling, dear, doctor, foreigner, friend, guest, journalist, lawyer, musician, orphan, owner, parent, passenger, person, pupil, relation, relative, scientist, singer, speaker, spouse, stranger, student, teacher, tourist, visitor, writer.

Write: Supply the correct pronouns in these sentences.

1 When I saw the doctor, ...*she*........ told me to go back and see her again next week.
2 Jennifer is a fine musician. .... plays in the Philharmonic.
3 My lawyer told me .... would ring me when he had the information I wanted.
4 Your visitor left .... glasses behind when he came here yesterday.
5 Professor Myers is a brilliant scientist. .... should be given the Nobel Prize for her work.
6 Mrs Carter, our English teacher, really knows .... grammar!
7 The artist, Rembrandt, painted several pictures of .... wife.
8 Anton Schmidt works as a cook at a large hotel. .... is famous for his cooking.
9 How would you describe her? – Well, ... is a student of about 18.
10 How do you know this passport belongs to a woman? – The owner has .... photo in it.
11 My daughter works as a journalist and .... has been very successful.
12 You don't know .... so you should begin your letter 'Dear Madam'.

2.7C Context

Write: Put in *actors, Miss, mother, Prince, princess, Sisters* and the missing words.

CINDERELLA AND THE UGLY SISTERS
Our local school recently put on *Cinderella* as a play and invited the Mayor of the town to see it. After the performance, the distinguished guest went backstage. [1].......*She*......... congratulated the young [2]....................... and actresses. [3]....................... spoke to Henry who played the part of [4]....................... Charming and Liz, who played the part of Cinderella. The Mayor asked Liz if [5]....................... would enjoy being a [6]....................... when she married Prince Charming and she blushed and giggled. The Mayor congratulated the Fairy God-[7]......................., and, of course, the teacher who produced the play, Miss Jones. [8]....................... Jones was very pleased because [9]....................... had worked hard to put on the play with a company of eleven-year-olds. The Mayor then approached us and said, 'Excellent ... excellent ... and ...-er ... you must be the Ugly [10].......................!' 'No, ma'am!' we cried. 'We're the children's mothers!'

You must be the Ugly Sisters!

2.8 The genitive

2.8A How to show possession with 's, s' and the apostrophe (') on its own
[> LEG 2.42-46]

Study:
★★

> 1 We show possession in English with the **genitive** form of a noun. This means we normally use *'s* and *s'* for people and some living creatures. We put the possessive before the noun it refers to: *Frank's car.* (Not **the car of Frank/the car of Frank's**)
>
> 2 The simplest rule to remember is: **Add 's to any personal noun unless it is in the form of a plural ending in -s, – in which case, just add an apostrophe (').** This means:
>
> – add *'s* to singular nouns and names not ending in *-s*: *a boy's tie, Tom's hat.*
> – add *'s* to singular nouns ending in *-s*: *an actress's career, a waitress's job.*
> – add *'s* to irregular plural nouns: *children's games, the men's club, sheep's wool.*
> – add an apostrophe (') after the *-s* of regular plurals: *the girls' uniforms.*
> – add *'s* to names ending in *-s*: *Charles's address, Doris's party, St James's Park.*
> Famous names ending in *s* just add ('): *Yeats' poetry.* This is pronounced /s/ or /ɪz/.

Write: Rewrite these sentences using *'s, s'*, or just an apostrophe (').

1 This bicycle is for a child. .....*This is a child's bicycle*.....
2 This pen belongs to the teacher. ....
3 He described the career of the actress. ....
4 That's a job for a stewardess. ....
5 These toys belong to the children. ....
6 This is a club for women. ....
7 It's a school for girls. ....
8 This is the lounge for residents. ....
9 This umbrella belongs to James. ....
10 That hat belongs to Doris. ....

2.8B Apostrophe s ('s/s'), compound noun, or 'of'? [> LEG 2.47-48, 2.50]

Study:
★★

> 1 When we want to show possession with things, we can use *of*: *the leg of the table.* However, we often prefer to use a compound noun instead of *of*: *the table-leg* [> 2.2B].
>
> 2 We must use *of* when we can't form a compound noun:
> *the book of the film* (Not **the film's book**); *the top of the box* (Not **the box's top**)
> You can only learn these from experience. If you are in doubt, use *of*.

Write: *Only where possible*, use an apostrophe to show possession in these sentences.

1 That's *the voice of a man*. .....*That's a man's voice*.....
2 I can't see *the bottom of the box*. ....
3 That's *the decision of the committee*. ....
4 It's *the fault of no one*. ....
5 This is a copy of *the poetry of Keats*. ....
6 That's *the leg of the table*. ....
7 Where's *the key of the car*? ....
8 That's *the bell of the village church* that you can hear. ....
9 These are *the stables of the horses*. ....

2.8C The use of 's and s' with non-living things: 'an hour's journey'
[> LEG 2.49-50]

Study:
★★

> We use 's and s' with some non-living things:
> – fixed phrases: *the earth's surface, journey's end, the ship's company*
> – time phrases (singular): *an hour's journey, a day's work, a month's salary*
> – time phrases (plural): *two hours' journey, two days' work, two months' salary*

Write: Use *'s or s' only where possible* with these.

1 a delay of an hour ..... *an hour's delay* ....
2 a journey of two days ....
3 the shade of the tree ....
4 the book of the film.......................................
5 the inside of the box ....

6 the price of success ....
7 work of seven years ....
8 the surface of the earth ....
9 at the door of death ....
10 an absence of a year ....

2.8D Omission of the noun after 's [> LEG 2.51]

Study:
★★

> We generally omit the noun after *'s* when referring to work-places, shops, and houses:
> *the doctor's*, rather than *the doctor's surgery*, *my mother's* rather than *my mother's house*.

Write: What could we use in place of the words in brackets?

1 Your mother has gone to (the shop owned by the hairdresser) ..... *the hairdresser's* ....
2 I'll meet you at (the shop owned by the chemist) ....
3 I'm going to spend the night at (the house owned by my aunt) ....
4 We were married in (the church dedicated to St Andrew) ....
5 I bought this at (the department store owned by Marks and Spencer) ....

2.8E Context

Write: Put in compounds and *'s and s'* constructions in this story.

MIND YOUR SKIN!
We have become very conscious of conservation these days. A lot of people won't buy any goods made from (skins of animals) [1] ..... *animal* ..... *skins* .... In many parts of the world, it is now unthinkable for a person to dress in (a coat made of the skin of a leopard) [2] .... We realize that (the wildlife of the earth) [3] .... needs protection. This affects such things as (clothing worn by children) [4] ....
.... and (coats worn by ladies) [5] ....
.... If (a fur coat worn by an actress) [6] ....
.... attracts admiration these days, it is probably created from man-made materials. Of course, we still farm animals for their skins, but the notice I saw in a shop recently must have been (the revenge of the crocodiles) [7] .... It was selling crocodile-skin bags and offering the following service: ('skins of customers) [8] .... *made up*'!

Mind your skin!

41

3 Articles

3.1 The indefinite article: 'a/an' (1)

3.1A General statements with 'a/an' and zero (Ø) [> LEG 3.7, 3.9.1-2, 3.19.1]

Study:
★★

> **1** *A* and *an* have exactly the same meaning. We use *a* in front of consonant sounds (*a man, a year*) and *an* in front of vowel sounds (*an umbrella, an eye, an hour*).
>
> **2** We can talk about people or things 'in general' with *a/an* or with the plural [> 3.5A].
> Instead of: ***Cats** are domestic animals.* (= 'cats in general')
> We can say: ***A cat** is a domestic animal.* (= 'cats in general')

Write: Make the singular sentences plural and the plural sentences singular.

1 A small computer isn't expensive. ...... *Small computers aren't expensive.* ......
2 A quartz watch doesn't last for ever. ....
3 I like plays with messages. ....
4 I admire politicians who are sincere. ....
5 A big city is always fascinating. ....
6 Even an efficient system can break down. ....
7 A road map is always out of date. ....
8 A rule is meant to be broken. ....
9 Restaurants shouldn't charge too much. ....
10 How much do car radios cost? ....
11 A bus leaves here every hour. ....
12 How long does a letter take to get here? ....

3.1B The 'plural form' of 'a/an' [> LEG 3.5-6, 3.9.1-2]

Study:
★★

> **1** The plural of *a/an* is *zero* (Ø) when we refer to 'things in general':
> ***A cat** is **a domestic animal**.* → (Ø) ***Cats** are (Ø) **domestic animals**.*
>
> **2** The plural of *a/an* is *some* or *any* when we refer to 'quantity' [but compare > 5.3A]:
> *There's **a sandwich** on the plate.* → *There are **some sandwiches** on the plate.* [> 5.3B]
> We use numbers in place of *a/an* and *some/any* only when we are counting:
> *There's only **one sandwich** left.*→ *There are only **four sandwiches** left.* [> 3.2B]

Write: Turn these sentences into the plural, making all necessary changes.

1 She's an architect. ...... *They're architects.* ......
2 Do you want a potato? ....
3 A doctor needs years of training. ....
4 How well can a cat see in the dark? ....
5 Have you got a cat at home? ....
6 Why should a compact disc be so dear? ....
7 I borrowed a compact disc. ....
8 Can you lend me a compact disc? ....
9 Why is a car so expensive? ....
10 There isn't a car in the street. ....

3.1C Describing people and things with 'a/an' + noun: 'He's a doctor'

[> LEG 3.9.3-4, App 49]

Study:

★★

1 We use some words as adjectives or nouns when we want to describe people.
   When we use them as countable nouns, we always put *a/an* in front of them [> 2.3A], e.g.
   – nationality: *She's **American**.* (adjective) or: *She's **an American**.* (noun) [> 3.3C]
   – religion: *She's **Anglican**.* (adjective) or: *She's **an Anglican**.* (noun)
   – politics: *He's **Conservative**.* (adjective) or: *He's **a Conservative**.* (noun)

2 We use some words only as countable nouns (people and things) and we always put *a/an* in
   front of them: *He's **a doctor**.* (Not **He's doctor.**) *It's **a tree**.* (Not **It's tree.**)
   We can also use adjective + noun: *She's **a good girl**.* (Not **She's good girl.**)

3 We can use *a/an* in front of proper nouns (names spelt with a capital letter) for:
   – members of a family: *He's **a Forsyte**.* (= a member of the Forsyte family)
   – literature and art: *It's **a Dickens novel**. It's **a Brecht play**.* Sometimes we can use the name
     on its own. We can say *It's **a Rembrandt painting*** or *It's **a Rembrandt**.*

Write: Write sentences using *He's ..., She's ..., It's ...* + noun for each of the following.

1 What does he do? He *drives a taxi*. *He's a taxi-driver.*
2 What's her religion? She's *Catholic*. ....
3 Where does he come from? He comes from *England*. ....
4 What's that? (*ant*) ....
5 What's that? (*kind of insect*) ....
6 What political party does she belong to? She's *socialist*. ....
7 What does she do? She *teaches* children. ....
8 What does she do? (*architect*) ....
9 What is it? (*sonnet by Shakespeare*) ....
10 What is it? (*painting by Picasso*) ....

3.1D Context

Write: Put in *a, some, any* or '-'. Alternatives are possible.

AT YOUR SERVICE, SIR!

[1] ....—........ robots are common in industry and perhaps they will soon be common in the home.
[2] .... robot working in the home must be able to behave like [3] .... human. You could
ask it to make breakfast for you. 'I'd like [4] .... pot of coffee, please and [5] .... boiled
eggs.' 'How many, sir?' 'Two please.' You wouldn't have to worry about bringing friends home to
dinner. 'I've brought [6] .... friends for dinner,' you would say, 'please prepare [7] .... meal
for six.' Your robot would be [8] .... cook, [9] .... servant and [10] .... cleaner, and
perhaps it could even do the shopping. 'We haven't got [11] .... tomatoes,' you would say. 'Be
[12] .... good robot and get some from the supermarket.' [13] .... robots would never need
to sleep, and would never complain. But I wouldn't want them wandering round the house at night!

Ask it to make breakfast for you.

3.2 The indefinite article: 'a/an' (2)

3.2A The use of 'a/an' when something is mentioned for the first time
[> LEG 3.8, 3.10.2]

Study:
⊡

> We use *a/an* to introduce a person or thing for the first time. This shows that the listener or reader doesn't know what we are referring to. After this first reference, we use *the*.
>
> *I watched* **a car** *as it came up our road.* **The car** *stopped outside our house and* **a man** *got out.* **The man** *was carrying* **a case** *in his hand. With* **the case** *in his hand,* **the man** *looked like* **a salesman**.

Write: Supply *a/an* or *the* in the following text.

During our journey we came to [1].....*a*...... bridge. As we were crossing [2]............. bridge, we met [3]............. old man and spoke to him. [4]............. man refused to answer us at first. He could tell at a glance that we had escaped from [5]............. prisoner-of-war camp and he was afraid of getting into trouble. We weren't [6]............. first prisoners of war to have escaped from [7]............. camp. As soon as Jim produced [8]............. revolver, [9]............. man proved very willing to answer our questions. He told us exactly where we were and directed us to [10]............. farm where we might find food.

3.2B The difference between 'a/an' and 'one' [> LEG 3.10.1, 3.11]

Study:
⊡⊡

> **1** We do not use *a/an* + noun and *one* + noun in the same way.
> We use *a/an* to mean 'any one': *I'd like* **a coffee**, *please.*
> We use *one* when we are counting: *It was* **one coffee** *I ordered and* **not two**.
>
> **2** We use *one* with *day, morning, evening* when we are telling a story:
> **One day**, *when I was working as a salesman, I received a strange telephone call.*
> Compare: *I had to stay in bed for* **a day**. (= any day, it doesn't matter which)
> *I had to stay in bed for* **one day**. (= one day and not two or more)
>
> **3** We use *a/an* or *one* with:
> **a** Whole numbers: *a/one hundred, thousand.* **c** Money: *a/one pound, dollar.*
> **b** Fractions: *a/one quarter, half.* **d** Weights, measures: *a/one kilo, foot.*

Write: Supply *a/an* or *one* in these sentences. Note where you can use either *a/an* or *one*.

1 I need ....*a*.......... picture-hook to hang this picture.
2 Did you say you wanted .... picture-hook or two?
3 .... nail won't be enough for this job. I need several.
4 You should use .... hammer to drive in those nails.
5 How many orange juices did you say? – Just .... orange juice, please.
6 You should get out into the fresh air on .... day like this!
7 .... day, many years later, I learnt the truth.
8 I was out walking late .... evening when I saw .... strange object in the sky.
9 He says he's going to be .... millionaire .... day.
10 There were over .... hundred people at the party.
11 Have you ever seen .... silent movie?
12 I've only ever seen .... silent movie.

3.2C 'A/an' for price, distance and frequency: '80p a kilo' [> LEG 3.12]

Study:
★★

price/weight: *80p a kilo*	**distance/speed**: *40 km an hour*
distance/fuel: *30 miles a* (or *to the*) *gallon*	**frequency/time**: *twice a day*

Write: Write complete answers to these questions.

1 How much are these apples? 90p/kilo .....*They're 90p a kilo.*.....
2 How often do you take these pills? once/day ....
3 What speed are we doing? 100 km/hour ....
4 How many miles a gallon do you do? 45 miles/gallon ....
5 How often is the rubbish collected? twice/week ....
6 What does olive oil cost? £3/litre. ....

3.2D 'A/an' or zero with reference to illnesses: 'a cold' [> LEG 3.15]

Study:
★★

1 We always use *a/an* with these illnesses: *a cold, a headache, a sore throat.*

2 We can use or omit *a/an* with these:
   catch (a) cold, have (a/an) backache/earache/stomach-ache/toothache.

3 We use no article at all with these plurals: *measles, mumps, shingles.*

4 We use no article with these: *(high) blood pressure, flu, gout, hepatitis.*

Write: Supply *a/an* where necessary. Note where you can use *a/an* or zero (-).

1 I'm going to bed. I've got ...*a*.... headache.
2 I was awake all night with .... toothache.
3 I think Gillian's got .... flu.
4 The children are in bed with .... mumps.
5 Mind you don't catch .... cold.
6 .... measles can be very unpleasant.
7 Don't come near me. I've got .... sore throat.
8 I think I've got .... cold!
9 I've had .... terrible backache.
10 I often suffer from .... backache.

3.2E Context

Write: Put in *a*, *the*, or *one* only where necessary.

HERE'S HEALTH!
'I think that's all, Mrs Grant,' Dr Grey said as she handed her [1].......*a*..... list of prescriptions. [2].............. list was very long and Mrs Grant almost fainted as she tried to read it. She had [3].............. headache and [4].............. cold and felt as if she was getting [5].............. flu. On top of this, one of her children was in bed with [6].............. mumps. 'I've prescribed some pills for [7].............. high blood pressure as well,' Dr Grey said. 'How many do I have to take – [8].............. pill [9].............. day?' 'No. One pill with each meal. Three pills [10].............. day.' Mrs Grant thanked [11].............. doctor and walked out of her surgery with some difficulty. She staggered into the local chemist's and handed [12].............. long prescription list to Mr Burt, [13].............. chemist. Mr Burt greeted her cheerfully. 'Good morning, Mrs Grant,' he said, glancing at [14].............. list. 'What a list! I trust you're keeping well!'

I trust you're keeping well!

3.3 The definite article: 'the' (1)

3.3A Form and basic uses of 'the' [> LEG 3.16, 3.18]

Study:

⭐

> 1 *The* never varies in form whether it refers to people or things, singular or plural:
>   **a** *That's **the man** we met last night.*   **d** *They're **the men** we met last night.*
>   **b** *That's **the woman** we met last night.*   **e** *They're **the women** we met last night.*
>   **c** *That's **the shirt** I bought yesterday.*   **f** *They're **the shirts** I bought yesterday.*
>
> 2 We use *the* to refer to something that is known. [> 3.2A]
>
> 3 *The* can combine with singular countable nouns (*the book*), plural countable nouns (*the books*), and uncountable nouns, which are always singular (*the furniture*).

Write: Supply *a* or *the* in the following text.

We wanted to reach ¹......*a*..... small village and knew we must be near. Then we saw ².............. woman just ahead and some children playing. When we stopped to ask the way, ³.............. woman said she was ⁴.............. stranger herself. We called out to ⁵.............. children, but they ignored us. Just then two men came along and we asked them the way. ⁶.............. men didn't know, but at least they were helpful. 'There's ⁷.............. signpost a mile along this road,' one of them said. We drove to ⁸.............. signpost eagerly. This is what it said: NORTH POLE 6,000 MILES.

3.3B 'A/an', 'the' and zero in front of abbreviations: 'the BBC'
[> LEG 3.7, 3.17, 3.24]

Study:

⭐⭐

> 1 We make abbreviations with the first letters of the most important words. We then treat these abbreviations like ordinary nouns and use them with *a/an*, *the* or zero [> 3.1C]:
>   *I've just bought **an LP**.* (= a Long Playing record).
>   We use *an* + vowel sound (*an LP*) and *a* + consonant sound (*a VW* = a Volkswagen).
>
> 2 We use *a/an* and full stops with titles: *She's **an M.A.*** (= Master of Arts)
>
> 3 We use *the* in front of institutions when we can't say them as single words. We don't use full stops: *I listen to the news on **the BBC**.* (= the British Broadcasting Corporation)
>   *We are members of **UNESCO**.* /juːˈnɛskəʊ/
>   (= the United Nations Educational, Scientific and Cultural Organization)
>
> 4 We use no article (zero) with chemical symbols: ***CO$_2$** stands for Carbon Dioxide.*
>
> 5 The first letters of some words are often used as normal words: e.g.
>   *Planes use **radar**.* (= RAdio Detection And Ranging)

Write: Supply *a/an*, *the* or '-'.

1 Jim got ....*a*.......... B.Sc. (= Bachelor of Science) from Durham University in 1988.
2 Celia is sure she's seen .... UFO (= Unidentified Flying Object).
3 .... EC (= European Community) does a lot of trade with the rest of the world.
4 I don't know how much .... MP (= Member of Parliament) earns.
5 Which countries belong to .... NATO /ˈneɪtəʊ/ ? (= North Atlantic Treaty Organization)
6 .... H$_2$0 is the chemical formula for water.
7 I've used my computer to learn .... BASIC (= Beginners' All-purpose Instruction Code).
8 .... NASA (= National Aeronautics and Space Administration) had a setback in 1986.

3.3C 'The' + nationality noun: 'the Chinese' [> LEG 3.19.2, App 49]

Study:
★★

> We use *the* in front of nationality nouns to refer to 'all the people in general'.
> We can divide nationality nouns into four groups:
>
> 1 *the* + *-ese* or *-ss*: *the Chinese, the Japanese, the Portuguese, the Sudanese, the Swiss.*
>
> 2 *the* + plural ending in *-s*:
> *-ian*: *the Austrians, the Belgians, the Brazilians, the Egyptians, the Russians.*
> *-an*: *the Americans, the Koreans, the Mexicans, the Venezuelans, the Zimbabweans.*
> other *-s* endings: *the Arabs, the Germans, the Greeks, the Poles, the Scots, the Turks.*
>
> 3 Two forms: *the Danes/the Danish, the Spaniards/the Spanish, the Swedes/the Swedish.*
>
> 4 *the* + *-ch* or *-sh*: *the British, the Dutch, the English, the French, the Irish, the Welsh.*

Write: Rewrite these sentences using nationality nouns to refer to 'the people in general'.

1 *The people from Portugal* are very different from *the people from Spain*.
   The Portuguese are very different from the Spaniards.

2 *The people from America* and *the people from Russia* understand each other better.
   ....

3 *The people from Brazil* speak Portuguese, but *the people from Mexico* speak Spanish.
   ....

4 *The people from Germany* and *the people from Japan* work very hard.
   ....

5 *The people from Greece* buy ships from *the people from Korea*.
   ....

6 *The people from Britain* and *the people from Holland* do a lot of foreign trade.
   ....

3.3D Context

Write: Put in *a* or *the*.

An ancient Egyptian drill

ANCIENT SECRETS

Mr Denys Stocks, [1].....*a*..... retired policeman, has just been given [2].............. B.Sc. for twelve years' research into ancient Egyptian industrial methods. Egyptologists have often wondered how [3].............. Egyptians were able to cut such hard stone and how they produced such fine jewellery. Mr Stocks has shown that [4].............. Egyptians used saws and drills. [5].............. saws and drills were made of copper, which is very soft. But [6].............. Egyptian craftsmen turned them into very powerful tools. First [7].............. craftsman made [8].............. cut in [9].............. stone with [10].............. soft saw. Then [11].............. craftsman poured sand into [12].............. cut. [13].............. hard sand got into [14].............. teeth of [15].............. saw and did [16].............. cutting. In this way, [17].............. worker could cut basalt, one of the hardest rocks. [18].............. sand he used turned into [19].............. very fine powder. [20].............. powder was then used by jewellers to cut precious stones and to make delicate jewellery.

3.4 The definite article: 'the' (2)

3.4A 'The' for specifying [> LEG 3.20]

Study:
★★

> 1 When we use *the*, the listener or reader knows or can understand what we are referring to. We can make a reference 'specific' or 'definite' by means of:
>   – **back reference**: *We stopped at a small village.* ***The village*** *was very pretty.* [> 3.2A, 3.3A]
>   – ***the + noun + of***: ***The life of Napoleon*** *was very stormy.*
>   – **a clause** (= part of a sentence): ***The Jones I'm referring to*** *is a colleague of mine.*
>   – **context**: The listener knows exactly what we are referring to from the context.
>   That's why we say: *It's* ***the postman***. (Not **a postman**)
>   *She's gone to* ***the butcher's***. (Not **a butcher's**) [> 2.8D]
>   *Running is good for* ***the heart***. (Not **a heart**)
>
> 2 We often say *the cinema, the theatre, the supermarket, the bank*, etc. even if we don't know exactly which: *He's gone to* ***the cinema/the theatre/the supermarket/the bank***.
>
> 3 We refer to *the country, the mountains, the seaside* even if we don't know exactly where: *We're spending the weekend in* ***the country****/in* ***the mountains****/at* ***the seaside***.
>
> 4 We use *the* to refer to 'one of a kind': *the earth, the sea, the sky, the sun, the moon, the solar system, the planets, the galaxy, the universe*: ***The earth*** *doesn't belong to us.*

Write: Supply *a/an*, *the* or '-'.

1 We were looking for ......*a*........ place to spend .....*the*..... night. .... place we found turned out to be in .... charming village. .... village was called .... Lodsworth.
2 .... individual has every right to expect personal freedom. .... freedom of .... individual is something worth fighting for.
3 Yes, my name is .... Simpson, but I'm not .... Simpson you're looking for.
4 Who's at .... door? – It's .... postman.
5 When you go out, would you please go to .... supermarket and get some butter.
6 I've got .... appointment this afternoon. I've got to go to .... doctor's.
7 We went to .... theatre last night and saw *Flames*. It's .... wonderful play.
8 We prefer to spend our holidays in .... country, ... mountains or by .... sea.
9 We have seen what .... earth looks like from .... moon.
10 This is the front room. .... ceiling and .... walls need decorating, but .... floor is in good order. We'll probably cover it with .... carpet.
11 You're imagining .... things. All your fears are in .... mind.
12 Look at this wonderful small computer. .... top lifts up to form .... screen; .... front lifts off to form .... keyboard and .... whole thing only weighs 5 kilos.
13 .... history of .... world is .... history of .... war.
14 Is there .... moon round .... planet Venus?
15 What's .... John doing these days? – He's working as .... postman.
16 .... exercise is good for .... body.
17 Could you pass me .... salt, please?
18 They're building .... new supermarket in .... centre of our town.
19 Where's your mother at .... moment? – I think she's in .... kitchen.
20 If you were a cook, you'd have to work in .... kitchen all day long.

3.4B 'The' to refer to things that are unique (not place names) [> 3.6C, LEG 3.22]

Study:
★★

1 We often use *the* to refer to 'things that are unique':
   a organizations: *the United Nations*
   b ships: *the Titanic*
   c documents: *the Constitution*
   d public bodies: *the police, the Government*
   e titles of books and films: *The Odyssey*
   f climate: *the weather*
   g historical events: *the French Revolution*
   h official titles: *the President*
   i political parties: *the Labour Party*
   j the press: *The Economist, The Times*
   k beliefs: *the gods*
   l the whole species: *the dinosaurs*

2 We treat other, similar, words as proper nouns [> 3.5A] and use no article (zero), e.g.
   a organizations: *Congress, Parliament*
   b titles of books and films: *Jaws*
   c beliefs: *God, Buddha*
   d official titles: *Queen Elizabeth*
   e the press: *Punch, Time magazine*
   f the whole species: *Man*

Write: Supply *the* or '-'.

1 I like to read newspapers like .....*The*.... *Times* and ....*The*.... *Washington Post*.
2 I read .... *Economist* every week and .... *Time* magazine.
3 Do you think .... *New Yorker* and .... *Punch* have much in common?
4 We can't be sure about the history of .... human race, but .... man developed earlier than we think, though we certainly weren't around at the time of .... dinosaurs.
5 I like watching old films. I recently watched .... *Graduate* and .... *Jaws* on video.
6 The Ancient Greeks believed in .... gods. The idea of .... God was not known to them.
7 I've read Homer's .... *Odyssey*, but I haven't read Joyce's .... *Ulysses*.
8 .... United Nations may be a talking shop, but so is .... Congress.
9 A lot of people object to attempts to bring up .... *Titanic*.
10 My oldest son joined .... Navy and now my youngest wants to join .... Army.
11 France celebrated the 200th anniversary of .... French Revolution in 1989.
12 In many countries, the head of state is called .... President.
13 Do you know who killed .... President Lincoln?
14 Because of 'the greenhouse effect' .... climate of the world is changing.

3.4C Context

Write: Put in *a/an* or *the*.

SUNRAYCER
I read recently in [1]....*The*.... *Times* that the big American company, General Motors, has developed [2].............. vehicle that uses [3].............. power of [4].............. sun instead of petrol. [5].............. vehicle is called Sunraycer. Sunraycer has just taken part in [6].............. race against 25 solar-powered vehicles. [7].............. route of [8].............. race was from Darwin to Adelaide, [9].............. immense distance. Sunraycer covered [10].............. distance in 45 hours at [11].............. average speed of 41 miles [12].............. hour in temperatures as high as 48°C. It beat all other cars by two and [13].............. half days! Sunraycer ('ray of the sun' + 'racer') is certainly [14].............. car of [15].............. future!

Sunraycer

3.5 The zero article (1)

3.5A Basic uses of the zero article (∅): 'Life is short' [> LEG 3.24-26, 3.27.1, 3.27.3-5]

Study:
★★

We often use no article at all (zero) in English where some other languages use *the*:

1 In front of **plural countable nouns** used in general statements [> 3.1A], e.g. for:
  – people: **∅ Women** need better pay.   – places: **∅ Museums** are closed on Mondays.
  – animals: **∅ Cats** don't like cold weather.   – plants: **∅ Trees** don't grow in the Antarctic.
  – food: **∅ Beans** are good for you.   – products: **∅ Watches** aren't expensive.
  (Not *The beans are good for you.* etc.) [compare > 5.3A]

2 In front of **uncountable nouns** (always singular) used in general statements, e.g. for:
  – food: *I like **∅ butter**.*   – substances: **∅ Oil** is produced in Alaska.
  – colours: **∅ Red** is my favourite colour.   – activities: **∅ Swimming** is good for you.
  – abstract: **∅ Life** is short.   – languages: **∅ English** is a world language.
  (Not *The life is short.* etc.) [compare > 5.3A]

3 In front of most **proper nouns** (names spelt with a capital letter) [> 3.1C, 3.6C]:
  Fritz Weber lives in Berlin. This was made by Jackson and Son.

  By comparison, we use *the* when the reference is specific, not in general statements:
1 In front of plural countable nouns: **The beans** I like best are kidney beans.
2 In front of uncountable nouns: I used all **the butter** that was in the butter dish.
3 In front of proper nouns: **The Fritz Weber** I know lives in Vienna.

Write: Supply *the* or '-'.

1 A lot of people are giving up ....—........ meat.
2 .... meat we had for lunch last Sunday was very tough.
3 As someone said, ... life is just one damned thing after another.
4 I don't know much about .... life of .... Napoleon.
5 .... running is supposed to be good for you.
6 I ought to be fit with all .... running I do, but I don't feel fit.
7 Which is your favourite colour? – .... Red.
8 I think .... red one will suit you best. .... Red is more your colour.
9 We learnt .... English at school, but .... English we learnt was useless.
10 .... London is a safe city today, but .... London of the 18th century was pretty rough.
11 .... watches have become very cheap and very attractive.
12 Most of .... watches you see today work on .... quartz.
13 .... indoor plants require a lot of effort and attention.
14 .... Bach gives me a great deal of pleasure.
15 .... Bach recording you bought for my birthday is first class.
16 What has been the longest period of .... peace in .... history?
17 If you study .... History, you've got to read a lot.
18 .... fasting during .... Ramadan is more difficult in the summer months.
19 .... journeys to unknown places require a lot of preparation.
20 .... lives of .... poets and .... musicians have often been unbearably difficult.
21 I'm not interested in the price of .... silver or the price of .... gold.
22 .... time is .... money.
23 I can never regret .... time I've spent enjoying myself.
24 I often listen to .... music and I like .... jazz best.

3.5B   The zero article with names and titles: 'Mr Pym' [> LEG 2.13, 3.27]

Study:
★★

1 We do not normally use articles in front of proper nouns (like *John, London*, etc.).

2 We use a surname or first name + surname after *Mr, Mrs, Miss* and *Ms* /məz/ : *Mr Pym, Mr John Pym*. We often write, but rarely say *Ms*, as in *Ms Joan Cartwright*.

3 We abbreviate *Doctor* to *Dr* in writing and use a surname after it: *I'm Dr Brown*, but we can use *Doctor* on its own as a form of address (written in full): *It's my liver, Doctor*.

4 In British English *Madam* and *Sir* can be used as forms of address, e.g. by shop assistants: *Yes, madam? Sir* is also a title in front of first name (+ surname): *Sir John (Falstaff)*, (Not **Sir Falstaff**). Americans use *Sir* on its own to speak to strangers.

5 We can say *Uncle* and *Auntie* (but not **Cousin** or **Sister**) to address our relations.

6 *Major* and *Professor* can be used with names or on their own.

7 *Nurse* and sometimes *Sister* can be used as forms of address for nurses.

Write: Mark with an X those sentences that are wrong or unacceptable and briefly say why.

1 Excuse me, Mr – can you tell me the way to the station, please? X
2 Good morning, Doctor. __
3 Don't ask me. Ask Mrs Elizabeth. __
4 Can I introduce you to Mrs Elizabeth Jackson? __
5 I have an appointment with Dr White. __
6 I've just received a letter from cousin Frank. __
7 Can I help you, Mrs? __
8 Can I help you, Madam? __
9 Sir Falstaff is a famous Shakespeare character. __
10 May I have a word with you please, Professor? __
11 I've addressed the letter to Professor John Williams. Is that right? __
12 Nurse, could I speak to you for a moment, please? __

3.5C   Context

Write: Put in *a/an, the* or '-'.

FOOD FIT FOR A KING!
[1].....:...... seeds dating from 1325 B.C. have been found at [2]............. Kew Gardens in [3]............. London. 'It's [4]............. exciting discovery,' [5]............. Professor Arthur Bell, [6]............. Director, said yesterday. [7]............. seeds were found in 30 cardboard boxes by [8]............. French student, [9]............. Christian Tutundjian de Vartavan. [10]............. seeds come from [11]............. tomb of [12]............. King Tutankhamun. Inside [13]............. tomb were *shawabtis*, that is, model human beings who would serve [14]............. King after [15]............. death. Inside [16]............. Tutankhamun's tomb, there was [17]............. wheat for making [18]............. bread, [19]............. barley, perhaps for brewing [20]............. beer, and spices like [21]............. coriander, [22]............. cumin and [23]............. sesame, as well as [24]............. grapes and [25]............. tropical fruits. [26]............. food had to be suitable for [27]............. King's last journey, but it was very tasty, too!

Inside Tutankhamun's tomb

3.6 The zero article (2)

3.6A Zero article for parts of the day ('at dawn') and for meals ('for lunch')
[> LEG 3.28.1-2]

Study:
★★

> 1 **Parts of the day and night**: We use no article when we refer to parts of the day and night:
> *at dawn/daybreak, at sunrise/sunset/noon/night, by day/night,*
> *at/by/before/after/till 4 o'clock: We left at dawn.*
> But compare: *I've never seen **a dawn** like it! I got up early to admire **the dawn**.*
>
> 2 **Meals:** We use no article with words like: *breakfast, lunch, tea, dinner, supper.*
> **Dinner** is served. He's **at lunch**. Let's **have breakfast**.
> But compare: **The breakfast** I ordered still hasn't arrived. (a specific reference)
> *That was **a very nice dinner**.* (simple description [> 3.1C])

Write: Supply *a/an, the* or '-'.

1 We're setting off at .... sunrise.
2 We must be home before .... midnight.
3 I'm often wide awake at .... night.
4 We reached the village before .... sunset.
5 .... lunch I ordered was burnt.
6 We're invited to the Smiths for .... lunch.
7 Let's have .... breakfast on the terrace.
8 Do you always have .... tea at four?
9 We've come here to see .... sunset.
10 I had .... nice lunch at the Ritz.

3.6B Zero article for e.g. 'She's at school' and 'He's in hospital'
[> LEG 3.28.3, Apps 21-23]

Study:
★★

> 1 We use no article in front of nouns like *school* and *hospital* in phrases like *to school, at school, in hospital* when we are referring to their normal purpose:
> *Jane's gone **to school**. Jane's **at school**.* (to learn); *John's **in hospital**.* (he's ill)
> (Not *Jane's gone to the school.* *Jane's at the school.* *John's in the hospital.*)
> Other nouns like this are: *bed, church, class, college, prison, sea, town, university, work.*
> For the use of *to, at* and *in* with these nouns [> 8.2A]. For *home* [> 8.2A, 10.2C].
>
> 2 We use *the* or *a/an* with these nouns when we are not referring to their 'purpose':
> *Jane's gone **to the school** for a meeting. There's a meeting **at the school**.*
> *Norton High is **a very good school**. I'm going to make **the bed**.*
>
> 3 Nouns which are not part of this special group behave in the usual way:
> *My wife's at **the office**.* (perhaps to work); *They are **at the mosque**.* (perhaps to pray)
> *John's **in the kitchen**.* (perhaps to prepare a meal) [> 3.4A]
> *My wife's firm has **an office** in Edinburgh.* (Not *My wife's firm has office* [> 3.1C])

Write: Supply *a/an, the* or '-'.

1 I'm really tired and I'm going to .... bed.
2 Your shoes are under .... bed.
3 Tim's been in .... bed for hours.
4 We've bought .... lovely new bed.
5 We took some photos outside .... church.
6 We always go to .... church on Sunday.
7 Have you ever worked in .... factory?
8 Susan's in .... class at the moment.
9 My father went to .... sea when he was 14.
10 When do you hope to go to .... university?
11 Martha's been taken to .... hospital.
12 How long wili she be in .... hospital?
13 There's a strike at .... hospital.
14 We've got .... fine new hospital.
15 When do you get home from .... office?
16 John's at .... work at the moment.

3.6C Zero article or 'the' with place names [> LEG 3.31]

Study:
★★

1 **General rule**: We use no article with proper nouns [> 3.5A], so this includes place names, but there is some variation. We use *the* with the words *bay, canal, channel, gulf, kingdom, ocean, republic, river, sea, strait(s), union, united: the United States of America*.

2 **Zero** for: countries (*Turkey*), states (*Ohio*), cities (*Paris*), streets (*Oxford Street*), parks (*Hyde Park*), addresses (*24 North Street*), buildings (*Westminster Abbey*), geographical areas (*Africa*), historical references (*Ancient Rome*), mountains (*Everest*), islands (*Malta*).

3 ***The*** for: some countries (*the USA, the USSR*), some geographical areas (*the Arctic, the Balkans*), some historical references (*the Dark Ages*), oceans and rivers (*the Pacific, the (River) Nile*), mountain ranges (*the Alps, the Himalayas*), deserts (*the Sahara, the Gobi*).

4 **Zero** or ***the***: theatres (*Her Majesty's/The Globe*), hotels (*Brown's/the Hilton*), restaurants (*Leoni's/the Café Royal*), hospitals (*Guy's/the London Hospital*).

Write: Supply *the* or '-'.

1 I've always understood ..*the*.. Dark Ages to refer specifically to ...—.... Medieval Europe.
2 Ferguson has travelled everywhere from .... Central Asia to .... Arctic.
3 I've been to .... Brazil and .... Argentina, but I've never been to .... USA.
4 I'd love to do a tour of European capitals and visit .... London, ... Paris, and .... Vienna.
5 What's your address? – I live in .... Montague Road, number 27.
6 I could never afford to stay at hotels like .... Brown's or .... Hilton.
7 Karl was born in .... Bavaria, but he now lives in .... Ohio.
8 You can't visit .... London without seeing .... Buckingham Palace.
9 I've been climbing in .... Alps, but I've never managed to get up .... Mont Blanc.
10 A lot of people have tried to cross .... Sahara without being properly prepared.
11 I'd love to travel down .... Nile as far as .... Luxor.
12 There's a splendid view of .... Lake Geneva from this hotel.
13 We had an early dinner at .... Leoni's and then went to a play at .... Globe Theatre.
14 Go down .... Oxford Street till you come to .... Oxford Circus, then turn right.
15 Do you know the song about .... London Bridge?

3.6D Context

Write: Put in *a/an, the* or '-'.

HIGH FLYER
I travel all over [1]...*the*..... world on business and my neighbour thinks my life is one long holiday. You know what [2].............. business travel is like: up at [3].............. dawn to catch [4].............. plane; [5].............. breakfast in [6].............. London, [7].............. lunch in [8].............. New York, [9].............. luggage [> 2.4B] in [10].............. Bermuda. When you're in [11].............. sky, you see only snow in [12].............. Arctic or [13].............. Greenland. You have glimpses of [14].............. Andes or [15].............. Pacific. You're always exhausted. Your wife or husband complains you're never there to take [16].............. children to [17].............. school or put them to [18].............. bed. When you get home, your neighbour says, 'Another nice holiday, eh?' Give me Home Sweet Home any day!

Home Sweet Home!

4 Pronouns

4.1 Personal pronouns

4.1A Subject and object pronouns [> LEG 4.1-6]

Study:

⭐

1 We use pronouns in place of nouns. They may be subject (*she*) or object (*her*).

2 We call *I, you*, etc. **personal pronouns** because they refer to 'grammatical persons':
1st person: *I, we*   **2nd person**: *you*   **3rd person**: *he, she, it, one, they*

3 In English, we must express the subject of a sentence, so we use a pronoun or a noun:
John (or **He**) *is here*. **Tim and Pam** (or **They**) h*ave arrived*. (Not **is here* *have arrived** etc.)

4 We do not have singular and plural forms of *you*. We can say *You're right* to someone we don't know at all or to someone we know very well, to a child or to an adult.

5 We use *it* to say who someone is: *Who's **that**? – **It**'s our new neighbour, Mr Groves*.
We use *he/she/they* to give information about someone:
*Who's **Mr Groves**? – **He**'s our new neighbour*.

6 We also use *it* when we don't know the sex of a baby or child: *Is **it** a boy or a girl?*

Write: Supply pronouns and underline the words they replace.

1 Your parcel has arrived. ....*It*.......... was delivered this morning.
2 Jane and I have already eaten. .... had a meal before we left home.
3 Who's that? – ....'s my mother. Would you like to meet her?
4 Who's Jane Wilson? – ....'s the woman who's just started working for our company.
5 So you've had a baby! Is .... a boy or a girl?
6 Whose cat is that? ....'s always in our garden.
7 When John comes in, please tell .... I phoned.
8 If you see Catherine, please give .... my regards.

4.1B Subject or object pronoun? [> LEG 4.7, 6.27.1]

Study:

⭐⭐

1 We often use object pronouns after *be*: *Who is it? – It's **me/him/her/us/them***.

2 We do not use *I, she*, etc. on their own in answer to questions with *Who?*. In everyday speech, we use object pronouns: *Who told him? – **Me/Not me***. Or we say: *I did/I didn't*.

3 We use object pronouns after *as* and *than*: *He's taller **than me**/as tall **as me***.
or we use subject + verb: *He's taller **than I am**/as tall **as I am***. [> 1.10D]

Write: Supply suitable pronouns in the following. Alternatives are possible.

1 Who's that? – It's *me/him/her/us/them* !
2 Who wants to know what we're having for dinner tonight? – .... !
3 Who wants to help me in the garden? – Not .... !
4 You can invite him to your place. – .... ! You must be joking!
5 It was .... who told you, not my brother.
6 She's taller than ...., but not as strong as .... am.
7 He's more intelligent than .... am, but not as good at sports as ....

4.1C Gender in relation to animals, things and countries [> LEG 4.8]

Study:
★★

1 We use *it* to refer to animals, as if they were things [> 1.6, 2.7A]. We only use *he, she* and *who* when there is a reason for doing so, for example, when we refer to a pet:
*Rover's a good dog. **He**'s my best friend. Bessie's a fine cow. **She** gives a lot of milk.*
Or in folk stories: *'It's late,' the hare said as **he** looked at **his** watch.*

2 We use *he* or *she* to refer to 'lower animals' when, for example, we regard their activities with interest: *Look at that frog! Look at the way **he** jumps!*

3 We sometimes refer to ships, cars, motorbikes and other machines as *she*, when the reference is 'affectionate': *My old car's not fast, but **she** does 50 miles to the gallon.*

4 Some writers refer to a country as *she* when they're thinking of it 'as a person':
*In 1941, America assumed **her** role as a world power.*

Write: Supply suitable pronouns in the following. Alternatives are possible.

1 What do you call your dog? – ......*She*......'s called Flossie.
2 There's a dog in our neighbourhood that barks all night. ....'s getting on my nerves.
3 They're launching a new ship in Portsmouth and I've been invited to see .... launched.
4 The *Titanic* may be at the bottom of the sea, but ....'s never forgotten.
5 I run a car in London, but I really don't need ....
6 This old car of mine may be falling to pieces, but ....'s all I've got.
7 Did you see that frog? .... jumped right in front of us!
8 I saw a frog in our garden. – Where did you see ....?
9 You can't see America in a week, you know. ....'s a big country!
10 In the 19th century America welcomed the European poor. .... opened her arms to them.
11 '....................'s a cunning fox,' the monkey said to the hen. 'Be careful!'
12 They've just found an old wreck off the coast of Florida. ....'s probably Spanish.

4.1D Context

Write: Put in the missing pronouns (including *who*).

TOO MUCH TO BEAR!
If you're on holiday in the Western Islands of Scotland and ¹....*you*... see a bear, avoid ²...............! It might turn out to be Hercules, the famous star ³.............. has appeared in TV ads, films and cabaret. Hercules disappeared when his owner, Andy Robbins, took ⁴.............. for a swim. Police and troops have joined in the search, but ⁵.............. haven't had any success. After all, Hercules is unlikely to appear suddenly, shouting, 'It's ⁶...............! Here ⁷............... am!' The search party are carrying yoghurt and bananas to offer the bear because that's what ⁸.............. likes best. '⁹.............. isn't dangerous, but ¹⁰..............'s very hungry,' a searcher said. So if you see a ten-foot bear in the Western Islands, make sure ¹¹.............. are carrying some bananas. ¹².............. may be just what a hungry bear is waiting for and if ¹³.............. don't find ¹⁴.............., you can always eat ¹⁵.............. yourself!

If you see a ten-foot bear ...

4.2 'One'

4.2A 'One' and 'you' [> LEG 4.9]

Study:
★★

We use *one*, as a pronoun meaning 'everyone/anyone', to refer to 'people in general' only when we want to be formal. In everyday speech, we use *you* in an informal way to mean 'everyone/anyone'. Compare:
A: *Is it easy to go camping in this country?*
B: *Yes, but* **one** *isn't allowed to camp where* **one** *likes.* **One** *can only use camp-sites.*
or: *Yes, but* **you** *aren't allowed to camp where* **you** *like.* **You** *can only use camp-sites.*
Don't use *one*, *one's* (= your) and *oneself* (= yourself) unless you want to sound formal.

Write: Rewrite this paragraph so that it sounds 'informal'. Use *you*.

The moment one gets into the mountains, one is on one's own. One has to rely on oneself for everything. This means one has to carry all one's own food, though, of course, one can get pure drinking water from mountain streams. One won't see any local people for days at a time, so one can't get help if one's lost. One has to do one's best to find sheltered places to spend the night.

The moment you get into the mountains ....

....

....

....

....

4.2B 'One' and 'ones' in place of countable nouns: 'Use this clean one'
[> LEG 4.10]

Study:
★★

1 We can't use an adjective on its own in place of a singular countable noun. We must use a noun after an adjective or we must use *one* to avoid repeating the noun [> 6.3A]:
Don't use that **cloth**. *Use this clean* **one**. (Not **Use this clean.**)

2 We use *ones* to avoid repeating a plural countable noun:
I don't want to wear my old **shoes**. *I want to wear my new* **ones**. (Not **wear my new**)

3 We can use *one* and *ones* for people as well as things:
Do you know **John Smith/Jane Smith**? – *Is* **he/she** *the* **one** *who phoned last night?*
Do you know **the Smiths**? – *Are* **they** *the* **ones** *who used to live in this house?*

4 We do not use *one* in place of an uncountable noun. We repeat the noun or use no noun at all:
Don't use that **milk**. *Use this* **fresh milk**. Or: *Use this* **fresh**. (Not **this fresh one**)

Write: Supply *one* or *ones* where necessary.

1 Have you met our new secretary? – Is she the .....*one*............................ who joined us last week?
2 You know the man I mean, the .... who lent you £50.
3 Which actresses did you meet? – The .... who appeared in Act 1.
4 Here are your stamps. These are the .... you paid for.
5 Which computer did you use? – The .... that is in your office.
6 The children I like to teach are the .... who like to learn.
7 Pour away that dirty water and get some clean ....
8 If I were you, I'd sell that old car and buy a new ....

4.2C 'Which one(s)?' – 'This/that (one)', etc. [> LEG 4.10]

Study:
★★

1 We use *one/ones* to refer to people and things after *Which?, this/that* and adjectives:
   Which one would you like? **This one** or **that one**? – I'd like the **large one**/the **red one**.
   We can also say **Which** would you like? **This** or **that**?

2 We sometimes omit *one* and *ones* after superlatives and in short answers:
   *Which one/ones would you like? – I'd like **the best** (one/ones).*
   *Which one/ones would you like? – **The large/the red**.*

3 We usually avoid *ones* after *these/those: I want **these**. I want **those**.* (Not **these ones**)

4 We normally use *one/ones* after *this/that/these/those* + adjective:
   *I want **this/that white one**. I want **these/those white ones**.*

5 We cannot omit *one/ones* in structures like: *Which woman? – **The one** in the green dress.*

Write:
  a Supply *one* or *ones*.
  b Put a tick beside the sentences where *one/ones* could be omitted.

  1 Which gloves would you like to see? – The ....*ones*........ in the window.
  2 Which shoes fit you best? – The large ....
  3 Which pullover do you prefer? – The red ....
  4 Which jeans are you going to buy? – The most expensive ....
  5 Please pass me that plate. – Which .... ?
  6 Two of those coats suit you very well. – Which .... ?
  7 I'd like to test-drive one of these two cars. – This .... or that ....?
  8 I'd like to see some rings, please. – These .... in silver or those .... in gold?
  9 I'd like to try one of these shirts. Please pass me that white ....
  10 I think, on the whole, I prefer these yellow ....

4.2D Context

Write: Put in *you, one* or *ones* where necessary.

HELP!
[1]....*You*..... can always tell the people who know all about cars. They're the [2].............. who can recognize all the latest models and who bore [3].............. silly with useless information. The [4].............. who don't know about cars are a bit like my friend, Robin. Robin is [5].............. of those people who believes that all car engines are in the front of a vehicle. He recently hired a car without even realizing that it was [6].............. of those with its engine at the back. Last week he was driving along a country road when he heard a strange noise coming from the car and he stopped to have a look. He raised the bonnet to examine his engine and you can imagine his surprise when he saw that he didn't have [7]..............! He waved to a passing car and a young man stopped. Robin explained that he had lost his engine. 'I don't suppose [8].............. can help me,' he said. 'Of course I can help [9]..............,' the young man said. 'I've got a spare [10].............. in the back of my car. You can use that [11].............. .'

A spare engine in the back.

4.3 'It' and 'one/some/any/none'

4.3A 'It' as in 'It's hot' and 'It's nice to see you' [> LEG 4.12-13]

Study:
★★

> **1 'empty subject': 'It's hot'** [> 1.2A, 4.1A]
> *It* carries no information in sentences like *It's hot, It's 8 o'clock,* etc. so we call it an 'empty subject'. We use *it* because a sentence must have a subject. (Not **Is hot**)
>
> **2 'preparatory subject': 'It's nice to see you'** [> 1.5B, 16.4A, 16.7A]
> We sometimes begin a sentence with *it* and continue with *to-, -ing* or *that.*
> The true subject is *to-, -ing,* or *that,* but we generally prefer to begin with *it:*
> ***To lie in the sun/Lying in the sun*** *is pleasant.* → ***It's*** *pleasant to lie/lying in the sun.*
> ***That he's arriving*** *today is certain.* → ***It's*** *certain (that) he's arriving today.*

Write: Here are some notes. Write them as sentences beginning with *It.*

1 Monday, 13th June today. .....*It's Monday, 13th June, today.*.....
2 Snowing now. Snows a lot here. ....
3 22° Celsius in London yesterday. ....
4 100 kilometres from here to Paris. ....
5 Important to get to the meeting. ....
6 Difficult making such decisions. ....
7 A pleasure to welcome you all here. ....
8 A pity that they couldn't come. ....

4.3B 'It' and 'one' as subjects and objects: 'I like it' [> LEG 4.16]

Study:
★★

> **1** We use *it* and *they* if we are referring to 'something particular':
> *Has **the letter** arrived this morning?- Yes, **it** has just arrived.*
> *Have **the letters** arrived this morning? – Yes, **they** have just arrived.*
>
> **2** We use *one, some* and *none* when we mean 'in general':
> *Has **a letter** arrived? – Yes, **one** has just arrived.*
> *Have **any letters** arrived? – Yes, **some** have arrived. No, **none** have/has arrived.* [> 5.7C]
>
> **3** We must use an object after verbs like *enjoy* and *like* [> 1.2B]:
> particular: *Do you like **this cake**? – Yes, I like **it**.* (Not **I like/I don't like**)
> general: *Would you like **some cake**? – Yes, I'd like **some**./No, I don't want **any**.*
> (Not **I'd like/I wouldn't like**)

Write: Supply *it, them, one, some, any* or *none* in the following.

1 Were any cars parked outside our house today? – Yes, ...*one*..... was parked there all morning.
2 Was that car parked outside our house today? – Yes, ... was parked there all morning.
3 Did any letters come for me this morning? – No, ... came for you.
4 Have the spare parts arrived yet? – Yes, ... of them have just arrived.
5 Do you like this dish? – Yes, I like .... very much.
6 Did you enjoy the strawberries? – Yes, I enjoyed .... very much.
7 Would you like some strawberries? – No, I don't want ...., thank you.
8 Would you like any cherries? – Yes, I'd like ...., please.
9 Have you got the maps with you? – No, I haven't got ....
10 Have you got a spare light bulb? – No, I haven't got ....

4.3C 'I hope/believe/expect so' [> LEG 4.17]

Study:
★★

1 We use *so* (not **it**) after these verbs when we are responding in the affirmative:
believe, expect, fear, guess, hope, imagine, say, suppose, tell someone and *think*:
*Is what you told me true? – I **believe so**.* (Not **I believe* *I believe it**)

2 We use *so* in the affirmative after *I'm afraid* and *It seems*:
The weather changing for the worse. – I'm afraid so. It seems so.

3 We can make a negative in two ways after these verbs:
believe, expect, imagine, suppose, think and *It seems*:
*Is that true? – **I don't think so**.* Or: ***I think not**.*

Write: Write questions or statements followed by responses using *believe*, etc.

1 Someone asks you if the next train goes to London. You believe it does.
   ....*Does the next train go to London? – I believe so.*..

2 Someone says the weather is going to improve. You hope it will.
   ....

3 Someone asks you if the letters have arrived yet. You don't think they have.
   ....

4 Someone says the rail strike hasn't ended. It doesn't seem to have ended.
   ....

5 Someone says it's a holiday tomorrow. You want to know who says this.
   ....

6 Someone says there's been a terrible air disaster. You fear this is the case.
   ....

7 Someone asks if the democrats will win the election. You don't expect they will.
   ....

4.3D Context

Write: Put in *one, any, it, they, them,* or *so*.

... because of rheumatism

SPELLING CAN BE A PAIN!
[1].....*It*.... was late in the afternoon when Mr Fox asked his ten-year-olds if
[2]............. would like to do a spelling test.

MR FOX: [3].............'s quite an easy [4]............. . I'll say the words and
           you'll spell [5]............. . Write [6]............. in your exercise
           books. If there are [7]............. words you can't spell, I'll write
           [8]............. on the blackboard. Do you like spelling, Liz?
LIZ: I love [9]............. .
MR FOX: What about you, Annie?
ANNIE: I think [10]............., but I'm not sure.

Annie was quite late getting home from school that afternoon. Annie's
granddad was worried.
GRANDDAD: Why are you late, Annie?
ANNIE: [11].............'s because of rheumatism.
GRANDDAD: Only older people have rheumatism, Annie.
ANNIE: No, I haven't got [12]............., granddad. I just can't spell
           [13].............!'

59

4.4 Possessive adjectives and possessive pronouns ('my/mine')

4.4A Basic differences between 'my' and 'mine', etc. [> LEG 4.19-21]

Study: ⭐

1 *My, your, his, her, its, one's, our, your* and *their* are **possessive adjectives**. This means they must go in front of nouns: *He's **my son**. It's **your house**.* etc.

2 They refer to the possessor, not to the thing possessed:
*John amused **his daughter**.* (= his own) *John amused **her daughter**.* (= someone else's)
*Jane amused **her son**.* (= her own) *Jane amused **his son**.* (= someone else's)
Its refers to possession by an animal or thing: ***The cat** drank **its** milk.* [> 2.7A]

3 *Mine, yours, his, hers, ours, yours,* and *theirs* are **possessive pronouns**. This means they stand on their own: *That book is **mine**.* (Not **That is mine book.**)
We cannot use possessives with *the*. (Not **That's the my car./That car's the mine.**)

Write: Supply the missing possessive adjectives and possessive pronouns.

1 What a beautiful baby girl! What's ....*her*............... name?
2 This is your towel: it's yellow. And that's your husband's. .... is blue.
3 This car isn't .... My car has a different registration number.
4 'Shall we have .... supper on a tray and watch TV?' my wife asked.
5 That umbrella doesn't belong to you. .... is the one with the leather handle.
6 Their flat and our flat may seem to be the same, but .... is different from ours.
7 One should put .... own interests last.
8 John's son wants to be an actor and .... daughter wants to be an actress.
9 Patricia's eldest daughter has just left school and .... youngest has just begun.
10 Has the cat been given .... milk yet?

4.4B The double genitive: 'He is a friend of mine' [> LEG 2.52]

Study: ⭐⭐

1 We can say: *He is **your friend**.*
or: *He is **a friend of yours**.* (No apostrophe: not **He is a friend of your's.**)
And note: *He is **a friend of mine**.* (Not **He is a friend of me.**)

2 We can say: *He is **my father's friend**.* [> 2.8A]
We still use *'s* after *of* if we say: *He is **a friend of my father's**.* (Not **of my father**)

3 We often use *this* and *that* with this construction, especially when we are criticizing:
***That boy of yours** is in trouble again. **That motorbike of yours** is very noisy.*

Write: Rewrite these sentences using phrases with *of*, making any necessary changes.

1 *Your brother* is always in trouble. That ...*brother of yours is always in trouble.*...........
2 He's not *my friend*. He's no ....
3 We watched *a play by Shakespeare*. We watched ....
4 Now tell me about *your problem*. Now tell me about ....
5 We've known him for years. He's *our friend*. He's ....
6 *Her loud music* drives me crazy! That ....
7 *My sister's friend* phoned from New York. A ....
8 *Their neighbours* have been complaining again. Those ....
9 *Your radio* keeps us all awake! That ....

4.4C 'My own' and 'of my own' [> LEG 4.22]

Study:
★★

> We can use *own* after possessive adjectives, not pronouns, in two ways:
> I have **my own room**. Or: I have **a room of my own**. (Not **mine own room/of mine own*)

Write: Complete these sentences in two ways.

1 I'd love to have a room. *my own room / a room of my own* . 3 The children have rooms. ....
2 Frank has started a business. .... 4 Our dog has a kennel. ....

4.4D 'The' in place of 'my', etc.: 'a pain in the neck' [> LEG 4.23]

Study:
★★

> We sometimes use *the* where we might expect *my, your*, etc., e.g. with parts of the body or with clothing after prepositions: *He hit me* **in the face**. *She pulled me by* **the sleeve**.
> We use *the* to refer informally to members of the family: *How are* **the children**?
> But avoid expressions like 'Meet the wife'.

Write: Supply *my* or *the*.

1 He hit me in ..*the*.... eye.
2 Something has got into .... eye.
3 You don't have to pull me by .... collar.
4 It's nice to see you. How's .... family?
5 What's wrong? – I've hurt .... arm.

6 .... collar is too tight. I can't bear it.
7 .... hair is getting too long. I must get it cut.
8 She looked me in .... face and said, 'No'.
9 What's worse than a pain in .... back?
10 The house is quiet with .... children away.

4.4E Context

Write: Put in *my, mine*, etc., or *the* where necessary.

It's been in the computer memory ...

REAL PERSONAL SERVICE

On [1] ....*our*....... last visit to London my wife and I stayed at the Magna Hotel. The Magna used to be a favourite hotel of [2] ...., but we hadn't stayed there for over sixteen years. The hotel is famous for [3] .... service and we weren't disappointed. 'The porter will show you to [4] .... room,' the Receptionist said with a smile and we were shown to a room on the first floor. 'This is [5] .... favourite room,' I exclaimed. 'I know sir,' the porter said. '[6] .... is the room with a view, isn't it?' 'That's right,' I said. 'You like milk in [7] .... tea in the morning and madam prefers lemon in [8] ....' 'That's right,' my wife said. She pulled me by [9] .... sleeve with pleasure when the porter had gone. 'Aren't they amazing! They remember [10] .... preferences after all these years. This is real personal service!' The next morning at breakfast, we were given raspberry jam with [11] .... toast instead of orange marmalade. 'Isn't there any marmalade?' I asked the waiter. 'We never eat raspberry jam in the morning.' 'Sorry sir,' the waiter said. 'You ordered some for breakfast on [12] .... last visit and it's been in the computer memory ever since!'

4.5 Reflexive pronouns ('myself')

4.5A Verbs commonly followed by reflexive pronouns: 'I enjoyed myself'
[> LEG 4.25]

Study:
★★

1 *Myself, yourself, himself, herself, itself, oneself, ourselves, yourselves* and *themselves* are **reflexive pronouns**. There aren't many verbs in English which we must always use with reflexive pronouns: *absent oneself, avail oneself (of)* and *pride oneself (on)*:
*Monica **absented herself** from work. Jim **prides himself** on his cooking.*

2 We often use reflexive pronouns with these verbs: *amuse, blame, cut, dry, enjoy, hurt*, and *introduce*: *I've **cut myself** with the bread knife.*
We can use these verbs without reflexive pronouns if we want to: *I've cut **my thumb**.*
We can use object pronouns (*me, him, her*, etc.) after these verbs only when we refer to someone else: *He **amused** me* (but not **I amused me/I cut me**, etc.)

Write: Supply the correct reflexive pronouns in the following.

1 I enjoyed ....*myself*............ very much at the party.
2 I see you've cut .... again. Won't you ever learn how to shave?
3 How did Tom dry ....? – He used your towel!
4 She has no reason to blame .... for what has happened.
5 I think that poor dog has hurt ....
6 'One prides .... on one's patience,' the boss said, in his usual pompous manner.
7 We amused .... playing football on the beach.
8 Our new neighbours knocked at our door and introduced ....
9 Sheila prides .... on her ability to judge people's characters.
10 Bill had to absent .... from work when his baby was born.

4.5B Verb + reflexive, or not?: 'I've dressed (myself)' [> LEG 4.26-27]

Study:
★★

1 We sometimes add reflexive pronouns after verbs like *dress, hide, shave* and *wash* for emphasis or to show that something has been done with an effort. For example, if we are referring to a child, we might say: *Polly's now learnt how to **dress herself***, but we could also say: *Polly has now learnt how to **dress**.* (without *herself*). The choice is ours.

2 Verbs such as *get up, sit down, stand up, wake up* and *get wet, get tired, get dressed, get married* [> 10.4C] are not normally reflexive in English: *I sat down with difficulty.*
We might use a reflexive only for emphasis:
*I **sat myself down** with difficulty. Old Bill has **got himself** married at last!*

Write: Write these sentences again using reflexive pronouns with the verbs.

1 We didn't know where to *hide*. .....*We didn't know where to hide ourselves.*.....
2 That kitten now *washes* every day. ....
3 She's just learning how to *dress*. ....
4 We *sat down* and waited. ....
5 I *got wet* watering the garden. ....
6 I *woke up* with a start. ....
7 Barry has just *got engaged*. ....
8 *Get ready* quickly! ....

4.5C   Reflexive pronouns used after prepositions and for emphasis

[> LEG 4.29-30]

Study:
★★

1 We can use reflexive pronouns:
   – after a preposition: *Look **after yourself**! Take care **of yourself**!*
   – in fixed expressions: *strictly between ourselves, just among ourselves, in itself.*

2 We use object pronouns when we refer to:
   – place: *Have you got any money **on you**?* (Not **Have you got any money on yourself?**)
   – after *with* (= accompanied by): *I brought the children **with me**.* (Not **with myself**)

3 We use *by* + reflexive to mean 'without help' or 'alone':
   *She made the dress **by herself**.* (= without help) *She lives **by herself**.* (= alone)

4 We sometimes use reflexive pronouns after nouns and pronouns for emphasis to mean 'that person/thing and only that person/thing':
   *The **film itself** is very good. **You yourself** saw it.*
   The reflexive pronoun can also go at the end of a sentence or clause:
   ***You** saw what happened **yourself**.* Or: ***You yourself** saw what happened.*

Write 1:   Use reflexive pronouns or object pronouns in the following.

1 Hargreaves knows how to take care of *himself*.
2 Have you got any money on ....?
3 Come and sit beside ....
4 Strictly between ...., she's wrong.

5 She's very certain of ....
6 There's a big truck in front of ....
7 Granddad doesn't like living by ....
8 Jimmy tied his shoelaces all by ....

Write 2:   Rewrite these sentences using reflexive pronouns for emphasis.

1 *I* didn't know about it till yesterday. *I didn't know about it myself till yesterday.*
2 *The building* is all right, I think. ....
3 *You* can't do that! ....
4 I can't fetch it – *you* fetch it. ....
5 Don't expect me to do it. *Do* it! ....

4.5D   Context

Write: Put in reflexive pronouns (*ourselves*, etc.) or object pronouns (*us*, etc.).

You're marvellous!

KEEP SMILING!
Psychiatrists have proved that happiness is the secret of good health. Mood really can affect the body [1]............ *itself* .... This means we all have to look after [2]............................ . We have to enjoy [3]............................ and take pride in [4]............................ and we'll rarely have to visit the doctor. Praise helps [5]............................ to learn and is good for us, too. We all know how pleased young children feel when they learn to dress [6]............................ and do things by [7]............................ . We should praise [8]............................ for their achievements. Bosses rarely have a good word for [9]............................ . Yet if we want to be happy and healthy, we need people around [10]............................ who keep telling [11]............................ how marvellous we are. Then we [12]............................ will believe that we are marvellous, too!

4.6 Demonstrative adjectives/pronouns ('this', etc.) 'Some/any/no' compounds ('someone', etc.)

4.6A Different uses of 'this' and 'that' [> LEG 4.32-36, App 7]

Study:
★★

1 The basic uses of *this, these* and *that, those* are:
 – *this* and *these* may refer to something that is close to you: **this** one here.
 – *that* and *those* may refer to something that is not close to you: **that** one there.

2 You can use *this* and *that* in many different contexts and situations. For example:
 when you are showing someone round the house: **This** is my room.
 when you recognize someone you are looking for: There he is – **that's** him!

Write: Say when you would use these sentences.

1 *This* is Mr Cooke. – How do you do. .... *Introducing someone* ....
2 Hullo. Is *that* George? *This* is Tom here. ....
3 We lost the match and *that* set us back. ....
4 I was robbed. – When did *this* happen? ....
5 You can't be too careful *these* days. ....
6 Quick! Run! It's *that* man again! ....
7 £50? It costs more than *that*! ....
8 There was *this* missionary. ....
9 I don't mean *that* Mrs Smith. ....
10 The fish I caught was *that* big. ....

4.6B Uses of 'some/any/no' compounds [> LEG 4.37-39]

Study:
★★

1 We use *some* compounds in [compare > 5.3B-C, 13.2A]:
 – the affirmative: **I met someone** you know last night.
 – questions expecting 'yes': **Was there something** you wanted?
 – offers and requests: **Would you like something** to drink?

2 We use *any* compounds in:
 – negative statements: There **isn't anyone** here who can help you.
 – questions when we're doubtful about the answer: **Is there anyone** here who's a doctor?

3 We use *no* compounds when the verb is affirmative: **There's no one** here. (= not anyone)

Write: Supply *anybody/anyone, nothing, anything, nobody/no one, somebody/someone* or *something* in these sentences.

1 There's .... *nothing* .... in the clothes basket. It's empty.
2 Is there .... in the clothes basket? – No, it's empty.
3 I've tried phoning, but every time I phone there's .... in.
4 I've prepared .... for dinner which you'll like very much.
5 I've never met .... who is as obstinate as you are.
6 Would you like .... to start with before you order the main course?
7 I know .... who can help you.
8 He sat at the table, but he didn't have .... to eat.
9 Is there .... here who can speak Japanese?
10 Does .... want a second helping?

64

4.6C 'Everyone', 'anyone', etc. with singular or plural pronouns [> LEG 4.40]

Study:
★★

1 We often use *anyone* to mean 'it doesn't matter who', especially after *if*.
The traditional rule is to use masculine pronouns with *anyone, everyone, no one*, etc., unless the context is definitely female (e.g. a girls' school).

According to this rule, you would address an audience of both sexes like this:
*If **anyone** wants to leave early, **he** can ask for permission.*
But you would address an audience of females like this:
*'If **anyone** wants to leave early,' the headmistress said, '**she** can ask for permission.'*

2 In practice, we use *they, them*, etc. without a plural meaning to refer to both sexes, though some native speakers think this is wrong:
Instead of: ***Everyone** knows what **he** has to do, **doesn't he**?*
We say: ***Everyone** knows what **they** have to do, **don't they**?*

Write: Change the words in italics into plural references.

1 Anyone planning to travel abroad should take *his* driving licence with *him*. ......*their*......*them*......
2 I suppose everyone believes *he* could be Prime Minister. ....
3 We knew that no one had done *his* homework. ....
4 If anybody wants to know the answer, *he* can ask me. ....
5 Everybody knows what the answer is, *doesn't he*? ....
6 If anyone wants help in an emergency, *he* can dial 999. ....
7 Everyone wants to have *his* cake and eat it. ....
8 Nobody wants to be told that *he is* going to be sacked. ....
9 Ask anyone you know what *he thinks* of war and *he'll* say it's evil. ....
10 Everyone gets what *he deserves*, even if *he doesn't like* what *he gets*. ....

4.6D Context

Write: Put in *they, this, that, nothing, something, anyone* or *no one*.

8%, but 4% for neatness

=4% for knowledge

4% was for neatness!

MY BEST PERFORMANCE
Everyone has studied subjects at school which [1] ......*they*...... weren't very good at. [2] .... can claim that some subjects aren't harder for them than others, however clever [3] .... are. I've never met [4] .... who's [5] .... clever. My weakest subject at school was certainly chemistry. I learnt formulas and experiments by heart, but there was [6] .... I could do to improve my performance. 'Is [7] .... the best you can do?' my chemistry teacher would say after every test he set us. 'It's time you did [8] .... about [9] .... subject!' 'I really do try, sir,' I would answer. Before my last chemistry exam, I made a big effort. 'I can't do better than [10] ....' I said to my teacher as I handed in my paper. 'It was my best performance.' Two weeks later I got my report and eagerly looked up my chemistry marks. I had got 8%! I couldn't believe it! 'Is [11] .... all I got, sir?' I asked. 'I'm afraid so,' my teacher said. 'Of course, 4% was for neatness!'

5 Quantity

5.1 Quantifiers + countable and uncountable nouns

5.1A Quantifiers + countable and uncountable nouns [> LEG 5.1-2]

Quantifiers are words like *few, little, plenty of*.
They show how many things or how much of something we are talking about.
Some quantifiers combine with countable nouns; some with uncountable and some with both kinds:

A + plural countable	B + uncountable	C + plural countable + uncountable	D + singular countable
both books	***a bit of bread***	***some books*** ***some ink***	***each book***
both	*a (small) amount of*	*some (of the)*	*all (of) the*
(a) few	*a bit of*	*any (of the)*	*any/some (of the)*
fewer	*a great deal of*	*enough*	*each*
the fewest	*a good deal of*	*a lot of/lots of*	*either*
a/the majority of	*(a) little*	*hardly any*	*every*
(not) many	*less* [but see 5.4D]	*more/most (of the)*	*most of the*
a minority of	*the least*	*plenty of*	*neither*
a number of/several	*(not) much*	*no, none of the*	*no, none of the*

Write:
a Choose the right word in brackets.
b Mark the quantifier **A**, **B**, **C** or **D**.

1 We have imported ......*fewer*...... videos this year than last year. (fewer/less) <u>A</u>
2 There has been .... demand for videos this year than last year. (fewer/less) __
3 .... vehicles have just been recalled because of a design fault. (a lot of/much) __
4 .... effort has been put into this project. (a lot of/many) __
5 There isn't .... hope of finding the wreck. (much/many) __
6 There aren't .... dictionaries that can compare with this one. (much/many) __
7 .... book was written by someone else. (most/most of the) __
8 .... magazines carry advertisements. (most/most of) __
9 .... metal is liable to rust. (most/most of) __
10 I'd like .... milk in this coffee, please. (a few/a little) __
11 This room needs .... pictures to brighten it up. (a few/a little) __
12 .... businesses have gone bankrupt this year. (a good deal of/several) __
13 There aren't .... chocolates left! (any/some) __
14 There isn't .... time to waste. (any/some) __
15 We've had .... trouble with this machine already. (enough/hardly any) __
16 There have been .... accidents on this corner this year. (a good deal of/hardly any) __
17 We can't accept the estimates. .... estimate is low enough. (either/neither) __
18 .... examples prove that I am right. (both/neither) __
19 There have been .... changes in the new edition. (no/any) __
20 There has been .... change in the new edition. (no/any) __

5.1B Quantifiers that tell us roughly how much and how many [> LEG 5.3]

Study:
★★

1 If we say *I bought **five magazines** to read on the train*, we are saying exactly how many.

2 If we say *I bought **some magazines** to read on the train*, we aren't saying how many.

3 If we say *I bought **a few magazines** to read on the train*, we are giving 'a rough idea'.
Some quantity words like *a few, a little* give us 'a rough idea'. If we arrange these on a scale, *too much* and *too many* are at the top of the scale and *no* is at the bottom.

Write: Arrange the quantifiers to show *most* at the top and *least* at the bottom. More than one answer is possible.

There are

enough eggs. 1a *too many eggs*
no eggs. 2a ....
too many eggs. 3a ....
hardly any eggs. 4a ....
a few eggs. 5a ....
plenty of eggs. 6a ....
very few eggs. 7a ....
a lot of eggs. 8a ....
not many eggs. 9a ....

There is

hardly any milk. 1b *too much milk*
too much milk. 2b ....
a little milk. 3b ....
no milk. 4b ....
not much milk. 5b ....
enough milk. 6b ....
a lot of milk. 7b ....
plenty of milk. 8b ....
very little milk. 9b ....

Now write sentences of your own using any six of the above quantifiers.

1 *There are plenty of apples in the bowl.*
2 ....
3 ....
4 ....
5 ....
6 ....

5.1C Context

Write: Put in *any, enough, few, hardly any, many, no, plenty of, some* or *very little*.

I'm asking for some NOW!

EXCUSES! EXCUSES!
You may be trying to buy a pair of shoes and there are too
[1] ...*many*... in your size and you can't choose, or there are too
[2] .... Shop assistants are good at inventing excuses. A few
days ago I was trying to buy [3] .... birthday cards for three
five-year-old children. There were [4] .... cards for children, but
[5] .... for five-year-olds. 'Five is a very popular age this year,'
the assistant said. 'We can't get [6] .... cards for this age-
group.' Then I went to a Do It Yourself shop and tried to buy some
orange paint. There was [7] .... paint in the shop, but in the
end I found [8] .... Then I asked for two small paint brushes.
'We don't have [9] ....,' the shop assistant explained. 'There's
[10] .... demand for them. No one ever asks for
[11] ....' . 'Yes, they do!' I exclaimed. 'I'm asking for
[12] .... now!'

5.2 General and specific references to quantity

5.2A 'Of' after quantifiers ('a lot of', 'some of', etc.) [> LEG 5.5]

Study:
★★

> **1** We always use *of* with these quantifiers when we put them in front of a noun or pronoun, and the reference is general:
> *a bit of, a couple of, a lot of, lots of, the majority of, a number of, plenty of*:
> ***A lot of people*** *don't eat meat.* (= a lot of people in general)
>
> **2** If we use words like *the* or *my* after *of*, the reference is specific:
> ***A lot of the people I know*** *don't eat meat.* (= the ones I know)
>
> **3** We use quantifiers like *some, any, much* and *many* without *of* in general references:
> ***Some people*** *don't eat meat.* (= some people in general)
>
> **4** If we use *of* + *the, my* etc., after *some* etc., the reference is specific [compare > 5.7C]:
> ***Some of the people I know*** *don't eat meat.* (= the ones I know)
> Note that *None of* is always specific: ***None of*** *my friends is here. I want **none of** it.*

Write:

  a Supply *of* where necessary.
  b Mark each sentence **G** (= General) or **S** (= Specific).

1 There have been a lot .....*of*..... changes to our plans. *G*
2 You only need to use a small amount .... salt in a dish like this. __
3 A lot .... the trouble was caused by a faulty switch. __
4 Have some .... tea. __
5 Would you like any .... cake?__
6 Would you like any .... this cake?__
7 We need a couple .... people to work in our new warehouse. __
8 There's plenty .... food for everybody. __
9 There were plenty .... complaints about the service. __
10 There's plenty .... this stew left, so we can have it again tonight. __
11 How much milk is there in the pan? – None .... __
12 How much of the milk have you used? – None .... it. __
13 Some .... students have complained about the canteen. __
14 Some .... my students have complained about the canteen. __
15 Would you like a bit .... butter on this toast? __

5.2B When to use quantifiers without 'of': 'I've got a lot' [> LEG 5.5]

Study:
★★

> If we use a quantifier on its own (not in front of a noun or pronoun) we do not use *of*:
> *Did you buy any fruit? – Yes, I bought **a lot/lots/plenty**.* (Not **a lot of* etc.)

Write: Use *a couple, a bit, a lot, lots* and *plenty* in short answers to these questions.

1 Are there any eggs in the fridge? – Yes, ...*there are a couple*...........................
2 Did you buy any cheese at the supermarket? – Yes, ...
3 Have we got enough potatoes for the weekend? – Yes, ...
4 Is there any milk in that jug? – Yes, ...
5 Were there many people at the meeting? – Yes, ...
6 Is there any ironing to be done? – Yes, ...

5.2C 'More' and 'less' after quantifiers: 'some more', 'a little less' [> LEG 5.6]

Study:
★★

We can emphasize quantity with *more* and *less* after quantifiers:
1 We can use *more* + plural nouns after:
some/any, a couple, hundreds, a few, hardly any, a lot, lots, many, no, plenty, several:
There are **a lot more students** studying English this year.

2 We can use *more* + uncountable nouns after:
some/any, a bit, a good deal, hardly any, a little, a lot, lots, much, no, plenty:
There's **a little more soup** if you'd like it.

3 We can use *less* + uncountable nouns after:
any, a bit, a good deal, a little, a lot, lots, much:
I'd like **a little less soup,** please.

Write: Choose *any more, any less,* etc. in the following sentences.

1 How much did we make yesterday? £200? – No, ...*much less*.... than that. (much less/a few less)
2 You've had enough food already and you can't have .... (any more/some more)
3 There are .... people giving up smoking these days. (much more/many more)
4 Newspapers have .... freedom than you think. (many less/much less)
5 .... young people are passing their driving test first time. (lots more/much more)
6 I'll help myself to .... of these vegetables. (some more/any more)
7 Have what you like. There are .... where these came from. (plenty more/much more)
8 There's been .... interest in this idea than we expected. (a lot less/many less)
9 We've had .... than forty applicants for this job. (no less/no fewer)
10 We need .... of this material, but it's hard to get. (many more/much more)
11 Do you want any more? – Yes, ..., please. (hardly any more/a lot more)
12 I've got .... experience in business than you think. (much more/many more)

5.2D Context

Write: Put a circle round the correct words in brackets.

SPARE THAT TREE!
How (¹many/much) lists is your name on? There must be (²plenty/plenty of) lists of names in every part of the world and they must be used to send information to (³millions/millions of) people. The (⁴number/amount) of letters ordinary people receive these days has greatly increased. (⁵A lot/A lot of) the people I know object to receiving unwanted letters. (⁶Much/Many) of the mail we receive goes straight into the waste-paper basket. That's why (⁷most/the most) people refer to it as 'junk mail'. It would be better for all of us if we received (⁸much/many) less junk mail and, as a result, saved (⁹many/much) more trees from destruction. (¹⁰A lot/A lot of) trees must be wasted each year to produce mountains of junk mail. Recently, I received a very welcome (¹¹bit/bit of) junk mail. It was a leaflet urging me not to waste paper and to return junk mail to the sender. 'If we all do this,' the leaflet said, 'we will reduce the (¹²number/number of) trees being destroyed.' I agreed with every word they said, but why did they have to send me four copies of the leaflet?

'Junk mail'

5.3 Uses of 'some', 'any', 'no' and 'none'

5.3A 'Some/any' or zero in relation to quantity [> LEG 3.6, 3.28.8, 5.3, 5.10]

Study:
★★

countable nouns

The plural of *a/an* is normally *any* or *some* when we are referring to **quantity** [> 3.1B]:
*Is there **a present** for the children?* → *Are there **any presents** for the children?*
*Here's **a present** for the children.* → *Here are **some presents** for the children.*
Sometimes we don't use *any* and *some*, even if we are referring to quantity.
The meaning is exactly the same, though we generally prefer to use *any* and *some*:
*Are there **any presents** for the children?* → *Are there **presents** for the children?*
*Here are **some presents** for the children.* → *Here are **presents** for the children.*

uncountable nouns

In the same way, we sometimes don't use *any* and *some* when referring to quantity:
*Is there **any milk** in the fridge?* is the same as *Is there **milk** in the fridge?*
*There's **some milk** in the fridge.* is the same as *There's **milk** in the fridge.*

general statements

We always use zero in general statements [> 3.1A-B, 3.5A]:
***Beans** are good for you. **Oil** is produced in Alaska. **Life** is short.*

Write: We can use zero in all these sentences. Put in *some* or *any* only where possible.

1 .... eggs are not nice to eat raw.
2 There are .... eggs in that basket.
3 .... life is full of surprises.
4 He's 89, but there's still .... life in him.
5 Get .... meat and salad for the weekend.
6 Some people don't eat .... meat.
7 .... biscuits are bad for the teeth.
8 You won't find .... biscuits in that tin.
9 We can't do without .... bread.
10 Get .... bread while you're out.
11 I don't like .... boiled cabbage.
12 Would you like .... boiled cabbage?
13 .... money has to be earned.
14 You need to earn .... money.
15 There isn't .... news of him.
16 I hate .... bad news.

5.3B Four basic uses of 'some' and 'any' [> LEG 5.10]

Study:
★

Some [compare > 4.6B]	Any [compare > 4.6B]
1 Affirmatives: *I want **some eggs**.*	1 Negatives: *I don't want **any eggs**.*
2 Questions + 'yes': *Do you want **some tea**?*	2 Uncertain questions: *Is there **any** ...?*
3 Requests: *May I have **some tea**?*	3 With *hardly*, etc.: *There's **hardly any ink**.*
4 (= certain): ***Some people** believe anything.*	4 With *at all*: *I haven't **any idea at all**.*

Write: Supply *some* or *any*.

1 Are there any more potatoes? – Yes, there are ....*some*............ potatoes in the dish.
2 Have we got any sugar? – I expect we have. Yes, there's .... sugar in this bowl.
3 May I have .... more tea? – Yes, of course.
4 .... people just don't know how to mind their own business.
5 I didn't get .... shoes at the sales. They were too expensive.
6 I think we've run out of sugar. Is there .... sugar in that bowl? – No, there isn't.
7 There are never .... taxis when you want one.
8 There isn't .... point at all in getting upset about it.

5.3C 'Not ...any', 'no' and 'none' [> LEG 5.11]

Study: ★★

1 We can use *no* instead of *not any*. We use an affirmative verb with *no* [> 13.2A]:
There **aren't any** buses after midnight. → There **are no** buses after midnight.
There **isn't any** milk. → There**'s no** milk.
2 *We* can also use *no* in place of *not a/an*: I'm **not an** expert. → I'm **no** expert.
3 *None* stands on its own as a pronoun: We have **no bananas**. We have **none**.

Write: Rewrite these sentences with *any, no* and *none*.

1 There are no buses after 12.30. There aren't ...... *any buses after 12.30.* ....
2 We haven't got any. We've got ....
3 I'm not an accountant, but these figures are wrong. I'm ....
4 There isn't any explanation for this. There's ....

5.3D Other uses of 'some' and 'any' [> LEG 5.12]

Study: ★★

Some and *any* also have special uses:
*I haven't seen Tom for **some years**.* (= I haven't seen Tom for several years.)
***Any fool** knows the answer to a question like that.* (= 'It doesn't matter who')

Write: Match the sentences on the left with the meanings on the right.

1 It took *some minutes* to see what had gone wrong. _f_
2 There were *some 500* people at the meeting. __
3 Monica's really *some actress*. __
4 There must be *some person* who knows the answer. __
5 You're *some help*, I must say! __
6 Albert isn't just *any hairdresser*, you know. __
7 *Any coat* will do. It needn't be a raincoat. __

a) it doesn't matter which
b) an extraordinary
c) an ordinary
d) not much
e) about
f) several
g) an unknown

5.3E Context

Write: Put in *some, any, no* or '-'.

Sardines for lunch.

CAUSE FOR ALARM!
'¹............—...... Children and ²............. grown-ups must do their best to keep the world clean,' Mr Fox said to his class. 'Sometimes we see ³.............
rubbish in the streets and we must pick it up. Sometimes we eat ⁴.............
sweets and we must put the wrappings in the bin. We must all work together so there's ⁵............. rubbish in the world. Never throw ⁶.............
plastic into the sea! There's ⁷............. tar on the beaches. There's
⁸............. oil in the sea. If we pour ⁹............. poison into our rivers,
¹⁰............. fish die. This is called ¹¹............. pollution. This weekend, see if you can find ¹²............. examples of pollution and write ¹³.............
sentences about it.' Jimmy looked very worried when he went home. On Monday, he handed in his composition. 'Yesterday we had ¹⁴.............
sardines for lunch. Mummy opened the tin, but all the fish were dead and the tin was full of oil!'

5.4 'Much', 'many', 'a lot of', '(a) few', '(a) little', 'fewer', 'less'

5.4A Basic uses of 'much', 'many' and 'a lot of' [> LEG 5.13-14]

Study:
⊡

The basic uses are:

1 *much* (+ uncountable, always singular) and *many* (+ plural countable) [> 5.1A]:
 – in **negative statements**: *We haven't got **much time**. There aren't **many pandas** in China.*
 – in **questions**: *Is there **much milk**? Have you had **many inquiries**?*

2 *a lot of* or the informal *lots of* (+ plural countable or singular uncountable):
 – in the **affirmative**: *I've got **a lot of time**/**lots of time**. I've got **a lot of**/**lots of books**.*

Write: Supply *much, many* or *a lot of* in these sentences.

1 I know old Mr Higgins has *a lot of* money.
2 Is there .... demand for silk stockings?
3 There isn't .... space in this flat.
4 There aren't .... portraits of Shakespeare.
5 I must say, you have .... books.
6 Will there be .... guests at your party?

5.4B Other common uses of 'much', 'many' and 'a lot of' [> LEG 5.13-14]

Study:
⊡⊡

1 We can also use *much* and *many* in the affirmative (like *a lot of*/*lots of*):
 – in formal statements: ***Much money** is spent on defence. **Many teachers** retire early.*
 – with *as ... as*: *Take **as much as** you like.*
 – in time references: *I've lived here **for many years**.*
2 We can use *Not much* and *Not many* to begin a sentence: ***Not many** know about this.*
3 We can use *not a lot of* for emphasis: *I haven't got **a lot of** time for people like him.*

Write: Supply *much* or *many* in these sentences.

1 ...*Much*.... depends on the outcome of the inquiry.
2 Don't be discouraged! .... have failed to run the marathon.
3 You can have as .... of this material as you like.
4 Take as .... of these tiles as you want.
5 He has lived here for .... of his life.
6 We have occupied the same house for .... years.
7 Not .... happens around here when the tourists leave.
8 Not .... doctors are prepared to visit patients in their own homes.

5.4C 'Few', 'a few', 'little', 'a little' [> LEG 5.15]

Study:
⊡⊡

1 We use *few* and *a few* with plural countable nouns: *few **friends**, a few **friends**.*
 We use *little* and *a little* with uncountable nouns: *little **time**, a little **time**.*

2 *Few* and *little* are negative (= hardly any): *I've got **few friends**. I've got **little time**.* (hardly any)
 We sometimes use *very* with *few* and *little*:
 *I've got **very few friends**. I've got **very little time**.* (hardly any at all)

3 *A few* and *a little* are positive (= some): *I've got **a few friends**. I've got **a little time**.* (some)
 We sometimes use *only* with *a few* and *a little*:
 *I've got **only a few friends**.* (not many) *I've got **only a little time**.* (not much)

Write: Supply *few, a few, little* or *a little* in these sentences.

1 There are very ....*few*.......................... scholarships for students in this university.
2 I'm sorry, but I'm going to have to ask you for .... more time to pay this bill.
3 If you don't hurry we'll miss our train. There's .... time to spare.
4 It's a difficult text. I've had to look up quite .... words in the dictionary.
5 I can't spare any of these catalogues. There are only .... left.
6 I can't let you use much of this perfume. There's only .... in the bottle.
7 There are .... who know about this, so keep it to yourself.
8 If what you say is true, there is .... we can do about it.

5.4D 'Fewer' and 'less' [> LEG 5.16]

Study:
★★

> 1 *Fewer* is the comparative of *few* (*few, fewer, the fewest*).
> *Less* is the comparative of *little* (*little, less, the least* [> 6.5C]).
>
> 2 *Fewer* goes with plural countables: ***Fewer videos*** *have been imported this year than last.*
>
> 3 *Less* goes with uncountables: ***Less oil*** *has been produced this year than last.*
>
> 4 Informally, we often use *less* with uncountables. Some native speakers think it's wrong:
> ***Less people*** *are travelling abroad this year.*
> *People are buying* ***less newspapers*** *than they used to.*

Write: Supply *fewer* or *less* in these sentences.

1 The .*less*. you pay, the *fewer* services you get.
2 We've had .... complaints this year.
3 I've had .... lessons than you.
4 New cars need .... servicing than old ones.
5 People have .... money to spend this year.
6 Sue's got .... homework than Tom.

5.4E Context

Write: Put in *a little, a lot of, a few, few, fewer, many* or *much.*

Which year?

DON'T CALL US, WE'LL CALL YOU!
Two years ago I moved to a new neighbourhood. There seem to be very [1].....*few*....... people in this area who are without telephones, so I expected to get a new phone quickly. I applied for one as soon as I moved into my new house. 'We aren't supplying [2]................... new phones in your area,' an engineer told me. '[3]................... people want new phones at the moment and the company is employing [4]................... engineers than last year so as to save money. A new phone won't cost you [5]................... money, but it will take [6]................... time. We can't do anything for you before December.' You need [7]................... patience if you're waiting for a new phone and you need [8]................... friends whose phones you can use as well. Fortunately, I had both. December came and went, but there was no sign of a phone. I went to the company's local office to protest. 'They told me I'd have a phone by December,' I protested. 'Which year?' the assistant asked.

5.5 'Both' and 'all'

5.5A 'Both/both the' and 'all/all the' with nouns [> LEG 5.18.1-2]

Study: ★★

1 We use *both* and *both the* (or *both my*, etc.) in exactly the same way to refer to two particular people or things (plural countable nouns):
Both children/Both the children are in bed. **Both cars/Both the cars** are very fast.

2 We use *all* + noun to refer to things in general: (= the whole number or amount):
All children like to play. (plural countables) **All advice** is useless. (uncountable nouns)

3 *All the* refers to particular people or things:
All the children in our street like to play. (*all the* + plural countable nouns)
All the advice you gave me was useless. (*all the* + uncountable noun)

Write: Supply *both (the)* or *all (the)*. There is often more than one possibility.

1 *Both (the)* tyres on my bicycle are flat.
2 .... people are mortal.
3 .... salt in this bag is damp.
4 .... drinking water must be pure.
5 .... windows in the house are open.
6 .... addresses in this list are out of date.
7 .... twins want to go to the party.
8 .... cars need regular servicing.
9 .... front legs of this chair are shaky.
10 .... earth and moon go round the sun.

5.5B 'Both' and 'all': word order with verbs [> LEG 5.19]

Study: ★★

Both and *all* have three basic positions in affirmative sentences [compare > 7.4A]:

a after *be* when it is the only verb in a sentence:
The girls **are both** ready. (= Both girls/Both the girls are ready.)
The girls **are all** ready. (= All the girls are ready.)

b after auxiliaries (*can*, etc.) or the first auxiliary when there is more than one:
The girls **can both** speak French. (= Both girls/Both the girls can speak French.)
The committee **should all have** resigned. (= All the committee should have resigned.)

c before the main verb when there is only one verb:
The girls **both left** early. (= Both girls/Both the girls left early.)
The girls **all left** early. (= All the girls left early.)

Write: Rewrite these sentences so that *both* and *all* are before or after the verbs.

1 All the customers are complaining. *The customers are all complaining.*
2 Both the patients had appointments at 10. ....
3 Both the directors have retired. ....
4 Both our secretaries can speak French. ....
5 All the customers should have complained. ....
6 Both the boys had haircuts. ....
7 All the pupils may leave now. ....
8 All the students wrote good essays. ....
9 All our employees work too hard. ....
10 All the children must go home early. ....
11 All the children here learn German. ....

5.5C 'Both' and 'all': word order with pronouns [> LEG 5.20]

Study:
★★

subject
Instead of: **We/They are both** ready.   We can say: **Both of us/them** are ready.
We/They all left early.   **All of us/them** left early.

object
Instead of: I love **you both/all**.   We can say: I love **both of you/all of you**.
He gave **us both/all** some money.   He gave some money **to both/all of us**.

Write: Rewrite these sentences using *both of* and *all of*.

1 We all took taxis. *All of us took taxis.*
2 They both turned left. ....
3 I know you both. ....
4 She's interested in them both. ....
5 It all went bad. ....
6 She's concerned about us all. ....
7 You all filled in the forms, didn't you? ....

5.5D 'None of' and 'neither of' [> LEG 5.21]

Study:
★★

The negative of **All the girls** left early.   is: **None of the girls** left early.
The negative of **Both the girls** left early. is: **Neither of the girls** left early.

Write: Rewrite these sentences in the negative.

1 All the passengers survived. *None of the passengers survived.*
2 We were both late. ....
3 Both tyres needed air. ....
4 We all knew the answer. ....

5.5E Context

Write: Put in *us, them, both, both the, all* or *all the*.

ALL ON BOARD?
[1] *All* of [2]................... who travel by plane probably find reasons to complain about airlines, but it is less common for airlines to complain about [3]...................! At 2.35 p.m. Flight 767 was ready to leave for Ibiza and nearly [4]................... passengers were on board. At 6.10 p.m. the plane was still on the runway. Two passengers hadn't boarded. If people check in but don't board [5]................... the luggage must be unloaded. [6]................... passengers had to get off the plane and [7]................... of [8]................... identified their luggage. At the end there were two pieces of luggage left. Just then, [9]................... missing passengers appeared. 'We [10]................... went to the bar and we had something to drink and a sandwich,' they explained. [11]................... of [12]................... had been sitting in the bar for hours! The captain scolded [13]................... [14]................... severely and the other passengers were very angry with [15]................... .

The plane was still on the runway

75

5.6 'All (the)', '(a/the) whole', 'each' and 'every'

5.6A 'All (the)' compared with '(a/the) whole' [> LEG 5.22]

Study:
★★

1 We use *the whole* and *a whole* with singular countable nouns:
*He ate **the whole loaf**. He swallowed **a whole banana**. **The whole film** was boring.*
We do not use *the whole* with plurals or uncountables. (Not **the whole books/bread**)

2 Some nouns combine only with *all*:
*He spent **all the money**. She's 90 and she's still got **all her teeth**.*
Some nouns combine only with *whole*:
*You must tell me **the whole truth**. I'd like to know **the whole history** of the world.*
Some nouns combine with *all* or *whole*:
*I've waited **all my life/my whole life** for such a moment as this.*

3 We also use *all* and *a/the whole* with time references: *all day, a/the whole night.*
Whole is stronger than *all* and also combines with words like *hour* and *century*:
a/the whole hour, a/the whole century. (Not **all the hour* *all the century**)

Write: Rewrite these sentences using either *all* or *whole*.

1 I'm losing my hair. ....*I'm losing all my hair.*..
2 He explained the situation to me. ....
3 The money was spent. ....
4 You didn't tell me the truth. ....
5 I heard the story. ....
6 It will take a century to clean up the atmosphere. ....

5.6B 'All' compared with 'everyone/everybody' and 'everything' [> LEG 5.24-25]

Study:
★★

1 We rarely use *all* on its own to mean 'everyone/everybody':
***Everyone/Everybody wanted** Marilyn's autograph.* (Not **All wanted**).

2 *All* means 'everyone/everybody' when we use other words with it:
***All of us/We all** agreed to sign the contract. **All those who were present** were in favour.*
(= Everyone/Everybody agreed to sign. Everyone/Everybody present was in favour.)

3 We often use *all* and *everything* with other words to refer to things:
***All/Everything I have** belongs to you. He taught me **all/everything I know**.*
But note: *He gave me **everything**.* (Not **He gave me all.**)

Write: Use *all, everyone* or *everything* in these sentences.

1 When the famous actress appeared, ...*everyone*.......... wanted to speak to her.
2 .... I invited came to my party.
3 I'm not buying anything. .... is too expensive.
4 .... those who know me can be sure I'm telling the truth.
5 .... of us felt that it had been a wonderful experience.
6 .... stood up when the President came into the room.
7 .... talked about the elections, but I'm not sure they .... voted.
8 .... in the building was destroyed in the fire. Some of the objects were priceless.
9 I wouldn't help you for .... the tea in China!
10 How much do you want for .... in the shop?

5.6C 'Each' and 'every' [> LEG 5.26]

Study:
⭐⭐

1 We often use *each*, like *both*, to refer to two people or things:
My wife and I each ordered avocado to start with. We cannot use *every* here.

2 We can use *each* and *every* to refer to more than two.
Each suggests 'one by one', 'separately'; *every* suggests 'all together':
Each child at the party had a piece of cake. (*Every* is also possible.)
Every child in the world loves the story of Cinderella. (*Each* is unlikely.)

3 We must use *every* (Not *each*) after *nearly* and after *not*:
Nearly every shop is shut today. **Not every** train driver is on strike today.

4 We cannot use *of* after *every* and we cannot use *every* at the end of a sentence:
Each of the children received a present. They received a present **each**.

5 We can use **every** with a few uncountable nouns:
My mother gave me **every encouragement** when I was a child.

Write: Supply *each* or *every* in the following sentences. Sometimes both are possible.

1 Nearly ....*every*..................... home in the country has television.
2 Here is something for .... of you.
3 Not .... student is capable of learning English.
4 Our motoring organization will give you .... assistance if you break down.
5 The admission ticket cost us £5 ....
6 They seem to be repairing .... road in the country.
7 .... road is clearly signposted.
8 There's a fire extinguisher on .... floor in the building.
9 .... floor in the building has its own fire extinguisher.
10 They are .... fortunate to have such a good start in life.
11 They both did well and they will .... receive prizes
12 You've been given .... opportunity to do well in this company.
13 I've phoned him twice, but he's been out on .... occasion.
14 I've been phoning him all week, but he's been out on .... occasion.

5.6D Context

Write: Put in *each, every, everyone, everything, all* or *whole*.

'It wasn't like meeting a stranger!'

JIM MEETS JAMES
I've just heard the [1].....*whole*........ story of the Lewis twins from Ohio, who were adopted by different families at birth and who met each other for the first time at the age of 39. [2]........................ wanted to know if they had anything in common. They had! They had [3]........................ married a woman called Linda. [4]........................ of them had been divorced and married another woman called Betty. The couples who adopted them had [5]........................ called them 'Jim'. Many similar things happened to them [6]........................ their lives. The [7]........................ list is endless. Almost [8]........................ experience they had had was the same: there were exact parallels for [9]........................ they had ever done. As Jim said when he first met James, 'It wasn't like meeting a stranger!'

5.7 'Another', '(the) other(s)', 'either', 'neither', ' each (one of)'

5.7A 'Another', 'other', 'others', 'the other', 'the others' [> LEG 5.27]

Study:
★★

> **1** *Another* doesn't refer to anything in particular. It can mean:
> – 'different': *Come **another day**.* (= any other day, no particular day)
> – 'additional': *We need **another day** to finish this.* (= one more day, no particular day)
>
> **2** We can contrast *some* and *other(s)* when we talk about things in general:
> ***Some holidays** are cheap and **other holidays** are expensive.*
> ***Some holidays** are cheap and **others** are expensive.* (= holidays in general)
>
> **3** We can contrast *one* with *the other* or *the others* when referring to particular things:
> ***This one** is mine and **the other one** is yours.* (Or: ... **the other** is yours)
> ***This one** is mine and **the other ones** are yours.* (Or: ... **the others** are yours)
>
> **4** We can use *the other(s)* to refer to people as well:
> *John went cycling and **the other boy/the other boys** went with him.*
> *John went cycling and **the others** went with him.*
>
> **5** *The other day* can mean 'a few days ago'; *the next day* refers to the following day:
> *I met your father in the street **the other day**.* (= a few days ago)
> *We spent our first night in Cairo and **the next day** we went to Alexandria.*

Write: Supply *another, other, the next, the other, the others* and *others.*

1 John came to see me ....*the other*........ day. It was last Friday, I think.
2 I met two strangers on the way to work. One of them greeted me and .... didn't.
3 Some people like to have the windows open all the time; .... don't.
4 I can't see him today. I'll have to see him .... day.
5 We spent the night in a small village and continued our journey .... day.
6 Bill and .... boy are playing in the yard. Jane and .... girls are in the front room.
7 There must be .... road that leads to the city centre.
8 There must be .... roads that lead to the city centre.
9 I can't let you have any of these plants, but you can have all ....

5.7B 'Either' and 'neither' + singular nouns [> LEG 5.29]

Study:
★★

> *Either* and *neither* refer to two people, things, etc. only. [compare > 1.4]
> *Either* means 'one or the other':
> *Which pot will I use? – **Either (of them)**. It doesn't matter which.*
> *Neither* means 'not one and not the other':
> *Which pot will I use? – **Neither (of them)**. Use this frying pan.*

Write: Supply *either* or *neither.*

1 When shall we meet: at 7 or at 7.30? – I don't mind. ....*Either*.......... time is convenient for me.
2 You can't use those screwdrivers. .... of them is suitable for the job.
3 I don't know who's on the phone. It's .... your mother or your aunt.
4 I met John a year ago, but I've .... seen him nor heard from him since.
5 Say what you like about those two applicants. I didn't like .... of them! [> 13.2A]
6 I know you sent us two letters, but we have received .... of them.

5.7C 'Each of', etc. [> LEG 5.5.2, 5.30-31]

Study:
★★

1 We can use *of the/my*, etc. after *any, some, another, each, either, neither, none* [> 5.2A]:
   Instead of: **Neither lift** *is working.*
   We can say: **Neither of the lifts** *is working.*

2 After *either, neither* and *none*, when the reference is plural, we can use a plural verb in everyday speech or a singular verb when we wish to sound 'correct' or formal:
   Neither of us is/are *happy about this.* **None of my friends has/have** *been invited.*

Write: Rewrite these sentences using *of the*.

1 Another teaspoon is missing. ....*Another of the teaspoons is missing.*........
2 Neither roadmap is much use. ....
3 Any roadmap you have will be OK. ....
4 Either road leads to the same place. ....
5 Each painting is perfect. ....
6 Neither boy is guilty. ....
7 I can't ask either secretary to do the job. ....
8 Give a tip to each porter. ....

5.7D 'One of' [> LEG 5.30]

Study:
★★

We can say: **Each of these** *answers is right.* Or: **Each one of these** *answers is right.*
We can use *of* or *one of* after *any, another, each, either,* and *neither.*
We must use a noun after *every* (*every room*) or we must use *one of* (*every one of*):
Every room *is booked.* **Every (single) one of** *the rooms is booked.* (Not **Every of**)

Write: Delete *one* where possible in these sentences.

1 Every one of these answers is wrong.
2 Each one of these pilots has been highly trained.
3 She came in here and criticized every single one of our products.
4 I'm not prepared to listen to another one of your complaints.
5 Any one of us might be asked to help in an emergency.

5.7E Context

Write: Put in *one, either, others, other, the other* or *some*.

He goes everywhere by bicycle

HALT!
The [1].....*other*.... day the Prime Minister appointed a new Minister of Transport.
[2].................. ministers like to travel everywhere by car; [3].................. prefer to use public transport. [4].................. of these means of transport is fine, but the new minister is [5].................. of those who goes everywhere by bicycle. When he arrived at the House of Commons yesterday, he was stopped by two security guards.
[6].................. of them was sure he had seen him before. 'I know you, don't I?' asked one of the guards. 'You're [7].................. of these messengers, aren't you?' 'Well, no, actually,' the minister replied. 'I'm [8].................. of the ministers.' 'I knew you were [9].................. or [10]....................!' the guard replied.

6 Adjectives

6.1 Formation of adjectives

6.1A Adjectives formed with suffixes: 'enjoy/enjoyable' [> LEG 6.2, App 8.1]

Study:
★★

Many adjectives related to verbs or nouns have a characteristic ending (or **suffix**):
We enjoyed the party. The party was very enjoyable.

-able (capable of being): *manageable*   *-ible* (like *-able*): *permissible*
-ful (full of): *boastful*   *-(i)an* (historical period, etc.): *Victorian*
-ic: *energetic*   *-ish* (have the quality of): *foolish, reddish*
-ive (capable of being): *attractive*   *-ly* (have this quality): *friendly* [> 7.1C]
-ant: *hesitant*   *-ous*: *humorous*

And note *-ing* forms used as adjectives: *running water* [> 2.2A, 6.3B, 16.5A].

Write: Supply the right adjectival forms. Refer to the box above only when you have to.

1 I'm *attracted* by this scheme. I find it very ....*attractive*.
2 A class of forty can be *managed*. It's just about ....
3 I know I *hesitated* before agreeing. I couldn't help being ....
4 I don't know where you find all that *energy*. You're tremendously ....
5 This piece of furniture was made in the reign of *Victoria*. It's ....
6 I don't know how to describe the colour of the sky. It's almost *red*, sort of ....
7 I've never met anyone who *boasts* as he does. He's extremely ....
8 What level of radiation can be *permitted*? How much radiation is ....?
9 The story is full of *humour*. I've rarely read anything that's so ....

6.1B Adjectives formed with prefixes: 'possible/impossible' [> LEG 6.2, App 8.2]

Study:
★★

A **prefix** (e.g. *im-*) added to an adjective generally has a negative effect:
*I think it's possible to solve the problem. I think it's **im**possible to solve the problem.*

un-: *un*cooked, *un*imaginable   *im-*: *im*moral, *im*practical
in-: *in*capable, *in*human   *dis-*: *dis*honest, *dis*agreeable
il-: *il*legal, *il*legible   *ir-*: *ir*responsible, *ir*regular

And note **pre-** (**pre**-*war*) and **hyper-** (**hyper**active), which do not create opposites but modify the meaning of the word in some way.

Write: Supply the right adjectival forms. Refer to the box above only when you have to.

1 I suspect he isn't *honest*. In fact, I think he's quite ....*dishonest*.
2 This arrangement isn't strictly *legal*. Some people would regard it as ....
3 Sometimes she doesn't behave in a *responsible* manner. She's quite ....
4 Such a situation is barely *imaginable*. It's quite ....
5 Bob's not very *capable*. He's .... of making sound decisions.
6 This fish hasn't been *cooked* enough. It's ....
7 This scheme isn't very *practical*. In fact, it's quite ....
8 This dates from before the *war*. It's ....

6.1C Compound adjectives of measurement, etc.: 'a twenty-year-old man'

[> LEG 6.3.2]

Study:
★★

1 We combine numbers with nouns in the singular to form compound adjectives with hyphens:
a twenty-year-old man (Not **a twenty-years-old man**).
We prefer compounds of this kind to phrases with *of*: 'a man of twenty years'.

2 Compound adjectives of this kind can refer to:
- age: *a three-year-old building*
- area: *a fifty-acre farm*
- volume: *a two-litre car*
- duration: *a four-hour meeting*
- length: *a twelve-inch ruler*
- depth: *a six-foot hole*
- price: *a $50 dress (a fifty-dollar dress)*
- time/distance: *a ten-minute walk*
- weight: *a five-kilo bag*

Write: Rewrite the following sentences using compound adjectives.

1 The office-block costs two million pounds. It's *a two-million-pound office-block.*
2 The woman is seventy years old. She's ....
3 The conference lasts two days. It's ....
4 The farm is eighty hectares. It's ....
5 The journey takes three days. It's ....
6 The bag weighs five kilos. It's ....
7 My engine is three litres. It's ....
8 It's a note for fifty pounds. It's ....
9 The fence is twenty miles. It's ....
10 The tunnel is fifty kilometres. It's ....

6.1D Context

Write: Refer to the words in brackets and put in the right adjectives.

... they broke into smiles

EAGER DRIVER
It's (*legal*) [1] *illegal* to drive under the age of seventeen in Britain,
but a (*boy of seventeen years old*) [2] .... managed to pass his
driving test on the day of his seventeenth birthday. Most people would
consider this (*possible*) [3] .... because you need a lot of
lessons to pass the test. David Livesey arranged to have (*a lesson of
eight hours*) [4] .... beginning at dawn on his birthday. At first
he was very (*care*) [5] .... and (*hesitate*) [6] ...., but
he had a (*wonder*) [7] .... teacher and his driving improved
amazingly during the day. By four in the afternoon, still feeling (*energy*)
[8] ...., he was ready to take his test and he passed first time!
He was almost in a state of shock after the test, and he drove home
very slowly in the (*red*) [9] .... light of the (*set*) [10] ....
sun. David's driving attracted the attention of two policemen, but they
broke into smiles and congratulated him warmly when he showed them
his certificate and told them his story.

6.2 Position of adjectives

6.2A Form and position of most adjectives [> LEG 6.4, 6.7]

Study:
⭐

1 Adjectives have the same form whether they refer to people or things in the singular or plural:
*He's a **tall man**.   She's a **tall woman**.   It's a **tall building**.*
*They're **tall men**.   They're **tall women**.   They're **tall buildings**.*

2 Most adjectives are used in two ways in English:
– before a noun: *He is an **old man**. This is an **old ticket**.*
– after *be, seem*, etc. the adjective stands on its own: *The man **is old**. The ticket **is old**.*

Write: Rewrite these sentences so that the adjectives come after *be*:

1 This is a big company. This company ...*is big*...
2 Kevin and Matthew are clever boys. Kevin and Matthew ....
3 Nina is a hardworking girl. Nina ....
4 These are busy streets. These streets ....
5 They're well-behaved children. The children ....

6.2B Adjectives that can change in meaning before a noun or after 'be'
[> LEG 6.7, 6.8]

Study:
⭐⭐

– before a noun: *John is an **old friend** of mine.* (= I've known him for a long time)
– after *be*:   *My friend, John, **is** very **old**.* (= old in years)

Some other common adjectives that can change meaning according to their position are:
early, faint, fine, heavy, ill, late, sick. Note that *sick* can go before a noun or after *be*, but *ill* (like *well*) comes after *be*. *Sick* means 'ill' and also means 'upset in the stomach'.

Write 1: Rewrite these sentences using adjectives with the same meaning as the words in italics.

1 John is a friend *whom I have known for a very long time*.
John is .....*an old friend*...
2 Some money was left to me by my uncle *who is dead*.
Some money was left ....
3 She drew a line *which I could hardly see*.
She drew ....
4 Your suitcase *weighs a lot*.
Your suitcase is ....
5 Susan *smokes a lot*.
She's ....

Write 2: Which words or phrases in B will replace words or phrases in A?

A
1 Her wedding dress is made of *beautiful* silk. _b_
2 The weather is *good* today. __
3 Something's upset me. I think I'm going to *throw up*. __
4 John is *extremely unwell*. __
5 I was born *at the beginning of the* 1960s. __
6 Martha is *not a healthy* woman. __

B
a) a sick
b) fine (twice)
c) very ill
d) in the early
e) be sick

6.2C Adjectives before and after nouns with a change of meaning [> LEG 6.11.2]

Study:
★★★

Adjectives go before nouns in English [> 6.2A], but there are a few adjectives which go before or after nouns and they change in meaning according to their position:
*This **elect body** meets once a year.* (before the noun = 'specially chosen')
*The **president elect** takes over in May.* (after the noun = 'who has been elected')

Write: Which words or phrases in B best explain the words or phrases in A?

A

1 The *concerned* doctor phoned for an ambulance. _b_
2 The doctor *concerned* is on holiday at the moment. __
3 It was a very *involved* question. __
4 The person *involved* has left the company. __
5 *Present* employees number 3,000. __
6 The employees *present* should vote on this. __
7 It was a *proper* question. __
8 The question *proper* has not been answered. __
9 Janet is a *responsible* girl. __
10 The girl *responsible* has been expelled. __

B

a) correct
b) worried
c) who was blamed
d) complicated
e) with a sense of duty
f) now employed
g) here now
h) connected with this (twice)
i) itself

6.2D Context

Write: Put in the missing adjectives. Alternatives are sometimes possible.

> *alive, asleep, beautiful, big, complete, fast, fresh, lovely, pleased, polished, poor, quick-drying, shiny, tall, young*

NOT A FAST LIFE!
Three and a half years ago Mr Bell received a ¹...*beautiful*... present from his ².......................
grandson. The boy had had a ³....................... holiday by the seaside and had bought his grandfather a present. It was a ⁴....................... sea-snail which had been stuck on top of an oyster and another shell. Mr Bell was very ⁵....................... with his gift and put it on a shelf. While he was dusting one morning, he accidentally knocked the ⁶....................... snail off the oyster. He went to find some ⁷....................... glue. When he came back, he couldn't believe his eyes. The snail had moved along the shelf. It was ⁸....................... ! 'It must have been ⁹....................... all these years and the shock woke it up.' Mr Bell said. He put the snail in a paper bag to show his friends. At first they thought the story was ¹⁰....................... nonsense, until they saw the snail. The ¹¹....................... creature was so hungry, it had eaten a hole in the bag. Mr Bell gave it a ¹²....................... meal of ¹³.......................
cabbage leaves which it really enjoyed. 'It's not such a ¹⁴....................... story,' a scientist explained. 'These creatures live on the seashore and don't lead a ¹⁵....................... life. They can hibernate for years without eating.'

It had eaten a hole in the bag

6.3 Adjectives that behave like nouns; '-ed/-ing' endings

6.3A 'The' (etc.) + adjective + noun: 'the blind' [> LEG 6.6, 6.12.2]

Study:
★★

> 1 We use a noun after an adjective or we use *one/ones* [> 4.2B-C, compare > 3.1C]:
> *He's a **young man**.* (Not **He's a young**) *You **poor** thing!* (Not **You poor!**)
> *I sold my **old car** and I've bought a **new one**.* (Not ** ... and I've bought a new**)
>
> 2 In the plural, we use no article (zero) [> 3.1A]:
> *They are **young men**. You **poor things**! We sold our **old cars** and bought **new ones**.*
>
> 3 We can use a few adjectives on their own after *the* to refer to 'the group as a whole':
> *the blind/the sighted, the deaf, the dumb, the living/the dead, the rich/the poor,*
> *the young/the old, the elderly, the healthy/the sick, the injured, the unemployed:*
> *We have opened a new school for **the blind**/for **blind people**.* (Not **for (the) blinds**)
>
> We say *He is **blind**.* or *He is **a blind man**.* (Not **He is a blind.**)
> We say *They are **blind**.* or *They are **blind people**.* (Not **They are blinds.**)

Write 1: Rewrite these sentences using the adjectives with *man, woman* or *people*.

1 He is *poor*. ....*He is a poor man.*..
2 They are *unemployed*. ....
3 She is *young*. ....
4 He is *elderly*. ....
5 She is *sick*. ....
6 They are *healthy*. ....

Write 2: Rewrite these sentences to refer to a group without using the word *people*.

1 Rich people should pay more tax than poor people.
.........*The rich should pay more tax than the poor.*...
2 What hope can the government give to unemployed people?
....
3 Will this new invention really help deaf people?
....
4 Old people usually have to live on a fixed income.
....
5 After the crash, the injured people were rushed to hospital.
....
6 This is a memorial to dead people.
....
7 We have interesting study courses for elderly people.
....
8 Healthy people never think about getting ill.
....
9 It's a nurse's job to look after sick people.
....
10 Blind people should have the same opportunities as sighted people.
....

6.3B Adjectives ending in '-ed' and '-ing': 'interested/interesting'

[> LEG 6.15, App 10]

Study:
★★

> **1** We use some past participles ending in *-ed* (e.g. *excited*) and some present participles ending in *-ing* (e.g. *exciting*) as adjectives. Common pairs of *-ed/-ing* adjectives are:
> *amazed/amazing, annoyed/annoying, bored/boring, enchanted/enchanting, excited/exciting, interested/interesting, pleased/pleasing, tired/tiring.*
> Similar pairs are: *delighted/delightful, impressed/impressive, upset/upsetting.*
>
> **2** We often use *-ed* endings to describe people:
> *The story interested* **John**. → **John** *was* **interested** *in the story.*
> We often use *-ing* endings to describe things, events, etc.: **The story** *was* **interesting**.
>
> **3** We can also use *-ing* endings to describe people: *Isn't* **John interesting**! Compare:
> **Gloria** *was* **interesting** *to be with.* (= that was the effect she had on others)
> **Gloria** *was* **interested**. (= that was the effect someone or something had on her)

Write: Rewrite these sentences using *-ed/-ing* or other endings. Make necessary changes.

1 The coincidence amazed *us*. We ...*were amazed by the coincidence.*....................
2 *The journey* tired us. The journey ....
3 The experience upset *Sylvia*. Sylvia ....
4 *The experience* upset us. The experience ....
5 *Gloria* enchanted me. Gloria ....
6 I enchanted *Gloria*. Gloria ....
7 *The children* delighted us. The children ....
8 The children delighted *us*. We ....
9 *The new building* impresses us. The new building ....
10 The new building impresses *everybody*. Everybody ....

6.3C Context

Write: Put in the correct forms of the words in brackets: *the* + adjective or *-ed/-ing* adjectives.

You'll never want to try another!

A HUMAN IDEAL
A just society is a human ideal. We would all like to live in a place where (*rich*)
[1].....*the rich*........ are not too rich and (*poor*) [2]........................... are not too poor;
where no one would be (*shock*) [3]........................... or (*embarrass*)
[4]........................... at the way (*old*) [5]........................... are cared for. (*blind*)
[6]........................... would have as much opportunity as (*sighted*)
[7]........................... . (*deaf*) [8]........................... would be able to develop their skills.
(*unemployed*) [9]........................... would not depend on the state, because no one
would be unemployed. (*healthy*) [10]........................... would take care of (*sick*)
[11]........................... . The most innocent people in society, (*young*)
[12]..........................., would be protected. In this happy place no one would feel
(*depress*) [13]........................... or (*distress*) [14]........................... . Unfortunately, in
the real world, life can be both (*distress*) [15]........................... and (*depress*)
[16]........................... . So let's be thankful for a sense of humour. I recently saw a
notice in an undertaker's window and I wasn't sure whether it was addressed to
(*living*) [17]........................... or (*dead*) [18]........................... . It said: 'Once you've tried
one of our funerals, you'll never want to try another!'

6.4 Adjectives after 'be', 'seem', etc.; word order of adjectives

6.4A 'Look good' compared with 'play well' [> LEG 6.17]

Study:
★★

1 After *be, look, feel, seem, smell, taste,* and *sound* we use adjectives:
*That egg **is/tastes bad**. (Bad* is an adjective describing the noun *egg.*) [> 1.2C]

2 After other verbs, we use adverbs: *John **behaved badly**.* [> 7.1]
(*Badly* is an adverb: it adds to the meaning of the verb *behave.*) Compare:
*John **looks good**.* (adjective) *John **looks well**.* (adjective [> 6.2B]) *John **plays well**.* (adverb)

Write: Supply adjectives or adverbs in the following.

1 He behaved ...*nicely*... (nice)
2 The music sounds .... (nice)
3 The play ended .... (bad)
4 This food smells .... (bad)
5 Your cooking is .... (good)
6 You cook .... (good)
7 The train went .... (smooth)
8 I've just shaved and my face feels .... (smooth)

6.4B Word order: two-word and three-word nouns: 'a teak kitchen cupboard' [> LEG 6.13, 6.20.1]

Study:
★★

1 Materials (nouns) behave like adjectives when we use them to form compound nouns:
a cupboard (noun) made of *teak* (noun) → *a **teak cupboard*** (compound noun) [> 2.2C]

2 We can have three-word compound nouns. 'Material' comes before 'purpose' or 'use':
a teak cupboard, used in the *kitchen* → *a **teak kitchen cupboard*** (compound noun)
Adjectives go in front of nouns [> 6.2A]. We cannot separate a compound noun by an adjective:
*a **fine** teak kitchen cupboard*. (Not **a teak fine kitchen cupboard**)

Write: Make two-word and three-word nouns.

1 a shirt made of cotton .... *a cotton shirt* ....
2 a shirt made of cotton/worn in the summer ....
3 a rake made of wire ....
4 a clock used in the kitchen ....
5 a clock made of plastic/used in the kitchen ....

6.4C Word order: past participle + noun: 'a handmade cupboard' [> LEG 6.20]

Study:
★★

An adjectival past participle (*damaged, handmade,* etc.) comes in front of a noun:
adjective + one-word noun: *a **handmade** cupboard*
adjective + two-word noun: *a **handmade** teak cupboard*
adjective + three-word noun: *a **handmade** teak kitchen cupboard*

Write: Add these adjectives to the nouns made in 6.4B above: *unused, damaged, worn, broken, handmade.*

1 .... *a worn cotton shirt* ....
2 ....
3 ....
4 ....
5 ....

6.4D Word order: adjective + noun: 'a big round table' [> LEG 6.20]

Study:
★★

The order of adjectives in front of a noun is as follows (in reverse order):

3 where from? + past participle: a *French handmade* kitchen cupboard
Or: **past participle + where from?:**   a *handmade French* kitchen cupboard

2 size/age/shape/colour + where from? + past participle:
a *large French handmade* cupboard

1 quality/opinion + size, etc. The most general adjective usually comes first:
a *beautiful large French handmade* teak cupboard

summary:

opinion	size	age	shape	colour	from?	past part.	noun
a valuable	–	–	–	brown	Victorian	handmade	teak cupboard
					Or: handmade	Victorian	

Write: You're looking for items you want to buy. Begin each sentence with *I'm looking for ...*

1 clock radio – white – Taiwanese – cheap – for my bedside table
...I'm looking for a cheap white Taiwanese clock radio for my bedside table.

2 sports car – well-maintained – second-hand – with a low mileage
....

3 polished – beautiful – antique – dining-table – mahogany – English
....

4 canvas – American – a pair of – trainers – grey and red – which I can use for jogging
....

5 cottage – stone-built – small – old – country
....

6 cotton – dress – summer – pink and white – for my holiday
....

6.4E Context

Write: Put in the right word order or choose the right forms.

NOT A DOG'S DINNER!! *Expensive handmade Italian leather shoes*
(*shoes leather Italian expensive handmade*) [1]........................: these are my pride and joy. I own a (*old beautiful pair*) [2]........................ – or I did until yesterday, when I discovered that one of the shoes was missing. I had left the shoes on my (*doorstep back*) [3]........................ to do some gardening. My neighbour has a (*dog friendly large*) [4]........................ called Sam. When I saw that one of my shoes had disappeared, I knew that Sam had taken it. I can't say he behaved (*bad/badly*) [5]........................ . He just behaved like a dog. Leather looks (*good/well*) [6]........................ and tastes (*good/well*) [7]........................, too. I unwillingly gave Sam the (*remaining Italian shoe*) [8]........................ and then followed him. I not only found one (*Italian unchewed shoe*) [9]........................, but also a pile of things Sam had been borrowing, including my wife's (*slippers fur-lined red*) [10]........................, which Sam had tried to have for dinner!

... had tried to have for dinner!

6.5 The comparison of adjectives

6.5A Common comparative and superlative forms: 'cold – colder – coldest'
[> LEG 6.5, 6.22-29]

Study:
⊠

> **1** We add *-er* and *-est* to form the comparative and superlative of most one-syllable adjectives: *clean – cleaner – the cleanest, cold – colder – the coldest*.
>
> **2** Adjectives like *hot* (*big, fat, sad, wet*) double the consonant: *hot – hotter – the hottest*.
>
> **3** Adjectives like *nice* (*fine, large, late, safe*) add *-r, -st*: *nice – nicer – the nicest*.
>
> **4** With adjectives like *busy* we use *-i* in place of *-y*: *busy – busier – the busiest*.
>
> **5** We use the **comparative** when comparing one person or thing with another.
>
> **6** We use the **superlative** when comparing one person or thing with more than one other.

Write:
1 My room's *big*. (in the house)
   My room's bigger than yours. It's the biggest in the house

2 My room's *cold*. (in the house)

3 My garden's *nice*. (in the street)

4 My desk is *tidy*. (in the office)

6.5B Adjectives with two or more syllables: 'clever', 'expensive' [> LEG 6.22-29]

Study:
⊠⊠

> **1** Some two-syllable adjectives like *happy* (*clever, common, narrow, pleasant, quiet, simple, stupid*) have two comparative or superlative forms:
>   – either with *-er/-est*:   She's clever**er** than you. She's the clever**est** person I know.
>   – or with *more/the most*: She's **more clever** than you. She's **the most clever person** I know.
> **2** We use only *more/the most* with most two-syllable adjectives: *careless, correct, famous*.
> **3** We use *more/the most* with three-syllable adjectives: *more beautiful, the most beautiful*.

Write: Give both forms where possible.

1 She's *happy*.
   than I am ......*She's happier / more happy than I am*.........
   person I have ever met ...*She's the happiest / most happy person I have ever met*......
2 His work was *careless*.
   than mine ....
   in the class ....
3 This problem is *simple*.
   than that one ....
   in the book ....
4 This watch is *expensive*.
   than that one ....
   in the shop ....
5 This engine is *quiet*.
   than mine ....
   ever built ....

6.5C Comparative and superlative forms often confused: 'older/elder'

[> LEG 6.24-26, 7.4-5, App 12]

Study:
★★

> 1 *Further* and *farther* refer to distance: *London is* **five miles further/farther**.
> *Further* (Not **farther**) can mean 'in addition': *There's no* **further information**.
>
> 2 We use *elder/eldest* before a noun only with reference to people in a family:
> *my* **elder** *brother/son,* **the eldest** *child, he's* **the eldest** (but not **He is elder than me.**)
> We use *older/oldest* for people and things: **He** *is* **older** *than I am. This* **book** *is* **older**.
>
> 3 **Irregular comparisons:** *good/well, better, the best; bad, worse, the worst; much/many, more, the most; little, less, the least.*
> *Good* is an adjective; *well* is adjective or adverb [> 6.4A].
>
> 4 *Lesser* is formed from *less* but is not a true comparative. We cannot use *than* after it.
> *Lesser* means 'not so great' and we use it in fixed phrases like *the lesser of two evils.*
>
> 5 *Latest/last*: *I bought* **the latest** (i.e. most recent) *edition of today's paper.*
> *I bought* **the last** (i.e. final) *edition of today's paper.*
>
> 6 The comparative and superlative of *little* is *smaller/smallest*: *a* **small/little** *boy, a* **smaller/the smallest** *boy.* Very young children often use *littler* and *littlest.*

Write: Circle the right forms in these sentences. In some cases both forms are right.

1 Is your house much (further/farther)?
2 Who is the (oldest/eldest) in this class?
3 Your driving is (worse/worst) than mine.
4 It's the (less/lesser) of two evils.
5 Have you heard the (last/latest) news?
6 We have no (further/farther) information.
7 Jane Somers writes (good/well).
8 His (latest/last) words were: 'The end'.
9 This is the town's (oldest/eldest) house.
10 My flat is (littler/smaller) than yours.
11 I've got (less/lesser) than you.
12 Jane is (older/elder) than I am.
13 This is the (more/most) expensive.
14 His English is (best/better) than mine.
15 It's the (better/best) in the shop.
16 It's the (furthest/farthest) point west.
17 It's the (oldest/eldest) tree in the country.
18 She's my (elder/older) sister.
19 I've got the (least/less)!
20 You've got the (more/most)!

6.5D Context

Write: Put in the right forms. Alternatives are possible.

King Karate was at the bar as usual!

THE CHAMP
The two men were sitting at the bar. The one (*near*) [1] .....*nearer*...... to me was the (*big*) [2] .... and (*strong*) [3] .... man I have ever seen. The one (*far*) [4] .... from me was the (*small/little*) [5] .... and (*weak*) [6] .... They were having the (*violent*) [7] .... argument I had ever heard. Suddenly the little man said, 'It's a case of the (*small*) [8] .... brain in the world fitted into the (*big*) [9] .... head!' They were his (*last/latest*) [10] .... words. The little man didn't know what hit him as he fell to the floor. 'When Shortie wakes up, tell him that was my (*better/best*) [11] .... Karate chop,' the big man told the barman as he left. The next evening, King Karate was at the bar as usual when Shortie crept in quietly, swung his arm and the champ fell to the floor. 'When Karate wakes up,' Shortie said, 'tell him it was my (*oldest/eldest*) [12] .... Land Rover starting handle.'

89

7 Adverbs

7.1 Adverbs of manner

7.1A Adverbs with and without '-ly': 'carefully', 'fast' [> LEG 7.7, 7.13, Apps 14, 15.1]

Study:
★★

1 An adverb adds to the meaning of a verb. Adverbs of manner tells us *how* something happens:
How did John behave? – (He behaved) badly.

2 We form adverbs of manner by adding *-ly* to an adjective: *slow/slowly*.
After a consonant, *-y* changes to *-i: heavy/heavily*.
It was a slow train./The train went slowly. It was heavy rain./It rained heavily.

3 We can use some words as adjectives or adverbs without adding *-ly* or *-ily*:
It was a fast train. → *The train went fast*.
Other examples are: *better, best, early, hard, high, last, late, monthly, near, wide, worse*.

Write: Supply the right adverb. Some adverbs end in *-ly* and some do not.

1 He's a *bad* driver. He drives ....*badly*........
2 She's a *hard* worker. She works ....
3 He's a *fast* runner. He runs ....
4 I'm a *better* player than you. I play ....
5 This is an *airmail* letter. Send it ....
6 He made a *sudden* move. He moved ....
7 She gave a *rude* reply. She replied ....
8 The train is *early*. It has arrived ....
9 Make your *best* effort. Do your ....
10 She's *glad* to help. She helps ....
11 He's a *quick* thinker. He thinks ....
12 She's an *eager* helper. She helps ....
13 My name is *last*. I come ....
14 The plane is very *high*. It's flying ....
15 Be *careful*. Act ....
16 The bus was *late*. It came ....
17 She was *brave*. She acted ....
18 The house was *near*. We went ....
19 What a *wide* window! Open it ....
20 I get a *monthly* bill. I pay ....

7.1B Two forms and different meanings: 'hard/hardly' [> LEG 7.14, App 15.2]

Study:
★★

Some adverbs have two forms, one without *-ly* and one with *-ly*.
These forms have different meanings and uses: e.g. *hard/hardly, last/lastly, late/lately*:
He played hard. He hardly played at all.

Write: Choose the right adverb in each sentence.

1 Farm workers have to work very ....*hard*........... during the harvest. (hard/hardly)
2 Farm workers earn .... enough money to pay their bills. (hard/hardly)
3 I got off first in the race but managed to come .... (last/lastly)
4 – and ...., I'd like to thank all those who made my success possible. (last/lastly)
5 We've been receiving a lot of junk mail .... (late/lately)
6 The postman brings my mail so .... I rarely see it before I go to work. (late/lately)
7 I'm sure the boss thinks very .... of you. (high/highly)
8 If you want to succeed, you should aim .... (high/highly)
9 I don't think you were treated very .... (just/justly)
10 I've .... been offered a job in Mexico! (just/justly)
11 Please don't go too .... the edge of the platform. (near/nearly)
12 I .... fell off the edge of the platform! (near/nearly)

7.1C Adjectives which end in '-ly': 'friendly' [> LEG 7.12]

Study:
★★

> Some adjectives end in -ly: *cowardly, friendly, lively, lovely, motherly, sickly, silly*:
> *Meg's a **friendly** girl. John gave me a **friendly** handshake.*
> If we want to use these words as adverbs we say *in a friendly way/manner/fashion*:
> *Meg always greets me **in a friendly way**.* (Not **greets me friendly/friendlily**)

Write: Change the adjectives into adverbs or adverbial phrases in the following sentences.

1 That was a *cowardly* thing to do. You acted ......*in a cowardly way*..
2 That was a *quick* response. She responded ....
3 The music was very *loud*. The band played far too ....!
4 That was a *silly* thing to do. You acted ....
5 The orchestra gave a *lively* performance. They performed ....
6 She's a *slow* runner. She runs ....
7 The singers gave a *bad* performance. They performed ....
8 She can't control her *motherly* feelings. Even though he's 40, she looks after him ....
9 She's a *lovely* teacher. She handles young children ....
10 She delivered a *careful* speech. She spoke ....
11 He looks pale and *sickly*. He always greets me ....
12 You don't have to be so *unfriendly*! You needn't look at me ....

7.1D Context

Write: Put in the missing adjectives and adverbs. Add -ly or make other changes where you need to.

> *beautiful, best* (twice), *careful, cheap, early, far, fast, full, hurried, important, last, new, past,*
> *quick, rapid, silly*

... threw them out of the window

A SPLASH OF COLOUR

[1]......*Last*...... Thursday I had an [2]....................... interview for a job. I
got up [3]...................... and dressed [4]....................... . I put on my
[5]...................... jacket and trousers, to look my [6]....................... . I had
to travel by train, so I walked to the station which isn't [7]......................
from my house. I was walking quite [8]....................... when I saw a man
just ahead painting his fence with red paint. He didn't notice me as I
walked [9]....................... . Then he turned suddenly and splashed my
[10]...................... trousers! He had acted [11]....................... and he
apologized, but the damage was done. There was a big store on the
corner, so I decided to buy a new pair [12]....................... . I could change
on the train. I [13]...................... found a nice pair, which I bought quite
[14]....................... . The shop was [15]......................, so I paid
[16]......................, grabbed my shopping-bag and left. On the train, I
went to the toilet to change. I took off my stained trousers and threw
them out of the window. Then I opened the bag to get my
[17]...................... ones, but all I found was a pink woollen sweater!

7.2 Adverbs of time

7.2A Points of time: 'Monday', 'this morning' [> LEG 7.21-22, App 48]

Study:
⭐

> 1 Adverbs of time tell us *when* something happens. 'Points of time' tell us 'exactly when': e.g. *today, yesterday, this/next/last week, on Monday, at 5 o'clock.*
>
> 2 We can refer to days of the week without *this, last, next* or *on*:
> *I'm seeing him **Monday**.* (= this/next/on Monday). (Not *I'm seeing him the Monday.*)
> *I saw him **Monday**.* (= last/on Monday). (Not *I saw him the Monday.*)
>
> 3 *This morning,* etc. (Not *today morning* *today afternoon* etc.) can refer to:
> – now: *I feel terrible **this morning**.*
> – earlier: *I spoke to him **this morning**.*
> – later on today: *I'll speak to him **this morning**.*
>
> 4 Note: *tonight, tomorrow night* and *last night* (Not *yesterday night*).
>
> 5 Note: *the day before yesterday, the day after tomorrow (in the evening),* etc.
>
> 6 We do not use *the* in phrases like *next Monday, last Monday: I'll see him **next Monday**.*
>
> 7 We normally put time references at the end of a sentence or clause, but we can also put them at the beginning: *(This morning) I went to the dentist (this morning).* [> 1.1A]

Write 1: Fill in the missing points of time.

1 ......*yesterday*......	today	......*tomorrow*......
2	this morning	....
3	at noon	....
4	this afternoon	....
5	this evening	....
6	tonight	....
7	this Monday	....
8	this January	....
9	this week	....
10	this year	....

Write 2: Today is Tuesday. Write sentences using the right points of time (*today,* etc.)

Monday	**Tuesday**	Wednesday

1 When is she arriving? (*Tuesday morning*) .....*She is arriving this morning.*..........
2 When can you see him? (*Tuesday*) ....
3 When did she arrive? (*Monday night*) ....
4 When are you expecting her? (*Wednesday night*) ....
5 When will you be home? (*Tuesday night*) ....
6 When can I make an appointment? (*Tuesday afternoon*) ....
7 When can I see you? (*Thursday*) ....
8 When did she leave? (*Monday in the evening*) ....
9 When can I see you? (*Thursday morning*) ....
10 When can I come to your office? (*Tuesday midday*) ....
11 When did he leave? (*Monday morning*) ....
12 When will she phone? (*Wednesday in the afternoon*) ....

7.2B 'Still' and 'yet' [> LEG 7.25, 7.27]

Study:
★★

1 *Still* and *yet* mean 'until now' and we often use them with the present perfect [> 9.5A].

2 We use *still* to emphasize continuity, mainly in affirmatives and sometimes in questions:
*I'm **still** waiting for my new passport. Is Martha **still** in hospital?*
We can also use *still* in the negative for special emphasis: *John **still hasn't** written to me.*
Still has the same position in a sentence as adverbs of frequency [> 7.4B].

3 We use *yet* mainly in questions and negatives and often put it at the end of a sentence:
*Has your new passport arrived **yet**? – No, not **yet**. It hasn't arrived **yet**.*

Write: Rewrite these sentences supplying *still* or *yet*. Sometimes both are possible.

1 The children are at the cinema. .....*The children are still at the cinema.*....................
2 I haven't met your brother. ....
3 Jim works for the same company. ....
4 Has she phoned you? .... – No, not ....
5 The new law hasn't come into force. ....

7.2C 'Already' and other adverbs of time [> LEG 7.23-24, 7.26, 7.28-29]

Study:
★★

1 *Already* means 'before now' or 'so soon'. We use it in questions and affirmatives, but not in negatives. We can put it in the middle [> 7.4B] of a sentence or at the end:
*Have you **already** finished lunch? Have you finished lunch **already**?*
*This machine is **already** out of date. It's out of date **already**.*

2 Other common adverbs of time are: *afterwards, at last, just, lately, now, once, recently, soon, suddenly, then, these days*. We often use these adverbs in story-telling.

Write: Rewrite these sentences using *yet* or *already*. Sometimes both are possible.

1 Have you had breakfast? – I've had it, thanks. .....*I've already had it, thanks.*.................
2 I haven't received an invitation to the party. ....
3 I have received an invitation to the party. ....
4 Have you finished eating? ....
5 Haven't you finished eating? ....

7.2D Context

Write: Put in *already, immediately, this week, still, then, yesterday, yet*. Use each word once only.

Not fit for pigs!

FIT FOR HUMANS, BUT NOT FOR PIGS!
[1].....*This week*..... there's going to be a festival of British Food and Farming in Hyde Park in London. The festival hasn't begun [2]............................ and farmers are [3]............................ bringing their animals. But a pig farmer has [4]............................ run into a serious problem. [5]............................ he arrived with his pigs from the Welsh Hills – hundreds of miles away. The pigs were very thirsty when they arrived in Hyde Park and the farmer [6]............................ gave them some London water. [7]............................ he got a big surprise because the pigs refused to drink the water. London water is fit for humans but not for pigs!

7.3 Adverbial phrases of duration

7.3A 'Since', 'for' and 'ago' [> LEG 7.31, 7.32, 9.18]

Study:
★★

1 **'Since' + a point of time** [> 7.2A] answers *Since when?* We use *since* with the present perfect to mark a period lasting till now: *I haven't seen him **since January**.* [> 9.5A, 10.2D]

2 **'For' + period of time** answers *How long?* We use *for* to refer to periods of time:
– in the past: *My wife and I worked in America **for five months**.*
– in the future: *John will be staying in New York **for two weeks**.*
– in the present perfect: *I've known Susan **for five years**.* [> 9.5A, 10.2D]

3 **Period of time + 'ago'** answers *How long ago?* and marks the start of a period going back from now. We use *ago* with the simple past [> 9.3C]: *I arrived here **two months ago**.*

Write 1: Show where *since* or *ago* will fit into these sentences.
Since when have...
1 When have you been interested in jazz?
2 I saw your mother a week.
3 I started work here seven months.
4 I saw her last week and haven't seen her.
5 I haven't been home 1987.
6 How long did you become a director?

Write 2: Show where *since* or *for* will fit into these sentences.
... for five years ...
1 They lived here five years before moving.
2 They have lived here 1984.
3 I've known him six years.
4 I've been expecting a letter weeks.
5 I've been expecting a letter last week.
6 I've enjoyed jazz I was a boy.

7.3B 'Till' (or 'until') and 'by' [> LEG 7.34]

Study:
★★★

1 Some verbs naturally refer to 'periods of time' or 'continuity' [> 9.5B]:
e.g. *learn, lie, live, rain, sit, sleep, stand, stay, wait* and *work*.

2 *Till* (or *until*) and *by* mean 'any time before and not later than'.
We cannot use *by* at all with these 'continuity' verbs. (Not *I'll wait here by 5 o'clock.*)
We can only use *till* (or *until*) with these verbs:
*I'll **wait** here **till** (or **until**) 5 o'clock. **I won't wait** here **till** (or **until**) 5 o'clock.*

3 We use *by* with verbs which do not refer to periods of time.
We can think of these as 'point of time verbs': e.g. *arrive, come, finish, go, leave*:
*She **will arrive by** 5.* (= any time before and not later than 5.)
*She **won't arrive by** 5. She'll arrive at 6.*

4 We use *till* or *until* with 'point of time verbs' only in the negative.
*She **won't arrive till** (or **until**) 5.* (But not *She will arrive till 5.*)

Write: Supply *by* or *till*.

1 I'll wait ....*till*.......... Monday before answering his letter.
2 I intend to stay in bed .... 10 o'clock tomorrow morning.
3 Your suit will be ready .... Friday.
4 Your suit won't be ready .... Friday. You can collect it then.
5 Your suit won't be ready .... Friday. You can collect it next Monday.
6 I'm sure I will have left .... Monday.
7 Your aunt says she won't leave .... Monday. Monday's the day she's going to leave.

7.3C 'During', 'in' and 'for' [> LEG 7.35]

Study:
★★

> **1** *During* means:
> – either: 'from the beginning to the end': *We had a lot of fun **during the holidays**.*
> – or: 'at some point during a period of time': *I'll mend the gate **during the weekend**.*
> *We watched a very nice film **during the flight** to New York.*
>
> **2** We use *in* like *during* to refer to time:
> *We had a lot of fun **in the holidays**.* (Or: ... *during the holidays*)
> But we cannot use *in* to refer to an activity or event:
> *We watched a film **during the flight**.* (Not **in the flight**)
>
> **3** *For* tells us 'how long' [> 7.3A]:
> *We stayed in Recife **for a week/for three weeks**.* (Not **during three weeks**)

Write: Supply *in, during* and *for*. Show which sentences take both *in* and *during*.

1 It was very hot ....*during*.......... August.
2 I was sent abroad .... my military service.
3 It rained .... the night.
4 I'll see you .... the lunch hour.
5 I woke up twice .... the night.
6 I tried to get a taxi .... a whole hour.
7 Many people gave up .... the course.
8 I suddenly felt ill .... my speech.
9 There was an accident .... the race.
10 I sleep .... the daytime.
11 I'm going abroad .... June.
12 Can you hold your breath .... two minutes?

7.3D Context

Write: Put in *during, in, by, till, since, for* or *ago*.

PEACE AND QUIET

I moved to this area seven years [1] ....*ago*.......... . [2] .... years I have had noisy neighbours. Ever [3] .... I moved into this flat, I've had to put up with noise [4] .... the night. I decided I'd had enough and I've been looking for a new flat [5] .... the beginning of the year. I haven't found anything [6] .... now. Every week I go to the local estate agent's office, but it's the same story. 'I might have something [7] .... the end of the week,' he says, or, 'Wait [8] .... next week. I think I might have a few flats [9] .... then.' I've seen a few flats [10] .... my search, but I don't like any of them. One flat I saw has been empty [11] .... two years. 'It's got a busy road on one side and a railway on the other!' I exclaimed. 'I want peace and quiet.' Last week I visited the agent again. 'I won't leave [12] .... you show me something,' I said. He smiled and said, 'I've got just the flat for you.' I went to see it and I was horrified. 'But it's next to a cemetery!' I cried. 'But you won't have noisy neighbours,' my agent said. 'It's ideal for peace and quiet!'

You won't have noisy neighbours!

7.4 Adverbs of frequency

7.4A Position of adverbs of frequency ('often') in affirmatives and questions
[> LEG 7.37-40]

Study:
★★

> 1 Adverbs of frequency generally answer the question *How often?*. The most common are:
> *always, almost always, generally, usually, normally, frequently, often, sometimes,*
> *hardly ever, seldom, ever, not ... ever, never.*
>
> 2 Adverbs of frequency have three basic positions in affirmative sentences:
> – after *be* when it is the only verb in a sentence: *I **am always** late.*
> – after the first auxiliary when there is more than one: *I **would always** have been late.*
> – before the main verb when there is only one verb: *You **never tried** hard enough.*
>
> 3 In questions, the adverb of frequency comes after the subject: *Are **you always** late?*

Write: Rewrite these sentences using any suitable adverb of frequency in each one.

1 I am late. ....*I am generally late.*..
2 I was late for work. ....
3 I can tell the difference between the two. ....
4 I would have been able to find a job like yours. ....
5 You tried hard enough. ....
6 You got good marks at school. ....
7 Are you late? ....
8 Have you lived in this town? ....
9 Did you get good marks at school? ....

7.4B The position of adverbs of frequency in negative statements [> LEG 7.40.2]

Study:
★★

> 1 These usually come after *not*: *always, generally, normally, often, regularly, usually*:
> *Public transport **isn't always** (etc.) very reliable.*
>
> 2 *Generally, normally, often* and *usually* can come after the subject for special emphasis:
> ***We normally** don't worry if the children are late.*
>
> 3 We use *sometimes* and *frequently* before *not* or before *isn't, doesn't, don't, didn't,* etc.:
> *Debbie is **sometimes not** responsible for what she does. He is **frequently not** at home.*
> *She **sometimes isn't** reliable. He **frequently doesn't** get home till 10.*
>
> 4 We can't use *not* to form negatives with *hardly ever,* etc. [> 13.2A]: *He **hardly ever writes**.*
> (Not **He almost always doesn't write.** or **He doesn't hardly ever write.**)

Write: Write these sentences again using the adverbs in brackets. Make changes where necessary.

1 Public transport isn't reliable. (always) ......*Public transport isn't always reliable.*...........
2 He wasn't late when he worked here. (often) ....
3 She doesn't arrive on time. (usually) ....
4 She doesn't arrive on time. (sometimes) ....
5 We don't worry if the children are late. (normally) ....
6 You don't phone. (hardly ever) ....
7 We don't complain. (generally) ....
8 You're not at home when I phone. (sometimes) ....

7.4C Adverbs of frequency at the beginning of a sentence [> LEG 7.40.4]

Study:
★★

For special emphasis, we can begin a sentence with *frequently, generally, normally, (very) often, sometimes* and *usually*.
We can say: *We **normally** don't worry if the children are late home from school.*
Or: ***Normally,** we don't worry if the children are late home from school.*

Write: Answer each question in full putting the adverb a) in the middle and b) at the beginning.

1 Do you ever bring work home from the office? (often)
I often bring work home from the office.   *Often, I bring work home...*

2 Does John leave home before his wife does? (normally)
....

3 Have you ever forgotten to lock the back door? (frequently)
....

4 Do you know when to wake up? (usually)
....

5 Are you the one who pays the bills? (generally)
....

6 Is the traffic heavy in the mornings? (often)
....

7 Do you ever have power cuts? (sometimes)
We ....

8 Are there complaints about the service? (often)
....

7.4D Context

Write: Show where the adverbs in brackets can go in the sentences that follow them.

People don't carry stuffed gorillas!

WHERE DID I PUT MY TEETH?
(¹*ever*) Have you forgotten something on a train or bus? *ever forgotten*
(²*never*) Don't say you have!
(³*always*) (⁴*occasionally*) We can't be careful with our things and most of us must have left something behind when getting off a bus or train.
(⁵*never*) There can't be anyone who forgets anything.
(⁶*regularly*) Over 150,000 items a year are dealt with by London Transport's Lost Property Office.
(⁷*normally*) People don't carry stuffed gorillas, but someone recently left one on a train.
(⁸*most* often) The things people lose are umbrellas and keys.
(⁹*sometimes*) But there are items that are not very common.
(¹⁰*ever*) Can you imagine losing a bed and not claiming it?
(¹¹*often*) Prams and pushchairs are lost.
(¹²*frequently*) But it is unbelievable that people forget false teeth and even glass eyes when they get off a train!
(¹³*often*) Yet they do!

7.5 Adverbs of degree

7.5A The two meanings of 'quite' [> LEG 6.5, 7.41-42]

Study:
★★

1 *Quite, fairly* and *rather* are common **adverbs of degree**. They can make the word they modify weaker or stronger and their effect depends on stress and intonation. If we say:

*The film is **quite/good**!* and our voice 'goes up', this means 'I enjoyed it on the whole'.

*The film is **quite\good**.* and our voice 'goes down', this means 'I didn't really enjoy it'.

We can put *quite* in front of ordinary adjectives (*quite good*), adverbs (*quite slowly*), and a few verbs (*I quite enjoy*). Regardless of stress, the meaning is 'less than'.

2 We can also use *quite* with 'absolute' adjectives (*dead, empty* and *full*), and with 'strong' adjectives like *amazing* and *wonderful*. Then it means 'completely'. The voice 'goes up'.

*The man was **quite dead**! The bucket is **quite full**! The film was **quite wonderful**!*

Write: Answer these questions in full with *quite*, and say whether *quite* means 'less than' or 'completely'.

1 What was the film like? (good) .....*The film was quite good. ('less than')*.....
2 How was the exhibition? (amazing) ....
3 What's Pam like? (wonderful) ....
4 How was the play? (awful) ....
5 How was your holiday? (quite enjoy) ....
6 Do you eat snails? (quite like) ....

7.5B 'Fairly' [> LEG 7.43]

Study:
★★

Fairly often goes with 'good' adjectives and adverbs (*good, nice, well*, etc.). It is generally 'less complimentary' than *quite*. We do not use 'enough' [> 16.4B] to mean *quite* or *fairly*.
*What's Yoko's English like? – It's **quite good**.* ('complimentary') Not *enough good*
*What's Yoko's English like? – It's **fairly good**.* ('less complimentary') Not *enough good*
We can't use *fairly* with some 'absolute' adjectives: Not *fairly dead/fairly wonderful*

Write: Add *quite* and *fairly*. Mark as 'complimentary', 'less complimentary' or 'completely'.

1 She sings ....*quite/ fairly*......... well. *('complimentary'/'less complimentary')*
2 The dinner is .... spoilt. ....
3 I feel .... sick. ....
4 She's .... clever. ....
5 I think he's .... mad. ....
6 You're .... incredible! ....

7.5C 'Rather' [> LEG 7.44]

Study:
★★

Rather is stronger than *quite* and *fairly* and suggests 'inclined to be'.
It often goes with 'bad' adjectives (*bad, poor, awful, unpleasant*, etc.).
When it goes with 'good' adjectives (*good, nice, tasty*, etc.) it often means 'surprisingly':
*This ice-cream is **rather good**.* (perhaps I didn't expect it to be)

Write: Add *quite* and *rather* to each sentence, where possible. Say if they mean 'inclined to (be)', 'less than' or 'completely'.

1 I'm afraid Jane's health is ......*quite/rather*...... poor. *('completely.'/'inclined to be')*
2 Don't worry! Your son is .... all right! ....
3 Your work has been .... unsatisfactory. ....
4 I'm afraid an appointment tomorrow is .... impossible. ....
5 Last night's documentary was .... interesting. ....

7.5D 'Much', 'any', 'far' and 'a lot' as adverbs of degree [> LEG 5.12.3, 7.45]

Study:
★★

1 We can use *much* and *far* with comparatives and superlatives to say 'to what degree':
   *Jane is **much better** today. London is **far bigger** than Edinburgh.*
   *This Indian cookery book is by **far the best**. London is **much the biggest** city in Britain.*

2 We can use *a lot* and *any* with comparatives: *It's **a lot bigger**. Is it **any better**?*

3 *Not much* and *not any* go with a few adjectives: *This battery isn't **much good/any good**.*

4 We can use *not much* and *(not) a lot* with verbs such as *like* and *enjoy*:
   *I **don't much like** fish. I **don't like** fish (very) **much**. I **(don't) like** fish **a lot**.*

5 We often use *much* and *far* with *prefer* and *would rather* [> 16.8B, 11.8]:
   *I **much prefer** tea to coffee. I**'d far rather** have tea than coffee.*

Write: Add *much, any, far* or *a lot* and give alternatives where possible.

1 I'm not *much/any* good at maths.
2 You're .... quicker than me.
3 This is .... more expensive.
4 This is ...., the best way to enjoy yourself.
5 I can't go .... faster.
6 Those two recordings aren't .... different.
7 I don't .... like people who show off.
8 I .... prefer swimming to cycling.
9 This machine isn't .... use.
10 You're .... thinner than when I last saw you.

7.5E Context

Write: Put in any suitable adverbs of degree (*any, many, much, rather, fairly, quite*, etc.).

The couple sat and sat and sat!

CAN WE GO HOME PLEASE?
It was [1]......*quite*...... late. The restaurant clock showed 1.30 a.m. The waiters were feeling [2]...................... tired and were beginning to yawn. There was one [3]...................... middle-aged couple left. They had clearly had [4]...................... a good meal. Now they were looking at each other across the table and were [5]...................... unaware of the world around them. The waiters wanted to go home. One of them asked the couple if they wanted [6]...................... more to eat or drink. He didn't get an answer. It clearly wasn't [7]...................... use asking questions! One of the waiters had [8]...................... a good idea. He began stacking chairs upside-down onto the tables. The others joined in. Another waiter turned off the lights. In the end, the restaurant was [9]...................... dim. The chairs were stacked on the tables round the couple who just sat and sat and sat!

7.6 Intensifiers

7.6A 'Very', 'too' and 'very much' [> LEG 6.8.2, 6.9, 6.28.2, 7.45, 7.48, 7.50-51]

Study:
★★

1 **Intensifiers** are words like *very* and *too* which strengthen adjectives and adverbs.

2 We use *very* to strengthen:
– the positive form of adjectives (not comparative/superlative): *Martha has been **very ill**.*
– adjective + noun: *John is a **very nice man**.*
– adverbs: *The wheels of bureaucracy turn **very slowly**.*
– many past participle adjectival forms: *I'm **very interested**. You're **very mistaken**.*
The very goes with *best/worst*: *It's **the very best/the very worst** meal I've ever had.*
and some nouns (*beginning/end*): *I waited till **the very end** of the film.*

3 *Too* goes before adjectives and adverbs and means 'more than is desirable' [> 7.7B, 16.4B]:
Compare: *It's **very hot**, but I can drink it. It's **too hot** and I can't drink it.*
It's often more polite to say *not very good* or *not too good* rather than 'bad':
*His work's **not very good/not too good**.* (There is no difference in meaning here.)

4 *Very much* goes with:
– comparatives: *She is **very much better**.*
– verbs: *I like your painting **very much**. This idea **has very much interested** me.*
– adjectives like *afraid, awake, alive* and *alone*: *Old Mrs Page is **very much alone**.*

Write 1: Supply *very, too*, or *very much* in these sentences. Two answers may be possible.

1 I hear Jack has been ...*very*... ill.
2 I can't go .... faster than I'm going.
3 Go slower. You're driving .... fast for me.
4 She didn't think my work was .... good.
5 I can't afford that. It's .... expensive.
6 If you think that, you are .... mistaken.
7 This project has .... interested our firm.
8 I didn't enjoy the meal ....
9 Susan's paintings have been .... admired.
10 I always try and buy the .... best.
11 She's .... intelligent to believe that!
12 The Antarctic would be .... cold for me.
13 I .... like your idea.
14 The new XJ6 is .... faster than the old one.
15 We were .... late, but we just got the train.
16 We were .... late, so we missed our train.
17 We have .... missed you.
18 Your children get .... much pocket money.
19 He hasn't got .... much money.
20 I've been .... alone lately.

Write 2: Complete these responses using *very, too, very much* and *too much*.

1 How did you enjoy last night's film? – I enjoyed it ...*very much*...
2 So you didn't buy the picture in the end! – No, it cost ....
3 I think you should take a coat with you. – Yes, I will. It's .... cold outside.
4 Is that lobster alive? – Yes, it's .... alive!
5 Was that car expensive? – Yes, ...!
6 Are you thirsty? – Yes, ...!
7 Did you spend a lot of time on it? – Yes, ...!
8 I don't like sitting in the smoking compartment. – I agree. There's .... smoke.
9 Why aren't you buying those shoes? – They're .... large for me.
10 Those shoes are very large! – Yes, but not .... large!
11 Are the children still awake? – Yes, they're .... awake!
12 How are you feeling? – Not .... well, I'm afraid.

7.6B Adverbs in place of 'very': 'extremely happy', 'fast asleep'
[> LEG 7.52-53, 6.8.2, App 16]

Study:
★★

1 We often use *extremely* and *really* for special emphasis instead of *very*:
I'm very sleepy. → *I'm **extremely sleepy**.* (more emphatic)

2 In everyday speech we often use *terribly* and *awfully* in place of *very*:
That hi fi is very expensive. → *It's **awfully/terribly expensive**.*

3 Note that we say *fast asleep* and *wide awake* (Not *very asleep/very awake*):
*Don't disturb the children – they're **fast asleep**.*

4 We use some -*ly* adverbs in fixed phrases: *deeply hurt, painfully embarrassed, highly respected, richly deserved, I greatly appreciate, badly needed, bitterly cold*:
*Mr Wilson is **highly respected** in our community.*
*A new playground for our children is **badly needed**.*

Write: Use suitable adverbs in place of *very*.

1 The traffic is *awfully* slow today.
2 I'm .... confused by the new regulations.
3 I .... appreciate all you've done for me.
4 We are .... interested in your proposal.
5 That radio talk wasn't .... interesting.
6 I was .... awake all night.
7 I was .... hurt by her answer.
8 Old Mr Ford is .... boring!
9 I'm .... annoyed about this.
10 Your success has been .... deserved.
11 We were all .... embarrassed!
12 Your friend works .... slowly.
13 I was .... bored by the play.
14 I didn't think the film was .... funny.
15 I'm .... sorry about this.
16 What you did was .... stupid.
17 Your staff have been .... helpful.
18 You didn't wake me. I was .... asleep.
19 It was .... cold last night.
20 You think you're .... clever.
21 A well is .... needed in that village.
22 This computer is .... fast.
23 She's still .... young.
24 We're .... grateful to you.

7.6C Context

Write: Use suitable words to complete this story. Don't use the same word more than twice.

A rude man sat in the empty seat

JUSTLY PUNISHED

There were ¹........*too*.......... many people on the bus for comfort and passengers were standing in the aisle. A young woman carrying a baby was ²...................... grateful when an old man offered her his seat. The baby was ³...................... asleep and she could now rest him on her lap. She thanked the old man ⁴...................... and was just going to sit down when a rude young man sat in the empty seat. Everyone was ⁵...................... embarrassed, and the young mother was ⁶...................... surprised to say anything. All the passengers ⁷...................... disapproved of the man's action. They were ⁸...................... angry with him, but he paid no attention. ⁹...................... later, the rude man wanted to get off the bus and tried to push past the passengers. They all stood closely together and wouldn't let him move. He was made to stay on the bus till it reached its terminus, a punishment he ¹⁰...................... deserved.

7.7 Focus adverbs

7.7A 'Even', 'only', 'just' and 'simply' for 'focusing' [> LEG 7.54-55]

Study:
★★

1 We can change the position in a sentence of adverbs like *even, only, just* and *simply* depending on where we want to 'focus our attention'. Compare:
Even I *understood Professor Boffin's lecture.* (i.e. even though I'm stupid)
I **even understood** *Professor Boffin's lecture.* (i.e. out of various things I understood)

2 In everyday speech, we often put these adverbs before the verb and other people can understand what we mean from stress and intonation: *I* **only asked** *a question means* 'that's all I did' rather than 'I was the only person who asked a question'.

Write: Write sentences to show how you interpret these statements.

1 *Only* I understood his lecture. ...... *I understood his lecture, but no one else did.* ....
2 I *only* listened to his lecture. ....
3 I understood his lecture *only*. ....
4 Set the table *simply*. ....
5 I *just* understood his lecture. ....
6 I understood *just* his lecture. ....
7 I understood his lecture – *just*! ....

7.7B Two meanings of 'too' [> LEG 7.48, 7.56]

Study:
★

Too changes its meaning according to position:
This coffee is **too hot** *to drink at the moment.* (= more than is desirable [> 7.6A, 16.4B])
The croissant is freshly-made and the coffee is hot, **too**. (= also)

Write:

1 I can't drink the coffee. (hot) ...... *It's too hot.* ....
2 The coffee is freshly-made and it is also hot. ....: ...... *and it's hot, too.* ....
3 I went to the bank and I also went to the supermarket. ....
4 I didn't walk to the supermarket. (far) ....
5 I didn't buy that jacket. (expensive) ....
6 I didn't buy that jacket. It was badly-made and also expensive. ....

7.7C 'Too' and 'not either' [> LEG 7.56]

Study:
★

We use *too* at the end of an affirmative sentence to mean *also*:
Billy can already read and he can write, **too**.
In the negative, we must use *either* in place of *too*:
Billy can't write yet and he can't read, **either**. (Not *He can't read, too.* [>13.4])

Write: Add *too* or *either*.

1 I like walking and I like cycling, ... *too.* .... 5 I can't knit and I can't sew, ...
2 I met John and I met his wife, ... 6 Don't drink tea and don't drink coffee, ...
3 I don't swim and I don't run, ... 7 I don't know and I don't care, ...
4 He runs a restaurant and a hotel, ... 8 I know John well and I like him, ...

7.7D 'Also' and 'as well' [> LEG 7.56]

Study:
★★

1 We use *also* and *as well* like *too*, that is in affirmative sentences. We replace them by *either* in negative sentences. We use *as well* only at the end of a a clause or sentence:
*I bought this handbag and I bought these shoes to go with it, **as well**.*

2 *Also* is more common in writing than in speech. It normally comes:
– after *be, have, can*, etc.: *Susan is an engineer. She is **also** a mother.*
– after the first auxiliary verb when there is one or more than one:
*I should have collected the letters from your office and I **should also** have posted them.*
– before the main verb: *I play volley-ball and I **also play** tennis.* [compare > 7.4A]

Write: Show where *also* goes in these sentences.

1 She can act and she can sing. ....*She can act and she can also sing*..............

2 I have had a rest and I have had a shower. ....

3 He writes novels and he writes TV scripts. ....

4 He has been arrested and he will be tried. ....

5 You should have phoned and you should have written. ....

6 I have to write a report and I have to file some letters. ....

7 I'd like a cup of coffee and I'd like some sandwiches, please. ....

8 Mr Mason owns the corner shop and he owns the flat over it. ....

9 We sell our products in the home market but we export a lot. ....

10 I'm not going to buy it because it's not what I want and it's too expensive. ....

7.7E Context

Write: Show where the adverbs in brackets will go in the sentences that follow them.

I screamed with surprise!

A SAFE PLACE

(¹*either*) My aunt, Millie, always said she had some jewels which she would leave to me, but when she died she didn't leave any money and she didn't leave any jewels. *either*.

(²*even*) My mother was surprised.

(³*too*) 'I know she had some rings and some lovely necklaces.

(⁴*only*) I saw them once, but perhaps she sold them.'

(⁵*as well*) My mother and I looked everywhere: we looked in the bedrooms, in the bathroom, and in the attic, but we found nothing.

(⁶*also*) 'Millie was very careful and was afraid of burglars,' mother said, 'but I don't think she hid her jewels anywhere.

(⁷*too*) Let's go home, and we'd better take all the food in the deep freeze.'

On Sunday, mother said to me, 'I'm going to cook this lovely goose which was in your aunt Millie's deep freeze. I'll prepare some stuffing and you can stuff the goose.'

(⁸*too*) Five minutes later I screamed with surprise: the goose was full of jewels and there were some gold coins!

7.8 Viewpoint adverbs, connecting adverbs and inversion

7.8A Viewpoint adverbs [> LEG 7.57, App 17]

Study:
★★★

We may express our 'viewpoint' in speech or in writing using adverbs like these:
– (= I'm sure): *clearly, definitely, honestly, naturally, obviously, really, strictly speaking.*
– (= I'm going to be brief): *anyhow, briefly, in brief, in effect, in a few words, in short.*
– (= I'm expressing my opinion): *as far as I'm concerned, frankly, in my opinion, I think.*

Write: Mark the 'viewpoints' (a-i) that are expressed in this text.

I was *agreeably* (¹.*d.*.) surprised to learn that I had passed my history exam. *Between ourselves,* (²......) I was expecting to fail. *After all,* (³......) I hadn't done any work and, *naturally,* (⁴......) I didn't think I deserved to pass. So when the results came, I was expecting the worst. *As a general rule,* (⁵......) you get what you deserve and this is *certainly* (⁶......) true of exams. *Frankly,* (⁷......) I deserved to fail, but, I not only passed, I even got very good marks. This only shows that luck can help; *at any rate,* (⁸......) it helped in my case. *In my view,* (⁹......) it just shows that passing exams is not always a matter of hard work.

a *I am making a generalization*
b *the reason for this was*
c *I don't want you to repeat this*
d *I was pleased*
e *as was to be expected*
f *I am sure*
g *the important thing is this*
h *I'm being honest*
i *I'm expressing my opinion*

7.8B Connecting adverbs [> LEG 7.58, App 18]

Study:
★★★

We can connect ideas in speech or writing using adverbs like these:
– (= I'm adding something): *in addition, again, apart from this, besides, moreover.*
– (= I'm comparing/contrasting): *as compared to, equally, however, in reality.*
– (= I'm summarizing): *all in all, and so on, essentially, in brief, in conclusion, in effect.*

Write: Mark the 'connecting ideas' (a-h) that are expressed in this text.

According to (¹.*h.*.) a lot of people I know, there are few things more terrifying than having to speak in public. The only way to succeed is to follow strict rules. *First of all,* (²......) you should be well-prepared. *Second,* (³......) you should have a few jokes ready. *As well as that,* (⁴......) you should have rehearsed your speech, preferably in front of a mirror. *In comparison with* (⁵......) being hit by a bus, public speaking isn't too bad, but it's bad enough. *However,* (⁶......) you can make things easier for yourself by being ready. *Alternatively,* (⁷......) you can do nothing and make a fool of yourself. *To sum up,* (⁸......) success depends entirely on you.

a *I am introducing a list*
b *I am making an addition*
c *I am pointing to a contrast*
d *I am stating an alternative*
e *I am summarizing*
f *I am making a second point*
g *I am making a comparison*
h *As stated by*

7.8C Inversion after 'negative adverbs', etc. [> LEG 7.59, App 19]

Study:
★★★

1 Some adverbs like *never* and *little* have a 'negative effect' and we sometimes refer to them as 'negative adverbs'. We can use them in the ordinary way [> 7.4]:
*I **have never seen** so much protest against a government.*
*Michael **little realizes** how important this meeting is.*

2 If we begin a sentence with a 'negative adverb' we must follow with the word order we use in a Yes/No question [> 13.1]. Beginning with a negative is very formal:
***Never have I seen** so much protest against a government.*
***Little does Michael realize** how important this meeting is.*

3 We use this kind of inversion, in formal style, after:
  – 'negative adverbs': e.g. *hardly, hardly ever, never, rarely, seldom.*
  – phrases with *only*: e.g. *only after, only then, only when (**Only then did I learn ...**).*
  – *so* + adjective: ***So difficult was this problem**, Einstein couldn't solve it.*

Write: Rewrite these sentences so that they begin with the words in italics.

1 There has *never* been such a display of strength by the workers.
  Never has there been such a display of strength by the workers ....

2 I realized what had happened *only later*.
  ....

3 You shouldn't sign the document *on any account*.
  On no account ....

4 You shouldn't answer the door when I'm out *in any circumstances*.
  In no circumstances ....

5 The papyrus was *so old*, we didn't dare to touch it.
  ....

7.8D Context

Write: Put in the right verb form and these adverbs: *according to, agreeably, however, in brief, moreover* or *ultimately*.

Don't ask for a room with a view!

DON'T ASK FOR A ROOM WITH A VIEW!
So high [1] (*be*)..............*is*............. the price of land in Tokyo, that its land area probably costs as much as the whole of California. Never, in any place in the world, (*there be*) [2]............................ such a demand for space! [3]............................ a newspaper report, this lack of space has led to 'capsule hotels'. The rooms are just capsules, measuring 1 metre high, 76 cms wide and 2 metres deep. [4]............................, you will be [5]............................ surprised to hear that they are equipped with phones, radio and TV. [6]............................, they are less expensive than ordinary hotels. [7]............................, they provide you with all you need for a comfortable night's sleep, even if they don't give you an automatic wash and dry as well! [8]............................, some people would argue, a small hole in the wall is preferable to a big hole in your pocket! But don't ask for a room with a view!

8 Prepositions, adverb particles and phrasal verbs

8.1 Prepositions, adverb particles and conjunctions

8.1A Words we can use either as prepositions or as adverbs [> LEG 8.4, 7.3.4]

Study:

1 There are many 'small words' in English such as *up, down,* and *by* which we call **prepositions**. In fact, we use these as **prepositions** or **adverb particles**. Understanding the difference between the two will help us to understand 'phrasal verbs' [> 8.6-8].

2 A **preposition** must have an **object** (a noun or a pronoun), so it is always related to a **noun**: *across the road, over the wall, up the hill, down the mountain.*

3 An **adverb particle** does not need an object, so it is more closely related to a **verb**: *walk across, drive over, come up, climb down.*

4 We can use the following words either as **prepositions** or **adverb particles**: *about, above, across, after, along, before, behind, below, beneath, between, beyond, by, down, in, inside, near, off, on, opposite, outside, over, past, round, through, under, underneath, up, without.* This means we can say:
*We drove **round the city**.* (*round* has a noun object, so it's a **preposition**)
*We drove **round**.* (*round* has no object, so it's an **adverb particle**).

Write: You are giving instructions to a young child. Give each instruction twice.

1 (run across the road) ......*Run across the road. Run across now.*...........................
2 (climb over the wall) ....
3 (come inside the house) ....
4 (go down the hill) ....
5 (go up the ladder) ....
6 (run past the window) ....

8.1B Words we can use only as prepositions or only as adverbs [> LEG 8.4.2-3]

Study:

1 We use some 'small words' only as **prepositions**, so they always have a noun or pronoun object: *against, among, at, beside, during, except, for, from, into, of, onto, on top of, out of, since, till/until, to, toward(s), upon, with.* This means we have to say: e.g.
*Sit **beside me**.* We can't say **Sit beside.**

2 We use other 'small words' only as **adverb particles**, so they do not have an object: *away, back, backward(s), downward(s), forward(s), on top, out, upward(s).* This means we have to say: e.g. *Don't go near the fire. Stay **away**!* (Not **Stay away the fire!**)

Write: You are answering the question *What did you do?* Supply suitable noun objects where possible.

1 We waited at ....*the station*................
2 We went to ....
3 We jumped back ....
4 We climbed out ....

5 We drove away ....
6 We ran into ....
7 We ran out of ....
8 We went upwards ....

8.1C Words we can use either as prepositions or conjunctions
[> LEG 8.4.4, 1.45.1]

Study:
★★

1 There are a few words we can use either as **prepositions** or **conjunctions**:
after, as, before, since and *till/until* [> 1.8, 1.9, 7.3A-B].

2 When we use them as **prepositions**, we have a noun or pronoun **object** after them:
*Let's have our meeting **after lunch**.*

3 When we use them as **conjunctions**, we have a **clause** [> 1.5] after them:
*Let's have our meeting **after we have had lunch**.*

Write: Complete these sentences with a) a noun object b) a clause.

1 I can't work before ......*breakfast / before I have had breakfast*..
2 I'll meet you after ....
3 I'll wait here till ....
4 I've been staying at this hotel since ....

8.1D Object pronouns after prepositions: 'between you and me' [> LEG 8.3]

Study:
★★

We use the object form of a pronoun, not the subject form, after a preposition [> 4.1A]:
***Between you and me**, I think he's a fool.* (Not **Between you and I**)

Write: Circle the right forms in these sentences.

1 The invitation is for my husband and (me/I).
2 She gave these presents to (us/we).
3 Share this between yourselves and (they/them).
4 For (we/us), the older generation, there have been many changes in society.
5 Employers are keen on people like (us/we) who work hard.
6 The news came as quite a surprise to a person like (me/I).

8.1E Context

Write: Circle 17 items (including in the title) and say whether they are prepositions or particles.

... legs sticking out of the boat!

TWO LEGS (IN) ONE BOOT   *preposition*
It was late in the afternoon. Inspector Mayhew had an hour to go before
he finished work for the day. He sat in his police car watching the traffic
go by. Suddenly, he sat up! A woman in a blue car drove slowly past
and the inspector clearly saw a pair of man's legs sticking out of the
boot! Inspector Mayhew immediately gave chase. The woman drove
round the town. The blue lamp on top of the police car was flashing, but
the woman paid no attention to it. The inspector finally got in front of her
and made her stop. 'What's the matter?' the woman asked. 'You've got
a body in the boot!' the inspector said. There was a loud laugh from the
boot. 'But I'm alive,' the voice said. 'I'm a car mechanic and I'm trying to
find the cause of a strange noise in the back of this car.'

107

8.2 Prepositions of movement and position Prepositions of time

8.2A 'At a point', 'in an area' and 'on a surface' [> LEG 8.6-9, Apps 21-23]

Study:
★★

1 We use *to/from* and *into/out of* to show direction with movement:
  – *to/from*:   She has gone **to Paris**. She has just come home **from Paris**.
  – *into/out of*:   I went **into the shop**. I came **out of the shop**.

2 We use *at, in, on* to show position after movement: *at a point, in an area, on a surface*.
  We can use *at* with some nouns to mean 'a (meeting) point' or *in* to mean 'inside':
  *I'll meet you **at the airport**.* (= that's the meeting point)
  *I'll meet you **in the airport**.* (= inside the building)
  Typical nouns like this are: *the cinema, the office, the bank, the library, (the) school*.

3 We use *at* mainly with:
  – public places/buildings: *at the airport, the bus stop, the Grand Hotel, the butcher's*.
  – addresses: *at his sister's, 24 Cedar Avenue*.
  – nouns with zero article: *at home, church, college, school, university* [> 3.6B]
  – events: *at a concert, a dance, a dinner, a funeral, a meeting, a party, a wedding*.
    *He's gone **to a party**. He is **at a party**.*
    *He's been **to a party**. He was **at a party**.* [> 10.2C]

4 We use *in* mainly with:
  – large areas: *in Europe, Asia, the Antarctic, the Andes, the Sahara, Texas, the Pacific*.
  – towns/parts of towns: *in Canterbury, Chelsea, Dallas, Manhattan, New York, Paris*.
  – outside areas: *in the garden, the park, Hyde Park, the street, the old town, the desert*.
  – rooms: *in the bathroom, his bedroom, the garage, the kitchen, the waiting room*.
  – nouns with zero article: *in bed, chapel, church, hospital, prison*. [> 3.6B]
    *He's gone **to Texas**. He is **in Texas**.*
    *He's been **to Texas**. He was **in Texas**.* [> 10.2C]

Write: Supply *at* or *in*.

1 He's gone to the station. He's probably .....*at*..... the station now.
2 She's gone to school. She's probably .... school now.
3 He flew from London. He's probably .... Paris now.
4 He's gone into the garden. He's .... the garden now.
5 She's gone to bed. She's .... bed now.
6 He's gone to a dinner party. He's probably .... the dinner now.
7 She's gone to a wedding. She's probably .... the wedding now.
8 He's gone to the kitchen. He's probably .... the kitchen now.
9 They've come out of the desert. They're probably .... the jungle now.
10 They've gone to New York. They're probably .... New York now.
11 She's gone to the waiting room. She's probably .... the waiting room now.
12 He's been sent to prison. He's probably .... prison now.
13 She's gone to the doctor's. She's probably .... the doctor's now.
14 He's gone home. He's probably .... home now.
15 She's gone to the old town. She's probably .... the old town now.
16 They've sailed to the Pacific. They're probably .... the Pacific now.
17 We live .... 14 Woodland Avenue.
18 She was taken to hospital. She's .... hospital now.

8.2B   Prepositions of time: 'at', 'on' and 'in' [> LEG 8.10-14]

Study:
★★

> 1   We use *at* for: exact time: *at 10 o'clock*; meal times: *at lunch time*; points of time: *at night* [> 3.6A]; festivals: *at Christmas*; age: *at the age of 14*; + 'time': *at this/that time*.
>
> 2   We use *on* for: days of the week: *on Monday, on Mondays*; parts of the day: *on Monday morning*; dates: *on June 1st*; particular occasions: *on that day*; anniversaries: *on your birthday*; festivals: *on New Year's Day*.
>
> 3   We use *in* for [> 7.3C]: parts of the day: *in the evening*; months: *in May*; years: *in 2050*; seasons: *in (the) spring*; centuries: *in the 20th century*; periods: *in Ramadan, in two years' time*.

Write: Supply *at, on* or *in*.

1   I'll meet you ....*at*....... 10.30 ....*on*....... Monday, June 14.
2   We're taking our holiday .... July.
3   I always finish work early .... Fridays.
4   Who knows what the world will be like .... the year 2030?
5   You don't want anything to go wrong .... your wedding day.
6   .... the 19th century many children died before they were a year old..
7   We got up .... dawn and reached the summit .... noon.
8   .... the age of 14 I realized I would never become a brain surgeon.
9   The birds don't find much to eat in our garden .... winter.
10   What will you be doing .... the holidays?
11   What will you be doing .... New Year's Day?
12   The year was 1986. .... that time I was working as a waiter.
13   We try to get away .... Christmas time.
14   I'll see you .... ten days' time.
15   They prepared a surprise for me at the office .... my birthday.

8.2C   Context

Write: Supply the missing prepositions.

'THE PROPHECY'
People who live [1] ....*in*....... California have every reason to be afraid of earthquakes. No one has ever forgotten the great quake that destroyed San Francisco [2] .... 1906. [3] .... May, 1988, the people of Los Angeles panicked. According to a prophecy made [4] .... the 16th century by a prophet called Nostradamus, the city would be destroyed early [5] .... 1988. During the panic, parents didn't send their children [6] .... school and people didn't go [7] .... work. No one stayed [8] .... home, either. The airlines did great business carrying people who fled [9] .... their 'doomed city'. Which is more puzzling: how Nostradamus knew that a city which didn't even exist [10] .... his time would be destroyed [11] .... the 20th century, or the behaviour of the people who believed 'the prophecy'?

The people of Los Angeles panicked

8.3 Particular prepositions, particles: contrasts (1)

8.3A Prepositions, particles, etc. often confused and misused [> LEG App 25.1-11]

Study:

★★

1 *about* and *on*
We can use *about* and *on* to mean 'concerning'. We use *on* in a formal way, e.g. to describe a textbook: *a textbook on physics*; *about* is informal: *a book about animals*.

2 *according to* and *by*
We use *according to* to refer to information coming from other people or sources: *according to him, according to this guide book*. When we refer to ourselves, we say *in my opinion* (Not **according to me***). We can use *by* or *according to* when we refer to a clock or a timetable: *By* or *According to my watch, it's 3.15*.

3 *across* and *over*
We can use both these prepositions to mean 'from one side to the other': *My house is **across/ over** the road/the river*. We cannot use *over* for large areas: *They're laying a pipeline **across Siberia***. (Not **over***) We use *over* after verbs like *wander* to mean 'here and there'. We use *across* to describe movement through water: *She swam **across the Channel***. (Not **over the Channel***) But we say *over a wall/a fence*. (Not **across***)

4 *across* and *through*
Through, meaning 'from one side to the other', refers to something like a tunnel (*through a pipe*) or something dense (*through the forest*); *across* refers to a large area (*across the desert*). With some nouns, like *park*, we can use either *across* or *through*.

5 *after* and *afterwards*
We generally use a noun or pronoun with *after*: *after lunch* [> 8.1A]. We use *afterwards* on its own: *We had a swim in the sea. **Afterwards** we lay on the beach*. (Not **After***)

6 *around* and *about*
We use both words to refer to 'lack of purpose': *We didn't have anything to do, so we started **fooling around/about***. But we say *He **lives (a)round** here*. (= near)(Not **about***)

7 *at, to* and *against*
We use *at* after adjectives like *good, clever*. After verbs like *throw*, *at* often means 'taking aim'. Compare: *throw at* (to hit) and *throw to* (for someone to catch). When there is no idea of 'taking aim', we use *against*: *throw the ball against the wall*. And note: *fight against*. We use *at* for speed or price: *at 100 miles an hour, at $2 each*.

8 *away*
Away [> 8.1B] combines with *far* (*far away*) and *from* (*away from*) and with verbs which give the idea of 'distance': e.g. *live, work: I live 5 miles **away***. (Not **I live 5 miles far away***)

9 *because* and *because of*
We use *because* to give a reason: *We left the party **because it was noisy***. [> 1.9] We use a noun or pronoun after *because of*: *We left the party **because of the noise***.

10 *before* or *in front of*
We often use *before* to refer to time (*before 7*); *in front of* (and its opposite, *behind*) refers to position. We can use either *before* or *in front of* after the verbs *come* and *go*.

11 *behind, at the back (of)* and *back*
We can put a noun or pronoun after *behind* (*behind this house*) or we can use it on its own (*there's a garden behind*). Or we can say: *at the back of this house, it's at the back*.
Do not confuse *back* with *again*: *invite them back* means 'return their hospitality'. Don't use *back* after *return*: *We returned early*. (Not **returned back***) Note *3 years back* (= ago).

Write: Supply suitable words. Refer to the notes only when you have to.

about or *on*?

1 Read this article ...*on/about*... the Antarctic.
2 I've read a lot of books .... animals.

according to or *by*?

3 .... Dr Pim, the sea is rising.
4 .... the timetable, the train leaves at 8.27.
5 It's 10.15 .... my watch.

across or *over*?

6 There's a newsagent's .... the road.
7 No one wants a pipeline .... Alaska.
8 We skated .... the frozen lake.
9 I'm going to swim .... the river.

across or *through*?

10 Nothing can flow .... this pipe.
11 We managed to get .... the jungle.
12 I've never walked .... the park.

away (add *far* where possible)

13 I see storm clouds .... in the distance.
14 London is 15 miles .... from here.

because or *because of*?

15 I couldn't get to work .... I was ill.
16 I couldn't get to work .... my illness.

before or *in front of*?

17 Make sure you're there .... 7.
18 I'll wait for you .... the shop.
19 You come .... me in the queue.

after or *afterwards*?

20 Come and see me .... work.
21 We tidied up. Our guests arrived soon ....
22 We had a swim and .... we sunbathed.

around or *about*?

23 We stood .... waiting.
24 I wish you'd stop fooling ....
25 Let me show you .... the house.
26 He lives somewhere .... Manchester.

at, to or *against*?

27 I'm not very good .... figures.
28 Throw it .... me so that I can catch it.
29 Jim is always throwing stones .... birds.
30 We fought .... the enemy.
31 Ron is driving .... 100 miles an hour.
32 We have combs .... $2 each.

behind, *at the back (of)* or *back*?

33 There's a garden in front and one ....
34 Keep this book. I don't want it ....
35 There's a garden .... the house.
36 I saw him four years ....
37 They invited us. We must invite them ....
38 We had to go .... early after the party.
39 Put it .... in its place.
40 I've fallen .... in my work.
41 I tried to lift it out of the hole but it fell ....

8.3B Context

Write: Put in *about, according to, across, after, at, away, because, before, behind, in front of, on*.

... the photographer's left ear

A GOOD EYE FOR A LEFT EAR

My friend Jonathan, who lives [1]......*across*...... the road, develops and prints films. [2]........................ Jonathan most of us take awful pictures. Usually, we fail to aim [3]........................ the subject so that the subject is not even in the picture. Sometimes the subject is too far [4]........................; sometimes too near. Some photos are spoilt because the sun is [5]........................ us, when of course, it should always be [6]........................ us. Some of us take blank pictures [7]........................ we take the lens cover off [8]........................ we have taken our shots. We take most of our pictures when we are on holiday and like to catch our friends when they are fooling [9]........................ . It's a pity we don't practise using our cameras [10]........................ we go on holiday. A good book [11]........................ photography would make us better [12]........................ taking pictures, but most of us are too lazy to bother. I asked Jonathan what was the worst film he had ever seen. He didn't have to think very hard [13]........................ the question. At once he answered, 'Twenty-four shots of the photographer's left ear!'

8.4 Particular prepositions, particles: contrasts (2)

8.4A Prepositions, particles, etc. often confused and misused
[> LEG App 25.12-19, 25.25]

Study:
★★

1 *beside* and *besides*
Beside + noun/pronoun means 'next to': *Sit **beside me**. Besides* with or without an object means 'in addition to' or 'as well as': *There were many people there **besides (us)***.

2 *between* and *among*
We commonly use *between* to show a division between two people, things, or times: *Divide this **between you both***. We use *among* + plural noun to refer to a mass of people, etc.: *Were you **among the people** present?* We sometimes use *between* to refer to more than two, if these can be viewed separately: *Don't smoke **between courses***.

3 *but (for)* and *except (for)*
But (for)/except (for) mean 'with the exception of': *Everyone has helped **but (for)/except (for) you***. We can use *except* and *but* without *for*, but not to begin a sentence: ***Except for/But for you**, everyone has helped. (Not **Except you/But you** everyone ... .*)
Except for/but for can mean 'if not': *We'd've been on time **except for/but for** the snow.*

4 *by, near* and *on*
By can mean 'right next to': *Sit **by** me*. We often use the words *right* or *close* in front of *by*: *The hotel is **right by/close by** the station. Near* (or *not far from*) usually suggests 'a short way from': *We live **near/not far from** London. On* means 'right next to' or 'beside' when we refer to 'a line': *Our house is right **on the road**. I can't see what is **on my left***.

5 *by* and *past*
We use either word after verbs of motion (*go, run, walk*, etc.) to mean 'beyond in space or time': *He **went right by/past me** without speaking. A few days went **by/past***.

6 *by, with* and *without* [compare > 8.5An.7]
We often use *by* in fixed phrases: *by bus, by car, by post*. We also use it to refer to 'method': *You can open it **by moving** the catch. By* can refer to time and rate: *I'm paid **by the hour**. With/without* refer to things (especially tools or instruments) which we need to use: *You can't open it **with/without a bottle-opener***.

7 *down, up, under* and *over*
Down is the opposite of *up* and shows direction towards a lower level, especially with 'movement verbs': *Let's **climb up/down***. We can also use *up* and *down* to show position: *He lives **up/down the street**. Under* suggests 'being covered': *Let's sit **under a tree**. Over* can have the meaning 'covering': *Keep this blanket **over you***.

8 *due to* and *owing to*
We often use either one or the other. However, *due to* is related to a noun + *be*: *Our delay* (noun) *was (+ be)* ***due to/caused by*** *the heavy traffic. Owing to* (= because of) is related to the verb: *The broadcast was cancelled* (verb) ***owing to/because of*** *the strike.*

9 *like* and *as*
Like (= to compare with) is followed by a noun or pronoun: *There's no one like **John/ you***. We can also use it to mean 'such as': *Invite people **like the Frys***. Like can also mean 'similar to/ in the same way as': *It was **like a dream**. He acts **like a king***.
We use *as* (Not **like***) + object to mean 'in the capacity of': *I work **as a receptionist***.
We also use *as* to give a reason [> 1.9]: ***As the last bus had left**, we walked home.*
We use *like* informally to introduce a clause, especially in American English: ***Like I told you**, it's an offer I can't refuse.* A lot of native speakers of English think this is wrong.

Write: Supply suitable words. Refer to the notes only when you have to.

beside or **besides**?

1 Who was sitting *beside* you?
2 Who's invited .... us?
3 It's a fast car. .... it's got four-wheel drive.

between or **among**?

4 Divide it equally .... the two of you.
5 Switzerland lies .... four other countries.
6 I saw you .... the crowd.

but (for) or **except (for)**?

7 The plane would've landed .... the fog.
8 Everyone sent flowers .... you.
9 .... you, everyone sent flowers.
10 Everyone's here .... John.
11 Who .... John would do a thing like that?

by, near or **on**?

12 I sat .... the phone all morning.
13 We live .... Manchester.
14 Our house is right .... the river.
15 .... my right I have Frank Milligan.

by or **past**?

16 The ball went right .... my head!
17 Several days went .... before I had news.
18 Stop .... here on your next visit.
19 Something flew .... my ear.
20 It's .... your bedtime.

by, with or **without**?

21 Our dog was hit .... a bus.
22 You can open it .... pulling this lever.
23 Dentists are paid .... the hour.
24 It won't open .... a bottle-opener.

down, up, under and **over**?

25 My mother lives .... the street.
26 The bus got stuck .... the bridge.
27 Put this blanket .... your knees.

due to or **owing to**?

28 Our success was .... luck.
29 Flights were delayed .... the strike.
30 He lost his job .... bad health.

like or **as**?

31 There's no business .... show business.
32 .... a lawyer, I would advise caution.
33 I once worked .... a bus conductor.
34 This motorway is .... a car park!
35 People .... the Joneses always copy us.
36 .... it was raining, I took a taxi.
37 .... I explained, it's a public holiday today.
38 He's more .... his mother than his father.
39 Who's used this knife .... a screw-driver?
40 You're just .... your brother.
41 He spends money .... a millionaire.

8.4B Context

Write: Put in *among, as, beside, between, by, down* (or *up*), *due, except, like, past, without*.

DELIVERED AND SIGNED FOR!
[1] .... *As* .... my grandmother used to say, 'Don't sign for anything
[2] .... checking it first.' I forgot this good advice when two
delivery-men brought my new sideboard yesterday. Delivery was very
late [3] .... to the heavy traffic on the road. I saw the delivery-
van go [4] .... the house and stop outside a neighbour's
[5] .... the street. Then I watched it reverse until it stopped
right [6] .... my house. I went outside to look into the back of
the van: there was my lovely sideboard [7] .... several pieces
of furniture! It was quite heavy, but the two men managed it
[8] .... them. Soon, the beautiful sideboard was in place,
[9] .... the dining-room wall. I had waited so long for it, it was
[10] .... a dream! It was only when the men left that I realized I
had checked everying [11] .... the keys. It had been delivered
[12] .... keys! It was too late to phone the shop, but I needn't
have worried because next morning the keys arrived in the post. I
unlocked the sideboard and found a note inside which said, 'Keys will
follow [13] .... post'!

Keys will follow

8.5 Particular prepositions, particles: contrasts (3)

8.5A Prepositions, particles, etc. often confused and misused
[> LEG App 25.26-37]

Study:
★★

1 of, out of, from and with after made
We use *made of* and *made out of* when we can actually recognize the material(s): *made of wood, iron*, etc. We use *made from* when the ingredients are not immediately obvious: *a cake made from eggs, milk and flour*. We use *made with* (= contains) to identify one or more of the ingredients: *These chocolates are **made with fresh cream***.

2 of and off
We never use *of* and *off* in place of each other. We always use a noun or pronoun object after *of*: *north of the river, a woman of 50*. We can use an object after *off*, or we can use it on its own to suggest separation: *just off the motorway, take the top off*.

3 on and in
We often use both of these to refer to the body. *On* refers to surface: *on your nose*. *In* suggests 'deep': *a speck in my eye*, or refers to pain: *a pain in my stomach*.

4 out of and outside
Out of is the opposite of *into* when we are describing movement: *We ran **out of the building***. In this sense, we can't replace *out of* by *outside*. Compare uses without movement: *He is **out of his office***. (= not here) *He is **outside the office***. (= waiting)

5 over, above and on top of
Over (= covering, sometimes touching): *Keep the blankets **over** you*. *Above* (= at a higher level and not touching): *a light above my head*. *On top of* (= touching): *on top of the TV*. We can use *over* and *above* in place of each other to mean 'vertically at a higher level': *a helicopter over/above a lifeboat*. We cannot use *over* and *above* in place of each other when all we are concerned with is 'a higher level' (not vertical). If, for example, we were referring to two cats on a tree we would say that A was *above* B, not *over* it. We also use both words to refer to rank, etc.: *over/above the rank of colonel*.

6 under, underneath and below
Under (= covered by, sometimes touching); *underneath* (= completely covered by): *a mat under/underneath a hot dish*. *Below* is the opposite of *above* and we can use it in place of *under/underneath*,. *Below* (Not *under*) refers to position (*below the knee*).

7 with and without
We use *with* and *without* to mean 'accompanied by' or 'not accompanied by': *with/without my sister*. *With* can suggest 'having': *with your hands in your pockets*, and 'taking into consideration': *with the high cost of living*. *With* follows common adjectives (e.g. *angry*) and we use it in expressions like *blue with cold*. *Without* + -ing can suggest 'and not do something': *Go into the room **without waking** the children*.

8 with, without, in and of
We can use *with* and *without* to mean 'carrying'/'not carrying': *with a handbag, without any money*. We can also refer to physical characteristics: *with a big nose*; and such things as hairstyles and make-up: *with pink lipstick*. We can use *in* to mean 'wearing': *the man in the blue suit*. We can also refer to voice quality: *in a loud voice*. *Of* can describe personal qualities: *a man of courage*; age: *a man of 65*; or wealth: *a woman of substance*.

Write: Supply suitable words. Refer to the notes only when you have to.

of, out of, from or *with* after *made*?

1 You rarely find toys made *of / out of* solid wood.
2 Beer is made .... hops.
3 Bronze is made .... copper and tin.
4 This sauce is made .... fresh cream.

of or *off*?

5 We live south .... the river.
6 Our house is just .... the main road.

on or *in*?

7 There's a black mark .... your nose.
8 I've got a speck of dust .... my eye.
9 I've got a deep cut .... my foot.
10 I've got a light scratch .... my arm.

out of or *outside*?

11 We ran .... the house, into the street.
12 Mr Ray's not here. He's .... his office.
13 Please wait .... the headmaster's study.
14 There was a big crowd .... the building.

with or *without*?

15 Enter the room .... making a noise.
16 .... all our expenses, we can't save.
17 She was very angry .... me.
18 I turned blue .... cold.
19 'Life .... father' is a famous book.
20 As an orphan, I grew up .... parents.
21 He stood .... his hands in his pockets.
22 I was green .... envy!

over, above or *on top of*?

23 I can't sleep with a light .... my head.
24 Don't put that cup .... my papers, please.
25 The helicopter was .... the lifeboat.
26 My bedroom is .... the kitchen.
27 We have the sky .... us.
28 We don't want a boss like that .... us.
29 Major is .... the rank of Captain.
30 His work is .... average.
31 The answer is on the next page. See ....

under, underneath or *below*?

32 There's nothing new .... the sun.
33 I think she's .... 17.
34 Put a mat .... that saucepan.
35 The stone hit me just .... the knee.
36 What's .... the rank of Captain?
37 She swam just .... the surface.
38 I have two people .... me at work.

with, without, in or *of*?

39 Who's the woman .... the green umbrella?
40 I can't pay. I'm .... any money.
41 The camera comes .... a case included.
42 Who's the woman .... the green blouse?
43 He spoke .... a quiet voice.
44 He's a man .... a red moustache.
45 She's a woman .... 38.
46 She's a woman .... intelligence.

8.5B Context

Write: Put in *with, out of, over, off, of, in, above, below, on top of*.

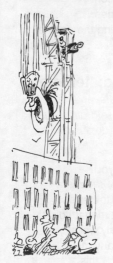

'Lost your hat, miss?'

THE AMAZING FLYING HAT

She was a striking woman [1]............*of*........ about 25, dressed for the races. [2]....................... her smart dress and fantastic hat made [3]....................... feathers, she drew admiring glances as she walked down the street. Her hat attracted even more attention when a gust [4]....................... wind lifted it [5]....................... her head and carried it into the air. We all stopped to watch as this amazing hat flew [6]....................... our heads. People came [7]....................... buildings and into the street. The young woman [8]....................... the smart dress was as entertained as the rest [9]....................... us. Suddenly, the hat rested [10]....................... a high building and we lost sight of it. Then the wind lifted it up again. 'There it is!' cried a man [11]....................... an umbrella. He jabbed his umbrella at the sky [12]....................... . Then an amazing thing happened. The hat simply disappeared! The mystery was solved when someone shouted [13]....................... a loud voice. There was a tall yellow crane [14]....................... a high building and the crane driver looked down at the crowd [15]....................... . 'Lost your hat, miss?' the crane driver cried and we all gasped [16]....................... surprise when we saw that the hat had been caught by his crane!

8.6 Phrasal verbs: Type 1, verb + preposition (transitive)

8.6A Introduction to phrasal verbs [> LEG 8.23-26]

Study:
★★

> We often combine verbs with prepositions and adverb particles [> 8.1A-B] to form **phrasal verbs**. These verbs can have non-idiomatic or idiomatic meanings and we use them a lot. So, for example, if someone knocks at the door, we would probably say 'Come in!' rather than 'Enter'. We would say 'take off' your jacket, rather than 'remove' it, and so on. We can define four types of phrasal verbs according to form. As you learn new verbs, get used to recognizing them as one of these four types so that you learn how to use them.
>
> Note the terms: **transitive** (= followed by a noun or pronoun object) [> 1.2B]
> **intransitive** (= not followed by a noun or pronoun object) [> 1.2B]
>
> Type 1: verb + preposition (transitive): e.g. **Listen to** this record. **Listen to** it. **Listen**!
> Type 2: verb + particle (transitive): e.g. **Take off** your hat. **Take** your hat **off**. **Take** it **off**.
> Type 3: verb + particle (intransitive): e.g. **Hurry up! Sit down!**
> Type 4: verb + particle + preposition (transitive): e.g. We've **run out of** matches.

8.6B Type 1: Verb + preposition + object, non-idiomatic: 'look at the camera'

Study: These verbs are used in their normal sense. [> LEG 8.27.2, App 28]

Write: Supply the missing prepositions.

1 I don't agree ...*with*... your proposal.
2 Mr Potter suffers .... asthma.
3 Please don't insist .... paying the bill.
4 I wouldn't think .... borrowing money.
5 These two pictures differ .... each other.
6 Choose .... the two.
7 Where did you read .... it?
8 I'm depending .... you.
9 We can only guess .... the truth.
10 Please wait .... me.
11 Knock .... the door.
12 Ask .... the menu.
13 I don't agree .... you.
14 How do you know .... this?
15 Does this jacket belong .... you?
16 Let's begin .... tomato soup.
17 Can you look .... the children for tonight?
18 I couldn't wish .... a nicer office.
19 We failed .... our attempt to win the race.
20 You can't reason .... him.
21 This pie tastes .... onion.
22 I don't believe .... fairies.
23 I succeeded .... starting the engine.
24 The police are looking .... the robbers.

8.6C Type 1: Verb + object + preposition + object, non-idiomatic: 'tell me about it'

Study: These verbs are used in their normal sense. [> LEG 8.27.3, App 29]

Write: Supply the missing prepositions.

1 I've arranged an excursion ....*for*..... you.
2 He accused me .... lying.
3 You can't hide the truth .... me.
4 Would you kindly explain this .... me?
5 Invest some money .... this company.
6 I can't advise you .... your private life.
7 Insure your house .... storm damage.
8 Translate this report .... Spanish for me.
9 I'll reserve a seat .... you.
10 You remind me .... my sister.
11 Don't associate me .... them.
12 Can you forgive me .... what I did?
13 They robbed me .... my wallet.
14 Don't repeat this .... anyone.
15 You can't blame me .... this.
16 He stole money .... the firm.

8.6D   Type 1: Verb + preposition + object, idiomatic: 'get over an illness'
[> LEG 8.27.4, App 30]

Study: We cannot relate the parts of these verbs to their literal meanings: e.g.
★★   *I don't know what **came over me**.* (= affected)

Write: Match these verbs (1-20) with the explanations on the right (a-t) after you have tried to explain them in
your own way.

1   Eggs don't *agree with* me. *f* ....   a) decide later
2   Please *call for* me at 6. ....   b) found (it) easy
3   I *came across* this old book. ....   c) found
4   The dog *went for* the postman. ....   d) reaches
5   Let's *go after* him. ....   e) supervise
6   Can I *count on* you for help? ....   f) have a bad effect on
7   I haven't *got over* my cold yet. ....   g) doing nothing with
8   This dress will *do for* Jane. ....   h) obtain
9   Where did you *come by* this information? ....   i) come and collect
10   You can't *dictate to* me. ....   j) resemble
11   I'll *sleep on* your suggestion. ....   k) serve
12   I can't *make* anything *of* this. ....   l) attacked
13   I won't *stand for* your rudeness. ....   m) give orders to
14   Is there anyone here to *wait on* us? ....   n) try and catch
15   The cost *runs into* millions. ....   o) inspect
16   She *took to* English quickly. ....   p) rely on
17   He's been *sitting on* my application. ....   q) understand
18   You *take after* your father. ....   r) tolerate
19   You can *look over* the house. ....   s) be all right for
20   You don't have to *stand over* me, you know. ....   t) recovered from

8.6E   Context

Write: Put in *at, for, from, in, of, on, out of* or *to*. Use each word at least once.

IS THERE ANYBODY THERE?
A dentist in Bavaria has been haunted by a voice which swears
[1].....*at*.... him all the time. The voice comes [2]............. light sockets,
washbasins and the telephone. It is a sharp, deep voice which laughs
[3]............. the dentist and mocks him. The poor dentist is suffering
[4]............. a bad case of nerves. Recently, the voice was recorded and
broadcast, so now everyone in Bavaria is looking [5]............. the ghost,
but so far no one has succeeded [6]............. finding it. People who don't
believe [7]............. ghosts think it is just a practical joke. The voice always
shouts [8]............. the dentist, but speaks sweetly [9]............. his 17-year-
old assistant, Claudia. But no one can blame Claudia [10]............. the
behaviour of the ghost or accuse her [11]............. playing tricks [12].............
her poor boss. Engineers don't know what to make [13]............. it. 'He's a
technical genius,' one of them said. The ghost has responded [14].............
all this activity by saying, in a thick Bavarian accent, 'You'll never get
hold [15]............. me!'

You'll never get hold of me!

117

8.7 Phrasal verbs: Type 2, verb + particle (transitive)

8.7A Type 1 and Type 2 phrasal verbs compared [> LEG 8.28, Apps 32, 33]

Study:
★★

1 We use prepositions after Type 1 verbs. We cannot separate the preposition from the verb: *I'm **looking at** the camera.* (Not **I'm looking the camera at.**)

2 We can separate the adverb particle from a Type 2 verb and put it immediately after the noun object: *She **gave away** her books. She **gave** her books **away**.*

3 If the object is a pronoun, we cannot put the particle in front of it: *Give **it** away.* (Not **Give away it.**) *Give **them** away.* (Not **Give away them.**)

4 Special note: In *She gave away her books, away* is an adverb particle [> 8.1B], not a preposition, even if it has an object after it. Unlike a preposition, a particle is 'mobile' and can be used before or after a noun object. [> LEG 8.28.2]

Write: Use arrows to show which adverb particles you can move in these sentences.

1 I'm looking for my glasses.
2 I read about it in the papers.
3 Did you turn the gas off?
4 Yes, I've just turned it off.
5 Have you given the papers out?

6 Yes, I've given them out.
7 Write the information down here please.
8 A crowd emerged from the cinema.
9 Don't associate with him.
10 We've dealt with the problem.

8.7B Type 2: Particles that extend the verb: 'write down' [> LEG 8.28.3-4, App 32]

Study:
★★

A single particle can strengthen or extend the meaning of a verb:
a *The scarecrow frightened the birds **away**.* (*away* refers to 'distance')
b *I was holding my hat and the wind snatched it **away**.* (*away* refers to 'detachment')
c *I got a cloth and wiped **away** the coffee I had spilled.* (*away* refers to 'disappearance')
d *Please put these dishes **away**.* (*away* refers to 'tidying')
The verb often has its non-idiomatic meaning, but the particle 'extends' this meaning: e.g. *pull out, push away, wash away, move back, burn down, bring in, cut off.*

Write: Match these meanings to the adverb particles in the sentences below.

a 'put on paper'	f 'movement out'	k 'removal'	p 'distribution'
b 'exclusion'	g 'permanence'	l 'reduction'	q 'inwards' ('destroy')
c 'addition'	h 'movement in'	m 'to the ground'	r 'up from the surface'
d 'out of bed'	i 'enclose'	n 'extension'	s 'confine'
e 'completely'	j 'clearly'	o 'into pieces'	t 'upwards direction'

out 1 drive the car *out* ..*f*..............
2 leave that word *out* ....
3 take that stain *out* ....
4 put *out* your hand ....
5 copy this *out* ....
6 give these *out* ....

in 7 let him *in* ....
8 lock him *in* ....
9 write this *in* ....
10 beat the door *in* ....

up 11 pull that line *up* ....
12 pick that *up* ....
13 fill this car *up* ....
14 chop that wood *up* ....
15 let the patient *up* ....
16 wrap this box *up* ....

down 17 cut the tree *down* ....
18 turn the heat *down* ....
19 close the shop *down* ....
20 write this *down* ....

8.7C Type 2: Verb + particle + object, idiomatic: 'bring about a change'
[> LEG 8.28.5, App 33]

Study:
⭐⭐
We cannot relate the parts of these verbs to their literal meanings: e.g.
*What **brought about** this change? What **brought** this change **about**? What **brought** it **about**?*
(= caused to happen)

Write: Match these verbs (1-15) with the explanations on the right (a-o) after you have tried to explain them in your own way.

1 When will they *bring* your article *out*? ...*e*....................................   a) get my revenge
2 So she's *broken off* her engagement! ....   b) discuss your grievance
3 Don't *bring* that subject *up* again please! ....   c) fill
4 Why don't you *call up* your mother? ....   d) give me accommodation
5 Shall I *do* your room *out*? ....   e) publish
6 What excuse did he *cook up* this time? ....   f) invent
7 They're sure to *find* him *out*. ....   g) destroyed
8 You've *given away* the secret. ....   h) make him stop talking
9 I can't *make out* what he means. ....   i) ended
10 If you're angry, *have it out* with her. ....   j) clean
11 I'll *pay* you *back* for this! ....   k) reveal his dishonesty
12 Can you *put* me *up* for the night? ....   l) mention
13 *Shut* him *up*! ....   m) revealed
14 The earthquake *wiped* the village *out*. ....   n) phone
15 Why don't you *top up* the battery? ....   o) understand

8.7D Context

Write: Look at the phrases in italics. Show with arrows which particles can be moved and where.

He got up to shake hands

NOT ONLY RED IN THE FACE!
Ken Rose is a company director and he has to sit at a desk all day. He likes to keep fit by running to work every morning. He [1]*arrives at the office* early, [2]*gets out of his shorts and vest* and [3]*puts on a business suit*. Last week, Ken [4]*got to his office* earlier than usual, dressed in red shorts and a red vest. He had just [5]*put on his shirt and tie*, when the phone rang. Ken [6]*picked up the receiver* and sat behind his desk. A business colleague [7]*had called him up* early. Could he see Ken later? Could he [8]*bring someone round*? Could they [9]*check over some figures*? Could they [10]*think of ways* of [11]*cutting down expenses*? Could they [12]*put off the meeting* till later in the week? Ken [13]*was writing down some notes* when he noticed the time. It was after 9. 'Excuse me,' Ken said. 'I'll [14]*call you back*.' He [15]*had just put the receiver down* when someone [16]*knocked at the door*. The Managing Director [17]*came into the room* with six important guests. 'Ah, Ken,' he said, 'I want to [18]*introduce you to our visitors* and I'd like you to [19]*show them round the company*.' 'Of course, sir,' Ken said and he got up to shake hands, forgetting he still [20]*had on his red shorts*!

8.8 Phrasal verbs: Type 3, verb + particle (intransitive)
Type 4, verb + particle + preposition (transitive

8.8A Type 3: Verb + particle, intransitive, non-idiomatic: 'hurry up' [> LEG 8.29.2]

Study:
★★
We use these verbs in their normal sense. Many combinations are possible:
Hurry up! Sit down! Stand up! Compare Type 1 [> 8.6A-B]: *Look!* (Not *Look at*)

Write: Combine the following verbs with the following particles in different ways:
come, go, hurry, sit, stand + along, away, down, in, up

1	*Come along*	5		9		13	
2		6		10		14	
3		7		11		15	
4		8		12		16	

8.8B Type 3: Verb + particle, intransitive, idiomatic: 'break down'

Study:
★★
We cannot relate the parts of these verbs to their literal meanings: e.g.
*She **broke down** when she heard the news* (= collapsed). [> LEG 8.29.3, App 36]

Write: Match these verbs (1-17) with the explanations on the right (a-q) after you have tried to explain them in your own way.

1 All this information doesn't *add up*. ....*b*................................   a) be careful!
2 I'm glad to say my plan *came off*. ....   b) make sense
3 I need the money and you'd better *cough up*. (informal) ....   c) improving
4 You're tired. You should *ease off*. ....   d) improving
5 When did the plane *take off*? ....   e) work less hard
6 Please don't *let on* I told you this. ....   f) reveal the secret
7 I'm going to *lie in* tomorrow morning. ....   g) happen
8 Is there sufficient food to *go round*? ....   h) succeeded
9 Business is *looking up*. ....   i) not working properly
10 You work and I'll *look on*. ....   j) pay
11 My car's *playing up* again. ....   k) start your journey
12 I'll be late, so don't *wait up*. ....   l) arrived
13 *Mind out*! He's turning left! ....   m) leave the ground
14 I waited for him, but he never *showed up*. ....   n) not go to bed
15 What time are you going to *set out*? ....   o) be enough
16 I'm glad to say business is *picking up*. ....   p) be a spectator
17 How did that *come about*? ....   q) stay in bed late

8.8C Type 4: Verb + particle + preposition + object, non-idiomatic: 'walk up to the top'

Study:
★★
These verbs are used in their normal sense. [> LEG 8.30.2, 8.8]

Write: Write sentences with the following.

1 (come down from) *The lift takes a long time to come down from the top floor.*
2 (drive on to) ....
3 (hurry over to) ....
4 (run along to) ....
5 (stay away from) ....

8.8D Verb + particle + preposition + object, idiomatic: 'put up with it'

[> LEG 8.30.3, App 37]

Study: We cannot relate the parts of these verbs to their literal meanings: e.g.

★★ *How do you **put up with it**?* (= tolerate)

Write: Match these verbs (1-20) with the explanations on the right (a-t) after you have tried to explain them in your own way.

1 Your argument *boils down to* this. ...*e*............................
2 I can't *go back on* my word. ....
3 Please *let* me *in on* the secret. ....
4 You'd better *talk* him *out of* his plan. ....
5 Some of his good luck has *rubbed off on* me. ....
6 I can't *live up to* my reputation. ....
7 I've *set up in* business ....
8 That *ties in* nicely *with* my plan. ....
9 Who *put* you *up to* this? ....
10 I don't *feel up to* this party. ....
11 This won't *make up for* the damage. ....
12 You've got to *face up to* reality. ....
13 The Cabots *look down on* us. ....
14 We've had to *fall back on* our savings. ....
15 I think it would be a good idea to *keep in with* her. ....
16 I'll *get on to* them immediately. ....
17 The bill *comes out at* £100 exactly. ....
18 If you're angry, you don't have to *take* it *out on* me. ....
19 I'm glad they've *done away with* that bad law. ....
20 I'm *looking forward to* the holidays. ....

a) use
b) allow me to share
c) expecting to enjoy
d) contact
e) can be summarized as
f) totals
g) started
h) treat unfairly
i) benefited
j) accept with courage
k) fits
l) fail to honour
m) abolished
n) maintain the high standard
o) consider us inferior
p) compensate for
q) gave you this idea
r) stay on good terms
s) feel well enough for
t) persuade not to do

8.8E Context

Write: Put in *about, down, down on, in, in on, up, up on, up to, up with* or *to*.

A CURE FOR SNORING

It's very difficult for people who sleep silently to [1]put ...*up with*... the sound of snoring. Some people are asleep the moment they [2]lie ....; others [3]stay .... half the night waiting for the miracle of sleep to [4]come .... Even insomniacs snore. Insomniacs are the ones who need to [5]lie .... in the morning to [6]catch .... lost sleep. Snorers will never admit to snoring. They know the rest of the world [7]looks .... them and they just can't [8]face .... reality. My friend, Henry, a champion snorer, has just found a cure and he [9]let me .... his little secret. He has just [10]coughed .... good money for a band with a stud on it. He wears the band round his head at night and if he tries to sleep on his back, the stud gives him a jab. I'm sure this news will [11]cheer .... all snorers, who now have a new experience to [12]look forward .... With one of these on their heads, all they have to lose is their sleep!

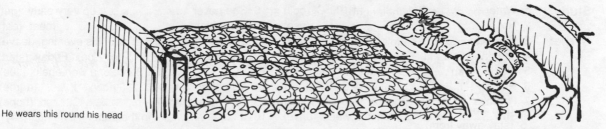

He wears this round his head

121

9 Verbs, verb tenses, imperatives

9.1 The simple present and present progressive tenses (1)

9.1A Pronunciation and spelling of the 3rd person, simple present [> LEG 9.6-7]

Study:
★★

> **1 Pronunciation** [compare plural nouns > 2.5A]:
> We pronounce -s as /s/ after these sounds: /f/ *laughs*; /p/ *drops*; /k/ *kicks*; /t/ *lets*.
> We pronounce -s as /ɪz/ after /z/ *loses*; /dʒ/ *manages*; /s/ *passes*; /ʃ/ *pushes*; /tʃ/ *stitches*, and /ks/ *mixes*.
> We pronounce -s as /z/ after all other sounds: /b/ *robs*; /d/ *adds*; /g/ *digs*; /l/ *fills*; /m/ *dreams*; /n/ *runs*; /ŋ/ *rings*; after vowels: *sees*; after vowel + *w* or *r*: *draws, stirs*.
>
> **2 Spelling**
> Add -s to most verbs: *work/works, drive/drives, play/plays, run/runs*.
> Add -es to verbs ending in -o: *do/does*; -s: *misses*; -x: *mixes*; -ch/-sh: *catches/pushes*.

Write:
a Give the third person forms of the verbs in these sentences.
b Show whether you would pronounce the third person form as /s/, /z/ or /ɪz/

1 They laugh a lot. He ....*laughs*........ / s /   8 I rush around a lot. She .... / /
2 I often drop things. She .... / /   9 I always saw the wood. She .... / /
3 We drink a lot of tea. She ..../ /   10 I wear old clothes at home. He .... / /
4 I often forget things. She ..../ /   11 I love sweets. She .... / /
5 We often lose things. He .... / /   12 I often see them. He .... / /
6 They manage all right. She .... / /   13 They pay £30 a week rent. He .... / /
7 I often pass your house. He .... / /   14 I cry at sad films. She .... / /

9.1B Uses of the simple present tense: 'I work/he works' [> LEG 9.8, 9.12]

Study:
★★

> There are seven basic uses of the **simple present tense** [compare > 11.11A]. We use it for:
>
> **1** Permanent truths: *Summer **follows** spring. Gases **expand** when heated.*
> **2** 'The present period' (= 'this is the situation at present'): *My sister **works** in a bank.*
> **3** Habitual actions: *I **get up** at 7. I sometimes **stay up** till midnight.*
> **4** Future reference (for timetables, etc.): *The concert **begins** at 7.30 next Friday evening.*
> **5** Observations and declarations: *I **hope** so. It **says** here that ... . I **love** you. I **hate** him.*
> **6** Instructions: *First you **weigh** the ingredients.*
> **7** Commentaries: *Becker **serves** to Lendl.*

Write: Give the correct form of the simple present of each verb.

1 Water ....*boils*........ at 100°C. (boil)
2 Hot air .... (rise)
3 My uncle .... in a factory. (work)
4 John and Sue .... glasses. (wear)
5 The children .... a lot of sweets. (eat)
6 He only .... at weekends. (work)
7 I always .... out on Saturdays. (go)
8 She .... to London once a week. (drive)
9 She never .... up very early. (get)
10 I occasionally .... meat. (eat)
11 The coach .... at 6 this evening. (leave)
12 The concert .... at 7 next Friday. (start)
13 I .... Barcelona won again. (see)
14 It's not right, you .... (know) – I .... (agree)
15 Can he manage? – I .... so. (hope)
16 It .... in the paper it'll be hot. (say)

9.1C Stative and dynamic verbs [> LEG 9.3, App 38]

Study:
★★

1 We call a few verbs like *love* **stative** because they refer to 'states'. A state has no beginning and no end. We don't 'control' it, so we don't normally use stative verbs in progressive tenses:
*She **loves** her baby more than anything.* (Not **is loving**)

2 Most verbs in English are **dynamic**. We can use them in two ways:
– in the simple present tense to describe habits, etc. [> 9.1B]: *I often **make** cakes.*
– in the present progressive to describe deliberate actions in progress [> 9.2B]:
*I'**m making** a cake.*

3 We can describe three classes of verbs:
a Dynamic verbs which have simple or progressive forms (most verbs in English):
*I often **listen** to records.* (simple present tense)
*I'**m listening** to a record.* (present progressive tense)
b Verbs which are always stative:
*This coat **belongs** to you.* (simple present tense) (Not **is belonging**)
c Verbs that have stative or dynamic uses:
*I'**m weighing** myself.* (a deliberate action: present progressive tense)
*I **weigh** 65 kilos.* (a state) (Not **I'm weighing 65 kilos.**)

4 There are five groups of stative verbs referring to: **a** feelings (*like, love*, etc.);
b thinking/believing (*think, understand*, etc.) **c** wants (*want, prefer*, etc.)
d perception (*hear, see*, etc. [> 11.2B]) **e** being/having/owning (*appear, seem, belong*, etc. [> 10.4])

Write: Tick the sentences that are right. Cross out the verbs that are wrong and correct them.

1a You're never ill. I envy you. ✓
1b You're never ill. I'm envying you. __
2a I understand English well. __
2b I'm understanding English well. __
3a You're knowing what I mean. __
3b You know what I mean. __
4a Is he seeming unfriendly? __
4b Does he seem unfriendly? __
5a I prefer fish to meat. __
5b I'm preferring fish to meat. __
6a Do you see that bird over there? __
6b Are you seeing John tomorrow? __
7a Why is he smelling his coffee? __
7b Something smells strange. __
8a She's weighing herself again. __
8b She weighs 75.5 kilos. __

9.1D Context

Write: Put in the simple present or the present progressive tenses.

CHOMP CHAMP!
[1](*you sit*) ...*Are you sitting*... comfortably? Good! I [2](*hope*) .... you [3](*study*)
.... this text carefully because I [4](*have*) .... news for you. The
Guinness Book of Records [5](*not include*) .... records for eating any more. People
who [6](*try*) .... to swallow 47 hard boiled eggs in half a minute will have to do it for
pleasure and not to get into the record book. 'We [7](*regard*) .... these records as
unhealthy,' said the book's editor, Mr Donald McFarlan. However, one record-holder will remain. He is
Michel Lotito of Grenoble ('Monsieur Mangetout'). Since 1966, he has chomped his way through 10
bicycles, 7 TV sets and a light aircraft. He's likely to remain world champ, unless you [8](*want*)
.... to challenge him, of course!

Chomp! chomp!

9.2 The simple present and present progressive tenses (2)

9.2A Spelling: how to add '-ing' to a verb: 'wait/waiting' [> LEG 9.10]

Study:
⊠

1 We add *-ing* to most verbs, without changing the base form: *wait/waiting*:
Wait for me. → I am **waiting** for you.

2 If a verb ends in *-e*, omit the *-e* and add *-ing*: *use/using*:
Use a broom. → I am **using** a broom.

3 A single vowel followed by a single consonant doubles the final consonant: *sit/sitting*:
Sit down. → I am **sitting** down. [> compare 6.5A]

4 We double the last consonant of two-syllable verbs when the second syllable is stressed:
be'gin/be'ginning. Compare the unstressed final syllable: 'differ/'differing:
Begin work. → I am **beginning** work.

5 *-ic* changes to *-ick*: *picnic/picnicking*; *-ie* changes to *-y*: *lie/lying*:
Lie down. → I am **lying** down.

Write: Add *-ing* to the verbs in these sentences.

1 I'm *making* the beds. (make) 4 I'm always .... things. (forget) 7 I'm .... the 9.04. (catch)
2 I'm .... a sandwich. (eat) 5 I'm .... on my coat. (put) 8 I'm .... of thirst. (die)
3 I'm .... a letter. (write) 6 I'm .... abroad. (travel) 9 I'm .... your case. (carry)

9.2B Uses of the present progressive tense: 'I am working/he is working'
[> LEG 9.11]

Study:
⊠⊠

There are four basic uses of the **present progressive tense**. We use it for:
1 Actions in progress at the moment of speaking: **He's working** at the moment.
2 Temporary situations/actions, not necessarily in progress at the moment of speaking:
My daughter **is studying** English at Durham University.
3 Planned actions (+ future adverbial reference): **We're spending** next winter in Australia. [> 9.9A]
4 Repeated actions with adverbs like *always, forever*: **She's always helping** people.

Write:
a Use the present progressive in the sentences below.
b Number the sentences 1, 2, 3 or 4 to show uses of the present progressive.

1 Don't rush me. *I am working (1)* .... as fast as I can. (I/work)
2 What ....? It looks awful. (you/drink)
3 .... to see the boss. (She/still wait)
4 .... to catch his train. (He/hurry)
5 ...., aren't you? Calm down! (You/constantly/panic)
6 .... more and more politically aware these days. (Young people/become)
7 What .... nowadays? (John/do) – .... for the British cycle team. (He/ride)
8 .... our holiday here very much. (We/enjoy)
9 .... people by asking personal questions. (He/always/upset)
10 What time .... tomorrow? (he/arrive)
11 .... to lock the front door. (She/forever/forget)
12 .... treatment on my bad back for a few weeks. (I/have)
13 You can't believe a word he says. .... (He/always/lie)
14 .... the 1,500 metres in the next Olympics. (She/run)

124

9.2C The simple present and the present progressive tenses in typical contexts [> LEG 9.12]

Write: a Use the correct present tense form.

b Say what the context for each extract could be, written and/or spoken.

1 Let me explain what you have to do. First you (take) ....*take*......... the photos and (sort) ....*sort*......... them into categories. Then you (file) ...*file*... them according to subject.

2 We (hope) .... you (enjoy) .... this marvellous weather as much as we are. We (sunbathe) .... and (go) .... swimming every day. Next week we (go) .... snorkelling.

3 The play is set in London in 1890. The action (take) .... place in Sir Don Wyatt's mansion. When the curtain (go) .... up, the hero and heroine (sit) .... in the lounge. They (argue) ....

4 The house is in a mess because we've got the workmen in. The plumber (put) .... in a new bath, the electricians (rewire) .... the system, and the carpenter (build) .... us some new bookshelves!

5 Dear Jane,
Sorry to hear about your problem at work I (think) .... you (do) .... the right thing, but I (doubt) .... whether your boss really (know) .... his job from what you (tell) .... me!

6 Pym (pass) .... to Smith, who (run) .... straight at the central defence and (shoot) ...., and Gomez (push) .... it over the bar for a corner.

9.2D Context

Write: Put in the simple present or present progressive. Note where both forms are possible.

A HOLIDAY JOB WITH A DIFFERENCE!
I (study)[1] *am studying*. English at Exeter University. I'm on holiday at the moment and I (work) [2]........................... in a public library. I'm lucky to have this job. I (not have to) [3]........................... get up early. The library (open) [4]........................... at 10 and (close) [5]........................... at 7. It's interesting work because people (always come in) [6]........................... and (ask) [7]........................... me to help them, so I (learn) [8]........................... a lot about different subjects. I (enjoy) [9]........................... the job and (find) [10]........................... it very amusing, too. People (use) [11]........................... the strangest things as bookmarks. I have found a rasher of bacon (uncooked!). Matchsticks (be) [12]........................... common and so (be) [13]........................... bus tickets. My colleagues (always find) [14]........................... things too – even a £10 note, but I haven't been so lucky! I often (think) [15]........................... of the photo of a beautiful woman which I found. On the back were the words: 'I (love) [16]........................... you. I (miss) [17]........................... you and I'll never forget you.'

The strangest bookmarks!

9 Verbs, verb tenses, imperatives

9.3 The simple past tense

9.3A The past form and pronunciation of regular verbs [> LEG 9.14, App 39]

Study: ★★

1 Regular verbs always end with a *-d* in the simple past, but we do not always pronounce the *-d* ending in the same way. We usually add *-ed* to the base form of the verb: *I play – I played, I open – I opened*. We do not pronounce *-ed* as an extra syllable. We pronounce it as /d/: *I played* /pleɪd/ Not * /pleɪ-ɪd/ *; *I opened* /əʊpənd/ Not * /əʊpənɪd/ *; *I arrived* /əraɪvd/ Not * /əraɪvɪd/ *; *I married* /mærɪd/ Not * /mæri-ɪd/ * [compare > 2.5A].

2 Verbs which end in the following sounds are pronounced /t/ in the past: /k/ *packed*; /s/ *passed*; /tʃ/ *watched*; /ʃ/ *washed*; /f/ *laughed*; /p/ *tipped*.

3 A few verbs are pronounced and spelt /d/ or /t/: *burned/burnt, dreamed/dreamt*.

4 Verbs ending in the sounds /t/ or /d/ have their past ending pronounced /ɪd/: *added, decided, counted, excited, needed, posted, shouted, started, tasted, wanted*.

Write:
a Give the past forms of these regular verbs.
b Show whether you would pronounce these past forms as /d/, /t/ or /ɪd/.

1 We *waited* an hour yesterday. (wait) /ɪd/
2 Joan .... her room on Friday. (clean) / /
3 I .... squash last night. (play) / /
4 She .... my letter yesterday. (post) / /
5 I .... at her. (smile) / /
6 She .... when she saw me. (stop) / /
7 I .... of you last night. (dream) / /
8 Who .... the cakes? (burn) / /
9 He .... a lot as a baby. (cry) / /
10 I .... TV all evening. (watch) / /
11 We .... when we saw them. (laugh) / /
12 He .... the sergeant's orders. (obey) / /
13 We .... into the house. (hurry) / /
14 You .... to me! (lie) / /
15 I .... early yesterday. (finish) / /
16 It's .... in the bill. (include) / /
17 I .... the door before I left. (lock) / /
18 We .... first class. (travel) / /

9.3B Irregular past forms [> LEG 9.15-16, App 40]

Study: ★

1 Some irregular verbs have the same form in all parts: *hit-hit-hit, cut-cut-cut*.

2 Some change one part only: *keep-kept-kept, make-made-made, sell-sold-sold*.

3 Some change two parts: *break-broke-broken, know-knew-known, ride-rode-ridden*.

Write: Supply the past forms of the irregular verbs in italics.

1 I often *see* Giulio. I .... *saw* .... him again only yesterday.
2 As teenagers, we always .... each other very well. We still *understand* each other now.
3 I hardly .... Ray's wife. Did you *know* her at all?
4 We always *meet* on Sunday. We .... last Sunday as usual.
5 I often *find* things on the beach. I .... this very old bottle yesterday.
6 Someone's always *leaving* that window open. Who .... it open this time?
7 I .... a lot of letters when I was young. I hardly ever *write* letters now.
8 They *sell* all kinds of rubbish now, but they once .... good handmade furniture.
9 She *is* very good at figures, you know. She .... first in maths at school.
10 I *have* the same car now that I .... five years ago.
11 I don't *keep* pets now, but I .... a dog when I was a boy.
12 Where did you *eat* last night? – We .... at a restaurant.

126

9.3C Uses of the simple past tense: 'I worked/he worked' [> LEG 9.17-18]

Study:
★★

We use the **simple past** to talk about events, actions or situations which happened in the past and are now finished. We always have to say (or imply) **when** the action happened, so we often use time references like *yesterday, ago, last summer* [> 7.2A].
We use the past:
– to describe actions which happened in the recent or distant past:
   *Sam **phoned a moment ago**.* (Not **Sam has phoned**) [> 9.5A]
   *The Goths **invaded Rome in A.D. 410**.* (Not **The Goths had invaded**) [> 9.6]
– to describe past habit: *I **smoked forty cigarettes a day** till I gave up.* [compare > 11.11]

If we do not use time references (*a moment ago, when I was young*, etc.) we imply them:
*I **saw** Fred in town.* (i.e. when I was there this morning)
*I **never met** my grandfather.* (i.e. perhaps he died before I was born)

Write: Give complete answers to these questions using the time references in brackets.

1 How long ago did you work as a civil servant? (five years ago)
   I worked as a civil servant five years ago.

2 When did you last play football? (when I was 14)
   ....

3 When did the Carters leave for their summer holiday? (last night)
   ....

4 What time did John arrive? (at 4)
   ....

5 When did you last see 'Gone with the Wind'? (recently)
   ....

6 How long did you wait at the airport? (till they arrived)
   ....

7 When did Sally tell you about her engagement? (when she was here)
   ....

9.3D Context

Write: Put in the correct forms of the simple past tense of the verbs in brackets.

... red eyes and green scaly skin

LIZARDMAN
Christopher Davis, a young driver from South Carolina, (*claim*)
[1].......*claimed*...... a monster (*attack*) [2]............................. him while he was driving along a lonely road. The monster (*be*) [3]............................. seven feet tall and (*have*) [4]............................. red eyes and green, scaly skin. It (*chase*) [5]............................. Christopher's car and (*jump*) [6]............................. on the roof. Many people (*believe*) [7]............................. the story and the newspapers (*call*) [8]............................. the monster 'Lizardman'. Seventy hunters recently (*set out*) [9]............................. to trap Lizardman and a local radio (*offer*) [10]............................. $1 million to anyone who (*capture*) [11]............................. him dead or alive. Lizardman had so much publicity that thousands of people (*visit*) [12]............................. South Carolina to find him. No one has found him yet. As everyone knows, monsters may or may not exist, but they are very good for the tourist industry!

9.4 The simple past and past progressive tenses

9.4A Irregular verbs with the same form in the present as in the past: 'put/put' [> LEG 9.16]

Study:
★★

A small number of irregular verbs have the same form in the present as in the past: e.g. *burst/ burst, cost/cost, cut/cut, hit/hit, put/put*. We have to remember, especially with such verbs, that the third person singular does not change in the past:
He put on *a clean shirt yesterday.* **(past)** ***He puts on*** *a clean shirt every day.* **(present)**
After *I, you, we,* and *they*, the context or the adverbial tells us the tense:
I put on *a clean shirt* **yesterday**. **(past)** ***I put on*** *a clean shirt* **every day**. **(present)**

Write: Do these sentences refer to the present or the past? Write 'present' or 'past'.
In a few cases both references are possible.

1 That shirt cost me £7.00. ....*past*..........
2 He often cuts himself. ....
3 She hurt her arm. ....
4 He let me drive his car. ....
5 She reads a lot. ....
6 I set the table every morning. ....
7 I set the table an hour ago. ....

8 She often hit him. ....
9 He shut the door with a bang. ....
10 I hurt my arm yesterday. ....
11 I often let him drive my car. ....
12 She always beat him at tennis. ....
13 The BBC broadcasts every day. ....
14 The BBC broadcast the talk yesterday. ....

9.4B Uses of the past progressive tense: 'I was working' [> LEG 9.20]

Study:
★★

There are five basic uses of the **past progressive tense**. We use it for:

1 Temporary actions in progress in the past: *I **was living** abroad in 1987.*
We often use *all* to emphasize continuity (*all day, all summer*): *It **was raining** all night.*

2 Actions which were in progress when something else happened:
*Just as/When I **was leaving**, the phone rang.*
These are often introduced by conjunctions like *when, as, just as* and *while*, but the shorter action can be introduced by *when*: *We **were having** supper when the phone rang.*

3 Actions in progress at the same time: *While I **was reading**, Joan **was playing** the piano.*

4 Repeated actions with e.g. *always*: *When I worked here, I **was always making** mistakes.*

5 Polite inquiries: *I **was wondering** if you could give me a lift.*

Write: Use the past progressive in the sentences below.

1 I ..*was not listening*.. , so I missed what he said. (not listen)
2 We stayed because we .... ourselves. (enjoy)
3 .... tennis yesterday? (they play)
4 He .... all weekend. (garden)
5 .... television all evening? (you watch)
6 It .... hard all day. (rain)
7 I .... whether you could lend me some money. (wonder)

8 .... when I left? (you still work)
9 I lived in France at the time you .... in Spain. (live)
10 When she was younger, she .... things for other people. (always do)
11 Bill and Sue .... their house, before they moved. (constantly improve)
12 .... when I rang you? (you read)
13 Just as I .... to an interesting part of the story, the doorbell rang. (get)

9.4C The simple past and the past progressive in story-telling [> LEG 9.21]

Study:
★★

> We often use past tenses (simple past, past progressive and past perfect [> 9.6]) for story-telling. We use the past progressive to set the scene at the beginning of the story.

Write:
    a Circle the simple past and the past progressive verbs in this story.
    b Number the past progressive verbs 1, 2, 3 to show their uses [> 9.4B].

THE SECRET AGENT
It (was) just before the Second World War. Tom was only 20 at the time and was living with his mother. He was working in a bank and travelling to London every day. One morning, he received a mysterious letter. It was addressed to 'Mr Thomas Parker'. The letter, which was signed, 'A Friend', asked Tom to go to The Crown Inn during his lunch hour. All morning, as he was dealing with customers, Tom was wondering whether he should do this. At lunch time he decided to go to the inn. It was full of people and Tom couldn't recognize anyone. He was just wondering if he should leave, when a stranger introduced himself and said he had known Tom's father, who had died when Tom was a baby. The stranger explained that Tom's father, Bill, was a secret agent in the First World War. Through this meeting, Tom was recruited to be a secret agent, too, and was already working in France when the war began.

9.4D Context

Write: Put in the simple past or past progressive. Note where both forms are possible.

TUG-OF-WAR WITH A HEDGEHOG
Mrs May, our District Nurse, (*drive*) [1] *was driving* home at 3 a.m. one night after an urgent visit to a sick patient. She (*drive*) [2] .... along a deserted country lane, when she (*see*) [3] .... a new kind of animal. She (*stop*) [4] .... her car and (*get out*) [5] .... The animal (*bc*) [6] .... clearly visible in the blaze of her headlights. It (*look*) [7] .... like a hedgehog with a tall white hat. It (*cross*) [8] .... the road without paying any attention to Mrs May. When Mrs May (*go*) [9] .... close to it, she (*notice*) [10] .... that there was a plastic yoghurt pot on the hedgehog's head. The poor creature had got its head stuck in the plastic pot! Her instincts as a nurse (*tell*) [11] .... her she would have to rescue it, so she (*pull*) [12] .... at the pot, but the hedgehog (*pull*) [13] ...., too. After a struggle, she (*pull*) [14] .... the pot off the hedgehog's head. Mrs May (*think*) [15] .... the hedgehog (*look*) [16] .... rather sad, when she (*notice*) [17] .... that the pot was half full of strawberry yoghurt. She (*give*) [18] .... it back to the hedgehog. The creature (*seize*) [19] .... it, (*put*) [20] .... it on its head again, and triumphantly (*continue*) [21] .... its journey across the road.

A hedgehog with a tall white hat

9.5 The simple present perfect and present perfect progressive

9.5A Uses of the simple present perfect tense: 'I have eaten/he has eaten'
[> LEG 9.22-27]

Study:
★★

> There are two basic uses of the **simple present perfect tense**. We use it to describe:
>
> 1 Actions beginning in the past and continuing up to the present moment:
>   – with time references like *before (now), ever, never ... before, up till now, so far*:
>   I **have received** 20 cards so far. I **have never tasted** papaya (before).
>   – with *since/for*: **I've lived** here since 1980. **I've lived** here for 20 years. [> 7.3A]
>
> 2 Actions which happened at an unspecified time in the past:
>   – with no time reference at all: **Have you passed** your driving test?
>   (Depending on context, this could mean 'very recently' or 'at any time up to now'.)
>   – with references to recent time, like *just, recently, already, still, yet*: **I've just eaten**.
>   – repeated/habitual actions: **I've watched** him on TV **several times. I've often met** her.

Write: Supply the simple present perfect tense of the verbs in brackets.

1 Up to now I *ive visited* twenty countries. (visit)
2 He .... six letters so far. (type)
3 .... couscous? (you ever eat)
4 They .... like this before. (never quarrel)
5 I .... to Marco since 1989. (not write)
6 We .... there since we were young. (not be)
7 I saw her in May, but .... her since. (not see)
8 She .... the same car for fifteen years. (drive)
9 I .... them for many years. (know)
10 She .... in that shop for ages! (be)
11 They .... a new car. (buy)
12 He .... all over the world. (travel)
13 .... your promise? (you forget)
14 I .... an elephant. (ride)
15 She .... in from Rome. (just fly)
16 She .... a director. (recently become)
17 They .... to me. (already speak)
18 I .... my tea yet. (not drink)
19 She still .... my letter. (not answer)
20 I .... her several times. (met)

9.5B The present perfect progressive tense: 'I have been eating' [> LEG 9.32-34]

Study:
★★

> 1 We use the **present perfect progressive** in place of the simple present perfect when we want
>   to emphasize that something has been in progress throughout a period:
>   Instead of saying: **I've typed** all day, we can say, for emphasis, **I've been typing** all day.
>   Depending on context, this may mean *I'm still typing* or *I've just recently stopped*.
>
> 2 Some verbs like *learn, lie, live, rain, sit, sleep, stand, study, wait, work*, naturally suggest
>   continuity [> 7.3B] and we often use them with *since* and *for* [> 7.3A].
>   We can use them in the simple present perfect tense:
>   **I've waited** here for two hours. **I've worked** here since 1987.
>   But we most often use them in the progressive:
>   **I've been waiting** here for two hours. **I've been working** here since 1987.

Write: Supply the present perfect progressive tense of the verbs in brackets.

1 I'm tired. I *have been digging* all day. (dig)
2 How long .... here? (you wait)
3 I .... here since 6 o'clock. (stand)
4 How long .... Chinese? (you learn)
5 She .... English for five years. (study)
6 You're out of breath. ....? (you run)
7 We .... here for twelve years. (live)
8 Your eyes are red. .... (You cry)
9 How long ....? (the children sleep)
10 What .... all afternoon? (you do)

9.5C The simple present perfect and the present perfect progressive compared [> LEG 9.34]

Study:
★★

The simple present perfect and the progressive forms mean different things here:
I've been painting this room. It will look good when it's finished. (the job is unfinished)
I've painted this room. Doesn't it look good? (the job is definitely finished)

Write: Supply the simple present perfect or the present perfect progressive.

1a I .....*I've typed*... all your letters. The job's done. (type)
1b I .... this report since yesterday and I'm only half way through. (type)
2a Your mother is still in the kitchen. She .... all morning. (cook)
2b I .... a lovely meal which I'll be serving in a couple of minutes. (cook)
3a We .... this garage ourselves and have just begun to use it. (build)
3b We .... this garage ourselves and hope to finish it within the next two months. (build)

9.5D The simple past and the simple present perfect compared [> LEG 9.23, 9.26.1]

Study:
★★

With the **simple past** we have to say or imply **when** something happenened [> 7.3A, 9.3C]:
*I **finished** the job **yesterday/an hour ago**,* etc. (Not **I have finished the job yesterday.**)
With the **present perfect**, we do not say 'exactly when': *I **have finished** the job.*
Even if we say *I **have just finished** the job,* we are still not saying 'exactly when' [> 9.5A].

Write: Supply the simple past or the simple present perfect in these pairs of sentences.

1a She ....*never read*.. a book until she was 25. (never read)
1b She is 80 and .... a book in her life. (never read)
2a I .... lunch an hour ago. (have)
2b I .... lunch. (just have)
3a .... to the bank yet? (he go)
3b .... to the bank at lunch time? (he go)

9.5E Context

Write: Put in the simple present perfect, the present perfect progressive or the simple past.

THE AUSTRALIAN SALUTE
Before I (*visit*) [1] .....*visited*...... Australia, an Australian friend in London (*tell*)
[2] .... me I'd learn 'the Australian salute'. 'What's that?' I (*ask*)
[3] .... 'You'll find out when you get there,' he (*say*) [4] I
(*arrive*) [5] .... in Perth last week. Since then, I (*stay*) [6] .... at a
nice hotel near a beautiful beach. I (*never visit*) [7] .... Australia before and
I am enjoying my stay. I (*swim*) [8] .... every day from the time I (*arrive*)
[9] .... Yesterday, an Australian friend (*suggest*) [10] .... a tour
into 'the bush'. I (*agree*) [11] .... at once. The first thing I (*notice*)
[12] .... when we (*be*) [13] .... in the bush (*be*) [14] ....
the flies. After a while I (*remember*) [15] .... the conversation I had had in
London before I (*come*) [16] .... here. 'What's the "Australian salute"?' I
(*ask*) [17] .... suddenly, as I waved my right arm to keep the flies away.
'That's it!' my friend said as he (*wave*) [18] .... back!

I waved my right arm

9.6 The simple past perfect and past perfect progressive tenses

9.6A Uses of the simple past perfect tense: 'I had worked' [> LEG 9.29-30]

Study:
★★

1 When we have two past references, we are not obliged to use the simple past perfect:
After I finished work, I went home. (simple past + simple past)

2 But we often need the past perfect for the event that happened first to avoid ambiguity:
When I arrived, Ann left. (i.e. at that moment)
When I arrived, Ann had left. (i.e. before I got there)

We use the past perfect to refer to 'an earlier past', that is to describe the first of two or more actions: ***First** the patient died. **Then** the doctor arrived.*
*The patient **had died** when the doctor **arrived**.*
We often introduce the past perfect with conjunctions like *when, after, as soon as, by the time that*. We use adverbs like *already, ever, never ... before*.

Write: Supply the simple past or the simple past perfect. Show when both are possible.

1 They ....*locked/had locked*.... the gates before I ....*got*................. there. (lock, get)
2 By the time we ...., the party .... (arrive, finish)
3 I .... the shop as soon as I .... the contents of the box. (ring, check)
4 After we .... it on the phone, I .... him a letter about it. (discuss, write)
5 We .... a good rest when our guests. .... (have, all leave)
6 When she .... the office this morning, Jim. .... (ring, already go out)
7 Before we .... Tim to the theatre, he .... a stage play before. (take, never see)
8 I .... the carpet when the dog .... in and .... himself. (just clean, come, shake)
9 He .... to do the job in an hour, but he still .... by 10 o'clock. (promise, not finish)

9.6B Uses of the present and past perfect progressive: 'I have/had been working' [> LEG 9.32-33]

Study:
★★

The past perfect progressive is the 'past' form of the present perfect progressive. [> 9.5B]
The progressive forms have the effect of emphasizing continuity.

1 We use them to describe actions in progress throughout a period:
present perfect progressive: *She is very tired. She **has been typing** all day.*
past perfect progressive: *She was very tired. She **had been typing** all day.*
Depending on context, she was still typing, or had recently stopped. (*then*, not now)

2 Some verbs like *learn, lie, live, wait, work*, naturally suggest 'continuity' [> 7.3B, 9.5B]:
We say: ***I've waited** for two hours.* (simple present perfect)
Or: ***I've been waiting** for two hours.* (present perfect progessive)
We say: ***I'd waited** for two hours before he arrived.* (simple past perfect)
Or: ***I'd been waiting** for two hours before he arrived.* (past perfect progressive)

3 Repeated actions:
present perfect progressive: ***He's been phoning** every night for a month.*
past perfect progressive: ***He'd been phoning** every night for a month.*

4 Drawing conclusions:
present perfect progressive: *Her eyes are red. It's clear **she's been crying**.*
past perfect progressive: *Her eyes were red. It was clear **she'd been crying**.*

Write: Supply the present perfect progressive or the past perfect progressive tenses. Show where both are possible.

1 I was tired. I *had been digging* .... all day. (dig)
2 We .... for your call all evening. (wait)
3 How long .... there? (you wait)
4 I .... there since 6 o'clock. (stand)
5 She .... English for five years before she visited Canada. (study)
6 It started raining last Monday and it .... ever since. (rain)
7 I .... to the firm regularly for a month before, but they still hadn't answered. (write)
8 They .... me about it every day for the past week. (ring)
9 I knew you .... – How did you know? – Your hair was covered with paint! (paint)
10 You were out of breath when you came in this morning. ....? (you run)

9.6C The simple past perfect and past perfect progressive compared
[> LEG 9.34]

Study:
★★

> The past perfect progressive can tell us that an action was uncompleted *then*:
> *When I got home, I found that **Jill had been painting** her room.* [compare > 9.5C]
> The simple past perfect can tell us that an action was completed *then*:
> *When I got home, I found that **Jill had painted** her room.*

Write: Supply the simple past perfect or the past perfect progressive.
had been cooking
1 We .... all day for the party that evening and by 8 o'clock we still weren't ready. (cook)
2 John .... a beautiful meal for his guests and they all enjoyed it. (prepare)
3 I knew she .... the washing because the machine was still working when I got in. (do)
4 I knew she .... the washing because when I got in she was ready to go out. (do)
5 By 10 o'clock the children .... their homework and were ready to go to bed. (do)
6 The children .... their homework and by 10 o'clock they still hadn't finished. (do)

9.6D Context

Write: Put in the past perfect simple or progressive or the simple past. Give alternatives where possible.

COOKING THE BOOKS?
Old Mr Williams was very concerned. He and his wife were pensioners and he (*spend*) [1] *had spent* the whole morning looking for their pension books. He (*look*) [2] .... everywhere, but he (*not be able*) [3] .... to find them. Meanwhile, his wife (*be*) [4] .... busy. She (*cook*) [5] .... all morning. She (*prepare*) [6] .... a delicious meal. She (*make*) [7] .... soup, followed by a lovely pie, which she (*bake*) [8] .... in the oven. Mr Williams (*always enjoy*) [9] .... his food, but he clearly wasn't enjoying his lunch. 'What's the matter, Tom?' his wife asked. Mr Williams (*have to*) [10] .... confess that he (*lost*) [11] .... their pension books. 'I know,' Mrs Williams (*say*) [12] ...., with a twinkle in her eye. 'I've got them'. 'You've got them?' 'Yes – and guess where I (*find*) [13] .... them!' Mr Williams suddenly remembered. 'In the oven! I (*put*) [14] .... them there for safe-keeping.' He (*smile*) [15] .... with relief as she (*fish*) [16] .... them out of her apron pocket!

He wasn't enjoying his lunch

133

9.7 The simple future tense

9.7A Some uses of 'will' and 'shall' [> LEG 9.37, 11.23, 11.38-40, 11.73]

Study:
★★

> **1** *Will* and *shall* are 'modal verbs', so they are like *can, must*, etc. [> Chapter 11].
>
> **2** We often use *will* and *shall* to make predictions (**the simple future tense**):
> *It **will rain** tomorrow. I don't know if I **shall see** you next week.*
>
> **3** We use *will* and *shall* in many other ways, apart from predicting the future: e.g.
> – intentions/promises [> 9.8A]: ***I'll** (= I will) **buy** you a bicycle for your birthday.*
> – requests/invitations [> 11.6D]: ***Will you hold** the door open for me, please?*
> – offers [> 11.6E]: ***Shall I get** your coat for you?*
> – suggestions [> 11.6F]: ***Shall we go** for a swim tomorrow?*
> – threats: *Just wait! **You'll regret** this!*
> – decisions [> 9.9A]: ***I'll stop** and ask the way.*

Write: Match the sentences on the left with the functions on the right.

A
1 We'll have a thunderstorm tonight, I'm sure. *d*
2 Will there be a general strike? __
3 I'll send you a card from Florida. __
4 Will you write to me? __
5 Shall I go to the post office for you? __
6 Shall we take a drive into the country later? __
7 I'll report you to the police next time. __
8 The wedding will take place next Friday. __
9 I hope you'll come and see us again. __
10 Tell them again. Perhaps they'll understand. __
11 Will you have lunch with us on Sunday? __
12 I'll be seeing John at the meeting tomorrow. __

B
a) making a formal announcement
b) making a request
c) stating a planned arrangement
d) making a prediction
e) making an invitation
f) asking for a prediction
g) promising/stating intention
h) expressing future hope
i) expressing future uncertainty
j) threatening
k) offering
l) making a suggestion

9.7B 'Will' and 'shall' to refer to the future [> LEG 9.35-37]

Study:
★★

> **Forms of 'will' and 'shall'**
> **1** When we are referring to the future, we use *will* with all persons (*I, you, he, she*, etc.), but in British English, we often use *shall* with *I/we*. (Not **he/she/it/you/they shall**):
> *I/We will (I'll/We'll) see you tomorrow.* Or: **I shall/We shall** *see you tomorrow.*
> **2** In speech, we weaken *shall* to /ʃəl/. We often use *'ll* in place of *will* in speech and sometimes in writing, especially after vowels: ***I'll/He'll** see you tomorrow.*
> We also use *'ll* after consonants: ***Tom'll** be here soon. **When'll** I see you?*
> **3** Negative short forms are: *'ll not, won't* (= will not) or *shan't* (= shall not):
> ***I'll not** be there/**I won't** be there/**I shan't** be there tomorrow.*
> In American English *shall* and *shan't* with a future reference are rare.
>
> **Uses of the 'will/shall' future**
> **1** Prediction: We invite prediction or we say what we think will happen:
> *Who **will win** on Saturday? Tottenham **will win** on Saturday.*
> **2** In formal style we say what will happen for events that have been arranged:
> *The wedding **will take place** at St Andrew's on June 27th.*
> **3** We use *shall* and *will* to express hopes and expectations:
> *I **hope she'll** get the job she's applied for. She'll get a surprise. – **I expect she will**.*

Write: Supply suitable forms of *will* and *shall*. Give alternatives where possible.
Situation: Jim is asking his friend Don for advice about a job interview.

JIM: What sorts of questions do you think they ¹ .....*'ll/will*..... ask?
DON: The same as they asked me. They ² .... ask you why you want to work for them.
JIM: That's easy. I want to earn more money.
DON: Yes, but you can't say that. You ³ .... have to think of some better reasons.
JIM: I can't think of any just now, but I expect I ⁴ .... think of something at the time. I hope I ⁵ .... anyway!
DON: I'm sure you ⁶ .... What time is your interview?
JIM: It's at three in the afternoon.
DON: I know it ⁷ .... help very much, but I ⁸ .... be thinking of you. Don't worry, everything ⁹ .... be OK!
JIM: When ¹⁰ .... I know if I've got the job?
DON: They ¹¹ .... let you know in a couple of days. That's what happened in my case. You ¹² .... get a letter which begins, 'We regret to inform you – !'

9.7C Context

Write: Put in suitable forms of *will* and *shall*.

RETIREMENT
I'm going to retire next week and I'm looking forward to it. For the first time in my life I ¹ .....*shall*.... be able to do all the things I've always wanted to do. I ² .... (*not*) have to travel to work any more. I ³ .... (*not*) have to earn a living. My firm ⁴ .... pay my pension into my bank account and I ⁵ .... (*not*) have to worry about earning money ever again. My wife and I ⁶ .... be able to spend more time together. We ⁷ ,................... take care of the house together. We ⁸ .... do the shopping together. I explained all these plans to my wife. 'Of course,' she said. 'I'm looking forward to your retirement, too, but you must remember that while you can retire, I can't. I've written out some simple rules for us both which ⁹ .... apply from the day you retire. Here they are:'

RULES OF THE HOUSE
1 We ¹⁰ .... take turns to do the cooking and the housework.
2 We ¹¹ .... (not) watch TV all day long.
3 We ¹² .... keep regular hours.
4 We ¹³ .... find interesting hobbies to keep us occupied.
5 We ¹⁴ .... spend time out of the house as well as in it.
6 We ¹⁵ .... keep fit in mind and body.

'They look like sensible suggestions,' I said. 'They are,' my wife answered. 'If we follow these rules I'm sure we ¹⁶ .... enjoy a long and happy life together.' 'I hope we ¹⁷ .... ,' I answered.

If we follow these rules ...

9.8   The simple future, the future progressive, the future perfect

9.8A   Simple future 'I will work' and progressive 'I will be working' compared
[> LEG 9.40-41]

Study:
★★

> There are three basic uses of the **future progressive**:
>
> **1** We use it to emphasize actions that will be in progress in the near or distant future, especially when we imagine ourselves doing something:
> *By this time tomorrow,* **I'll be lying** *on the beach.* (Not **I will lie**)
>
> **2** The progressive 'softens' the effect of *will* + verb and sounds more polite:
> *When will* **you finish** *these letters?* (e.g. boss to assistant)
> *When* **will you be seeing** *Mr White?* (e.g. assistant to boss)
> *If we say* **I'll work** *on this tomorrow we may be stating an intention.*
> *If we say* **I'll be working** *on this tomorrow, we are simply referring to future time.*
>
> **3** We use the future progressive like the present progressive for planned actions [> 9.2B]:
> **We'll be spending** *the winter in Australia* is the same as:
> **We're spending** *the winter in Australia.*

Write 1:   Supply *will* + verb or *will be* + *-ing*. Where both are possible, see if you can 'feel' the different effect of the simple future compared with the progressive.

1 Sit down and fasten your seat belt. We *will take off* in a few minutes. (take off)
2 When .... to the bank to draw some money? (you go)
3 Do you think you .... here in five years' time? (still work)
4 They .... from Dover, not Folkestone. (sail)
5 The President .... the Prime Minister before flying back home. (meet)
6 So you're stopping off in Dubai on your way to Beijing. How long .... there? (you stay)
7 We .... to London next Monday morning. (drive)
8 By this time next year, I .... my memoirs. (write)
9 In five years' time a permanent space station .... the moon. (circle)
10 I don't think I .... him tonight. (see)

Write 2:   Supply *will* + verb or *will be* + *-ing* – whichever 'feels' appropriate in this dialogue.
Situation: Susan and her family will be setting out on holiday tomorrow morning.

MEG: So you're off on holiday tomorrow. How exciting! What time (*you leave*) [1] *...will you be leaving...*?
SUE: We (*leave*) [2] .... the house at about 6 a.m.
MEG: 6 a.m.! Why so early? You don't have to check in till 9.45. You (*arrive*) [3] .... at the airport terribly early!
SUE: I know, but the airport is very busy at this time of the year and we want to avoid the rush. We (*check in*) [4] .... as quickly as we can, then we (*have*) [5] .... breakfast at the cafeteria.
MEG: I'm sure that's wise of you. Imagine! By this time tomorrow evening you (*lie*) [6] .... on the beach and I (*do*) [7] .... the ironing or something!
SUE: I hope you're right! I hope we (*not sit around*) [8] .... at the airport. You never know these days!

9.8B The future perfect simple and the future perfect progressive tenses
[> LEG 9.43-44]

Study:
★★

> 1 We often use the **future perfect simple** with *by* and *not ...till/until* [> 7.3B] to show that an action will already be completed by a certain time in the future.
> We use it with verbs which point to completion, like *complete, finish* and *retire*:
> I **will have retired** by the year 2020. I **won't have retired** till the year 2020.
>
> 2 We often use the **future perfect progressive** with verbs like *learn, lie, live, rain, sit, wait* and *work* which naturally suggest continuity [> 7.3B, 9.5B, 9.6B] to say that what is in progress now will be in progress in the future:
> By this time next week, I **will have been working** on this book for a year.

Write: Supply the future perfect simple or progressive. Note where both are possible.

1 They .....*will have completed*...... the new bridge by the end of the year. (complete)
2 By the end of this week, I .... seventeen weeks for my phone to be repaired. (wait)
3 Do you realize that on August 15, we .... in this house for fifty years? (live)
4 I hope I .... this report by the end of the day. (finish)
5 She .... for work before the children get home from school. (leave)
6 We .... non-stop for fourteen hours before we get to Calcutta. (fly)
7 They .... work on the great dam by the end of this decade. (complete)
8 Radio waves from earth .... for light years before anyone picks them up. (travel)

9.8C Context

Write: Put in the simple future, the future progressive or the future perfect simple.

FLYING JUNK
By the middle of the 21st century we (*build*) [1] .....*will have built*...... space stations which (*circle*) [2] .... the earth and (*probably circle*) [3] .... the moon, too. We (*establish*) [4] .... bases on planets like Mars. At present, we use radar to 'watch' nearly 8,000 objects in space. In addition, there are at least 30,000 bits of rubbish from the size of marbles to the size of basket balls flying round the earth. These (*increase*) [5] .... in number by the year 2050 and (*orbit*) [6] .... the earth. All these bits and pieces are watched by NORAD (North American Radar Defence Command). NORAD (*have*) [7] .... more and more rubbish to watch as the years go by. Some bits fall back to earth, like the Russian satellite C954, which crashed in the Northern Territories of Canada in 1978. Crashing junk could give us a bad headache. Most of the stuff (*stay*) [8] .... up there (we hope)! The sad fact is that we who are alive today (*not clear up*) [9] .... our own junk tomorrow. Perhaps we (*just watch*) [10] .... from some other (safe) place as it goes round and round the earth!

Perhaps we'll be watching ...

137

9.9 'Going to' and other ways of expressing the future

9.9A Uses of the 'going to'-future compared with 'will' [> LEG 9.44-46]

Study:
★★

There are three basic uses of the **'going to'-future**:

1 Predictions: We often use *going to* to predict the future, especially when we can see something that is about to happen: *Look out!* **She's going** *to faint.* (Not **will**)
Or we can describe something which we know will take place in the future:
Angus and Margaret **are going to** *be married in May.*

2 Intentions: We often use *going to* rather than *will* in informal style:
I'm going to *practice the piano for two hours this evening.*
I'm going to *be successful one day.*

3 Planned actions: We use *going to* like the present progressive or future progressive:
We're going to spend *the winter in Australia.*
Or: **We're spending** *the winter in Australia.* [> 9.2B]
Or: **We'll be spending** *the winter in Australia.* [> 9.8A]

4 We use *will* when we decide to do something at the moment of speaking:
We're lost. **I'll stop** *and ask the way.* (= I've just decided to do this.)

Write: Supply *be going to* or *'ll* in this dialogue.
Situation: Mr Sims is driving. His wife is sitting beside him.

HE: Where (*we spend*) [1] *are we going to spend* the night?
SHE: Cardiff. I've booked us in at the Angel Hotel. Why do you ask?
HE: That's another thirty miles away. We (*run*) [2] .... out of petrol before we get there. I (*stop*) [3] .... at the next filling-station.
Half an hour later.
SHE: This road goes on forever.
HE: We (*get*) [4] .... stuck. The car's stopping. We (*have to*) [5] .... walk.
SHE: Come on then. Perhaps someone (*give*) [6] .... us a lift.
HE: Not a filling-station in sight and look at those black clouds. It (*rain*) [7] ....
SHE: Look! A car's coming. I (*wave*) [8] .... to the driver.
HE: Oh good!. He's slowing down. He (*stop*) [9] ....

9.9B 'am/is/are to', 'be about to', 'be due to' [> LEG 9.47-48]

Study:
★★

1 We use *to be to* for:
– formal arrangements/duties: *OPEC representatives* **are to meet** *in Geneva in May.*
– formal appointments/instructions: *Three tablets* **are to be taken** *twice a day.*
– prohibitions: *You're not to tell* him anything about our plans.

2 *to be about to* refers to the immediate future:
Look! The race **is** just **about to** *start.*

3 We often use *to be due to* to refer to timetables:
The plane **is due to** *land at 2.15.*

Write: Supply the correct forms of the verb phrases in brackets.

1 The conference delegates .... *are to* .... meet again later today. (to be to)
2 You .... take these new tablets four times a day. (to be to)
3 They .... open their instructions until midnight. (not to be to)
4 You'll have to hurry. The train .... leave. (to be (just) about to)
5 I can't talk now. I .... go out. (to be (just) about to)
6 There's not much longer to wait. Their plane .... land in ten minutes. (to be due to)
7 Don't be so impatient. She is .... arrive until teatime. (not to be due to)

9.9C The future-in-the-past [> LEG 9.49-50]

Study:
★★

> Sometimes we want to refer to events which were 'destined' or planned to take place in the past ('the future-in-the-past'). We use *was going to, was about to, was to* and *was due to*. We use these forms for:
> – events we couldn't foresee: *They didn't know they **were to be reunited** ten years later.*
> – events which were interrupted: *We **were just going to leave**, when Jean had an accident.*
> We also use *would* for 'destiny' in story-telling:
> *They had already reached 9,000 feet. Soon they **would reach** the top.*

Write: Supply suitable 'future-in-the-past' forms.

1 I .... *was to* .... meet them at the station at 4, but I was held up in the traffic.
2 She .... phone later, but she must have completely forgotten.
3 She was still young. She didn't realize she .... be world famous before she was 20.
4 He thought his life's work was finished. He didn't know he .... win the Nobel Prize.
5 The plane .... take off at 4.25, but it was delayed.

9.9D Context

Write: Supply suitable future forms (*will, going to*, etc.). Alternatives are possible.

THE ADVENTURES OF ORLIK
The plane had been privately hired to transport Orlik the bull from one part of the country to the other. 'What (*do*) [1]*are we to do* with him, sir?' the co-pilot asked. 'We (*deliver*) [2]........................ him to a farm in Wales,' the captain said. 'I (*just check*) [3]........................ the wooden crate,' the co-pilot said. A few minutes later, he reported that it looked safe. 'I've just heard from Ground Control,' the pilot said. 'Our flight (*be*) [4]........................ due in ten minutes. We (*take off*) [5]........................ from Runway Number 7.' Little did both men know how dramatic their flight (*be*) [6]........................ They couldn't have imagined that when they were in the air, Orlik the bull (*break*) [7]........................ loose from his crate and smash his way into the flight cabin! 'I (*take over*) [8]........................, sir!' the co-pilot cried as the captain grabbed Orlik's nose-ring and pulled him away. The co-pilot made an emergency landing in a field. Both men jumped to safety, while Orlik crashed about inside the tiny plane, smashing everything to pieces!

Orlik the bull

9.10 The imperative

9.10A Some uses of the imperative to express different functions [> LEG 9.51-2]

Study:
⭐

1 We don't use the imperative just for 'giving orders'. We can use it e.g. for:
  – offering: ***Have*** *another sandwich.*   – prohibiting: ***Do not walk*** *on the grass.*
  – directing: ***Take*** *the next turning left.*   – warning: ***Look out!*** *A bus is coming!*

2 We can make an imperative more polite or more urgent with *Do*. Compare:
  – ordinary imperative: ***Help*** *yourself!*
  – polite imperative: ***Do help*** *yourself!*
  – negative imperative: ***Don't help*** *yourself!*

Write: Make these imperatives more polite or more urgent.

1 Have a cup of coffee. ...*Do have a cup of coffee.*...........
2 Make yourself at home. ....
3 Stop talking! ....
4 Hurry! ....
5 Try and ring us. ....
6 Help me with this letter. ....

9.10B The imperative to address particular people [> LEG 9.54]

Study:
⭐⭐

1 When we say e.g. *Wait here!* we might be addressing one person or several. We are really saying '*You* (singular or plural) *wait here!*'

2 If we want to speak to someone in particular, we can:
  – add *you* (unstressed) for an instruction: ***You wait*** *here for a moment.* (= I want you to)
  – add *you* (stressed) to express annoyance: '***You keep*** *quiet!*
  – use *you* with (or without) a name: ***You wait*** *here, Henry.* Or: ***Henry, you wait*** *here.*
  – add *yourself/yourselves* to verbs like *help, enjoy, behave:* ***Help yourself!***

3 If we are talking to groups of people, we can use the imperative with:
  – *everybody:*   ***Everybody keep*** *quiet.* ***Keep*** *quiet,* ***everybody***.
  – *somebody/nobody:*   ***Somebody answer*** *the phone!* ***Nobody say*** *a word!*
  – *Don't .. anybody:*   ***Don't say*** *a word,* ***anybody!*** ***Don't anybody say*** *a word!*

Write: Write these imperatives again to address particular people. Alternatives are possible.

1 Enjoy ...*Enjoy yourself / Enjoy yourselves*..........
2 Try teaching 40 noisy children every day! ....
3 Make the coffee today! (Meg) ....
4 Turn off that TV! ....
5 Don't turn the lights on! ....
6 Carry this case! (John) ....
7 Sit down! ....
8 Have a short break! ....
9 Don't move! ....
10 (John) Post these letters! ....
11 Don't listen to her! ....
12 Enjoy .... (children)!

9.10C The imperative with question tags [> LEG 9.55]

Study:
★★★

> We can make a request [> 11.6D] by adding a 'tag' like *will you?* to an imperative:
> 1 We add *will you?/won't you?/can't you?* to express annoyance: **Stop** shouting, **will you**?
> 2 We add *would you?/could/can you?* for neutral requests: **Post** this for me, **would you**?
> 3 We add *will you?/won't you?* for friendly offers: **Take** a seat, **will you**?
> We show our feelings not just by adding a tag, but through stress and intonation.

Write: Rewrite each request as an imperative + tag.

1 Will you stop whistling? .....*Stop whistling, will you?*.....
2 Can't you do something useful? ....
3 Won't you stop asking questions? ....
4 Could you post this letter? ....
5 Would you hold this bag? ....
6 Can you get me some stamps? ....
7 Won't you come in? ....
8 Will you take a seat? ....

9.10D Double imperatives joined by 'and' [> LEG 9.56]

Study:
★★

> When we have two imperatives together, we join them with *and* (Not **to**):
> **Go and buy** yourself a new pair of shoes. (Not **Go to buy**)
> The only exception is *try*. We can say: **Try and help** or **Try to help**.

Write: Write double imperatives joined by *and* with the following.

1 Come/see .....*Come and see us soon.*.....   3 Sit here/wait ....
2 Try/lift it ....   4 Wait/see ....

9.10E Context

Write: Put in the missing imperatives.

| ASK | AVOID | COME AND ASK | DO | KEEP | MIND | THINK! | DON'T WASTE |

The kitchen sink

THINK!
It's a case of [1].........*DO*......... AS YOU'RE TOLD in our company! I work for a small firm and my boss is so *bossy* that we all call him 'Napoleon'. He doesn't mind a bit. Wherever you look in our building there's a notice of some kind. The first thing you see when you arrive is [2]....................... OFF THE GRASS! You come into the building and see [3]....................... THE STEPS! The walls are covered with advice. IF IN DOUBT [4]....................... ME! [5]....................... MAKING MISTAKES! [6]....................... ME FIRST! [7]....................... TIME! We have learnt to ignore this advice, but lately notices have begun to appear in every part of the building. We have a small kitchen at the back where we make coffee. Yesterday there was a new notice over the kitchen sink. It said: [8]....................... I was pleased to see it wasn't long before someone added another notice under it which said THOAP!

10 Be, Have, Do

10.1 'Be' as a full verb (1)

10.1A Some uses of the imperative of 'be': 'Be careful!' [> LEG 10.1, 10.5, App 41]

Study:
★★

> 1 *Be* is a 'helping' (or auxiliary) verb when it 'helps' other verbs, for example to form the present or past progressive [> 9.2B, 9.4B]: *He **is** reading. He **was** sleeping.*
>
> 2 *Be* is a full verb when we use it with nouns (*She's **a teacher***) or adjectives (*She's **tall***).
>
> 3 *Be* + noun or adjective in the imperative has limited uses.
> We use *be* with nouns to mean 'act like': ***Be** a dear and answer the phone!*
> or to mean 'become': ***Be** a better cook!* or 'pretend to be': ***Be** a monster, granddad!*
> *Don't be* is more common: ***Don't be** silly! **Don't be** a fool!*
>
> 4 We use *be* only with adjectives that describe 'passing behaviour':
> ***Be** + careful, patient, quiet,* etc. ***Don't be** + careless, impatient, silly,* etc.
> But not with adjectives which describe 'states', like *hungry, thirsty, pretty.*

Write 1: Rephrase the words in italics using *be.*

1 *Act like* an angel and fetch my newspaper, please. ...*Be an angel!*........................
2 *Don't act like* a silly idiot! ....
3 The advertisement said: '*Become* the proud owner of a new sports car!' ....
4 *Don't become* a writer. You'll regret it. ....
5 You *play the part of* Batman and I'll *pretend to be* Robin. ....

Write 2: Using *(Do) be ...* or *Don't be ...*, what would you say to these people? Write two sentences for each, choosing from: *afraid, brave, careful, careless, critical, friendly, generous, mean, noisy, quiet.*

1 Some children who are making a lot of noise. ...*(Do) be quiet!*....................
2 Someone who has just broken a cup. ....
3 A friend who refuses to give any money to charity. ....
4 A friend who is always criticizing other people. ....
5 Someone who is afraid of going to the dentist. ....

10.1B The use of 'aren't' [> LEG 10.7n.3]

Study:
★★

> The full form *Am I not* is rare. We use *Aren't I ...?* (Not **Amn't I***) in:
> – negative questions: ***Am I not** late?* → ***Aren't I** late?*
> – negative Wh-questions: *Why **am I** not invited?* → *Why **aren't I** invited?*
> – negative question tag: *I'm late, **am I not**?* → *I'm late, **aren't I**?* [> 13.3]
> We use *aren't I* only in negative questions and negative question tags, never in negative statements: ***I am not** late.* → ***I'm not** late.* (Not **I aren't late***)

Write: Supply negative forms of *be.*

1 You ....*aren't*......... cold, are you?
2 I'm right, ... I?
3 You're American, ... you?
4 She's here already, ... she?
5 We're late again, ... we?
6 They're French, ... they?
7 He .... angry, was he?
8 You were early, ... you?

10.1C   'Be' in the simple present and simple past [> LEG 10.6-9]

Study:
★

> In the **simple present** and **simple past** we use *be* as a full verb with nouns and adjectives. Be careful of instances when English makes use of *be* where other languages sometimes don't. For example: *I am hungry* (Not **I have hunger**), *It's cold* (Not **It makes cold**)

Write: Supply *am, is, are, was, were* or *weren't*.

1   Her family name is now Jones, but it ..*was*.. Smith before she got married.
2   The name of the country .... previously Rhodesia, but it .... now Zimbabwe.
3   I .... hungry. – You can't be. We only had breakfast an hour ago.
4   It .... very cold and windy today, so wear a coat.
5   She .... a very nice woman, but her late husband .... a very unpleasant man.
6   This .... a beautiful blue dress. Buy it.
7   Today .... 23rd March: yesterday .... the 22nd.
8   I'm sure the twins .... 18 today: they .... 17 last year.
9   Whose .... these? – They .... Sue's, but she gave them to me, so they .... mine now.
10 Here, this book .... yours, and that one .... Jim's. They were both on the floor.
11 The other students .... here already. They .... all downstairs in the canteen.
12 The party .... next Saturday evening at Petra's house.
13 .... Mr James in? – No, I'm sorry, he .... here not long ago, but now he .... out.
14 .... Fred and Carmen at home when you called? – No, they ...., but they .... home now.
15 It .... quite foggy tonight, but it .... far worse last night.
16 It .... only 2 miles to the shops now. It .... 20 miles to any shops from our old house.
17 My ambition .... to start my own window-cleaning business, but it didn't work out.
18 Her dream .... to dance with the Royal Ballet Company.

10.1D   Context

Write: Put in the correct forms of the verb *be*. Use contracted forms (e.g. *I'm*) where you can.

... her class of five-year-olds

YOU TRY TEACHING FIVE-YEAR-OLDS!
Yesterday, it ¹....*was*.... Mrs Ray's first day at school with her class of five-year-olds.
MRS RAY: Now, you ².............. Liz, ³.............. you?
LIZ 1:   Yes, I ⁴.............. Liz
LIZ 2:   I'm Liz, too, ⁵.............. I?
MRS RAY: Yes. You ⁶.............. Liz, too. You ⁷.............. another Liz.
LIZ 2:   I ⁸.............. not Another Liz. I ⁹.............. Liz.
MRS RAY: Of course. Well, Liz, ¹⁰.............. a good girl and fetch some chalk from the cupboard.
BOY: ¹¹.............. careful! Don't drop it!
MRS RAY: What ¹².............. your name?
BOY: I ¹³.............. Don.
MRS RAY: Don ¹⁴.............. a nice name. What do you want to ¹⁵.............. when you grow up, Don?
DON: A racing driver. Brrrm, brrrm, brrrm ...!
MRS RAY: ¹⁶.............. yourself again! (Brrrm! Brrrm!) Stop it, Don, or I'll tickle you. ¹⁷.............. you ticklish?
DON: No, I ¹⁸.............. Scottish!

10.2 'Be' as a full verb (2)

10.2A Progressive forms of 'be' for 'temporary behaviour' [> LEG 10.10-11, App 41]

Study:
★★

> We use the progressive forms (*he is being/he was being*) with adjectives that describe 'passing behaviour' like *naughty* and *silly* [> 10.1A], not states, like *hungry* and *thirsty*. We often imply that this behaviour is deliberate: *He **is being naughty***. We can use the progressive of *be* with a few nouns as well: *He's **being a (silly) fool***.

Write: Tick the temporary behaviour in these sentences.

1 They're both being very greedy. ✓
2 They aren't normally greedy. __
3 You're being a nuisance. __
4 You aren't generally a nuisance. __
5 He was being very childish at the party. __
6 He isn't often childish at parties. __

10.2B 'Has been', 'have been', 'had been' + adjectives and nouns [> LEG 10.12-13]

Study:
★★

> The rules for the **present** and **past perfect** apply to *have been* and *had been* [> 9.5-6].
> The actions or states begin in the past and continue into the present (*have been*) or they refer to an earlier past (*had been*). We use *was/were* when we have a time reference:
> – behaviour/states/moods: *She**'s been** very **quiet**. I said she **had been** very **quiet**.*
> – the weather: *It**'s been** very **cold** lately. I said it **had been** very **cold** lately.*
> – professions, behaviour: ***Have** you ever **been a teacher**? She **has been a real angel**.*
> Compare: *The baby **was** very **quiet** while you were out.* (the past + exact time reference)

Write: Supply *has, have* or *had*.

1 Your brother *has* been very annoying.
2 How long ...:... you been a bus conductor?
3 I .... been terribly tired lately.
4 She said she .... never been seasick before.
5 It .... been a beautiful day, hasn't it?
6 She ...... been so good. She ...... been an angel!
7 You said you .... been a teacher.
8 I .... been a real fool.

10.2C 'Have been' and 'have gone' [> LEG 10.13.4]

Study:
★★

> 1 *Have been* and *has been* have the sense of 'visit a place and come back':
> *Where **have you been**? – **I've been home**.* (= and now I'm back)
>
> 2 *Have gone* and *has gone* have the sense of 'be at a place or on the way to a place':
> *Where's John? – **He's gone home**.* (= he's either there now or on his way there)
>
> 3 *Have been* and *have gone* combine with *to* + noun [> 8.2A]:
> ***I've been to** a party.* (= and I'm back) *John's **gone to** a party.* (= he's there/on his way)
> *Have been* combines with *at* and *in* [> 8.2A]: *I've **been at** a meeting. I've **been in** Paris.*
>
> 4 *Have been* and *have gone* combine with adverbs like *out* and *away*:
> ***I've been out/away**.* (= and I'm back) *John's **gone out/away**.* (= he's not here)
> and with *home*. (Not **gone/been to home** and not **to the** to mean 'my own home').
> Compare: *He's **been**/He's **gone** home.* (his own place) *He's **been to** the home of a friend.*

Write: Supply *have/has been* or *have/has gone*.

1 Isn't Jack here? – No, he *'s gone* home.
2 Where have you been? – I .... home.
3 The Smiths .... to Paris for the weekend and have just returned.
4 The Smiths .... to Paris for the weekend and are coming back on Monday.

5 It's nice to see you. I hear you .... away.
6 He doesn't live here. He .... away.
7 The boss won't be in the office till tomorrow. He .... to a meeting.
8 The boss wasn't here earlier, but he's back now. He .... at a meeting.

10.2D 'Have been' with 'since' and 'for' [> LEG 10.13.5]

Study:
★★

> We often use *How long ...?* with *have been* in questions and we use *since/for* in answers:
> 1 **How long have you been** a nurse? – **I've been** a nurse **for** nearly a year.
>   **I've been** a nurse **since** January. [> 7.3A, 9.5A]
>
> 2 *Have been* can have the following meanings [> 9.5B]:
>   – have lived/have been living: **I've been in this flat** for five years.
>   – have worked/have been working: Jane**'s been in the civil service** since she was 23.
>   – have waited/have been waiting: We**'ve been outside the bank** since 9.15.

Write: What do *have been* and *has been* mean in these sentences?

1 She's been in the waiting-room for over an hour. .... *She has been waiting* ....
2 I have been with this company for most of my life. ....
3 We have been in this district since 1982. ....
4 How long have we been under this clock? ....
5 How long has Silvia been with this publishing company? ....
6 How long has your brother been in Australia? ....

10.2E Context

Write: Put in *have been, have gone, has been, is being* or *were*.

IT'S BEEN A WONDERFUL EVENING!
This is what Angela wrote in her diary last night:
Mr and Mrs Lucas [1] .... *have gone* .... to the theatre. They
[2] .... away for two hours now and I [3] .... with
Jenny. This is the first time I [4] (*ever*) .... a baby-sitter and
I'm not finding it easy. Jenny is seven years old. She is very nice, but she
[5] .... a real nuisance. She won't stay in bed and she won't sit
still. I really don't know what to do.'
    This is what happened next:
Mr and Mrs Lucas [6] .... home at 11.30. The house was very
quiet and all the lights [7] .... on. Jenny was sitting on the
floor, playing with her toys. Her mother rushed up to her. 'Hullo, Jenny.' she
said. 'Are you all right? I hope you [8] (*not*) .... naughty.
Where's Angela?' 'She's sitting at the kitchen table,' Jenny answered. 'She
[9] .... asleep for the last two hours. She [10] .... a
very good girl. I've had a lovely time. It [11] .... a wonderful
evening!'

'I've had a lovely time'

10.3 'There' + 'be'

10.3A 'There' + 'be' as a 'natural choice' [> LEG 10.19]

Study:
⭐

1 We use *there is*, etc. (Not *it has* or *it is*) when we are talking about or asking about the existence of people, things, etc. It is more 'natural' to say:
There's a man at the door. than to say: *A man is at the door.*

2 We use *there is, there was, there will be, there has been/had been* when we want to:
– announce or report events: **There'll be** *a meeting tomorrow.* **There's been** *an accident.*
– set a scene for story-telling: **There had been** *no rain for months. The earth was bare.*

Write:
a Tick the sentences which sound more idiomatic or 'natural'.
b Rephrase the unticked sentences using *There*.

1 There are two men at the door. ✓ ....
2 A good clothes shop is not far from here. __ ... *There is a good clothes shop not far from here.*
3 There was an interesting article about that in yesterday's paper. __ ....
4 A photograph of that girl was in last week's magazine. __ ....
5 A new security system will be in operation from next week. __ ....
6 There'll be a lot of supporters at the match. __ ....
7 A public holiday is on May 1st. __ ....
8 A meeting between the two world leaders will be in Helsinki. __ ....

10.3B 'There is', etc. compared with 'it is', etc. [> LEG 10.20]

Study:
⭐⭐

First we show existence with *There is*, then we use personal pronouns (*he, she, it* or *they*) to give more details:
There was a concert *in our village last night.* ('existence')
It (= The concert) **was** *in the village hall.* ('more details')

Note how this happens in the following sentences:
There's a bus *coming, but* **it's** *full.*
There's a man *at the door.* **It's** *the postman.* [compare > 3.4A, 4.1A]
There's a man *at the door.* **He** *wants to speak to you.*
There are some children *at the door.* **They** *want to see Jimmy.*
There's a van *stopping outside.* **It's someone** *delivering something.*

Write: Supply *there* and a personal pronoun (*it, he, she* or *they*) in the blanks.

1 ...*There*... were a lot of people at the concert, and ...*they*... all enjoyed it.
2 ....'s a policewoman waiting to see you. ....'s in your office.
3 ....'s a parcel here for you. I think ....'s that book you've been waiting for.
4 ....'ll be a new boy in your class today. ....'s just arrived from Hong Kong.
5 .... has been a lot of argument about the plan. .... has all centred on traffic problems.
6 .... have been serious riots in this country. .... have all been about the price of food.
7 ....'s a review in today's paper of the film we saw last night. ....'s very favourable.
8 ....'s a dog in our garden. ....'s our next door neighbour's.
9 Is .... a route to the town centre from here and is .... more direct?
10 Are .... any applicants for the job and are .... suitable?

10.3C   Combinations with 'there' + 'be' [> LEG 10.17, 10.21-2, 11.76]

Study:
★★

1 *There is, there are, there was* and *there were* are the most common combinations:
   There's *a phone call for you.* **There was** *a phone call for you this morning.*

2 We also use *there* with different tenses, for example [compare > 11.13D]:
   perfect tenses: ***There has (there's) been*** *an accident.*
   He said ***there had (there'd) been*** *an accident.*
   There haven't been *many earthquakes in England.*
   future tenses: ***There will (there'll) be*** *a letter for me tomorrow.*
   There'll have been *an answer by Friday.*

3 *There* also combines with *seem to be* and *appear to be*:
   There seems to be *a mistake in our bill.* **There appears to be** *no one in.*

Write: Complete these sentences with the correct forms of *there + be* or *seem*.

1 ....*There was*..... an exhibition of Venetian glass last month.
2 .... days when I don't feel like going to work.
3 .... any letters for me today? – No, ... none. Oh, yes, sorry. .... some here.
4 .... anything I can do to help? – Yes, ... something. You can file those reports.
5 We'll have to rearrange the room. .... a lot more people here than we thought.
6 I've just driven down South Street. .... a terrible accident on the corner.
7 .... more jobs for everybody if more money is invested by large companies.
8 Where can I put these cherries? – .... my shopping bag. You can put them in there.
9 What did he say? – He said .... no news from Fred for months.
10 There's a big match on TV tonight, ...?
11 .... to be fewer teaspoons in the drawer than there should be.
12 .... to be less money in my pay packet than I had expected.

10.3D   Context

Write: Put in the correct combinations with *there* and *it*.

'I've never seen anything like this before'

WHERE TIME STOOD STILL
Miss Margaret White shut down her chemist's shop in the West of England in 1970, never to open it again. [1]*There had been*.. a chemist's shop in her family since the 19th century when [2] (*first*) ....
opened by her grandfather William. After Miss White's death, the auctioneers moved in. They couldn't believe their eyes. [3].................. an old-fashioned cash-register and [4].................. still old pennies in it. At the back of the shop [5].................. old medicine bottles covered with dust, and 127 little drawers. [6].................. full of herbal remedies. [7]................. unusual products like 'Allcocks Powder – Guaranteed Not to Contain Opium or Any Poison Whatsoever'. [8].................. a copy of a newspaper for April 16, 1912. [9].................. the issue that described the sinking of the Titanic. '[10] (*never*) .... anything like this before and [11] (*never*) .... again.' one of the auctioneers said.

10.4 Verbs related in meaning to 'be'

10.4A Certainty and uncertainty with 'be', 'seem', etc. [> LEG 10.23-24]

Study:
★★

1 These verbs have nearly the same meaning as *be*:
appear, feel, look, seem, smell, sound, taste, and also *chance/happen/prove to be*.

2 When we are certain about something, we use *be* or an ordinary verb:
He **is** ill. He **knows** the answer.

3 When we are uncertain about something, we can use 'modal verbs' [> 11.1C, 11.4]:
He **may/might/could be** ill. He **may/might/could know** the answer.
or we can use verbs related to *be*:

He **is** ill.	→	He **seems/appears** (to be) ill.
He **knows** the answer.	→	He **seems/appears to know** the answer.
He **was** rich.	→	He **seemed/appeared** (to be) rich.
He **is** working hard	→	He **seems/appears to be working** hard.
He **was working** hard.	→	He **seemed/appeared to be working** hard.
He **has been** hurt.	→	He **seems to have been/appears to have been** hurt.

Write: Rewrite these sentences using appropriate forms of *seem*.

1 They are very happy. ....*They seem (to be) very happy.*.................
2 He was a genius at maths. ....
3 She's finding the job difficult. ....
4 They were looking for something. ....
5 He's been knocked out. ....
6 It's very dark outside. ....
7 It's raining very hard outside. ....
8 My watch has stopped. ....

10.4B 'To be' or not 'to be'? [> LEG 10.25]

Study:
★★

1 We can leave out *to be* after *appear* and *seem* in the simple present and simple past:
He **appears/seems** (to be) **ill**. He **seemed** (to be) **a fool**.

2 We usually include *to be* before adjectives like *afraid, asleep* and *awake*:
They **seem to be** asleep. He **seems to be** afraid.

3 We cannot use *to be* after *feel, look, smell, sound* or *taste*:
He **feels hot**. You **look cold**. (Not *He feels to be hot.* *You look to be cold.*)

Write: Add *to be* where necessary in these sentences. Where you can't use *to be*, put a dash (-). Where *to be* is optional, put brackets (*to be*).

1 It seemed ....*(to be)*........................ a good idea at the time.
2 These things often appear .... a little strange.
3 All the old people seem .... asleep.
4 Doesn't he look .... stupid in that hat?
5 I think it feels .... quite hot in here.
6 That goulash smells .... good, doesn't it?
7 The choir sounded .... very good to me.
8 She seemed to me .... too young for the job.

10.4C   'Process verbs' related to 'be' and 'become' [> LEG 10.26]

Study:
★★

1   Process verbs describe a change in state: *When I asked him about it, **he grew angry**.*
Typical process verbs are: *become, come, fall, go, get, grow, run, turn, wear.*

2   The most common process verbs are *get, become* and *grow*:
*I'm **getting tired**. You're **becoming lazy**. It's **growing dark**.*
We often use other verbs in fixed phrases: e.g. *come true, fall ill, go bad, run dry, turn sour.*

3   We often use *get* + adjective: *get annoyed, get bored, get depressed, get ill, get wet.*

4   Nouns are not so common after process verbs, but note *become* and *make*:
*The ugly frog **became a handsome prince**. Cynthia will **make a good nurse** one day.*

Write: Supply suitable forms of verbs other than *be* in these sentences.

1   When I ......*grow*............................... old, I hope I'll have lots of grandchildren.
2   You must be very careful you don't .... ill when you're travelling.
3   I think this milk .... sour.
4   Food .... bad very quickly in hot weather.
5   It hasn't rained for months and our local river .... dry.
6   It's no good .... impatient every time I ask you a question. [> 16.7C]
7   She always wanted to retire before the age of 40 and her dream .... true.
8   I had to cut my trip short because I .... ill.
9   I must get these shoes repaired. The soles .... rather thin.
10   Don't you .... bored listening to political broadcasts?
11   My son is determined to .... a pilot when he grows up.
12   Personally, I think he'll .... a very good pilot.

10.4D   Context

Write: Put in *appeared, became, feel, got, looked, looks, proves, seemed, seems* or *smelt*.

This flower seizes anything

NOT AS INNOCENT AS IT SEEMS TO BE!
It was Katy's birthday last Thursday. Her husband, Paul, bought her a beautiful bouquet with what [1].....*seemed*..... to be an unusual flower as the centre piece. Katy was delighted with the flowers. They [2]........................ wonderful and [3]........................ wonderful, too. Katy [4]........................ very excited when she saw the beautiful flower in the centre of the bouquet. She bent over to smell it when it [5]........................ to punch her in the nose! Paul was amazed. He [6]........................ so interested in the flower that he took it to the botanical gardens at Kew to find out about it. An expert examined the flower and told him that it was a kind of orchid called a Cymbidium. This flower seizes anything that [7]........................ like an insect so that it will carry its pollen. If you try to smell it, the Cymbidium will try to grab your nose! So next time you [8]........................ like sniffing a rare orchid, hold your nose – just in case it [9]........................ to be a Cymbidium. It's not as innocent as it [10]........................ to be!

10.5 'Have' as a full verb = 'possess'; 'have got' = 'possess'

10.5A 'Have got' = 'own' and 'have got' = 'obtain' [> LEG 10.30]

Study:
★★

> 1 In British English, we often use *have* or *have got* to mean 'possess':
> *I **have** a new car. I **have got** a new car.* (= I own, I possess a new car)
>
> 2 In British English, we also use *have* (*just*) *got* (American English *have gotten*) as the normal present perfect form of the verb *get* to mean 'have obtained' or 'have received':
> *I've just got(ten) a letter from Pam.* (= I have just received)

Write: What does *have got* mean in these sentences? Tick the columns.

	'have received/obtained'	'possess/own'
1 I've just got a letter from Pam.	✓	—
2 I've got a black sweater.	—	—
3 They've got a villa near the beach.	—	—
4 They've just got a puppy.	—	—
5 Don't come near me. I've got a bad cold.	—	—
6 I think I've just got a cold!	—	—

10.5B Uses of 'have' and 'have got' to mean 'possess' [> LEG 10.30]

Study:
★★

> 1 We often use *have got* in place of *have* in the present:
> *I've got a good job. **Have you got** a good job? **I haven't got** a good job.*
>
> 2 *Do you have?* and *I don't have* are also common especially in American English:
> *Do you have a good job? I don't have a good job.*
>
> 3 We use the correct forms of *have*, not *have got*, in other tenses to mean 'possess':
> *I **have had** this car for three years. By June, I **will have had** this car for three years.*
>
> 4 In other tenses, *have got* means 'obtained':
> *When I saw him, he **had just got** a new car. By May I **will have got** a new car.*

Write: Replace the phrases in italics by a phrase with *have* or *have got*.
If you think it is possible to use *have* and *have got*, give two versions.

1 *They own* an apartment near the beach. ..... *They have./ They've got an apartment.* ....
2 *I don't possess* a party dress. ....
3 *Do you possess* a motorbike? ....
4 *My uncle owned* a Rolls Royce once. ....
5 *I've owned* this bike for five years. ....
6 *We'll possess* a new apartment soon. ....
7 *I will have owned* this suit for ten years by my next birthday. ....
8 She said *she had possessed* the car for some time. ....
9 That's a marvellous little invention. *I must own* one. ....
10 If he can't hear very well, *he should own* a hearing-aid. ....
11 *Does your brother possess* a bicycle? ....
12 *Will you own* this house one day? ....
13 *Have you owned* this house for a long time? ....
14 *Do you own* a car? ....

10.5C Common uses of 'have' and 'have got' [> LEG 10.31]

Study:
☆

> We can use *have* and *have got* to say we own or possess something (***I have/I've got** a car*).
> But note how we can extend this idea of 'possession':
> ***I have/I've got a good dentist. I have/I've got an appointment** at 4.30.* etc.

Write: Supply correct forms of *have* and *have got*. Give alternatives where possible.

1 *Have.* you *got....* a new car yet? *Do. you. have*
2 They .... a nice apartment. ....
3 .... you .... any spare pencils? ....
4 .... you .... today's newspaper? ....
5 She .... ten dresses. ....
6 He .... plenty of money. ....
7 He .... long black hair. ....
8 This tree .... red leaves in autumn. ....
9 I (not) .... any faith in him. ....
10 She (not) .... much patience. ....
11 How many sisters .... you ....? ....
12 They .... three sons. ....
13 I .... a good accountant. ....
14 We .... a very good butcher. ....
15 That's a smart suit he .... on. ....
16 What .... she .... on last night? ....
17 I .... a temperature, I think. ....
18 When .... you last .... a cold? ....
19 I .... a meeting in town today. ....
20 She .... a date tonight. ....
21 I .... no idea what to do. ....
22 .... you .... a better suggestion? ....
23 You .... mud on your shoes. ....
24 She .... something in her eye. ....

10.5D Context

Write: Put in the correct forms of *have* or *have got*.

Ole Ez

OLE EZ

I work as a journalist and today I was lucky [1].....*to have*... an interview with Ezra Pryme, the famous English eccentric. I say 'lucky', because Ole Ez (as the locals know him) [2]....................... (*not*) much time for the human race and he rarely [3]....................... visitors. Ole Ez Is very rich and he [4]....................... an immense country house with a large garden. He [5]....................... a large family, but he never sees any of his children or grandchildren. 'I [6]....................... (*not*) any time for them,' he says. Ole Ez [7]....................... the largest collection of Art Deco objects in the world, but he is the only one who ever sees them. I knocked at the door of the mansion at exactly 3 p.m. Ez's butler opened the door for me. I was led through a large hall which [8]....................... all sorts of paintings on the walls and then into a library. I waited for a while and at last a very short man appeared. He [9]....................... white hair and twinkling grey eyes. He [10]....................... a beautiful green velvet suit on and a pink bow tie. He also [11]....................... a smile on his face, which surprised me. As soon as he saw me, he held out his hand. Not expecting this, I hesitated for a moment. 'You can shake hands,' he said, 'I [12]....................... (*not*) any diseases! Mind the steps!' he cried, leading me down some steep steps. 'I don't say that to all my visitors, you know!'

10.6 'Have' as a full verb meaning 'eat', 'enjoy', etc.

10.6A 'Have' (= 'eat', 'enjoy', etc.) compared with 'have' (= 'possess')
[> LEG 10.32-36, App 42.1]

Study:
★★

1 *Have* can mean 'eat, enjoy, experience, drink, take', etc. In these senses, we use *have* like any other verb, in all tenses, including the progressive:
I'm having a drink. (= I'm drinking something at the moment)
By comparison, *have* meaning 'possess' does not have progressive forms [> 9.1C]:
I have a drink. I have got a drink. (= e.g. I have one in my hand)
I have a car. I have got a car. (Not *I'm having a car.*)

2 In the simple present and simple past of *have* (= eat, etc.), we use *do, does* and *did* to form questions and negatives:
Do you have milk in your tea? (= Do you take ...?)
Compare: ***Have you/Do you have/Have you got** any milk in your tea?* (= Is there any?)

3 Note how *have* can be both an auxiliary and a full verb in:
I have had my lunch. (= I have eaten)
He said he had had his lunch. (= He said he had eaten)

Write 1: Replace the words in brackets by a suitable phrase with *have got* or *have*.

1 (Do you take) sugar in your coffee? ...*Do you have*......
2 (There are) some beautiful fir trees in their garden. ....
3 (We own) a new apartment. ....
4 (She takes) a hot bath the moment she comes home from work. ....
5 Would you like a coffee? – No, thanks. (I've just drunk) one. ....
6 (We enjoyed) a very pleasant evening with them. ....
7 (She's suffering from) a very bad cold. ....
8 (I receive) a letter from them about once a year. ....
9 (I don't often eat) breakfast. ....
10 (Are there) any large envelopes in your drawer? ....
11 They told me (they had enjoyed) a pleasant holiday. ....
12 What (did you eat) for breakfast this morning? ....

Write 2: Supply the correct forms of *have* in these sentences.

1 Please help yourself. ......*Have*......... another sandwich.
2 She never .... milk in her coffee.
3 Where's John? – Oh, he .... a long talk with Simon in the garden.
4 I .... a lovely cycle ride in the country last Sunday.
5 We .... dinner when a salesman came to the door.
6 I .... a lot of bad luck recently.
7 She .... German lessons for about two years now.
8 He .... already .... interviews for two other jobs before he came to see me.
9 She .... trouble with her back before she went to see a specialist.
10 Don't phone between 6 and 7. I .... a rest then.
11 They .... supper if you don't get there before eight o'clock.
12 By August he .... 25 years with this company.

10.6B   Common 'have' + noun combinations [> LEG 10.37-39, App 42.1]

Study:
★★

> 1 *Have* combines with many nouns: *Let's **have lunch**! I've had a good trip*, etc.
>   We often use it in the imperative: ***Have** a sandwich! **Have** a good time!*
>
> 2 In place of common verbs like *to sleep* or *to swim*, we often prefer to use *have* + noun:
>   Instead of: *I **danced twice** with Molly*. We can say: *I **had two dances** with Molly*.

Write 1:   Make good sentences with *have* + the words in brackets.

1 (a meal) .... *We had an awful meal at the Station Hotel.* ....
2 (a dream) ....
3 (a haircut) ....
4 (an appointment) ....
5 (a good trip) ....
6 (a lovely day) ....
7 (a pain) ....
8 (a sense of humour) ....

Write 2:   Rewrite these sentences with *have*.

1 Those twins are always fighting. .... *Those twins are always having fights* ....
2 Look at this! ....
3 I want to rest this afternoon. ....
4 Can I ride in your car? ....
5 I talked to Jim about it. ....
6 Come and swim with us. ....
7 I must wash before lunch. ....
8 Sleep and you'll feel better. ....

10.6C   Context

Write: Put in the correct forms of *have got* or *have*.

NOT A MAN OF STRAW!
Our neighbour, Mr French, [1] .... *has (got)* ... a very large farm and he
[2] .... trouble with birds all his life. Birds eat his vegetable crops
and cost him a lot of money, so Mr French has just bought a computerized
scarecrow called Worzel. Worzel is more than two metres tall and [3] ....
.... four legs. He [4] .... a round head and arms that swing
from right to left. '[5] .... Worzel .... any success?' I
asked Mr French recently as I watched him [6] .... a walk in a
vegetable field. 'He [7] .... a tremendous effect on birds,' Mr
French said. 'Come and [8] .... a look at him. An ordinary
scarecrow [9] .... a head full of straw, but Worzel [10] ....
a brain!' Just then I heard a loud moan and saw a blinding flash. 'You
[11] (*not*) .... a dream,' Mr French said. 'He does this to frighten
the birds!' Of course, there wasn't a bird in sight! 'I must leave now, Mr
French,' I said as I saw Worzel coming towards me. 'I [12] .... an
appointment.' 'He's harmless,' Mr French said, but I wasn't going to wait to
find out!

I saw Worzel coming towards me!

153

10.7 'Do' as a full verb

10.7A Forms and uses of 'do' as an auxiliary and as a full verb [> LEG 10.40-44]

Study:
★★

> 1 We use *do* as an auxiliary verb to form questions and negatives in the simple present and simple past tenses: ***Do** you **like** Italian opera?* etc. [> 13.1]
>
> 2 *Do* is also a full verb meaning 'perform an activity or task'. We use it like any other verb in all tenses. This means *do* can be auxiliary verb and full verb at the same time:
> *What **did** (auxiliary) you **do** (full verb) this morning? – I **wrote** a lot of letters.*
>
> 3 We often use *do* to avoid repeating a previous verb:
> *The washing machine often **stops** suddenly. I don't know why it **does** that.*
>
> 4 *Do* can also mean 'be in the wrong place' in: *What are these clothes **doing** on the floor?*
>
> 5 We often use *do + -ing* for 'named tasks': *I've just **done the ironing**.*

Write 1: Match the phrases in column A with the phrases in column B.

A	B
1 Do *l*	a) the same job for thirty years!
2 She always does __	b) the job by the time I get back?
3 Are you still doing __	c) 140 kilometres an hour.
4 I did __	d) a great favour for me.
5 They were still doing __	e) this time tomorrow?
6 He's just done __	f) all the ironing by the time Sue came home.
7 He's been doing __	g) the cleaning on Thursday.
8 John had done __	h) quite a few little jobs yesterday.
9 She had been doing __	i) the same job for ten years by next month.
10 This car will do __	j) the same job?
11 What will you be doing __	k) the housework when their guests arrived.
12 Will you have done __	l) this exercise now, please.
13 I will have been doing __	m) the gardening for an hour when she remembered she should have been at the bank.

Write 2: Supply the correct forms of *do* in the sentences below.

1 What ...*are you doing?*...? – What does it look like? I'm reading the paper.
2 She loves cooking, but she (never washes up) ....
3 Shall I make the beds? – No, ... that. Dust the furniture first.
4 What (that flowerpot/do) .... in the kitchen sink?
5 A lot of people in Britain (wash their clothes) .... on Mondays.
6 Cut the grass first. Then, when .... that, start weeding the flower beds.
7 Whatever business he's in, he always makes a success of it. How .... it?
8 It's a shame (he doesn't read) ....
9 What ....? – I've just reversed the car into the garage door!
10 What (those suitcases/do) .... in the entrance hall?
11 What have you been doing all afternoon? – I (do/a bit of gardening) ....
12 What (that car/do) .... in the middle of the motorway?
13 Phone your mother. – I (already/so) ....

10.7B   'Do' and 'make' compared [> LEG 10.45, App 43]

Study:
★★

1 *Do* often means 'be engaged in an activity'; *make* has the sense of 'create':
*What are you **doing**? – I'm **making** a cake. What are you **making**? – A cake.*

2 We often use *do* and *make* in 'fixed phrases'. *Do* and *make* go with particular nouns:

do + :   (me) a favour, damage, good, no good, harm, the housework, a lesson, justice,
one's teeth (= clean).

make + :   an accusation, an agreement, a demand, a loss, a mess, a mistake, a promise,
a proposal.

3 Sometimes both *make* and *do* are possible:
*I'll **make**/I'll **do** the beds this morning, if you like.*

Write:
a Put *do* or *make* in front of these words.
b Then write sentences using these phrases with correct tenses.

..*Do*.. one's best; .... an appointment; .... business with someone; .... an experiment;
.... an arrangement; .... research; .... one's hair; .... an attempt;
.... a noise; .... something for a living; .... progress; .... an impression;
.... somebody a service; .... a journey; .... a fortune; .... war.

1 *You should always try to do your best.*   9 ....
2 ....   10 ....
3 ....   11 ....
4 ....   12 ....
5 ....   13 ....
6 ....   14 ....
7 ....   15 ....
8 ....   16 ....

10.7C   Context

Write: Put in the correct forms of *do* or *make*.

Meet the wolfman!

JUST HAIR-RAISING!
Last Saturday I [1] .....*did*....... a few jobs round the house and then decided
to go into the town. 'Shall I take the dog for a walk?' I asked my wife. 'No,
[2] ....,' she answered. 'I'll [3] .... that. You can [4] ....
some shopping for me.' I got the shopping [5] .... quickly and then
[6] .... a sudden decision to have a haircut. My barber was as
cheerful as ever. 'The usual?' he asked. 'I don't have much choice,' I said.
'Do you know,' my barber said, 'that scientists have been [7] ....
experiments with a new kind of product which will [8] .... miracles? It
will even grow hair on a head as bald as yours. It's called minoxidil.' 'You'll
[9] .... a lot of money,' I said. He ignored me. 'All you have to
[10] .... is rub it into your scalp.' 'That's hair-raising news!' I said. 'But
what happens if hair grows on my fingertips instead?' 'Meet the wolfman!'
my barber said.

155

11 Modal auxiliaries and related verbs

11.1 The two uses of modal verbs

11.1A The first use of modal verbs (1) [> LEG 11.1-2]

Study:
★★

1 Verbs like *can* and *may* are **modal auxiliaries**. We often refer to them as **modal verbs** or just **modals**. We use them with other verbs [> 16.1A], for example, to ask for permission:
Can I use your phone, please? ***May I borrow*** your car, please?
There are ten modals: *can, could, may, might, will, would, shall, should, must, ought to* and three 'semi-modals': *need, dare* and *used to*.

2 In their **first use**, modal verbs have basic meanings which are given in dictionaries:
– *can/could* (= ability):   ***I can lift*** 25 kg./***I can type***.
– *may/might* (= permission):   You ***may leave*** early.
– *will/would* (= prediction): It ***will rain*** soon. [> 9.7]
– *shall* after *I/We* (= prediction): ***Will we find*** our way? – I'm sure ***we shall***.
– *should/ought to* (= duty):   You ***should do*** as you're told.
– *must* (= total obligation): You ***must be*** quiet.
– *needn't* (= no obligation): You ***needn't wait***.

Write: What do these sentences express? Match A and B.

A
1 I can type twenty-five words a minute. _c_
2 You should do as you're told. ___
3 You needn't wait. ___
4 It will rain soon. ___
5 You may leave now if you want to. ___
6 You must be quiet. ___

B
a) prediction
b) permission
c) ability
d) no obligation
e) total obligation
f) duty

11.1B The first use of modal verbs (2) [> LEG 11.4, 11.6.1]

Study:
★★

1 Modal verbs are not 'complete verbs'. For example, we use verbs like *must* and *can* to refer only to the present or the future:
*I **must go** to the bank **now**. I **must go** to the bank **tomorrow**.*
This means we have to make up the 'missing parts' of *must* with *have to*.
So if we want to express the past of *must*, we say: *I **had to go** to the bank yesterday*.
In the same way, we use *be able to* to make up the 'missing parts' of *can* [> 11.2A,C].

2 Other important points about modal verbs:
We can't use them as *to*-infinitives: *I want **to be able to** type very fast*. (Not **to can*)
We do not use the *to*-infinitive after modals: *You **must/mustn't phone***. (Not **to phone*) [> 16.1A]
There's no *-(e)s* in the 3rd person singular: *The boss **can see** you now*. (No *-s* on *can*)

Write: Use suitable forms of *have to* only when it is impossible to use *must*.

1 You .... take a taxi if you intend to catch the next train.
2 Since the new boss took over, we ....*have had to*.... change our working methods.
3 We .... talk about this again tomorrow.

4 If you .... bring up a large family, you wouldn't have had so much money to spend.
5 I was late for work this morning because I .... go to the bank first.
6 I (not) .... speak French since I was at school.
7 I hate .... wait for people who don't know how to keep appointments. [> 16.8B]
8 He .... get up early tomorrow morning if he wants to see the sunrise.

11.1C The second use of modal verbs [> LEG 11.3-4, 11.8]

Study:
★★

1 The second way we use modals is to express degrees of **certainty** or **uncertainty**. We use nine of the modals for this purpose (not *shall*), but we don't use them in a fixed order. We express the greatest uncertainty with *might*; the greatest certainty with *must/can't*:
He **might be** right. He **might know** the answer. (very uncertain)
He **could be** right. He **would know** the answer. (fairly certain)
He **must be** right. He **must know** the answer. (almost certain)
He **can't be** right. He **can't know** the answer. (almost certain)

We use *be* or an ordinary verb, not a modal, for 'absolute certainty' [> 10.4A, 11.4A]:
You **are** right. You **know** the answer. (certain)

2 In their second use, modals have only two forms:
– present form: He **must be** right. He **must know** the answer. (now)
– perfect or past form: He **must have been** right. He **must have known** the answer. (then)

Write: Put 'certain', 'almost certain', 'fairly certain' or 'very uncertain' beside these sentences.

1 The phone's ringing. It's Roland. ....*certain*...
2 The phone's ringing. It might be Roland. ....
3 A car is parking outside our house. That will be the Kennedys. ....
4 A car is parking outside our house. That must be the Kennedys. ....
5 From your description, the person you met would have been my cousin, Jeff. ....
6 From your description, the person you met can't have been my cousin Jeff. ....
7 If I have understood you correctly, Jeff should be my second cousin. ....
8 Are you saying it mightn't be possible for me to get a visa to visit the USA? ....
9 If he spent five years in America, he must speak English, I suppose. ....

11.1D Context

Write: Put in *am, can, can't, couldn't, have had to, haven't been able to, may, must, must be* or *must have.*

Remember me?

REMEMBER ME?
There was a knock at the door. I opened it and saw a stranger. 'Hullo, Fred,' he cried. '[1]...*May / Can*........ I come in?' 'How do you know my name?' I asked. 'We met ten years ago on a ferry-boat and you gave me your card.' 'You [2]............................. mistaken,' I said. 'No, I [3]............................. not,' the stranger said. He produced my card: Fred Ames. I [4]............................. given it to him ten years ago, but I [5]............................. remember it!' 'I [6]............................. remember you,' I said. 'We exchanged cards years ago,' the stranger said. 'You said, "You [7]............................. come and stay with us for as long as you like any time you're in England." I'm sorry I [8]............................. wait so many years before coming to visit you. I've been so busy, I [9]............................., but here I am at last! Better late than never! I've just arrived on the ferry. My wife and children are in the car and we wonder if we [10]............................. stay with you for a month.'

11.2 Uses of modals (etc.) to express ability and inability

11.2A Expressing present and past ability: 'can' and 'be able to' [> LEG 11.10-12]

Study:
★★

1 We can use *can* (or sometimes *am/is/are able to*) to describe natural or learned ability:
I can (*I am able to*) *run* 1500 metres in 5 minutes. (natural ability)
I can't (*I am not able to/I am unable to*) *drive*. (learned ability)

2 We can use *could, couldn't* or *was/were (not) able to* to describe 'general ability in the past':
I could (*I was able to*) *run* very fast when I was a boy. (i.e. general ability)

3 We use *was/were able to* or *managed to* (Not **could**) to describe the successful completion of a specific action:
We *were able to* (we *managed to*) *get* tickets for the match yesterday. (Not **could**)

4 However, we can use *couldn't* to describe a specific action not successfully completed:
We *couldn't get* tickets for the match yesterday. Or:
We *weren't able to/didn't manage to get* tickets for the match yesterday.

Write: Supply *can, can't, could, couldn't, was/were able to, managed to*. Alternatives are possible.

1 A good 1500-metre runner ....*can*.......... run the race in under four minutes.
2 Bill is so unfit he .... run at all!
3 Our baby is only nine months and he .... already stand up.
4 When I was younger, I .... speak Italian much better than I .... now.
5 .... she speak German very well? – No, she .... speak German at all.
6 He .... draw or paint at all when he was a boy, but now he's a famous artist.
7 After weeks of training, I .... swim a length of the baths underwater.
8 It took a long time, but in the end Tony .... save enough to buy his own hi-fi.
9 Did you buy any fresh fish in the market? – No, I .... get any.
10 For days the rescuers looked for the lost climbers in the snow. On the fourth day they saw them and .... reach them without too much trouble.

11.2B 'Can/could' with verbs of perception: 'I can see' [> LEG 9.3, 11.13, App 38.4]

Study:
★★

1 **Verbs of perception** are verbs like *see, hear, smell*, etc. [> 9.1C]

2 When we are describing something that is happening now, we do not use the progressive with these verbs: *I see* a bird in that tree. (Not **I'm seeing**)

3 We often use *can* + verb in place of the simple present with verbs of perception:
I can see a bird in that tree. (= I see) *Can you see* it? (= Do you see)
We often use *could* + verb in place of the simple past with verbs of perception:
I looked up, but couldn't see anything. (= didn't see)

Write: Rewrite these sentences using *can, can't, could* or *couldn't*.

1 Do you see that man over there? ....*Can you see that man over there?*...........
2 I smell something burning. ....
3 I understood what he said. ....
4 Did you understand what he said? ....
5 I don't see anyone. ....
6 I didn't understand what he said. ....

11.2C Ability in tenses other than the present and the past [> LEG 11.16]

Study:
★★

> *Can* and *could* are not 'complete verbs', so we use *be able to* and sometimes *manage to* if, for example, we want to express the future or the present perfect [> 11.1B]:
> ***I'll be able to*** pass my driving test after I have had a few lessons. Not **I can/I will can**

Write: Supply suitable forms of *be able to* in these sentences.

1 Our teacher says we ....._will be able to_.......... speak English fluently in a few months.
2 I've been trying for hours, but so far I (not) .... get through on the phone.
3 If he had asked me earlier, I .... help him.
4 I'm sure she would have helped you if she ....
5 I think I .... play table tennis better after a bit of practice.
6 He has managed to live in England for years without .... speak English.
7 I'm practising hard because I want to .... pass my driving test first time.
8 If I .... sing, I would have loved to be an opera singer.

11.2D 'Can/could' in place of 'is often' and 'was often' [> LEG 11.18]

Study:
★★

> Instead of: ***It's often*** cold in January.   We can say: ***It can be*** cold in January.
> Instead of: ***He was often*** naughty when he was a boy.
> We can say: ***He could be*** naughty when he was a boy.

Write: Rewrite these sentences with *can be* or *could be*.

1 The sea is often rough in the harbour. ...._The sea can be rough in the harbour._...........
2 She is bad tempered at times. ....
3 She was often rude when she was a girl. ....
4 It is often cold here in winter. ....
5 He was often helpful when he wanted to be. ....

11.2E Context

Write: Put in suitable forms which express ability.

I'm Chief Naga

JOURNEY'S END
The journey to Western Papua had been very hard. We [1] *had not been able to* make much progress in the heavy rain and we [2]........................ only cross rivers with great difficulty. After two month's journey, we [3]........................ see smoke in the distance and knew we must be near a village. There was another boiling river in front of us, but we [4]........................ cross it by using a rope bridge we had brought with us. At last we approached the village and wondered how we [5]........................ communicate with the chief. None of us [6]........................ speak the local language. Soon, a young, dignified and smiling man approached us. '[7]........................ you speak English?' I asked hopefully. 'Of course,' the young man replied. 'I was educated at Oxford University. I'm Chief Naga. Welcome to my village!'

11.3 Uses of modals (etc.) to express permission and prohibition

11.3A Asking for permission with 'can', 'could', 'may' and 'might' [> LEG 11.20-22]

Study:
★★

We use *can, could, may* and *might* to ask for permission, depending on the situation.

1 *Can* is the commonest and most informal: **Can I borrow** your umbrella (please)?

2 *Could* is more polite than *can*: **Could I borrow** your umbrella (please)?

3 *May* is more 'respectful' than *can* and *could*: **May I borrow** your umbrella (please)?

4 *Might* is the most polite but the least common: **Might I borrow** your umbrella (please)?

5 We can add *possibly* and use expressions like *Do you think* and *I wonder if* to make requests even more polite:
Can/Could/May/Might I possibly borrow your umbrella?
Do you think I could/Do you think I might (possibly) borrow your umbrella?
I wonder if I could/I wonder if I might (possibly) borrow your umbrella?

Write: Make suitable requests for permission in these situations.

1 You are visiting a close friend and you want to make yourself some coffee.
...... *Can I make myself some coffee (please)?* ......

2 You are visiting an acquaintance and want to use the lavatory.
....

3 You are at a party given by people you hardly know. You want to see their garden.
....

4 You are visiting people you know reasonably well. You want to make a phone call.
....

5 You are visiting a close friend and want to borrow his new car.
....

11.3B Giving and refusing permission/Expressing prohibition [> LEG 11.19, 11.23]

Study:
★★

We personally give or refuse permission in everyday situations in the following ways:

You { *can (not)* / *may (not)* } *watch TV for as long as you like.* (Not *could*) (Not *might*)

We refer to 'some other authority' that gives/refuses permission like this [> 11.10A, 16.5A5]:
You can/cannot or *You're allowed to/not allowed to*
You can/cannot or *You're permitted to/not permitted to* } *smoke here.*
You mustn't or *You're forbidden to*

Write: Rephrase these notices to give or refuse permission. Begin each sentence with *You* ...

1 Thank you for not smoking .... *You may not smoke.* ....
2 No camping or picnicking ....
3 Fishing strictly forbidden ....
4 Campers welcome ....
5 Private – Keep Out ....
6 Do not lean out of the window ....
7 Leave your litter here ....
8 No stopping ....

11.3C Permission/prohibition in tenses other than present and future
[> LEG 11.24, 11.4, 11.6.1]

Study:
★★

> *May* and *must* are not 'complete verbs', so we use *be allowed to* to make up their 'missing parts'
> [> 11.1B]:
> The children **were allowed to watch** TV last night. (Not *could* > 11.2A)

Write: Supply the correct tense form of *be allowed to*.

1 The children ....*were allowed to*...... stay home from school yesterday because of the weather.
2 I .... never .... stay up late when I was very young.
3 She .... only .... go to parties in the last few months.
4 He .... just .... go home after three hours at the police station.
5 Since he was admitted to hospital, we (not) .... visit him.
6 His doctor (not) .... him ...... take any exercise in the year before he died.

11.3D 'Can' (= ability) and 'can/could' (= have permission, be free to)
[> LEG 11.10, 11.16, 11.26]

Study:
★★

> We use *can/could* in the sense of 'am/is/are free to' to refer to the future:
> **Mr Jones can/could see** you tomorrow, if you are free. Or *Mr Jones is able to see you ...*
> But we must use *will be able to* (not *can/could*) to describe future ability [> 11.2C]:
> **Baby will be able to stand up** in two weeks' time. (Not *can/could*)

Write: Replace *will be able to* with *can* where possible in the sentences below.

1 She'll be able to drive by the end of next week. ....
2 We'll be able to go to the seaside tomorrow. .....*We can go to the seaside tomorrow*.........
3 She'll be able to drive you home tomorrow. ....
4 I'll be able to play chess soon. ....
5 I'll be able to play a game of chess with you tomorrow. ....
6 You will be able to use my computer during the weekend. ....
7 You will be able to operate this computer after a bit of practice. ....

11.3E Context

Write: Supply suitable forms which express permission, prohibition or ability.

WHAT WOULD YOU ADVISE? *Am I allowed to*
Mrs Wilkins is on a strict diet. '¹....................... eat toast and butter for breakfast?'
she asked her doctor. 'I'm afraid not, Mrs Wilkins. You ²....................... only have
half a grapefruit and a glass of water. You certainly ³....................... eat any kind of
fat and you ⁴....................... eat biscuits or sweets. But don't worry, you
⁵....................... eat what you like after two months of this diet.' Mrs Wilkins was very
determined and took a lot of exercise as well. After two months' diet and exercise
she said to her husband, 'I still ⁶....................... touch my toes as I ⁷.......................
before we married.' 'Don't worry, my love,' he said kindly. 'Perhaps your fingernails
were longer in those days!'

Perhaps your fingernails were longer ...

11.4 Uses of modals (etc.) to express certainty and possibility

11.4A Certainty and possibility [> LEG 11.27-30]

Study:
★★

> 1 If we are certain of our facts, we use *be* or any full verb [> 11.1C]:
> Jane **is** at home. Jane **works** at home. (certain facts)
>
> 2 If we are referring to possibility, we use *may, might* or *could* + *be/have been*:
> Jane **may/might/could be** at home now.
> She **may/might/could have been** at home yesterday.
> Or we use *may, might, could* + full verb:
> Jane **may/might/could work** (or ... **may/might/could be working**) at home.
> She **may/might/could have worked** (or ... **have been working**) at home yesterday.

Write 1: Read these sentences and write C (= Certain) or P (= Possible) against each one.

1 My boss is away on holiday. *C*
2 His wife may be with him. __
3 She will be back next week. __
4 He could reply by the weekend. __
5 He wasn't here last week. __
6 She might have been to Paris. __
7 She's returned from Paris. __

8 He could be swimming right now. __
9 He'll come back in a good mood. __
10 He might leave this evening. __
11 They've been staying at a big hotel. __
12 They may have been dancing all night. __
13 He borrowed my ladder. __
14 He could have borrowed my ladder. __

Write 2: Turn these 'certain' statements into 'possible/less than certain' statements.

1 He is at home now. .... *He may/might/could be at home now.*
2 He will be at home tomorrow. ....
3 He was at home yesterday. ....
4 She leaves at 9. ....
5 She will leave tomorrow. ....
6 She has left. ....
7 She left last night. ....
8 She will have left by 9. ....
9 He is working today. ....
10 He will be working today. ....
11 He was working today. ....
12 He has been working all day. ....

Write 3: Write uncertain answers to these questions.

1 Where's Jim today? .... *He may/might/could be at home.*
2 Where was Jim yesterday? ....
3 Where will Jim be tomorrow? ....
4 What time does the train leave? ....
5 What time did the train leave last night? ....
6 What's Sue doing at the moment? ....
7 What was Sue doing yesterday? ....
8 What will Sue be doing tomorrow? ....
9 What has Sue been doing this week? ....
10 What has John had for breakfast? ....
11 Where has Ann parked the car? ....
12 What did that car cost? ....

11.4B   Certain and uncertain answers to questions [> LEG 11.31, 13.5-6]

Study:
★★★

1 A 'certain' question may produce an 'uncertain' answer [compare > 13.1C]:
*Does he like fish? – He **might (do)**. He **may (do)**. He **could (do)**. He **may not**.*

2 An 'uncertain' question may produce a 'certain' answer:
*Can he still be working? – Yes, **he is.***

3 We use *be* and *have been* to answer questions with *be*:
*Is he ill? – He **may be**. Was he ill? – He **may have been**.* (Not **he may**)

4 We use *do/done* to replace other verbs, though this is optional:
*Will you catch the early train? – I may./I may **do**.*
*Has he received my message? – He could have./He could have **done**.*

5 We also answer *Wh*-questions with 'certainty' or 'uncertainty':
*What's his name? – **It's** Smith. (certain) **It may/might be** Smith. (uncertain)*
*What was his name? – **It was** Smith. (certain) **It may/might have been** Smith. (uncertain)*

Write: Give uncertain answers to these questions.

1 Does she still live in London? .... *(Yes,) she may (do).* ....
2 Where does she live? ....
3 Did he catch the early train? ....
4 Which train did he catch? ....
5 Are they still living abroad? ....
6 Where are they living? ....
7 Has he finished work? ....
8 When did he finish work? ....
9 Will you leave tomorrow? ....
10 When will you leave? ....

11.4C   Context

Write: Put in suitable forms which express uncertainty or possibility.

Decisions! Decisions!

OLDER AND WISER?
We make decisions all the time, but we [1] ....*can*........ never be certain
whether we are right or wrong. The work you choose to do
[2] .... be suitable for you or it [3] .... not. The person
you marry [4] .... be a perfect match or [5] .... be the
worst possible choice. Suppose you have saved money for the future.
You [6] .... invest it wisely so that it grows in value or you
[7] .... lose the lot in a foolish moment. You think you have a
healthy diet, but the food you eat [8] .... actually be very bad
for you and [9] .... be the cause of terrible illness. Perhaps you
travel a lot by plane. All the flights you make are routine, but one of
them [10] .... be your last. Decisions! Decisions! But we don't
learn from experience. Experience is the quality that allows us to go on
making the same mistakes with more confidence!

11.5 Uses of modals to express deduction

11.5A Certainty or deduction? [> LEG 11.27, 11.32-33]

Study:

1 We express certainty with *be* or any full verb: *He is here. He lives here. He is leaving*.

2 We express deduction with *must be/can't be, must have been, can't/couldn't have been*:
He must be at home. He can't be out. He must have been at home yesterday.
or with verbs other than *be*: *He must live abroad. He must have lived abroad*.

Write: Read these sentences and write C (= Certainty) or D (= Deduction) against each one.

1 John Wright is a man of action. *C*
2 He was in the Galapagos ten years ago. __
3 Now he lives in an enormous house. __
4 He is writing a book. __
5 He has been writing this book since he came back from the Galapagos. __
6 He must be writing about his travels. __
7 He must have seen the giant tortoises and the iguanas on the Galapagos. __
8 He can't have seen any elephants on the Galapagos. __
9 He can't have been working very hard on his book. __
10 He must have taken a lot of photos while he was on the islands. __
11 He must have done a lot of research for his book. __
12 He must enjoy life. __

11.5B Two kinds of 'must be' [> LEG 11.33, 11.46-48]

Study:

1 We use *must be* in the present to express deduction [> 11.1C]:
You haven't eaten for hours. You must be hungry!

2 The negative of *must be* (= deduction) is *can't be*, not **mustn't be**:
You've only just eaten. You can't be hungry again! (Not **mustn't be**)

3 We can also use *must (be)* to express total obligation [> 11.1A]:
This is a hospital. You must be quiet.

4 The negative of *must (be)* (= total obligation) is *mustn't (be)* (= prohibition [> 11.3B]):
You mustn't be noisy outside a hospital.

Write:
a Supply *must be, can't be*, or *mustn't be*.
b Write D (= Deduction) or O (= Obligation) beside each sentence.

1 The meeting is at 10 o'clock sharp and you ...... *mustn't be* .... late. *O*
2 You .... at the station ten minutes before the departure of the train. __
3 The children .... tired already! We've only been walking for ten minutes. __
4 The children .... thirsty. They haven't had a drink for hours. __
5 Did you hear that? It .... someone walking about in our garden. __
6 I don't recognize the handwriting on this envelope. It .... from anyone we know. __
7 Your handwriting .... clear, otherwise no one will be able to read it. __
8 You .... a nuisance when you're a guest in someone's house. __
9 Don't panic! We .... late for the train. It doesn't leave till 10.05. __
10 We .... late for the train or we'll miss our connection. __

11.5C 'Must have been', 'can't/couldn't have been'; 'had to be/didn't have to be' [> LEG 11.32-33]

Study:
★★

1 We express deduction about the past with *must have been*:
   *You hadn't eaten for hours. You **must have been** hungry!*

2 The negative of *must have been* is *can't/couldn't have been*, not **mustn't have been**:
   *You had already eaten. You **can't/couldn't** have been hungry!* (Not **mustn't have been**)

3 *Must* (= total obligation) is not a 'complete verb' [> 11.1B]. We use *had* to in the past:
   *The meeting was at 10 this morning and I **had to be** there.* (Not **must have been**)

4 The negative of *had to* is *didn't have to*:
   *It was a holiday yesterday, so I **didn't have to be** at work.* (Not **mustn't have been**)

Write: Supply *must have been, can't/couldn't have been, have to/had to (be), didn't have to (be)*.

1 He knows a lot about flying planes. He ....*must have been*............ a pilot when he was young.
2 Vera .... at the supermarket this morning. I didn't see her there.
3 John .... at the bank till 10, so he only arrived here five minutes ago.
4 When .... (she) .... at the hospital? – Early this morning.
5 We had enough foreign currency left at the end of the holiday, so I .... buy any more.
6 Monica knew exactly what to do. I .... tell her twice.
7 There are so many nice things for tea, I think you .... expecting us.
8 There .... an accident on South Street because the road is closed off.
9 You .... waiting long. After all, I'm only five minutes late.
10 When I was a boy we .... sitting at our desks working before the boss got in.
11 I left a message on your answer phone last night. You .... out.
12 The fire alarm went and we .... out of the building in two minutes.

11.5D Context

Write: Put in *must be/must have been, can't be/can't have been, had to be* or *didn't have to be*.

THE MYSTERY OF THE TALKING SHOE
Tracy Evans [1]*didn't have to be* at work till ten, so she ignored her alarm clock. But she woke up with a start when she heard a strange sound coming from her wardrobe! What was it? It [2]........................... a mouse, Tracy thought. No, it [3]........................... . She knew there were no mice in her room. I [4]........................... careful, Tracy said to herself as she opened the wardrobe. There, in front of her, was the lovely pair of wedge-shaped sandals she had bought the day before. Then she heard the sound again! 'It [5]........................... coming from my sandals!' she cried. She picked them up and, sure enough, one of them was 'talking'! Tracy [6]........................... at work at ten, but she still had enough time to vist Mr Lucas, her shoemaker. He removed the wooden heel and they were both amazed to see a white larva eating the wood. Mr Pope, of the Natural History Museum, solved the mystery. 'These shoes [7]........................... (*import*) from Brazil. An insect [8]........................... (*lay*) its eggs in the tree from which the shoes were made,' he explained.

One of the shoes was talking!

11.6 Uses of modals for offers, requests and suggestions

11.6A Offering things and substances [> LEG 11.35]

Study:
★★

Offering:	e.g. **Would/Wouldn't you like** a sandwich/some coffee?
Yes/No responses:	e.g. Yes, I'd like one/some, please. No, thank you.

Write: Make offers for the following things and substances.
a sandwich, some coffee, a slice of toast, some potatoes, an orange, some fruit

1 ...... *Would you like a sandwich?* ......
2 ....
3 ....
4 ....
5 ....
6 ....

11.6B Requests for things and substances [> LEG 11.36]

Study:
★★

Requesting [> 11.3A]:	e.g. **Can/Could/May/Might I** have a sandwich/some sugar, please?
Yes/No responses:	e.g. Of course you can/may. No, you can't/may not, I'm afraid.

Write: Make requests for the following things and substances.
a sandwich, some coffee, a slice of toast, some potatoes, an orange, some fruit

1 ...... *Can I have a sandwich, please?* ......
2 ....
3 ....
4 ....
5 ....
6 ....

11.6C Making suggestions, inviting actions [> LEG 11.37]

Study:
★★

Making suggestions, inviting actions: e.g. **Would/Wouldn't you like to** come with us?
Yes/No responses: e.g. Yes, I'd like to/love to. No, I'd prefer not to, thank you.

Write: Make suggestions/invite actions for the following situations.

1 Your friend has nowhere to stay for the night. *Would you like to stay with me?*
2 You want your friends to join you for a meal. ....
3 You want your friend to come on an excursion. ....
4 You want your friends to have a holiday with you. ....

11.6D Requesting others to do things for you [> LEG 11.38]

Study:
★★

Requesting others to do things for you: e.g. **Will/Would you** please **open** the door **for me**?
Yes/No responses: e.g. Yes, of course I will. No, I'm afraid I can't at the moment.

Write: Make requests for the following situations. You want someone to …

1 hold the door open for you. *Will / Would you hold the door open for me, please?*
2 dial a number for you. ....
3 translate a letter for you. ....
4 deliver some flowers for you. ....

11.6E Offering to do things for others [> LEG 11.39]

Study:
★★

> Offering to do things for others: e.g. **Shall I carry** that **for you**?
> Yes/No responses: e.g. *Can/Could you? That's very kind of you. No, thank you.*

Write: Make offers for the following situations.

1 An old lady clearly wants to put her large suitcase on the luggage rack.
   Shall I put the suitcase on the rack (for you)?
2 A young woman is shivering and the window is open.
   ....
3 Your friend accidentally drops some sheets of paper on the floor.
   ....

11.6F Making suggestions that include the speaker [> LEG 11.40]

Study:
★★

> Making suggestions that include the speaker: e.g. **Shall we go** for a swim? [> 16.1B]
> Yes/No responses: e.g. *Yes, let's./Yes, let's, shall we? No, I'd rather we didn't.*

Write: Make suggestions to a friend for the following situations. You feel like …

1 driving to the coast. *Shall we drive to the coast?*
2 having a meal out this evening. ....
3 travelling first class. ....
4 having a holiday in Bahia. ....

11.6G Context

Write: Put in the missing requests, offers, etc.

And I'd like to send you there!

PLEASE BE NICE TO NIGEL!
'Please be nice to Nigel,' his mother said to Jenny, the baby sitter, before she went out. Jenny is doing her best.

JENNY: [1] *Would you* like something to eat, Nigel?	NIGEL: No!
JENNY: [2] .... build a castle for you, Nigel?	NIGEL: No!
JENNY: I'm cold. [3] .... shut the window for me?	NIGEL: No!
JENNY: [4] .... like to watch TV with me, Nigel?	NIGEL: No!
JENNY: [5] .... borrow your crayons, Nigel?	NIGEL: No!
JENNY: [6] .... play a game together?	NIGEL: No!
JENNY: [7] .... get a glass of water for you, Nigel?	NIGEL: No!
JENNY: [8] .... get a glass of water for me?	NIGEL: No!
JENNY: [9] .... you like to go to the moon, Nigel?	NIGEL: Yes!
JENNY: And I'd like to send you there in a rocket!	

11.7 Expressing wishes, etc.: 'I wish', 'if only', 'it's (high) time'

11.7A Present and past reference with 'I wish', 'if only' and 'it's (high) time'
[> LEG 11.41-43]

Study:
★★

> After *(I) wish, if only, it's (high) time* and *it's (about) time*, we 'go one tense back':
> 1 The past tense refers to the present: ***I wish I had*** a better watch! (i.e. NOW)
> 2 The past perfect tense refers to the past: ***If only you had asked*** me first! (i.e. THEN)

Write: Tick the sentences that refer to 'present' or 'past'.

	present	past
1 I wish I had a better watch!	✓	—
2 If only I knew the answer to the problem!	—	—
3 It's high time/about time he learnt more manners!	—	—
4 I wish you hadn't done that!	—	—
5 If only you had phoned me yesterday!	—	—

11.7B Expressing wishes and regrets with 'I wish' and 'if only' [> LEG 11.41-42.1-3]

Study:
★★

> 1 We often use *I wish* for things that might (still) happen:
>   ***I wish I knew*** the answer! (= it's possible I might find out the answer)
>   *If only* is stronger. We use it to express regret for things that can (now) never happen:
>   ***If only your mother were*** alive now! (Of course, *I wish* is also possible.)
>
> 2 We may use the simple past of *be* after *wish* and *if only*, especially in everyday speech:
>   ***I wish I was*** on holiday now. ***If only Tessa was*** here now!
>
> 3 If we want to be more formal, we use *were* in all persons [> 11.13B, 14.2B]:
>   ***I wish I were*** on holiday now. ***If only Tessa were*** here!
>
> 4 We may use the past perfect of *be* for things that can never happen:
>   ***I wish I had been*** on holiday last week. ***If only Tessa had been*** here yesterday!
>
> 5 We use the past or past perfect forms of other verbs:
>   ***I wish I knew*** the answer to your question. ***I wish I had known*** then what I know now!

Write: Express wishes and regrets about these situations. Refer to yourself where possible.

1 You're not very fit. .....*I wish / If only I was/were fit/fitter!*.....................
2 It's very hot today. ....
3 It's raining. ....
4 You were too impatient. ....
5 You wasted a lot of time watching TV. ....
6 They don't have a lot of friends. ....
7 We didn't lock the back door! ....
8 He is abroad. ....
9 Jane has read your letter. ....
10 John didn't take your advice. ....

11.7C   'Would' and 'could' after 'I wish' and 'if only' [> LEG 11.42.4]

Study:
★★

We must use *could*, not *would*, after *I* and *we*. Compare:
I can't swim.   →   **I wish I could** swim.
We weren't together!   →   **I wish we could have been** together.
We sometimes use *I wish you* (*he, she,* etc.) *would(n't)* like an imperative:
(I am making a lot of noise!)   →   **I wish you wouldn't** make so much noise!
(He is making a lot of noise!) →   **I wish he would be** quiet!

Write: Supply *would, wouldn't* or *could*.

1 I wish they ....*would*................ be quiet.
2 We wish you .... drive so fast.
3 We wish we .... come to London with you.
4 I wish I .... have seen the film with them.
5 We really wish she .... change her mind and come on holiday with us.
6 If only we .... have good weather like this the whole year.

11.7D   'It's (high) time' and 'It's (about) time' [> LEG 11.41, 11.43]

Study:
★★

We use *It's time, It's high time* and *It's about time* to express present or future wishes, or to express our impatience about things that haven't happened yet:
Kim can't even boil an egg. – I know. **It's time/high time/about time** *she learnt to cook!*

Write: Respond to these sentences with *It's high time* or *It's about time*.

1 John and Julie have been engaged now for over ten years.
   It's high time they got married!..
2 We haven't been out for an evening together for ages, have we?
   ....
3 It's very late. You should both really go now.
   ....
4 The boys' room is terribly untidy.
   ....

11.7E   Context

Write: Put in the right forms for the words in brackets.

'I wish I could have my friends back!'

HAVING A WONDERFUL TIME! WISH YOU WERE HERE!
While trying to sail round the world in a small boat, Harry, Sandy and Joe were shipwrecked one night. 'I wish there (*be*) [1] ....*was/were*..... an island nearby,' Harry said. By morning, they were washed up on to a desert island. For six months they lived on fish, nuts and fruit. One day, they saw a bottle on the shore. 'If only it (*contain*) [2] .... a note or something!' Sandy said. They opened it and a genie appeared. 'It's high time someone (*open*) [3] .... that bottle!' the genie gasped. 'I'm so grateful, I'll give you one wish each. You first,' the genie said, pointing to Harry. 'That's easy,' Harry said. 'I wish I (*be*) [4] .... with my family.' And (whoosh!) he disappeared. 'Me too,' Sandy said. 'If only I (*can be*) [5] .... in dear old Glasgow.' And (whoosh!) off he went. 'And you, sir?' the genie asked Joe. 'I wish I (*have*) [6] .... my friends back!' Joe said.

169

11.8   Expressing preferences: 'would rather' and 'would sooner'

11.8A   Expressing personal preference with 'I'd rather'/'I'd sooner' [> LEG 11.44, 16.5]

Study:
★★

1 We use *would rather* and *would sooner* in exactly the same way to express preference.
We can refer to the present or the future:
I'd rather/I'd sooner be a builder than an architect.
Or we can refer to the past:
If I could choose again, *I'd rather/sooner have been* a builder than an architect.

2 We can omit the verb in negative short answers:
Are you coming with us? – No, I'd rather/sooner not.
Would you rather have been a builder? – No, I'd rather/sooner not (have been).

Write 1:   Supply the correct forms of the verbs in brackets.

1 Which would you sooner ....*be*.........? A pilot or a passenger? (be)
2 My career is nearly over, but I'd much rather .... in the navy than in the army. (be)
3 If I had lived in the past, I'd sooner .... a peasant than a king. (be)
4 I'd rather .... in the eighteenth century than in the nineteenth century. (live)
5 I like my job. I'd rather .... my living as a teacher than anything else. (make)
6 I wish my job were secure. I'd sooner .... worry about it. (not have to)
7 Jim had to break the bad news to her. I know he'd rather .... do it. (not have to)

Write 2:   Supply negative short answers with *I'd rather/I'd sooner* to these questions.

1 Are you coming with us? No, ...*I'd rather not. / I'd sooner not.*...........................
2 Would you rather have been invited to the party? No, ...
3 Do you want to catch the next train? No, ...
4 Would you rather have lived in the past than the present? No, ...

11.8B   Expressing preferences about other people's actions [> LEG 11.45]

Study:
★★★

1 We can refer to other people after *I'd rather* or *I'd sooner*. Compare:
I'd rather leave on an earlier train. (= I'm referring to myself)
I'd rather Jack (etc.) *left* on an earlier train.

2 We use the past tense form after *I'd rather* to refer to the present or future. Compare:
I'd rather be happy. *I'd rather not sit* next to her. (= now – I'm referring to myself)
I'd rather she were/was happy. (= now) *I'd rather she didn't sit* next to me. (= now)

3 We use the past perfect form after *I'd rather* to refer to past time. Compare:
I'd rather have been present. (= then – I'm referring to myself)
I'd rather you had been present. (then) *I'd rather you hadn't told me* about it. (then)

Write: Supply the correct forms of the verbs in brackets.

1 You might be late for the meeting. I'd rather you ...*caught*......... an earlier train. (catch)
2 I won't be home till very late. I'd sooner you .... for me. (not wait up)
3 He took a risk investing money with them. I'd rather he .... it. (not do)
4 I don't mind your borrowing my ladder, but I'd sooner you .... me first. (ask)
5 I know our daughter is enjoying herself, but I'd rather she .... here than abroad. (be)
6 I'd rather you .... present when we signed the agreement. (be)

11.8C 'I'd rather he didn't', etc. [> LEG 11.45]

Study:
★★★

> We generally omit the main part of the verb in short responses:
>
> 1 negative responses: *Frank is going to buy* a motorbike. – I'd rather **he didn't**.
> *I've told* everyone about it. – I'd rather **you hadn't**.
>
> 2 affirmative responses: *Frank won't give up* his present job. – I'd rather **he did**.
> *I haven't told* anyone about it. – I'd rather **you had**.
>
> 3 We do not have to repeat the main verb in a complete sentence:
> *You always go* without me and I'd rather **you didn't**.

Write: Supply negative short responses or continuations to these sentences.

1 Joan wants to become self-employed. *I'd rather/sooner she didn't.*
2 I've told everyone about it. ....
3 Susan has moved her account to another bank. ....
4 Bill takes sleeping pills. ....
5 I often drive fast. ....
6 Frank went to live in Australia last year. ....
7 Our neighbours keep a large dog. ....
8 Our neighbours have cut down all the trees at the back of their garden. ....
9 I know you've already booked our holiday, but ....
10 Jane cycles to work every day, but ....
11 Alan retired early last year, but ....

11.8D Context

Write: Put in the missing preferences.

W.C. Fields

KNOW YOURSELF!

Most parents (*their children not decide*) [1] *would rather their children didn't decide* to join the acting profession because it is so hard to earn a living. They (*their children choose*) [2].. secure, well-paid jobs. But if you ask actors themselves, they always tell you there is nothing they (*do*) [3].. . An actor is a person who (*be*) [4].. a different man or woman. An actor (*talk, walk, and behave*) [5].. like someone else. That's what acting is about. Many actors (*be called*) [6].. something other than their real names. The great American comic actor Claude William Dukenfield (*be called*) [7].. W.C. Fields, which was the name he adopted when he became an actor. Fields was eccentric and (*live*) [8].. in a world in which there were no dogs or children. He used to wear a funny top hat and carry a walking-stick. He loved to pretend to be other people in real life as well. He opened bank accounts all over America using comic names. He died in 1946 and the epitaph he wrote for his tombstone clearly expressed a healthy preference for life: 'On the whole, I (*be*) [9].. in Philadelphia!'

11.9 'It's advisable ...'/'It's necessary ...'

11.9A 'It's advisable' → 'It's necessary': 'a scale of choice' [> LEG 11.47]

Study:
★★

We can say what, in our opinion, is advisable or necessary on a scale which shows how much choice there is. We use the following words to give advice or say what is necessary:

1 *Should* and *ought to* (= in my opinion it's advisable, but there is some choice):
You **should see** a doctor. You **ought to vote** in the next election.
(= That's my advice, but ignore it if you want to.)

2 *Had better* is stronger, even a warning: **You'd better see** a doctor.
(= That's my urgent advice. There may be consequences if you ignore it.)

3 *Have to, have got to* (less formal) and *must* (= in my opinion, you have no choice):
You have to/have got to/must see a doctor.
(= That's the strongest advice I can give you. Don't ignore it!) [compare > 11.10A]

Write: Tick the sentences that mean 'it is/it was advisable' or 'it is/it was necessary'.

	advisable	necessary
1 You should listen more carefully.	✓	—
2 I must get to the meeting before 7.30.	—	—
3 I'd better hurry, or I'll be late.	—	—
4 They should have taken umbrellas with them.	—	—
5 She had to complete the test in ten minutes.	—	—
6 We ought to have stopped for a meal on the way.	—	—

11.9B 'Must', 'have to' and 'have got to' [> LEG 11.48]

Study:
★★

1 We often use *must, have to* and *have got to* in place of each other, but sometimes not.

2 We tend to prefer *must*:
– when we refer to ourselves (with *I/we*): *I* really **must weed** this garden.
– with *you* to express urgency: **You must phone** home at once.
– in public notices, etc.: **Cyclists must** dismount.
– (= Can't you stop yourself?): **Must you** interrupt?
– pressing invitations or advice: **You must come** and see us. **You must repair** that fence.

3 We often use *have to* (or *have got to*) to refer to outside authority:
I **have (got) to pay** my road tax soon.

Write: Supply the forms *must* or *have (got) to* which 'feel right' in these sentences.
Sometimes more than one form is possible.

1 We really .... *must* .... do something about having this house decorated.
2 We .... pay this electricity bill by the end of the week.
3 You .... write and let us know you've arrived safely.
4 I .... be at my desk by 9.00 every morning.
5 We always .... clock in when we arrive at work.
6 ALL VISITORS .... REPORT TO THE DUTY OFFICER.
7 .... you always slam the door when you come in?
8 You really .... come and see the new extension to our house some day.

11.9C Expressing necessity in other tenses [> LEG 11.50-51, 11.46]

Study:
★★

1 *Must* can refer to the present or the future:
I must speak to him **today**. *I must speak* to him **tomorrow**.

2 *Must* is not a 'complete verb', so we use *have to* to make up its 'missing parts' [> 11.1B]:
I shall/will have to phone her tomorrow. (or *I must phone* her tomorrow.) (future)
I had to spend the day in a meeting. (past)
I have had to tell you before. (present perfect)
I am having to/I have been having to get up earlier this year. (progressive forms)

3 *Had to* shows that we couldn't avoid doing something: *I had to leave* at six. (and I did)
Should have shows we've failed to do something: *I should have left* at six. (and I didn't)

Write: Use a construction with *have to* in place of the words in italics.

1 *It will be necessary for him* to try harder if he wants to win the prize. ....*He will have to*............
2 *It has been necessary for them* to save hard to buy their new hi-fi. ....
3 Because of the snow *she has been finding it necessary* to walk to college. ....
4 *It had already been necessary for us* to clear the office floor twice before the
boss asked us to clear it again. ....
5 *It would have been necessary for me* to pay twice as much to travel first class. ....
6 *We are finding it necessary* to cut back on staff because of a shortage of orders. ....

11.9D Context

Write: Put in *will have to, must, having to, has to, should, had to, have to* and *should have*.
Use each one at least once.

ARIJABA!
The Post Office in Britain is famous for getting letters and parcels to their destinations. The problem is
that we the public [1]....*have to*.......... observe the rules. For example, we [2]............................ put a
stamp on a letter. If we don't, the recipient [3]............................. pay double. We often see the sign ALL
LETTERS [4]............................ BE CORRECTLY ADDRESSED. These days, this means
[5]............................ use postcodes. If you didn't use a postcode, it's no good complaining that your
letter [6]............................ arrived sooner. Parcels are a problem because they [7]............................ be
correctly packaged. If Aunt Sophie is going to send you a jar of your favourite jam, she
[8]............................ wrap it up well. The most important thing we [9]............................ do is to address
our letters and parcels legibly and correctly. This means clear handwriting and correct spelling. What
we [10]............................ do and what we actually do are often miles apart. Recently, the Post Office
[11]............................ deliver a letter which showed a name followed by the word ARIJABA. What is this,
do you think? Arabic? Hindustani? Wrong both times! Say it out loud and you'll see it's just plain
(misspelt!) English: HARWICH HARBOUR!

Arabic? Hindustani?

11.10 'It isn't advisable ...'/'It isn't necessary ...'/'It's forbidden ...'

11.10A 'It isn't advisable' → 'It's forbidden': 'a scale of choice' [> LEG 11.54]

Study:
★★

We can say what, in our opinion, is not advisable, or what is forbidden on a scale which shows how much choice there is. We use the following words [compare > 11.9A]:

1 *Shouldn't* and *oughtn't to* (= in my opinion it isn't advisable, but there is some choice):
*You **shouldn't drive** too fast. You **oughtn't to drive** too fast.*
(= That's my advice, but ignore it if you want to.)

2 *Had better not* is stronger, even a warning: ***You'd better not lose** your passport.*
(= That's my urgent advice. There may be consequences if you ignore it.)

3 *Can't* and *mustn't* (= you have no choice: it's forbidden [> 11.3B]):
*You **can't stop** on a motorway. You **mustn't stop** on a motorway.* (= it's against the law)

Write: Match A and B to show the effect of the verbs.

A
1 You mustn't park near a zebra crossing. _b_
2 You shouldn't eat so much chocolate cake. __
3 You can't use that footpath. It's closed. __
4 You had better not be late for the lecture. __

B
a) 'not advisable' – warning
b) 'forbidden' – law
c) 'not advisable' – personal
d) 'not possible'

11.10B 'Mustn't', 'needn't', 'don't have to', 'haven't got to' [> LEG 11.55]

Study:
★★

1 *Must, have to, have got to* generally mean the same in the affirmative [> 11.9B].
But *mustn't* **never** means the same as *don't have to/haven't got to*.

2 *Mustn't* means 'it's forbidden' [> 11.3B, 11.5B]: *Life belts **must not be removed**.* (no choice)

3 We can use *needn't, don't have to* and *haven't got to* in place of each other to mean 'it isn't necessary': ***I needn't/don't have to/haven't got to go** to the office tomorrow.* (choice)

Write: Supply *mustn't* or *needn't/don't have to/haven't got to*.

1 You ....*don't have to*.......... work such long hours. You won't earn any more.
2 They .... wear a uniform. It's not obligatory.
3 She .... leave the office last. She can go when she's ready.
4 You really .... waste money like that. It worries your parents.
5 Visitors .... enter the laboratories without permission.
6 We .... always wear protective clothing in the factory.
7 You .... go to the party if you don't want to. Nobody's forcing you.
8 He .... do the job today, as long as it gets done some time this week.
9 Surely we .... leave home yet. It's far too early to go to the station.
10 Passengers .... smoke in the toilets.
11 'Are you going to read the report?' – 'No, I .... It's confidential.'
12 'Are you going to read the report?' – 'No, I .... I already know what it says.'
13 You .... attend the meeting tomorrow. It's for union officials only.
14 You .... attend the meeting tomorrow. It's not important.
15 You .... forget to pay the electricity bill, or we'll be cut off.
16 We .... worry about Tom. He's just phoned to say he's all right.

11.10C 'Needn't have', 'didn't have to', 'didn't need to' [> LEG 11.57.1]

Study:
★★★

1 These sentences mean 'I went there, but it wasn't necessary':
*I **needn't have gone** to the office yesterday (but I went).*
*I **didn't have to/didn't need to** go to the office yesterday (but I went).*
(*have* and *need* are stressed in speech)

2 Compare *didn't have to* and *didn't need to*, without stress:
*I **didn't have to go** to the office yesterday. I **didn't need to go** to the office yesterday.*
(= I knew in advance it wasn't necessary to go to the office and I didn't go.)

Write: Supply *needn't have* or *didn't have to* and the correct form of the verbs in brackets.

1 I *needn't have phoned* the plumber. I learnt later that John had already phoned him. (phone)
2 I .... the plumber. I knew John had already phoned him. (phone)
3 You .... your umbrella after all. It hasn't rained. (bring)
4 The forecast was for fine weather so I knew I .... my umbrella. (bring)
5 I .... these clothes. I didn't know they had already been washed. (wash)
6 I .... a meal last night because we went out and the food I prepared was uneaten. (cook)

11.10D 'Shouldn't have' and 'oughtn't to have' [> LEG 11.57.2]

Study:
★★

We often use *shouldn't have (done)* or *oughtn't to have (done)* to criticize our own actions or someone else's: *I/You **shouldn't have paid/oughtn't to have paid** the plumber in advance.*

Write: Respond to these statements with *shouldn't have done that* or *oughtn't to have done that*.

1 I had to stop on the motorway. *You shouldn't have done that.*
2 John read your letter. ....
3 Frank and Jane sat in the sun all day. ....
4 Jane left the front door unlocked. ....
5 I borrowed your car this morning. ....

11.10E Context

Write: Put in *didn't need to*, *must not*, *shouldn't have* and *should have*.

Mr Paul Blake?

HOW TO CATCH YOUR MAN
'Candidates ¹ ...*must not*.... attempt more than four questions.' The young candidate for the law exam was very well-prepared and ² .... be told what to do. The results were brilliant. The paper achieved the third highest score out of 7,000 papers! But the examiners were puzzled. Mr Paul Blake ³ .... achieved such a high score. This candidate had failed this exam three times already. Then the truth became known. The candidate was not Mr Paul Blake, as it ⁴ .... been. His wife had gone instead. Mrs Alison Blake, a brilliant lawyer, had dressed up as a man. The fraud was discovered because an examiner had noticed that the candidate was visibly pregnant!

175

11.11 Modals to express habit: 'used to', 'will' and 'would'

11.11A The form of 'used to' [> LEG 11.59]

Study:
★★

> 1 *Used to* is a simple past form only. If you want to say 'I am in the habit of', you must use the simple present [> 9.1B]: *I get up* early every day. (Not *I use to get up early*)
>
> 2 We often use *do* and *did* + *use* (Not *used*) to form questions and negatives: *Did you use to* smoke? *I didn't use to* smoke. (Not *Did you used to* *I didn't used to*)
> We also use *never* to form the negative: *I never used to* smoke. (*Used not to* is rare.)
>
> 3 Note the use of *did*: *He used to* live in Manchester, *didn't he*? (rather than *usedn't he*?)
> *Did you use to* live here? – Yes, *I did*./No, *I didn't*. *He used to* live here and *so did I*.

Write: Supply the missing forms in the following.

1 She used to be a singer, ... *didn't* .... she?
2 He never used to have grey hair, ... he?
3 We .... enjoy physics, did we? (not/used to)
4 .... smoke when you were young? (you/used to)
5 Did you use to smoke? – Yes, I ....
6 He used to work here and so .... I.
7 Where .... live? (you/used to)
8 You .... (not/used to) eat so much.

11.11B Uses of 'used to' [> LEG 11.60-62]

Study:
★★

> 1 We use the simple past or *used to* to refer to past habit.
> We need a time reference with the simple past [> 9.3C], but not with *used to*:
> *I collected* stamps *when I was a child*. *I used to collect* stamps (when I was a child).
> (Not *I was collecting stamps when I was a child* [> 9.4B])
>
> 2 We use *used to* to make a contrast between past and present with expressions like:
> *but now ..., but not any more, but not any longer*:
> *I used to eat* a large breakfast, *but I don't any longer*.
>
> 3 *Used to* can also refer to past states:
> She *used to be* very *punctual* (but she isn't any more).

Write: Fill in the blanks with forms of *used to* or the past progressive (e.g. *was living*).

1 We ... *used to go* .... for long walks in the country when my father was alive. (go)
2 I .... getting up early when I was very young. In fact, I still don't like it. (like)
3 .... you .... eating vegetables when you were young? (like)
4 I .... drive to get to work, but I don't any longer. (have to)
5 I never .... Sundays, but I do now. (enjoy)
6 I .... a bath when you phoned me. (have)
7 She .... an employee at the post office before she started her own business. (be)
8 There .... open fields all round our town when I was a boy. (be)
9 John and I .... abroad last year. (work)
10 .... it .... here yesterday? (rain)

11.11C 'Would' in place of 'used to' and in place of the simple past [> LEG 11.61]

Study:
★★

When we are 'remembering the past', we sometimes use *would* in place of *used to*.
First we set the scene with *used to*, then we continue with *would*:
*When I was a boy we always **spent/used to spend** our holidays on a farm. We **would** get up at 5 and **we'd** help milk the cows. Then **we'd** return to the kitchen for breakfast.*

Write: Underline instances where we could use *would* in place of the simple past or *used to*.

From the time he was very young, Gerald used to spend all his spare time collecting birds, animals and insects of all kinds. Every morning he <u>used to</u> get up early and go first to the beach. There he caught small crabs and sometimes small fishes, which he put into a large jar and took home with him. On the way, he always used to go to an ruined fisherman's cottage where he was often lucky enough to find some unusual insect that he had never seen before.

11.11D 'Will/would' to describe 'usual behaviour' [> LEG 11.63-64]

Study:
★★

We sometimes use *will* in place of the simple present [> 9.1B] and *would* in place of the simple past [> 9.3C] to refer to a person's 'usual behaviour':
*In fine weather **he will often sit** in the sun for hours.* (= he often sits)
*As he grew old, **he would often talk** about his war experiences.* (= he often talked)

Write: Use a phrase with *will* or *would* in place of the words in italics.

1 She *always used to* tell us a story before we went to bed. *would always tell* ....
2 She *still tells* us a story occasionally. ....
3 They *only used to* discuss family matters with the priest. ....
4 He's very good, you know. He *plays* with that toy for hours on end. ....
5 When he needed extra money, he *used to* work overtime. ....
6 She *doesn't* always tell the truth, I'm afraid. ....

11.11E Context

Write: Put in appropriate forms of the past, *used to, will* or *would*. Alternatives are possible.

I can feel it in your bones!

WATER, WATER, EVERYWHERE!
The thing I remember most about my childhood was my visits to my aunt Charlotte in her lovely country house. She (*be*) [1] ....*was*........ a remarkable woman by any standards. She (*be*) [2] .... really skilled at water-divining and she (*find*) [3] .... water on the most unpromising bits of land. The farmers (*love*) [4] .... her, especially as she (*never accept*) [5] .... money for water-divining. 'Water (*always find*) [6] .... its own level,' she (*say*) [7] .... 'and I know exactly where that level is. Water-divining is a gift from God and you don't accept payment for that.' She had a gift for noticing changes in the weather, too. 'It's going to rain soon,' she (*say*) [8] ...., 'I can feel it in my bones,' and she (*always be*) [9] .... right! In her later years, she developed a bad back and (*often visit*) [10] .... her osteopath. She (*never tire*) [11] .... of telling us that her osteopath (*say*) [12] ...., as he massaged her painful back, 'It's going to rain, Charlotte. I can feel it in your bones!'

11.12 'Need' and 'dare' as modals and as full verbs

11.12A 'Need' as a modal and as a full verb [> LEG 11.49]

Study:
★★

1 We use *need* as a modal (without *to* after it) mainly in the negative to mean 'it isn't necessary' [> 11.10B-C]: *I **needn't go** to the meeting today. **I needn't have gone** to the meeting yesterday.*

2 In the affirmative, we use *need* as a modal:
– in questions: ***Need you go*** *so soon?* ***Need you have told*** *him the truth?*
– with 'negative adverbs' (e.g. *hardly*): ***I need hardly tell*** *you how important this is.*

3 Otherwise, we generally use the full verb *need to* (used like any regular verb):
I need to/I don't need to/I needed to/I didn't need to go *to the dentist this morning.*

Write: Replace the phrases in italics with modal *need* or the full verb *need to*.

	modal	full verb
1 *Is it necessary for you to go so soon?*.	*Need you go*...?	*Do you need to go*...?
2 *Is it necessary for me to* wait till you return?		
3 *It's not necessary for them to* wait.		
4 *It wasn't necessary for you to have said* that.		
5 *It's hardly necessary for me to* explain it. [> 13.2A]		
6 *There is no need for him to* learn about this.		
7 *All that is necessary for you to* do is to agree.		
8 *I don't think there is any need for you to* explain.		

11.12B The form of 'dare' as a modal and as a full verb [> LEG 11.65-66]

Study:
★★

1 We use *dare* as a modal (that is, without *to* after it) mainly in the negative to express lack of courage: ***I daren't tell*** *him the truth.* ***I daren't ask*** *for more money.*

2 In the affirmative, we use *dare* as a modal:
– in questions: ***Dare you do*** *it?*
– with 'negative adverbs' (e.g. *hardly*): ***I hardly dare tell*** *him what happened.*

3 We also form questions with *do/does/did*: ***Do you dare tell*** *him?* ***I don't dare tell*** *him.*

4 We can use *dare to* as a full verb: ***Do you dare to tell*** *him?* ***I don't dare to tell*** *him.*

5 And note: *I didn't like the meal ...,*
but ***I daren't say*** *so/**I daren't have said** so/**I didn't dare (to) say** so/**I dared not say** so.*

Write: Supply *dare, daren't, dare not have (done), didn't dare (do)*, etc.

1 I ....*daren't*........ tell them I've just broken their favourite vase.
2 I .... tell them I had broken their favourite vase.
3 I hardly .... mention this, but you still haven't paid for those tickets.
4 .... we ask for more money after what he has just said?
5 I knew I was right, but I .... say so at the time.
6 I'm going to tell your mother what you've just said! – Just you ....!
7 She'd like to wear more unconventional clothes, but she ....
8 We didn't like the meal they gave us, but we .... said so. It would have been rude.
9 They offered me something strange to eat which I .... refuse.

11.12C Uses of 'dare' [> LEG 11.67-69]

Study:
★★

> We use *dare* in four ways to express:
>
> 1 courage: *Very few climbers have **dared (to) attempt** Mount Everest without oxygen.*
> *Dare (to)* is in the affirmative here, and this use is relatively rare.
>
> 2 lack of courage: *I **don't dare (to) tell** the children that our holiday has been cancelled.*
> This use of *dare (to)*, in the negative, is the most common.
>
> 3 challenge: *I **dare you to jump** off that wall.* (Not **I dare you jump**)
> We use *dare* only as a full verb with *to* for challenging. We use it in the affirmative and negative
> like any other verb. 'Challenging' is common in the language of children.
>
> 4 outrage: *How **dare you read** my private diary!* (Not **How dare you to read**)
> We use *dare* only as a modal without *to* when expressing outrage.

Write: What do the sentences below express? Choose **a**, **b**, **c**, or **d**:
a courage **b** lack of courage **c** challenge **d** outrage

1 You dare raise your voice! *d*
2 I dare you to put a spider in her desk. __
3 How dare you speak to me like that? __
4 He's the only person who'll dare (to) stand up to her! __
5 I wanted to ask for some time off, but I didn't dare. __
6 Jill's friends dared her to bring her pet snake to class. __
7 I daren't ask for any more money. __
8 He lost his job because he dared (to) speak out. __
9 Don't you dare do anything like that in public again! __
10 I daren't have said so at the time, but I was very bored. __
11 John never dares to stand up in public and say what he thinks. __
12 I'm going to break the door down! – Just you dare! __

11.12D Context

Write: Combine the correct forms of *dare* and *need* with the verbs in brackets.

UNWELCOME FRESH AIR!
It was a routine flight from Hilo on Hawaii to Kahului 110 miles away. Suddenly, there was a
tremendous noise and the top of the plane was torn away! Ninety-four passengers (*not move*)
¹ *dared not move*, wondering what would happen next. They (*not worry*) ²............................ because
Robert Schornsteimer, the pilot, was firmly in control. For 25 minutes they hardly (*breathe*)
³............................, though there was plenty of unwelcome fresh air! 'I (*not open*) ⁴............................
my mouth,' one of the passengers said later. 'I hardly (*tell*) ⁵............................ you how terrified I was.'
The passengers embraced the pilot who had brought the plane down safely. 'I've heard of a plane
flying off a roof,' joked one of them later, 'but never of a roof flying off a plane!'

Plenty of unwelcome fresh air!

11.13 'Would/wouldn't'; 'that ... should'; 'there' + modal

11.13A 'Would' and 'wouldn't' in place of the simple present tense or 'will' future [> LEG 11.74.2]

Study:
★★

We often use *would* and *wouldn't* in place of the simple present (and sometimes in place of *will/won't*) when we want to sound less definite, or when we want to be very polite:

That **seems** to be a good idea.	→	That **would seem** to be a good idea.
I **think** Friday will be OK.	→	I **would think** that Friday will be OK.
Thursday **isn't/won't** be convenient.	→	Thursday **wouldn't** be convenient.

Write: Replace the verbs in italics with *would* and *wouldn't*.

1 £100 *is* rather expensive for a pair of gloves. ....*would be*
2 I'm sure your proposal *isn't* acceptable to the committee. ....
3 Does my idea seem reasonable to you? – I *think* so. ....
4 This new law *doesn't seem* to be fair to pensioners. ....
5 I'm not free on Thursday, but I'*m* free on Friday. ....
6 She's offered to help, but I *don't imagine* she's serious. ....
7 *Does* that *seem* a reasonable price to offer for a used car? ....

11.13B 'That ... should' after verbs like 'suggest' [> LEG 11.75, App 45.3]

Study:
★★★

If we put *that* after verbs like *ask, propose, recommend, suggest*, we continue like this:
– with *should*:   I suggest that he should apply/shouldn't apply for the job.
– with the simple present: I suggest that he applies/he doesn't apply for the job.
– with the 'subjunctive': I suggest that he apply/not apply for the job.

Note on the 'subjunctive': In the 'subjunctive', the base form of the verb (*be, go, run*, etc.) remains the same in all persons. The present form is rare in British English:
I suggest you go/he go/they (etc.) *go to the meeting tomorrow.*
The subjunctive form *were* is used in all persons in the past [> 11.7B, 14.2B].

Write: **a** Supply suitable verb forms in these sentences.
  b Then mark your answers **a** (= should), **b** (= simple present) or **c** (= 'subjunctive').

1 Marion proposed that ....*we should buy*........ a gift for Jim who would soon be leaving the firm. (we/buy) *a*
2 The travel agent recommended that .... driving abroad during the holidays. (we/avoid) __
3 I suggest that .... this matter during the meeting. (he/not raise) __
4 All I ask is that .... the rules. (they/not break) __
5 What does he advise ....? (she/do) __
6 It's no good demanding that .... our performance. We're doing our best. (we/improve) __
7 I would only request that .... good care of this flat while you're living in it. (you/take) __
8 Her solicitor insisted that she .... in signing the contract. (not/delay) __
9 I suggest .... a taxi if we want to get to the meeting on time. (we/take) __
10 He asks that .... to visit his children once a week. (he/be allowed) __

11.13C 'That ... should' after adjectives like 'essential' [> LEG 11.75.3, App 44]

Study:
★★★

If we put *that* after adjectives like *essential, urgent, vital*, we continue like this:
- with *should*:   **It's urgent that he should send** the information at once.
- with the simple present: **It's urgent that he sends** the information at once.
- with the 'subjunctive':   **It's urgent that he send** the information at once.

Write:
  a Supply suitable verb forms in these sentences.
  b Then mark your answers **a** (= should), **b** (= simple present) or **c** (= 'subjunctive')

1 It's urgent that .....*we should send*.................................... the information now. (we/send) *a*
2 It's essential that .... home now. (she/return) __
3 It's vital that .... (he/be inform) __
4 I'm eager that .... present at the meeting. (she/be) __

11.13D 'There' + modal auxiliaries [> LEG 11.76]

Study:
★★★

Just as *there* will combine with *be* (*there is, there was, there has been*, etc. [> 10.3]), it will combine with modals:
There could be no doubt about it. **There must be** a mistake.
There can't have been any doubt about it. **There might have been** a mistake.
There never used to be anyone living next door. **There might have been** someone outside.

Write:
Supply appropriate modal combinations. More than one answer is possible in each case.

1 There (be) a problem about this. ....*There could be a problem about this*........................
2 There (be) a witness present. ....
3 There (never be) a better opportunity. ....
4 (there be) a reason for this delay? ....
5 (there be) another election soon? ....
6 Why (there be) so much red tape? ....
7 Why (not there be) more university places? ....

11.13E Context

Write: Supply suitable forms of the verbs and insert *could be, may be, will be, would seem.*

You've been painting the ceiling!

MEDICAL DETECTIVE?
'For the time being,' Dr Grey said, 'it's important that (*you take*) [1] *you (should) take*. it easy. Immediately after a heart attack, I suggest (*you get*) [2] .... plenty of rest. After a month, I recommend (*you begin*) [3] .... taking a little exercise.' Mr Fry blinked through his glasses. 'I [4] .... dead!' he protested. 'If you don't do as I tell you, you will be,' Dr Grey said. 'It's vital that (*you follow*) [5] .... my advice.' 'But I've always been so active, Doctor.' 'And you [6] .... active again, but not yet. Come and see me in a fortnight.' Of course, Mr Fry didn't follow his doctor's advice. 'There [7] .... people who can sit around,' he said to his wife, 'but I can't!' He spent the morning before his next appointment painting the kitchen ceiling. In the afternoon, he visited Dr Grey. 'It [8] .... you have been painting the ceiling!' Dr Grey said sternly. 'How can you possibly know, Doctor?' 'You've got paint on your glasses!' the doctor said.

12 The passive and the causative

12.1 General information about form

12.1A Basic forms of the passive [> LEG 12.1-3]

1 In the **active** voice, the subject of the verb is the person or thing that does the action:
John burnt the dinner last night.
In the **passive** voice, the action is done to the subject: ***The dinner was burnt** last night.*

2 We form the passive with a suitable form of *be* + past participle. Only verbs which take an object (**transitive verbs** [>1.2B]) can go into the passive:
*The dinner **was burnt**.* (But not **The plane was arrived.**)

3 Basic tense forms are a tense of *be* + past participle:

present:	*he writes*	→	*it is written*
past:	*he wrote*	→	*it was written*
present/past perfect:	*he has/had written*	→	*it has/had been written*

4 Basic modal forms are: modal + *be/have been* + past participle:

will:	*he will write*	→	*it will be written*
may:	*he may write*	→	*it may be written*
may have:	*he may have written*	→	*it may have been written*, etc.

5 Infinitive: *to be/to have been* + past participle [> 16.1A]:
he is/was to write → *it is to be written/it was to have been written*

Write 1: Mark with a P those sentences which will go into the passive.

1 Someone will drive you to the airport. _P_
2 Goldfish live in fresh water. __
3 The Egyptians built pyramids. __
4 We walked for miles yesterday. __
5 They arrived at 7 last night. __

6 They informed me about it. __
7 I slept till 8. __
8 It's raining. __
9 You must obey the rules. __
10 He's sneezing again. __

Write 2: Rewrite these sentences in the passive.

1 *They owe* a lot of money to the bank.
...... *A lot of money is owed to the bank.* ....

2 *They have proved* that there is no life on the moon.
It ....

3 *You can buy* videos like this one anywhere.
....

4 *Someone has to write* the history of the European Community one day.
....

5 *Someone may have already written* the history of the European Community.
....

6 When we arrived home, we found that *someone had broken* one of our windows.
....

7 *They have sold* their car to pay their debts.
....

8 *They hold* a meeting in the village hall once a week.
....

12.1B The passive with progressive forms: 'She is being interviewed'
[> LEG 12.3n.6]

Study:
★★

> Only the present and past progressive [> 9.2B, 9.4B] are common in the passive. We form the passive with the progressive form of *be* (*am/is/are/was/were being*) + a past participle:
> **present progressive:** *They **are interviewing** her now.* → *She **is being interviewed** now.*
> **past progressive:** *They **were interviewing** her here.* → *She **was being interviewed** here.*

Write: Rewrite these sentences beginning with the words provided.

1 The manager always welcomes new employees.
New employees ...... *are always welcomed by the manager.* ....

2 They're building a new supermarket near the church.
A new supermarket ....

3 They fought the battle in 1623.
The battle ....

4 Someone was cleaning the windows while I was there.
The windows ....

5 Someone has moved my desk!
My desk ....

6 They are taking the refugees to a camp outside the village.
The refugees ....

7 Someone had signed all the documents before I arrived.
All the documents ....

8 They were questioning us and searching our vehicle at the same time.
We .... and our vehicle ....

9 They will post our letters when the ship arrives at the next port of call.
Our letters ....

10 They are opening the case again because they're not satisfied with the verdict.
The case ....

12.1C Context

Write: Put in the correct forms, active or passive, of the verbs in brackets.

HOW THE OTHER HALF LIVES (?)
Lord Manners was a rich and famous banker. When he (*die*) [1] .... *died* ...... recently, he (*give*)
[2] .... a magnificent funeral which (*attend*) [3] .... by hundreds of famous people.
The funeral was going to (*hold*) [4] .... in Westminster Abbey. Many ordinary people (*line*)
[5] .... the streets to watch the procession. The wonderful black and gold carriage (*draw*)
[6] .... by six black horses. The mourners (*follow*) [7] .... in silence. Lord Manners
(*give*) [8] .... a royal farewell. Two tramps were among the crowd. They (*watch*)
[9] .... the procession with amazement. As solemn music (*could hear*) [10] .... in the
distance, one of them (*turn*) [11] .... to the other and (*whisper*) [12] .... in admiration,
'Now that's what I call really living!'.

That's what I call really living!

183

12.2 Uses of the passive

12.2A Uses of the passive [> LEG 12.1, 12.4.1-3]

Study:
★★

1 The passive is not just a different form of the active. It has its own uses and is very common in English. It would be hard to think of the active forms of sentences like:
*Rome wasn't built in a day. **The origin of the universe will never be explained**.*

2 We use the passive mainly in three ways:
– when we don't want to take responsibility for something:
***The matter will be dealt** with soon.* (We don't know or want to say who'll deal with it.)
– when we want to focus on a happening, not who or what did it:
***Our roof was damaged** in last night's storm.* (We're concerned about the roof.)
– when we want to avoid 'vague subjects' like *one, someone, they*, etc.:
***The form has to be signed**.* (Not **Someone/One has to sign the form.*)
***English spoken**.* (Not **One speaks English*) ***Shoes repaired**.* (Not **One repairs shoes*)

Write: Supply suitable active and passive forms in these sentences using the verbs in brackets. Some variations in tenses may be possible.

1 It isn't clear how far the ozone layer (damage) ....*has been damaged*.... by aerosol sprays. It may be possible to tell whether the hole over the Antarctic (widen) .....*has widened*... after the area (investigate) *has been investigated* ..... by high-flying planes.
2 These days, even the most remote places on earth (visit) .... by tourists. Package tours (can/arrange) .... for almost anywhere, from the Himalayas to the Amazonian jungle.
3 Notices such as (English/Speak) .... and (Shoes/Repair) .... are common. Sometimes they (translate) .... into different languages for the benefit of tourists.
4 We (constantly remind) .... of the way the world (become) .... smaller when events taking place in different parts of the globe (flash) .... on our television screens.
5 If you (involve) .... in a car accident and someone (hurt) ...., you (have to) .... report the matter to the police. If only the vehicles (damage) ...., drivers should exchange names and addresses.

12.2B The use of 'by' + agent (= 'doer') after a passive [> LEG 12.5]

Study:
★★

1 We use *by* only when we need to say who or what is responsible for an event:
*The window **was broken** last night.* (We don't know or want to say who or what did it.)
*The window **was broken by a slate** that fell off the roof.* (We wish to give information.)

2 We often use *by* + agent with the passive of verbs like *build, compose, damage, design, destroy, discover, invent, make* and *write* to identify who or what is/was responsible:
***Who designed** St Paul's? – It **was designed by Christopher Wren**.*

Write: Supply passive forms with *by* + agent where necessary.

1 When Jasper Morgan died his collection of pictures (sell) ....*was sold*.... to raise enough money to pay his taxes. Tremendous interest in the sale (show/the general public) *was shown by the general pu*
2 The music that (compose/Beethoven) .... towards the end of his life is very different from his early music. The music (write) .... in extremely difficult conditions.
3 Many beautiful old buildings in cities (replace/modern ones) .... If this replacement (not control), ... it isn't very long before a city loses its character.

12.2C The passive with verbs of 'saying' and 'believing': 'It is said (that) ...'
[> LEG 12.8]

Study:
★★★

> We need to be sure of our facts when we say: e.g. *He was* a spy in World War II.
> If we are not sure of our facts, we can express caution by saying:
> *It is said (that) he was* a spy in World War II./*He was said to be* a spy in World War II.
> We can express caution in three ways, with:
>
> 1 *It* (+ passive + *that*-clause) with e.g. *agree, believe, consider, decide, hope, know, say*:
> *It is said (that)* there is plenty of oil off our own coast.
>
> 2 *There* (+ passive + *to be*) with e.g. *allege, believe, fear, know, report, say, suppose, think*:
> *There is said to be* plenty of oil off our own coast.
>
> 3 Subject (not *it*) (+ passive + *to*-infinitive) with e.g. *allege, believe, consider, know, say*:
> *Jane is said to know* all there is to know about chimpanzees.

Write: Begin these sentences with *It, There* or a name/a noun + passive construction.

1 *It is expected* .... that prices will rise again this month. (expect)
2 .... that all the passengers had died in the crash. (fear)
3 .... to be an expert in financial matters. (suppose)
4 .... to have committed the crime. (think)
5 .... that the sea level is rising. (think)
6 .... to be a lot of coal in the Antarctic. (think)
7 .... to be honest and reliable. (consider)
8 .... to be thousands of people waiting to renew their passports. (say)
9 .... that thousands of new jobs will be created in the computer industry. (say)
10 .... to be a fall in house prices, but I haven't noticed it. (suppose)

12.2D Context

Write: Use the correct tenses and passive forms of the verbs in brackets.

A beautiful mermaid?

FISHY TALES
Mermaids (*see*) *have been seen* by sailors for centuries. The basis of all mermaid myths (*suppose*) [2]........................... to be a creature called a Manatee: a kind of walrus! Mermaids used (*to show*) [3]........................... in funfairs until recently. It all began in 1817 when a 'mermaid' (*buy*) [4]........................... for $6,000 by a sailor in the South Pacific. She (*eventually sell*) [5]........................... to the great circus-owner Barnum. She (*exhibit*) [6]........................... in 1842 as 'The Feejee Mermaid'. It (*say*) [7]........................... that she earned Barnum $1,000 a week! The thousands who saw this mermaid (*must/disappoint*) [8]........................... . She (*cleverly make*) [9]........................... by a Japanese fisherman. A monkey's head (*delicately sew*) [10]........................... to the tail of a large salmon. The job (*so skilfully do*) [11]........................... that the join between the fish and the monkey was invisible. Real imagination (*must/require*) [12]........................... to see this revolting creature as a beautiful mermaid combing her golden hair!

12.3 Form and use of the causative

12.3A Form of the causative: 'have something done' [> LEG 12.10-11]

Study:
★★

1 Note the difference between these two sentences:
*I **had built** a house.* (past perfect tense = 'I did it myself' [> 9.6A])
*I **had** a house **built**.* (the causative = 'I arranged for it to be done' [> 12.3B])

2 We form the causative with *have* + noun or pronoun object + past participle.
We use the causative in different tenses and with modals:
*I **am having** a house **built**. I **had** a house **built**. I **have had** a house **built**.*
*I **will have** a house **built**. I **must have** a house **built**. I **can't have** a house **built**.* etc.

Write: Complete these sentences with the correct forms of the verbs in brackets.

1 They've just had their living room .... *decorated* .... (decorate)
2 Your car engine sounds dreadful. You ought to have it .... (look at)
3 Have you had your eyes .... recently? (test)
4 He's going to have his hair .... at the weekend. (cut)
5 Can I have this letter ...., please? (photocopy)
6 This letter is so important, I'm going to have it .... by a lawyer. (write)

12.3B The causative compared with the active and passive [> LEG 12.12]

Study:
★★

1 We use the **active** to describe jobs we do ourselves or when we know who's doing a job:
I'm servicing the car. Jack is servicing the car.

2 We use the **passive** to say that a job is being done for us, but we don't know or don't want
to say who is doing it:
***The car is being serviced**.* (We're focusing on the car [> 12.2A])

3 We use the **causative** to stress the fact that we are 'causing' someone to do a job for us:
***I'm having the car serviced. I have had my car serviced. I'm going to have my hair cut**.*
Not **I'm going to cut my hair** which means 'I'm going to cut it myself'. [compare > 16.2B]
We often use the causative with verbs that have to do with services: e.g.
build, clean, decorate, develop (a film), *mend, photocopy, press, print, repair, service.*

Write 1: Supply the correct forms of the verbs in brackets.

1 What are you doing? – I ..... *'m cleaning* .... the car. (clean)
2 Where's your car? – It .... at the moment. I'll collect it in an hour. (clean)
3 I never find time to clean the car myself, so I .... (clean)
4 Did you decorate the room yourselves? – No, we .... (decorate)
5 We can't use the living room. It .... at the moment. (decorate)
6 You .... They look quite worn. (must/repair your shoes)
7 My shoes .... It was an expensive job! (just repair)
8 The heel came off my shoe and I .... it myself. (repair)
9 'I'd like this film ....,' I said. 'Certainly,' the assistant said. (develop and print)
10 'Can I use the photocopier .... this document?' I asked. (photocopy)
11 Who .... the children's clothes, in this house? – Who do you think? I do! (mend)
12 What's happened to my report? – It .... at the moment. (photocopy)

Write 2: Today is Wednesday. Look at the notes Maria wrote yesterday and early today. Then write:
a what she had done yesterday; **b** what she is having done today;
c what she is going to have done tomorrow.

Tuesday	Wednesday (today)	Thursday
best skirt cleaned	eyes tested	a tooth extracted
two trees planted	a film developed	two teeth filled
car serviced	some furniture delivered	hair done

1a *She had her best skirt cleaned yesterday* ....
 b *She's having her eyes tested today* ....
 c *She's going to have a tooth extracted tomorrow* ....
2a ....
 b ....
 c ....
3a ....
 b ....
 c ....

12.3C 'Get' in the causative: 'get something done' [> LEG 12.11, 12.13]

Study:
★★

> We sometimes use *get* in place of *have* in the causative to say something is urgent:
> *Have* that car repaired! (causative) *Get* that car repaired! (more urgent causative)

Write: Use *get* in place of *have* in these sentences.

1 I must have .... *I must get* .... this report photocopied and sent off straightaway.
2 They're finally having .... their central heating repaired.
3 We'll be having .... the job done by a local builder.
4 Why don't you have .... that suit cleaned? It's filthy!
5 Have .... your hair cut!

12.3D Context

Write: Put in causative forms for the verbs in brackets.

... customers promptly executed!

CONSTANT MAINTENANCE!
The more you own, the more there is to go wrong. You invest in a new hi-fi system and in no time you have to (*it repair*) [1] *get it repaired* . You (*a new washing machine install*) [2] .... and you have to buy expensive insurance to maintain it. You buy a car and need to (*it service*) [3] .... regularly. You buy a camera and then spend a fortune (*films develop and print*) [4] .... It's not only things that need constant attention. How often we have to (*our eyes test*) [5] ...., (*our teeth fill*) [6] .... and (*our chests X-ray*) [7] ....! But I had to smile last time I went to (*my hair cut*) [8] .... A bold notice in the window announced: 'All our customers promptly executed!' You certainly wouldn't need to (*any jobs do*) [9] .... after that!

13 Questions, answers, negatives

13.1 Yes/No questions, negative statements, Yes/No answers

13.1A Yes/No questions (expecting 'Yes' or 'No' in the answer) [> LEG 13.1-3]

Study:
★

1 We make Yes/No questions from statements. In the case of *be, have* (auxiliary) and modal verbs like *can* and *must* [> 11.1A] we do this by **inversion**, that is by putting *be, have* or *can,* etc. in front of the subject: ***He is*** *leaving.* → ***Is he*** *leaving?*
   She can *drive a bus.* → ***Can she*** *drive a bus?*

2 With all other verbs, we form Yes/No questions with *Do* and *Does* in the simple present and *Did* in the simple past. The form of the verb is always the bare infinitive:
   We turn *left here.* → ***Do we turn*** *left here?*
   He works *well.* → ***Does he work*** *well?*
   They arrived *late.* → ***Did they arrive*** *late?*

Write: You want to know if ... What do you say?

1 you're late. *Am I late?*
2 this is the London train. ....
3 your photos are ready. ....
4 John is working in the garden. ....
5 the children are studying. ....
6 Jane gives piano lessons. ....
7 Tony was enjoying himself. ....
8 they live in the south. ....

9 she should be here. ....
10 she could ask a question. ....
11 it will be fine tomorrow. ....
12 my friend will be staying. ....
13 they would like an invitation. ....
14 they often argue like that. ....
15 I run a mile every morning. ....
16 Sheila went to the lecture. ....

13.1B Negative statements [> LEG 13.2, 13.4]

Study:
★

1 When a sentence contains *be, have,* or a modal like *can,* we form the negative by putting *not* after the auxiliary: *He **is** leaving.* → *He **is not** (**He isn't** or **He's not**) leaving.*
   *He **can** leave.* → *He **cannot** (**can't**) leave.*

2 With all other verbs we use *do not* (*don't*) and *does not* (*doesn't*) after the subject in the simple present and *did not* (*didn't*) after the subject in the past. The verb is always a bare infinitive:
   *We **turn** left here.* → *We **do not** (**don't**) **turn** left here.*
   *He **works** well.* → *He **does not** (**doesn't**) **work** well.*
   *They **arrived** late.* → *They **did not** (**didn't**) **arrive** late.*

Write: Say 'no', disagree or contradict with full negative statements.

1 Are you ready? *No, I'm not ready.*
2 She's right. ....
3 They're late. ....
4 You're being silly. ....
5 He's working in London. ....
6 They're playing tennis. ....
7 I'm going to fail. ....
8 She was waiting for you. ....

9 He can speak Russian. ....
10 He'll be leaving soon. ....
11 It would be a very good idea. ....
12 It looks like rain. ....
13 They always win. ....
14 They missed the last lesson. ....
15 She's always been good at sport. ....
16 You've met her. ....

13.1C Yes/No short answers [> LEG 13.5-7]

Study:
⭐

1 When answering with *Yes* or *No*, we usually repeat the first word in the question:
   Was *James late?* – *Yes, he **was**./No, he **wasn't**.*
   Can *he play chess?* – *Yes, he **can**./No, he **can't**.*
   Note: ***Are*** *you ...?* – *Yes, I **am**./No, I'**m not**.* ***Were*** *you ...?* – *Yes, I **was**./No, I **wasn't**.*
   where we repeat the verb, but in a different form.

2 We do not usually answer a Yes/No question in full:
   Did James go out last night? – ***Yes, he did./No, he didn't**.*
   rather than 'Yes, he went out last night.' 'No, he didn't go out last night.'
   We do not usually answer a Yes/No question with just *Yes* or *No*:
   Do you like dancing? – ***Yes, I do./No, I don't**.* Not **Yes./No.** which can sound rude.

3 We can put a lot of expression into short answers and use them to give information, agree,
   disagree, confirm, etc. e.g.
   Did you lock the back door? – ***Yes, I did./No, I didn't**.*   *It's hot.* – ***Yes, it is./No, it isn't**.*

Write: Answer these questions with either *Yes* or *No*.

1 Are you ready? *...Yes, I am....*
2 Is she still at college? ....
3 Are they on their way here? ....
4 Are you still learning French? ....
5 Is Carla applying for that job? ....
6 Are we staying at the same hotel? ....
7 Are you going to help me? ....
8 Was she joking? ....
9 Were they living there then? ....

10 Should I go with them? ....
11 Will you be at the meeting? ....
12 Would you do that if you were me? ....
13 Does she still write to you? ....
14 Do you like curry? ....
15 Did he tell you about the party? ....
16 Has he finished yet? ....
17 Have you ever eaten swordfish? ....
18 Has she been working here long? ....

13.1D Context

Write: Put in suitable Yes/No questions, negatives or short answers.

GUESS WHAT!
Before setting out on holiday, the Weeks family sat in their car and went through their usual quiz.
MR WEEKS: (*we/turn off*) [1] *...Did we turn off / Have we turned off...* the electricity?
MRS WEEKS: (*Yes*) [2] .... I turned it off myself.
MR WEEKS: (*all the taps off*) [3] ....?
JIMMY: (*Yes*) [4] .... I checked every one of them, dad.
SALLY: You (*not remember*) [5] .... my teddy-bear!
MRS WEEKS: (*Yes*) [6] ...., darling. I packed him in your case.
MR WEEKS: (*there any windows open*) [7] ....?
JIMMY: (*No*) [8] .... I shut them all, dad.
MRS WEEKS: (*the front and back doors/lock*) [9] .... ?
MR WEEKS: (*Yes*) [10] .... I've just locked them.
After they had been on the road for an hour, Mr Weeks suddenly turned pale and said, 'Guess what! I
(*not/got*) [11] .... my house keys. They're still in the back door!'

They're still in the back door!

13.2 Alternative negative forms and negative questions

13.2A Negative statements with 'negative adverbs': 'never', etc. [> LEG 13.8-10]

Study:
★★

> 1 We can make negative or near-negative statements with adverbs like *never, hardly, hardly ever, seldom* and *rarely* [compare > 7.4A-B, 7.8C]. *Never* is more emphatic than *not*. Compare: *I **don't drink** coffee.* (negative) with: *I **never drink** coffee.* (emphatic negative)
>
> 2 We can't use a negative adverb with a negative verb to make a 'double negative':
> *I **can hardly** recognize him.* (Not *I can't hardly recognize him.*)
> ***Nobody phoned.*** (Not *Nobody didn't phone.*)
>
> This is especially true for *no, any* and their compounds [> 4.6B]:
> | | | |
> |---|---|---|
> | *I've got **no** time.* | → | *I **haven't got any** time.* |
> | *I've seen **no one/nobody**.* | → | *I **haven't seen anyone/anybody**.* |
> | *I've bought **none** of them.* | → | *I **haven't bought any** of them.* |
> | *I've done **nothing** today.* | → | *I **haven't done anything** today.* |
> | *I've been **nowhere** today.* | → | *I **haven't been anywhere** today.* |

Write: Make negative or near-negative statements using the adverbs in brackets.

1 I don't go to the cinema. (never) *I never go to the cinema.*
2 She doesn't watch TV. (hardly ever) ....
3 I can't get him on the phone. (seldom) ....
4 They didn't greet me. (barely) ....
5 We don't go out. (scarcely ever) ....
6 We can't wait till tomorrow. (hardly) ....
7 We don't see our neighbours. (rarely) ....
8 It's not worth the trouble. (scarcely) ....
9 I haven't bought any eggs. (no) ....
10 I didn't speak to anyone. (no one) ....
11 I don't want any of them. (none) ....
12 She didn't say anything. (nothing) ....
13 We didn't go anywhere. (nowhere) ....
14 Please don't tell anybody. (nobody) ....
15 She doesn't understand English. (hardly) ....

13.2B Cancelling what has just been said: 'No, not Wednesday' [> LEG 13.12]

Study:
★★

> We can cancel what we have just said with *not*:
> *See you Wednesday – no, **not** Wednesday, Thursday.* (Not *No Wednesday*)

Write: Cancel the following by referring to the words in italics.

1 Ask *Diana*. *(No,) not Diana, Josephine.*
2 I'll see you at *5*. ....
3 The plane leaves from *London*. ....
4 The film you want to see is on *today*. ....
5 I'd like a cup of *coffee*. ....
6 Please pass me the *salt*. ....

13.2C Negative questions: 'Can't you ...?' [> LEG 13.14-16]

Study:
★★

1 In negative questions, the word order of the full form is different from the short form:
  full form: **_Did he not_** explain the situation to you?
  short form: **_Didn't he_** explain the situation to you?
  We normally use the short form in conversation and the full form only for emphasis.

2 Depending on the stress and intonation we use, we can:
  – express disbelief, surprise: **_Can't you_** really ride a bicycle?
  – invite the answer 'Yes': **_Don't you_** remember our holiday in Spain?
  – persuade: **_Won't you_** please help me?
  – express annoyance: **_Can't you_** ever shut the door behind you?
  – make exclamations: **_Isn't it_** hot in here!

Write: Rewrite these negative questions using short forms.

1 Am I not too early? [> 10.1B] _Aren't I too early?_
2 Is she not very well? ....
3 Are those answers not wrong? ....
4 Is he not waiting for you? ....
5 Are they not living in Canada? ....
6 Was she not a famous actress? ....
7 Were you not at my old school? ....
8 Are you not going to be there? ....
9 Can you not walk faster? ....
10 Could you not do this for me? ....
11 Do you not like fish? ....
12 Does she not go to church? ....
13 Did he not enjoy the film? ....
14 Have you not finished yet? ....
15 Has he not gone yet? ....
16 Have I not been invited? ....
17 Should you not let him know? ....
18 Am I not invited? ....

13.2D Context

Write: Put in *anything, anywhere, everyone, hardly ever, no, no one, nothing.*

NOT YETI

A Yeti is supposed to be a strange creature that lives in the Himalayas. Nearly [1] _everyone_ has heard of Yetis, but [2] .... has actually seen one. Recently, a party of climbers went up Mount Jaonli looking for Yetis. Unlike more famous mountains, Jaonli has [3] .... been climbed. The party saw [4] .... Yetis [5] .... There was a moment's excitement one night when a climber heard a strange, two-note sound. He rushed out of his tent and asked his Tibetan guide, Chewang Thundup, if he had heard [6] .... 'No, I heard [7] ....,' the guide replied. 'But I just heard a strange sound,' the climber said. 'That was no Yeti,' Chewang laughed. 'It was me, blowing my nose!'

... a strange two-note sound

191

13.3 Tag questions and echo tags

13.3A Tag questions 1: 'It is ..., isn't it?'/'It isn't ..., is it?' [> LEG 13.17-19, 13.22.1-2]

Study:
★★

1 A tag question is a short question (e.g. *have you?/haven't you?*) that follows a statement. We form tag questions with auxiliaries (*be, have, can, may*, etc.) and *do, does, did*.

2 They are **affirmative – negative**: *John **was** annoyed, **wasn't** he? You **like** fish, **don't** you?* or **negative – affirmative**: *John **wasn't** annoyed, **was** he? You **don't** like fish, **do** you?*

3 Many languages have a phrase which means 'Isn't that so?' In English, we use tags to say this, but we also use expressions like *don't you think?, right?* etc.

4 If our voice goes up on the tag, we are asking a real question which needs an answer: *You **left** the gas on, **didn't** you? – Yes, I **did**./No, I **didn't**. You **didn't** leave the gas on, **did** you? – Yes, I **did**./No, I **didn't**.*

5 If our voice goes down on the tag, we want the listener to agree with us and we don't usually expect an answer: *You **locked** the door, **didn't** you?* (= I assume you did.) *You **didn't** lock the door, **did** you?* (= I assume you didn't.)

Write: You want the listener to agree with you. Do the exercise orally, then in writing.

1 She's late, ...*isn't she*............? 10 She isn't late, ...?
2 They're on holiday, ...? 11 They aren't on holiday, ...?
3 I'm early, ...? [> 10.1B] 12 I'm not early, ...?
4 Carla was at home, ...? 13 Carla wasn't at home, ...?
5 We were all ill, ...? 14 We weren't all ill, ...?
6 You've finished, ...? 15 You haven't finished, ...?
7 Marc has gone out, ...? 16 Marc hasn't gone out, ...?
8 I always do the wrong thing, ...? 17 I don't often do the right thing, ...?
9 Tessa works hard, ...? 18 Tessa doesn't work hard, ...?

13.3B Tag questions 2: 'You painted it yourself, did you?' [> LEG 13.20-21, 13.22.3]

Study:
★★

Tag questions can also be **affirmative – affirmative**.
If our voice goes up on the tag, we mean 'Tell me more', etc.:
She's getting married, **is she**? (= I'd like to know more about it.)
If our voice goes down on the tag, we express negative feelings like disappointment, disapproval or suspicion. We don't usually expect an answer:
I'll get my money back, **will** I? (= I don't believe it.)

Write: Say the sentences under A aloud and match them with a statement under B.

A
1 You painted it yourself, did you? *e*
2 You couldn't give me a hand, could you?__
3 Someone broke that vase, did they?__
4 You'll give me a call, will you?__
5 So they're selling their house, are they?__
6 You didn't leave the garage open, did you?__
7 He says he's innocent, does he?__

B
a) I don't believe it.
b) Tell me more.
c) I hope you can.
d) I hope you didn't.
e) I'm impressed.
f) I hope you will.
g) I'm sorry to hear that.

13.3C   Echo tags: 'Is he?'/'He is?' [> LEG 13.24-26]

Study:
★★

1 An echo tag is a response, in tag form, to an affirmative or negative statement.

affirmative
He's resigning.
– Is he? He is?
– He is, isn't he?
– He is, is he?

negative
He isn't resigning.
– Isn't he? He isn't?
– He isn't, is he?
–

2 If our voice goes up on the echo, we want more information:
I've just won £500! – Have you?/You have?/You haven't, have you? (= Tell me more!)

3 If our voice goes down on the echo, we confirm what we know or have guessed:
I'm afraid he's made a bad mistake. – He has, hasn't he? (= I confirm what you say.)
or we express anger, surprise, disbelief, etc.:
I've got the sack! – You haven't!/You haven't, have you?/You have, have you?

Write: Supply different echo tags in response to these statements.
Say the echo tags aloud with different intonation and describe what they express.

1 John's paying. .....*Is he?*...............................
2 They aren't very happy. ....
3 Suzy was 30 yesterday. ....
4 I wasn't very well last week. ....
5 He works very hard. ....

6 They don't eat much. ....
7 You shouldn't be here. ....
8 I can afford a new car now. ....
9 We can't go tomorrow. ....
10 There'll be trouble about this. ....

13.3D   Context

Write: Put in appropriate question tags and echo tags.

You could have knocked me down!

YOU COULD HAVE KNOCKED ME DOWN WITH A FEATHER!
I asked for my favourite perfume at the perfume counter of a large department store. 'We don't have that, ¹ .....*do we*.......?' the snooty assistant asked her colleague, as if I had just tried to buy a bag of onions. I was about to leave the counter when I saw a girl of about twelve slip away from her mother, seize a huge bottle of perfume from the counter and put it into her carrier bag. I gasped! 'Excuse me,' I said. 'Your daughter has just stolen a large bottle of perfume!' The mother looked at me in amazement. 'She ²......................?' 'That's right,' I said. She turned to her daughter. 'You didn't steal that big bottle that was on display, ³......................?' The girl nodded. 'You did, ⁴..................?' 'Yes, mum,' the girl confessed. 'I've told you hundreds of times, ⁵......................, that the big one on display is a *dummy*'. She angrily took the bottle from her daughter and put it back on display. 'You should always take one of the boxed ones at the back, ⁶......................? You do understand that, ⁷......................?' She helped herself to a boxed one and both she and her daughter disappeared into the crowd quick as a flash.

193

13.4 Additions and responses

13.4A Additions and contrasts: 'John can ... and I can, too/but I can't'
[> LEG 13.28-29]

Study:
★★

We can add to statements or make contrasts in the following ways:		
statement	**parallel addition**	**contrast**
John **can** speak French	and I **can**, too.	but I **can't**.
John **can't** speak French	and I **can't**, either. [> 7.7C]	but I **can**.
John **speaks** French	and I **do**, too.	but I **don't**.
John **doesn't speak** French	and I **don't**, either.	but I **do**.
John **can** speak French	and so **can** I.	but I **can't**.
John **can't** speak French	and neither/nor **can** I.	but I **can**.
John **speaks** French	and so **do** I.	but I **don't**.
John **doesn't speak** French	and neither/nor **do** I.	but I **do**.

Write: Rudi and Roxanne are brother and sister. Read this information about them, then write good sentences, beginning each sentence with 'Rudi ...'.

Rudi
He can speak English, but not Italian.
He plays tennis and goes skiing.
He doesn't like classical music.
He visited London last year.

Roxanne
She can speak English and Italian.
She plays tennis, but doesn't go skiing.
She doesn't like classical music.
She visited Rome last year.

1 *Rudi can speak English, and Roxanne can, too*
2 ....
3 ....
4 ....
5 ....
6 ....
7 ....
8 ....
9 ....
10 ....
11 ....
12 ....

13.4B Parallel responses: 'John can ...'/'I can, too/So can I' [> LEG 13.28-29]

Study:
★★

1 We repeat the auxiliary and if there is no auxiliary, we use *do*, *does* or *did*:

statement	**parallel response**		
John **can** speak French.	I **can**, too.	or:	So **can** I.
John **can't** speak French.	I **can't**, either.	or:	Neither/Nor **can** I.
John **speaks** French.	I **do**, too.	or:	So **do** I.
John **doesn't speak** French.	I **don't** either.	or:	Neither/Nor **do** I.

2 We often say *So'm I, Neither'm I, Nor'm I*, but we usually write them in full:
So am I, Neither am I, Nor am I. Neither and *Nor* are exactly the same.

Write: People say things and you respond.

1 I can swim quite well. *I can, too./So can I.*
2 I can't speak Danish. ....
3 I really should study more! ....
4 I won't be at college tomorrow. ....
5 I love Spanish food. ....
6 I don't like red wine. ....
7 I once had a holiday in Ireland. ....
8 I didn't enjoy that film. ....
9 I was hoping to get home early. ....
10 I've had a terrible cold. ....
11 I haven't been very well. ....
12 I thought the concert was awful! ....

13.4C 'So have you' and 'So you have!' [> LEG 13.29.4]

Study:
★★

> Note the difference between:
> *I've got a rash on my arm and **so have you**.* (parallel addition)
> *I've got a rash on my arm. – **So you have!*** (confirmation or surprise)

Write: Tick which statements are additions and those which show confirmation/surprise.
Then continue with similar sentences of your own.

		addition	confirmation/surprise
1 She's wearing that funny hat again! – So she is!		__	✓
2 He's doing very well at work. – So is she.		__	__
3 Maria visits us quite often. – So does Sandro.		__	__
4 Sandro looks just like his uncle. – So he does!		__	__
5 I've got something in my eye. – So you have!		__	__
6 Rosa's got a new bicycle. – So have I.		__	__
7		__	__
8		__	__
9		__	__
10		__	__
11		__	__
12		__	__

13.4D Context

Write: Put in suitable additions and responses.

... a monkey's tail in my soup!

CRAZY STORY
'What are you having to start with?' I asked my wife. 'I don't know,' she said. 'I'm not very hungry.' '1 *Nor am I.*,' I answered, 'but I think I'll start with soup,' '2 ....,' my wife said. The waiter took our order. 'My wife would like some soup and 3 ....,' I said. When the waiter brought the soup, I noticed a monkey sitting on a chair beside me. Suddenly, the monkey's tail was in my soup! 'Waiter! Waiter!' I cried. 'There's a monkey's tail in my soup!' '4 ....!' the waiter exclaimed. 'I can't remove it,' I said. '5 ....,' the waiter said. 'This monkey belongs to the restaurant pianist and he won't let anyone touch it.' I spoke to the pianist. 'Do you know there's a monkey's tail in my soup?' I asked. 'No,' the pianist answered, 'but if you hum it to me, I'll be glad to play it for you.'

13.5 Question-word questions (1): 'Who(m) ...?', 'What ...?'

13.5A Form of question-word questions (except subject questions [> 13.8])
[> LEG 13.30-32]

Study:
⭐

The word order of question-word questions is: question-word + auxiliary + subject:

statement: *He is working.*   *He arrives at 8.*
Yes/No question: *Is he working?*   *Does he arrive at 8?* [> 13.1A]
question-word: ***Why is he working?***   ***When does he arrive?***
                    (Not **Why he is working?**)   (Not **When he arrives?**)

Write: Make two questions from each statement:
a a Yes/No question; **b** a question-word question.

1 She is arriving today.   a   *Is she arriving today?*
   (When)   b   *When is she arriving?*
2 He has written a letter.   a ....
   (Why)   b ....
3 She can help us.   a ....
   (How)   b ....
4 They live in Jamaica.   a ....
   (Where)   b ....
5 He arrives at 10.   a ....
   (What time)   b ....
6 You can't tell us.   a ....
   (What)   b ....

13.5B 'Who(m) ...?' as a question-word [> LEG 13.33]

Study:
⭐⭐

1 *Who(m) ...?* asks for the object of a sentence, usually a person's name or a pronoun:
   statement: *Frank met **Alice**.*   **question**: *Who(m) did Frank meet? – **Alice**.*

2 *Who(m) ...?* refers only to people and can be used to ask about masculine, feminine, singular
   or plural: ***Who(m)** did you see? – **Tim/Ann/The Robinsons***.

3 We still use *Whom ...?* in formal English, spoken or written, but we often prefer *Who ...?* in
   everyday style:
   ***Whom** did you meet at the party?* (formal) ***Who** did you meet at the party?* (informal)

4 We often use *Who(m) ...?* in questions with verbs followed by *to* or *for*:
   ***Who(m)** did you give it **to**? **Who(m)** did you buy it **for**?*

Write: Write questions using the past tense with *Who(m) ...?* to produce the answers given.

1 you invite to your house? – The Frys. *Who(m) did you invite to your house?*
2 Jane see this morning? – Her mother. ....
3 you speak to? – The manager. ....
4 they employ? – Miss Johnson. ....
5 she buy this present for? – Her son. ....
6 John phone? – His brother. ....
7 you complain to? – The headmaster. ....
8 she write to? – Her sister. ....

13.5C 'What ...?' as a question-word [> LEG 13.34]

Study:
★★

> 1 *What ...?* asks for a whole sentence: ***What** are you **doing**? – **I'm reading**.*
> or for the object of a sentence: ***What** are you **reading**? – **'Gone with the Wind'**.*
>
> 2 *What ...?* also combines with nouns:
> *What book/books? What boy/boys? What girl/girls?* [compare *Which?* > 13.6B]
>
> 3 We can use *What?* on its own (*What do you prefer?*) or in a variety of combinations:
> *What('s) ... like?, What('s) ... called? What make ... ? What nationality?,*
> *What ... do (for a living)?, What time/date/year?, What('s) ... for?,*
> *What kind(s)/sort(s) of ...?, What colour ...?, What size ...?.*

Write: Complete the questions on the left to fit the answers on the right.
Think about the combinations you can make with *What's ...?* or *What ...?*.

1 What *What are you doing / looking at* ......? I'm looking at some travel brochures.
2 What ....? I work as an assistant in a book shop.
3 What ....? I use 'Woodland' shampoo. It's lovely.
4 What ....? She's good-looking, but very unpleasant.
5 What ....? Wonderful! Lots of sunshine and no rain.
6 What ....? It's called a 'spade' in English.
7 What ....? It's a Saab.
8 What ....? He's Nigerian.
9 What ....? I think they're leaving at 9.00.
10 What ....? It's March 13th.
11 What ....? It's for scraping paint off windows.

13.5D Context

Write: Supply questions with *Who(m) ...?* and *What ...?*.

I don't mind the risk!

TAKING RISKS
MAGISTRATE: (*What/his name?*) [1] ...*What's his name?* ....
POLICEMAN: James Denyer.
MAGISTRATE: Not Denyer again! If he's not in gaol, he's in and out of
of this court. (*What/he/do this time?*) [2] ....
POLICEMAN: He stole 25 pence.
MAGISTRATE: (*Who(m)/steal it/from?*) [3] ....
POLICEMAN: An old lady. He took it out of her purse.
MAGISTRATE: (*What date/it?*) [4] ....
POLICEMAN: March 24th.
MAGISTRATE (to Denyer): (*What/do that for?*) [5] ....
DENYER: I'm sorry, sir. It won't happen again.
MAGISTRATE (to policeman): (*What/the chances*) [6] ....
if I let him go?
POLICEMAN: It would be a risk, sir.
MAGISTRATE: Do you hear, Denyer? It would be a risk. (*What/say*)
[7] .... to that?'
DENYER: It's a risk I'd be glad to take. Honest, I don't mind the risk!
(*The court falls about with laughter.*)
MAGISTRATE: In that case, I'd better let you go!

197

13.6 Question-word questions (2): 'When?', 'Where?', 'Which?', 'Whose?'

13.6A 'When ...?' and 'Where ...?' as question-words [> LEG 13.35, 13.38]

Study:
★★

> 1 We use *When ...?* to ask about time in the present, past or future.
> The answers are usually adverbs of time or prepositional phrases:
> ***When** is your flight? – **Tomorrow morning./At 4**.*
>
> 2 We use *Where ...?* to ask about place.
> The answers can be whole sentences, phrases or single words:
> ***Where** is he? – **He's over there. Over there! There!***
> *Where ... from?* asks about people and things: ***Where** are you **from**?/do you come **from**?*

Write: Read these situations. Then write questions with *When?* or *Where?*.

1 It's Jim's birthday soon. You can't remember when it is. Ask.
When is / When's Jim's birthday?

2 You like your friend's T-shirt. You'd like to know where he/she got it. Ask.

3 You're going on a coach trip but can't remember the departure time. Ask a friend.

4 Someone mentions a place called Kyzyl. You have no idea where it is. Ask.

13.6B 'Which ...?' as a question-word [> LEG 13.36]

Study:
★★

> 1 *Which* + noun asks about people: ***Which boy/boys/girl/girls** did you see?*
> or things: ***Which book/books** do you prefer?* [> 4.2C and compare > 13.5C]
>
> 2 *Which* always refers to a limited choice and we don't always use a noun after it:
> ***Which** is the longest river in the world?* (Or: ***Which river** is the longest?*)
> We also use *Which of* for two or more items: ***Which of the two/of them** do you prefer?*
>
> 3 *Which* combines with the comparative/superlative: ***Which** is **the cheaper/the cheapest**?*
>
> 4 *Which* combines with *day*, *month* or *year*: ***Which*** (or *What*) ***day*** was it?
>
> 5 *Which way ...?* asks for more exact information than *Where?*: ***Which way** did they go?*

Write: Complete the questions on the left to fit the answers on the right.
Think about combinations you can make with '*Which ...?*'.

1 Which *film did you go to* ....? (We went to see) 'Star Wars'.
2 Which ....? Oh, I like novels best.
3 Which ....? She always uses 'Smooth' soap.
4 Which ....? I met Jill and Sue there.
5 Which ....? I think the Nile's the longest.
6 Which ....? Oh, this desk is definitely the cheapest.
7 Which ....? Of the three, I prefer the leather one.
8 Which ....? That's easy. I'll always remember 1989.
9 Which ....? Oh, July is definitely the hottest.
10 Which ....? I think they went towards the station.

13.6C 'Whose?' [> LEG 13.39]

Study:
★★

> 1 *Whose?* asks about possession. The possessor is always a person and we expect the answer to be somebody's name + *'s* (*Kate's*) or a possessive pronoun (*mine*).
>
> 2 When the possession is a thing or a substance, we can omit the noun after *Whose*:
> *Whose (umbrella/coffee) is this? – It's mine.*
>
> 3 When the 'possession' is a person, we normally use a noun after *Whose*:
> *Whose son/daughter is he/she? – Kate's.* ***Whose children** are they? – The Lakers'.*
>
> 4 We can also phrase questions with *Whose* in the following way:
> ***Whose** is this **umbrella**?* (Compare: ***Whose umbrella** is this?*)
> ***Whose** are those **children**?* (Compare: ***Whose children** are they?*)

Write: Fill in the blanks with *Whose?* or *Who?*.

1 *Who* .... does this pen belong to? – It's John's.
2 .... pencil is this? – It's Kate's.
3 .... do those books belong to? – They're both mine.
4 .... are those socks on the floor? – They're Karl's.
5 .... book is this? – It's Maria's.
6 .... gloves are these? – They're Suzanne's.
7 .... children are they? – My neighbour's.
8 .... son is he? – He's John and Jean's.
9 .... 's at the front door?
10 .... are these children? – They're Mike and Shona's from next door.

13.6D Context

Write: Put in *When?*, *Where?*, *Which?*, *Who?* or *Whose?*.

He never came back!

WHO DID WHAT AND WHEN?

What we believe depends on our view of the world. For example, if we ask, '[1].....*When*.... was America discovered?', most of us would think of Christopher Columbus in 1492. But Chinese children learn that Hui Shen, a Buddhist monk, got to America 1000 years earlier than Columbus. [2].................... was printing invented by and [3].................... year was it invented? You immediately think of Gutenberg in 1436, but Chinese children learn that it was invented by Bi Shen in 1041. [4].................... invention is spaghetti? It's the invention of the Italians, you will say. Wrong again. The Chinese had it before them. [5].................... and [6].................... was the compass invented? Answer: in China in 200 B.C. [7].................... was silk-making invented? Not in Persia, as you might think, but in China. [8].................... was the first country to put a man into space and [9].................... was he? The Soviet Union, you will say and the man's name was Yuri Gagarin. But according to the Chinese, Wan Hu made an attempt long before Yuri. [10]...................., do you think? – In A.D. 1500! He sat in a chair attached to 47 rockets, holding a giant kite which would help him return to earth. He never came back!

13.7 Question-word questions (3): 'Why?', 'How?'

13.7A 'Why ...?' as a question-word [> LEG 13.37]

Study:

> 1 *Why ...?* asks for a reason and we answer with *Because* (Not **Why**) or a *to*-infinitive.
>
> 2 We can use *What ... for?* in place of *Why?*: **What** did you do that **for**? (= Why did you do that?)
>
> 3 We use *Why don't/doesn't ...?* (*Why don't you?/Why doesn't she?*) to make suggestions.
>
> 4 We may use *Why?* or *Why not?* + bare infinitive: **Why wait** for him? **Why not wait** a bit?

Write: Write suitable questions with *Why?* on the left to fit the answers on the right.
Think of possible combinations with *Why?*: *Why don't ...?*, *Why not ...? Why (wait) ...?* etc.

1 Why *are you still downstairs* ....?   Because I want to watch the late-night film.
2 Why ....?   That's a good idea.
3 Why ....?   Because I didn't want to trouble you.
4 Why ....?   I phoned to let him know I had arrived.
5 Why ....?   I'm sorry I shouted at you.
6 Why ....?   To find out his address.
7 Why ....?   I'm already late for my appointment.
8 Why ....?   All right. I'll put the job off till tomorrow.
9 Why ....?   To check that I had locked the back door.

13.7B 'How ...?' as a question-word; 'How much?/How many?' [> LEG 13.40]

Study:
★★

> 1 We use *How?*, basically, to ask about manner:
> **How** did you get on in the exam? – **Quite well**, I hope!
> *How* combines with *much, many*, and with adjectives and adverbs (*How far?* etc.).
>
> 2 We use *How much?* + uncountable to ask about quantity: **How much** bread/milk/time?
> We also use *How much?* to refer to cost: **How much** does this cost? **How much** is it?
>
> 3 We use *How many?* + plural noun to ask about number: **How many** people/books ...?

Write: Use *How much ...?* or *How many ...?* in these sentences.

1 *How much* .... time do we have?   4 .... did that car cost you?
2 .... coffee do you drink every day?   5 .... people came to the meeting?
3 .... times do I have to tell you?   6 .... slices of bread do you want?

13.7C 'How' + adjective or adverb: 'How far?' [> LEG 13.40.2, 13.34.8, 6.16]

Study:
★★

> We can use *How* + adjective (*How long?*) in place of *What* + noun (*What length?*):
> **How long** is that skirt? **What length** is that skirt?

Write: Change these *What* + noun questions into *How* + adjective questions.

1 What's the age of this building? How *old* ..?   4 What size is your briefcase? How ....?
2 What's the depth of this pool? How ....?   5 What length is this room? How ....?
3 What distance is Rome from here? How ......?   6 What height is this house? How ....?

13.7D 'How long ... (for)?' and 'How long ago?' [> LEG 13.40.5]

Study:
★★

> *How long ...?* (with or without *for*) asks about duration: ***How long*** *are you here* ***(for)?***
> *How long ago?* + past tense refers to a point of time: ***How long ago*** *did it happen?* [> 7.3A]

Write: Supply *How long ... (for)?* or *How long ago?*

1 ....*How long*...... are you here?   3 .... did Queen Victoria die?
2 .... was the great fire of London?   4 .... did the Victorian age last?

13.7E Social uses of 'How ...?' [> LEG 13.40.6]

Study:
★★

> We ask questions with *How ...?* for:
> – introductions: *How do you do?*, answered by *How do you do?* (Not e.g. **Fine, thanks**)
> – health: *How are you? How have you been?*, answered by e.g. *Fine, thanks.*
> – personal reactions: *How was the film?* (= What was the film like?)
> – offers and suggestions: *How about a drink?* (= What about a drink?)

Write: Match the questions and the answers.

A

1 How do you do? *d*
2 How are you?___
3 How have you been?___
4 How's life?___
5 How's the garden?___
6 How about going to the cinema?___
7 How was the concert?___
8 How would you like to have lunch
   with us?___

B

a) I'd love to. That's very kind of you.
b) It was very enjoyable.
c) Not bad, but I had a cold last week.
d) How do you do?
e) Yes, that's a nice idea. Let's.
f) Coming along nicely. The tulips are
   just coming out.
g) Very well, thank you. And you?
h) Fine! How's life with you?

13.7F Context

Write: Put in the correct question forms.

'It's a little gold mine!'

RENT-A-SPACE
My son, Len, is only twelve, but I think he's going to be an advertising
tycoon. He had an accident during a football match last week and since
then his leg has been in plaster. Len has been going round our local shops
selling advertising space on his leg. (*'What/charge?'*) [1] *What do you charge?*
I asked him. 'It depends,' he answered. (*'How much space/want?'*)
[2]............................ (*How long/want it (for)?*) [3]............................ (*Want/box*)
[4]............................ or just a few lines? (*Want*) [5]............................ "prime
position", or not?' His plastered leg was covered with ads, so he was
obviously doing well. (*'How much/make*) [6]............................ so far?' I
asked. 'I'm not saying,' he said. (*'How/your leg*) [7]............................ coming
on, anyway?' 'Fine, thanks,' he answered. (*'Why/you ask?'*)
[8]............................ 'I hope you're getting better and we can have that
plaster off,' I remarked. 'I don't want it off too soon,' he grinned. 'It's a little
gold mine!'

201

13.8   Subject-questions: 'Who?', 'What?', 'Which?', 'Whose?'

13.8A   Subject or object? [> LEG 13.41-43]

Study:

★★

> **1** A subject-question asks for the identity of the subject.
> There is no inversion and the question has the same word order as a statement:
>
> | | subject | verb | object | subject-answer |
> |---|---|---|---|---|
> | statement: | *Someone* | *paid* | *the waiter.* | |
> | subject-question: | *Who* | *paid* | *the waiter?* | *John* (did). |
>
> Compare a *Who(m)*-question which asks for the object of a statement [> 13.5B]:
>
> | | subject | verb | object | object-answer |
> |---|---|---|---|---|
> | statement: | *John* | *paid* | *the waiter*. | |
> | *Who(m)*-question: | *Who(m) did John pay?* | | | *The waiter*. |
>
> **2** Answers to subject-questions often echo the auxiliary verb used in the question:
> *Who **can** play the piano? – I **can**./I **can't**.*
> When no auxiliary verb is present in the question, we use *do, does* or *did* in the answer:
> *Who **wants** a lift? – I **do**. Who **won**? – We **did**.*
>
> **3** *What, Which, Whose* and *How much/How many* can combine with other subject-words:
> *What number is ...? Which boy likes ...? Whose car is ...? How many students are ...?*

Write 1:   Does the question-word ask for the subject or the object in each question?
Write **S** or **O** against each one.

1 Who spoke to you? *S*
2 Who did you speak to?__
3 Who will she leave her money to?__
4 Who'll lend you the money?__
5 What frightened you?__
6 What did she see?__
7 Which hat does he like?__
8 Which hat suits him best?__
9 Whose number did you ring?__
10 Whose telephone rang?__
11 How many people did you invite? __
12 How many people came to your party? __

Write 2:   Supply suitable subject question-words on the left and suitable answers on the right.

1 .... *Who* .... can play chess?   .... *Mary can.* ....
2 .... wants to have a day off?   ....
3 .... broke the big glass vase?   ....
4 .... 'll help tomorrow?   ....
5 .... made this mark on the table? A knife ....
6 .... will make you happy?   A new car ....
7 .... teacher took you for maths? ....
8 .... tie goes best with this shirt? ....
9 .... dog bit you?   My neighbour's ....
10 .... dog bit you?   The ....
11 .... suitcase got lost on the journey? ....

Write 3: What questions would you ask in these situations?

1 You and some other students are planning a beach party. You need someone who can play the guitar.

Who can play the guitar? / Which of you can play the guitar?

2 You're entertaining some friends. You've just made another pot of coffee.

....

3 A friend has just seen a film and you want to know the story-line.

....

4 You have organized a weekend walk. Ten of the class have said they'll come, but you're worried because you want to know the exact number.

....

5 You are discussing a film with a friend. You were most impressed by one actor. What about your friend's opinion?

....

6 You're sitting chatting with friends. A chair is squeaking. You find it annoying.

....

7 You are at a party and want to go home, but someone's car is blocking your exit. You want to identify the owner of the car.

....

8 You want to identify the students who want to come with you on an excursion.

....

13.8B Context

Write: Put in the right questions and verb forms.

... the wrong Mr Berlin!

PLAY IT AGAIN, WINSTON!
(*Who/compose*) [1] ...*Who composed*.. some of the most famous songs of the 20th century? The answer is Irving Berlin. (*What songs/compose*) [2] ....? Famous ones, like *Alexander's Rag Time Band* and *White Christmas*. There is a well-known story about the famous British Prime Minister, Winston Churchill, who read in a paper that Mr Berlin was in London, so he asked his aide to invite the great man to lunch. Over lunch, Mr Churchill asked question after question. (*Which party/win*) [3] .... the next American election? (*Who/be*) [4] .... the next president of the USA? (*What/papers say*) [5] ....? (*Which papers/be*) [6] .... the most influential? (*Which country/have*) [7] .... the better political system, Britain or America? (*Whose system/Mr Berlin prefer*) [8] ....? (*What/Mr Berlin/think*) [9] .... of party politics in Britain? Mr Churchill was very disappointed with Mr Berlin's answers. Mr Berlin didn't have strong political opinions and Mr Churchill decided he was rather dull. The fact is that Mr Churchill's aide had invited the wrong Mr Berlin to lunch. Mr Churchill thought he was speaking to Isaiah Berlin, the famous philosopher, but his aide had invited Irving Berlin, the song-writer instead!

13.9 Questions about alternatives
Emphatic questions with 'ever'

13.9A Questions about alternatives (1): 'Did you laugh, or cry?' [> LEG 13.44-45]

Study:
★★

> We can abbreviate questions after *or*.
> Instead of: *Did you laugh, or **did you cry** when you heard the news?*
> We can say: *Did you laugh or **cry** when you heard the news?*

Write: Join these full questions with *or* to make single questions.

1 Did they listen to records? Did they go for a walk?
 ...Did they listen to records, or go for a walk?...............
2 Can she dance? Can she sing? Can she play the piano?
 ....
3 Do you buy clothes when you need them? Do you wait for the summer sales?
 ....
4 Has she gone to church? Has she stayed at home?
 ....
5 Will you phone her? Will you wait till she rings back?
 ....

13.9B Questions about alternatives (2): 'Did you take it, or didn't you?'
[> LEG 13.44-45]

Study:
★★

> We can ask two questions, one affirmative and one negative, about the same thing without
> repeating the verb in full.
> Instead of: ***Did you take** it, or **didn't you take** it?*
> We can say: ***Did you** take it, or **didn't you**?*
> or: ***Did you or didn't you** take it? **Did you, or didn't you**?*
> or: ***Did** you take it, **or not**? (Not *or no*)*

Write: Rephrase each question in three ways without repeating the verb in full.

1 Do you like fish, or don't you like fish?
 a *Do you like fish, or don't you?*...........................
 b *Do you or don't you like fish?*...........................
 c *Do you like fish, or not?*...........................
2 Can you help me, or can't you help me?
 a ....
 b ....
 c ....
3 Have you sent a card, or haven't you sent a card?
 a ....
 b ....
 c ....
4 Will you phone the plumber, or won't you phone the plumber?
 a ....
 b ....
 c ....

13.9C Emphatic questions with 'ever', etc. [> LEG 13.46-47]

Study:
★★

1 We ask emphatic questions with *ever* to express admiration, anger, concern, etc.
We write *ever* as a separate word from question-words. Compare:
Where ever did you buy that tie?   *Wherever* you go, take your passport. [> 1.8C]
How ever did you manage it?   *However*, I managed to persuade him. [> 7.8B]
What ever does she see in him?   *Whatever* she sees in him, she'll marry him. [> 1.9C]

2 We use *ever* after all question-words except *Which?* and *Whose?* and we often put heavy
stress on it in spoken questions: *Where 'ever* did you pick that up?

3 We can ask questions with *ever*:
– to get a subject or an object: *What ever* made you late? *What ever* did he say?
– in short responses: *What ever for? Why ever not?*
or we use a phrase like *on earth* for extra emphasis: *How on earth* did you know?

Write: Make these questions more emphatic to express admiration, surprise, concern, etc.

1 Who gave you permission to do that? ..*Who ever gave you permission to do that?*....
2 Why didn't you ask an expert to look at it? ....
3 When did they go to Iceland? ....
4 What will she say next? ....
5 Where shall I put this wet umbrella? ....
6 How do you expect me to carry all this? ....
7 How did you get into this mess? ....

13.9D Context

Write: Use forms with *ever*, etc. and ask questions about alternatives.

THE MAN I'VE BEEN WAITING FOR!
Colonel Blimp is a short-tempered man. He pays good money to his
motoring organization and he expects instant service. He broke down on
a lonely road recently and was ready to explode when he had to wait for
two hours before help arrived. Even before the driver got out of his car,
the Colonel was muttering, '(*What*) [1] ....*What ever*.... took you so
long? (*What*) [2] .... do we pay good money for? I don't
break down often, but (*when*) [3] .... I do, I expect real
service.' The driver leaned out of the window. (*'Have you broken down?
Have you run out of petrol?*)' [4] .... 'Can't start the
engine!' the Colonel said sharply. 'Let's have a look at it,' the man said.
(*'Have you tried to start it? Haven't you tried to start it?'*)
[5]... The Colonel, now red in the face, didn't
reply. 'Well, (*have you? haven't you?*) [6]... the
man asked. 'Oh, I see, you've flooded the engine. Got a cloth?' 'Haven't
you even brought a cloth?' the Colonel yelled. The man smiled. 'Oh, this
isn't my job, you know. I'm just a passing motorist. I stopped because
you looked as if you needed help.'

This isn't my job, you know

205

14 Conditional sentences

14.1 Type 1 conditionals

14.1A Type 1 conditionals, basic uses: 'If the weather clears, we'll go for a walk' [> LEG 14.4-6]

Study:
★★

1 We can use all present tenses after *if*, not just the simple present, for example:
If **she finishes** work early, **she will go** home. (*if* + simple present + *will*)
If **she has finished** work by 4 o'clock, **she will go** home. (*if* + present perfect + *will*)

2 We can use all future tenses in the main clauses, not just the *will*-future:
If **he doesn't hurry**, the plane **will have left** by the time he gets to the airport.

3 We use Type 1 conditionals to describe what will or won't (probably) happen:
If **the weather clears, we'll go** for a walk. (Not *If the weather will clear*)

Write: Supply the correct forms of the missing verbs.

1 If it ......*is*...... (be) fine tomorrow, we *will go*.. (go) for a picnic.
2 If I .... (have) time tonight, I .... (finish) the novel I'm reading.
3 If it .... (rain) next weekend, we .... (not able to) plant the vegetables.
4 If he .... (be leaving) at 6 o'clock, I .... (ask) him to give me a lift.
5 If she .... (have drive) all that way since this morning, ... (be) tired and hungry.
6 If they .... (have/be working) all afternoon, they .... (probably need) a cup of tea.
7 If I .... (can't/finish) the job this weekend, I .... (try) to get it done during the week.
8 If John .... (be picked) for the team, he .... (be boasting) about it for weeks!
9 If you .... (have/forget) to phone, they .... (will have/go) without you.
10 If we .... (stay) in this flat till May, we .... (will have/be living) here for twenty years.

14.1B 'If' + present + modal: 'If it's fine tomorrow, we may go for a swim' [> LEG 14.7]

Study:
★★

When we use *will* in the main clause, we are expressing certainty or near-certainty:
If *the weather clears*, **we'll go** for a walk. (certain, or nearly certain) [> 11.4A]
If we do not feel 'certain' enough to use *will*, we can use another modal to say what is possible, necessary or desirable, for example:
If *it's fine tomorrow*, **we may go** for a swim. (it's possible)
If *it's fine tomorrow*, **we must go** for a swim. (it's necessary or desirable to do this)

Write: Supply the correct forms of the missing verbs, but use these modals in the main clause: *can, could, may, might, should, ought to*, or *must*. Alternatives are possible.

1 If you ......*are*...... (be) still ill tomorrow, you *ought to*.. stay at home.
2 If you .... (finish) work early, you .... come for a drink with us.
3 If she .... (have) too much to do, she .... ask someone to help her.
4 If he .... (not be coming) tonight, he .... come next week.
5 If he .... (have only just arrive), he .... not have heard the news.
6 If they .... (have be/waiting) longer than an hour, they .... be getting impatient.
7 If we .... (can't/go) next week, we .... manage to go the week after.

14.1C   'If + should' instead of 'if + present' [> LEG 14.8]

Study:
★★

> *If + should*, instead of *if + present*, makes the condition more doubtful or very polite:
> *If **I should** see him, **I'll ask** him to ring you.* (= *If **I see him, I'll ask** him to ring you.*)

Write: Rewrite these sentences using *should* in the *if*-clause.

1 If you see him, please give him this message. *If you should see him,.....*
2 If she asks you, please don't tell her anything. ....
3 If he phones, please say I'm out. ....
4 If the temperature falls, turn up the heating. ....
5 If you receive a letter, let me know. ....
6 If you go out, get me a paper. ....

14.1D   Imperative + 'and/or' + clause: 'Fail to pay and ...' [> LEG 14.9]

Study:
★★

> We can use the imperative in place of an *if*-clause to comment, threaten, request, etc.
>
> 1 We follow the imperative with *and* in place of an *if*-clause in the affirmative:
> *If you fail to pay, **they'll cut off** the electricity.* →
> **Fail** to pay **and they'll cut off** the electricity.
>
> 2 We follow the imperative with *or* in place of an *if*-clause in the negative:
> *If you don't stop borrowing money, **you'll be** in trouble.* →
> **Stop** borrowing money, **or you'll be** in trouble.

Write: Change these sentences to begin with an imperative.

1 If you ask me nicely, I'll mend it for you. *Ask me nicely and I'll mend it for you.*
2 If you crash my car, I'll never forgive you. ....
3 If you work late tonight, I'll pay you well. ....
4 If you don't hurry, you'll be late. ....
5 If you don't take a taxi, you'll miss your train. ....
6 If you don't stop shouting, I'll slap you. ....

14.1E   Context

Write: Put in the missing verb forms.

Here's the doctor!

AN URGENT CASE
The family party was in full swing when the phone rang. Dr Craig answered it. He listened carefully for a moment, then said, 'I'll come right away.' 'Do you *have* to go out?' his wife asked. 'If it [1] .....*is*..... an urgent case, I have to go,' Dr Craig answered. 'If I (*should*) [2] .... late, please don't wait up for me.' Dr Craig drove into the night. If I don't hurry, he thought, I (*might*) [3] .... too late. The thought made him drive faster. After driving for an hour, he arrived at a house. All the lights were on. If all the family is up, the doctor thought, the situation (*must*) [4] .... serious. A woman opened the front door immediately. 'Thank God you've come, doctor,' she cried. 'It's my daughter.' A sleepy child of about six appeared in a nightdress. 'I told her,' her mother said, ' "(*go*) [5] .... to bed, or I'll fetch the doctor". See,' she shouted at the child. 'I've done it. Here's the doctor!'

14.2 Type 2 conditionals

14.2A Type 2 conditionals, basic uses: 'If you went by train, you would ...'
[> LEG 14.10-12]

Study:
★★

> We form Type 2 conditionals with *if* + past (or *if* + *could*) + *would*.
>
> 1 We can use Type 2 conditionals in place of Type 1 to describe something that is reasonably possible. The past tense form does not refer to past time:
> *If you go* by train, *you will* (*you'll*) *get* there earlier. (Type 1: reasonably possible)
> *If you went* by train, *you would* (*you'd*) *get* there earlier. (Type 2, 'more tentative')
>
> 2 We often use Type 2 conditionals to describe what is totally impossible:
> *If you had* longer legs, *you would* be able to run faster. (Not *If you would have*)
> *If you could run* fast, *you'd be* an Olympic champion.

Write: Write Type 2 conditionals to match these situations.

1 I don't have a spare ticket. I can't take you to the concert.
If I had a spare ticket, I could / would take you to the concert

2 She drinks too much coffee. She doesn't feel calm.
....

3 He can't type. He isn't able to operate a computer.
....

4 They don't understand the problem. They won't find a solution.
....

5 He sits around too much. He isn't fit.
....

14.2B 'If + were/was' + 'would': 'If I were you, I would ...' [> LEG 14.13]

Study:
★★

> 1 We can use *were* in place of *was* after *if* in all persons: 'the subjunctive' [> 11.13B].
> *Were* is formal. We also prefer *were* when expressing doubt or imagining something:
> *If I was* better qualified, *I'd apply* for the job. (*If I was*: less formal)
> *If I were* better qualified, *I'd apply* for the job. (*If I were*: more formal)
> How *would she be managing*, if *she were running* a large company? (progressive forms)
> *If I were* the Queen of Sheba, *you would be* King Solomon. (*were* is preferable here)
>
> 2 We use *If I were you* and *If I were in your position* to give advice. (Not *If I was*)
> We can also refer to somebody else: *If I were in Jane's position*, I'd look for a new job.

Write: Write Type 2 conditionals to match these situations.

1 She is not in your position. She isn't able to advise you.
If she were in your position, she would be able to advise you.

2 I am in a hurry. I won't stay to dinner.
....

3 He's not a millionaire. He won't buy you a palace.
....

4 The weather isn't sunny. We won't stay indoors.
....

5 I am fit. I will go climbing.
....

14.2C 'If' + past + modal: 'If he knew the facts, he might ...' [> LEG 14.14]

Study:
★★

> When we use *would* in the main clause, we are expressing as much certainty as possible:
> *If he knew the facts, **he would tell us** what to do.* (certain or nearly certain [> 14.1B])
> If we don't feel 'certain' enough to use *would*, we can use another modal to say what would be possible or necessary, for example:
> *If he knew the facts, **he might tell us** what to do.* (it's possible)
> *If he knew the facts, **he should tell us** what to do.* (it's necessary)

Write: Supply the correct forms of the missing verbs. Use *could, ought to,* or *might* in the main clause.

1 If she ...*were/was*... (be) here now, she ...*could give*... (give) us some advice.
2 If he .... (fail) in his present job, he .... (think) about another career.
3 If you .... (can play) a musical instrument, you .... (help) with the school orchestra.
4 If they .... (have) the right qualifications, they .... (be able to) apply for better jobs.
5 If she .... (can have) some lessons, she .... (improve) her performance.
6 If we .... (run) our own business, we .... (be) more independent.
7 If John .... (go) to his home town, he .... (visit) his mother.
8 If Susan .... (borrow) your book, she .... (return) it.
9 If Frank .... (want) advice, he .... (ask) his bank manager.

14.2D Context

Write: Put in Type 2 conditionals throughout.

LYING IN THE SUN
Two tramps, Eugene and Sergio, were lying in the sun.
EUGENE: What (*we/doing*) [1] *would we be doing* if the sun (*not shining*) [2] .... ?
SERGIO: Well, (*we/not be*) [3] .... lying here for a start. But that's not the important question. The important question is: what (*we do*) [4] .... if (*we/be*) [5] .... rich?
EUGENE: If (*we/be*) [6] .... rich, we (*can/travel*) [7] .... everywhere.
SERGIO: True, but we travel everywhere already.
EUGENE: Yes, but not in style. If (*we/have*) [8] .... money, our chauffeur, James, (*can/drive*) [9] .... us round in our Rolls. Imagine, if (*we/be*) [10] .... in that position! (*We/return*) [11] .... to our fine mansion in the country.
SERGIO: Yes, the butler (*put out*) [12] .... fresh clothes for us, the cook (*prepare*) [13] .... a fine meal for us. We [14] .... not just be eating carrots all the time.
EUGENE: Yes. If (*we/own*) [15] .... a house like that, (*we/also have*) [16] .... a fine swimming-pool.
SERGIO: Yes! Yes! If (*we/have*) [17] .... a fine swimming-pool, (*we can/swim*) [18] .... as much as we liked.
EUGENE: If (*we/be*) [19] .... really really rich, (*we can/lie*) [20] .... in the sun!
SERGIO: But we are lying in the sun!

Lying in the sun

14.3 Type 3 conditionals

14.3A Type 3 conditionals, basic uses: 'If you had gone by train, ...'
[> LEG 14.16-19]

Study:
★★

> We form Type 3 conditionals with *if* + past perfect (or *if* + *could have*) + *would have*.
> We often use Type 3 conditionals to express regret, etc. about things that can now never happen. We can use simple or progressive forms of the past perfect in the *if*-clause:
>
> **If I'd** (= I had) **been** taller,   **I'd** (= I would) **have joined** the police force.
> **If I had had** any sense,   **I wouldn't have bought** a second-hand car.
> **If we had gone** by car,   **we would have saved** time.
> **If I had been trying** harder,   **I would have** succeeded.
> **If I could have stopped,**   **there wouldn't have been** an accident.

Write: Comment on the following situations with *if* (expressing regret, etc.).

1 John ate too much birthday cake, so he was sick.
If John hadn't eaten too/so much birthday cake, he wouldn't have been sick.

2 We came home from our holiday early because we ran out of money.
....

3 The house didn't burn down because the fire brigade came immediately.
....

4 The men were wearing protective clothing, so they were all quite safe.
....

5 I had an accident because I wasn't watching the road.
....

6 I was sweating because it was so hot.
....

7 My father didn't earn much money, so life wasn't easy for us.
....

8 I didn't enjoy school, so I didn't do very well.
....

14.3B 'If I had been you/If I had been in your position' [> LEG 14.18.1]

Study:
★★

> We often use *If I had been you* and *If I had been in your position* to describe what we would have done in someone else's position:
> **If I had been you/If I had been in your position**, I would have accepted their offer.

Write: Comment on these situations. Begin each sentence with *If I had been ...*

1 Marie paid £200 for a dress.
If I had been Marie, I wouldn't have paid £200 for a/that dress.

2 Franz didn't take that job he was offered.
....

3 Ali didn't study at all, so he failed his exams.
....

4 Sandra walked to work in the rain and got wet.
....

14.3C 'If' + past perfect + modal: 'If he had known the facts, he might have ...'
[> LEG 14.19]

Study:
★★

> When we use *would have* in the main clause, we are expressing as much certainty as possible:
> *If he had known the facts, **he would have told us** what to do.* (certain or nearly certain)
> If we don't feel 'certain' enough to use *would have*, we can use another modal to say what would have been possible:
> *If he had known the facts, **he might have told us** what to do.* (it's possible)
> *If he had known the facts, **he could have told us** what to do.* (he would have been able)

Write: Supply the correct forms of the missing verbs. Use *could have (done)* and *might have (done)* in the main clause.

1 If I *had managed* (manage) to repair my car earlier, I *could have driven* (drive) you to London.
2 If I .... (know) last week that she was ill, I .... (visit) her.
3 If you .... (not want) to drive straight home, we .... (miss) all this traffic.
4 If you .... (ask) politely, I .... (help) you.
5 If the weather forecast .... (be) different, we .... (stay) at home.
6 We .... (be) at the airport for hours, if we .... (not know) that the flight was delayed.
7 I .... (make) a bad mistake, if I .... (not read) the instructions.
8 We .... (have) an accident, if our car .... (not be) properly serviced.
9 If he .... (fasten his seatbelt), he .... (not be) hurt.
10 She .... (not hear) the news, if she .... (not turn on) the radio this morning.
11 If they .... (could see) us, they .... (laugh).
12 If you .... (tell) me you needed money, I .... (lend) you some.
13 I .... (save) some food for you, if I .... (know) you were going to be late.
14 They .... (play) better, if they .... (have) more training.

14.3D Context

Write: Put in Type 3 conditionals throughout.

BOTH RIGHT AND BOTH WRONG
The black car screamed round the corner on the wrong side of the road and passed a white car doing exactly the same thing in the other direction. Both drivers stopped and got out of their cars. 'If I (*be*) [1] *had been*... on my side of the road, you (*kill*) [2].......................... me,' driver A shouted. 'But you weren't on your side of the road,' driver B shouted back. 'If you (*... driving*) [3].......................... more carefully, you (*not be*) [4].......................... on the wrong side of the road.' 'If I (*know*) [5].......................... what was round the corner, I (*keep*) [6].......................... to my side of the road,' driver A said. 'If you (*know*) [7].......................... what was round the corner, you (*... not driving*) [8].......................... so carelessly.' Suddenly, both men stopped shouting and driver A said, very quietly, 'If we both (*not be*) [9].......................... on the wrong side of the road, we (*be*) [10].......................... dead now.' Without speaking a further word, both men shook hands and drove away.

... doing exactly the same thing

14.4 Mixed conditionals; 'unless/if ... not', etc.

14.4A Mixed tenses in conditional sentences [> LEG 14.3]

Study:
★★★

We do not always have to stick rigidly to the 'three types of conditional sentences'. There are occasions when we can use any tenses in *if*-clauses, depending on the context:
If I am as clever as you say I am, *I would have been* rich by now.   Type 1 + Type 3
If you knew me better, *you wouldn't have said* that.   Type 2 + Type 3
If I had had your advantages, *I'd be* better off now.   Type 3 + Type 2

Write: Use mixed tenses in these sentences.

1 If I *were* .... (be) you, I *would have checked.* (check) my facts before I wrote that letter.
2 If you .... (be) so hungry, you .... (not miss) breakfast.
3 If he .... (not catch) the 5.30 train, he .... (not arrive) for another two hours.
4 He .... (feel) very tired today if he .... (play) rugby yesterday.
5 If the snake bite .... (be) poisonous, you .... (feel) very ill now.
6 If I .... (be) in your position, I .... (answer) his letter by now.

14.4B 'If not' and 'unless' [> LEG 14.20]

Study:
★★★

1 We can use *if ... not* and *unless* in place of each other when we are saying 'except if'.
Unless is 'stronger' than *if not* and we sometimes use it in 'threats':
If you don't change your mind I won't be able to help you. (= Except if you change ...)
Unless you change your mind, I won't be able to help you. (= Except if you change ...)

2 We cannot use *unless* in place of *if not* when *if not* doesn't mean 'except if':
I'll be surprised *if he doesn't win*. (*if not* doesn't mean 'except if')
She'd be better company *if she didn't complain* so much. (*if not* doesn't mean 'except if')

3 We often use *unless* (never *if ... not*) to introduce an afterthought:
I couldn't have got to the meeting – *unless*, of course, I had caught an earlier train.

Write 1: Tick the sentences where we could use either *if not* or *unless*.

1 I won't do it if you don't help me. ✓
2 Unless he chooses his words more carefully, he'll be in trouble. __
3 She'd have more friends if she didn't criticise everyone so much. __
4 I'll be surprised if they don't get married one day. __
5 She couldn't have stolen the jewels unless she had had inside help. __
6 She couldn't have stolen the jewels – unless of course someone had helped her. __
7 I'd be very pleased with this car if it didn't break down all the time. __

Write 2: Supply *if not* or *unless* in these sentences. Note where you could use either.

1 (you/tell) *Unless you tell / If you don't tell* me the whole story, I won't be able to help you.
2 He would be happier and healthier (he/have) .... so many worries.
3 We couldn't have caught the plane – (we/break) .... the speed limit getting to the airport.
4 (management and unions/become) .... more flexible, there'll be a lot more strikes.
5 I'll be there by 7 o'clock (I/get held up) .... in the traffic.
6 (we/have) .... more rain soon, the plants will all die.
7 (you/not warn) .... me, I would have fallen into the same trap as you.

212

14.4C   Conjunctions we can sometimes use in place of 'if' [> LEG 14.21]

Study:
★★

> We can introduce conditionals with conjunctions which do not always have exactly the same meaning as *if*, for example: *assuming (that), even if, on (the) condition (that), provided* (or *providing*) *that, so long as, suppose* and *supposing*:
> **Assuming (that) it's** fine tomorrow, we'll go for a swim.

Write: Rewrite these sentences using the conjunctions in brackets.

1 If you gave me $10,000, I still (not go) down a coal mine. (even if)
   Even if you gave me $10,000, I still wouldn't go down a coal mine.

2 I (lend) you my book if you let me have it back by Monday. (on (the) condition (that))
   ....

3 If you look after it, I (let) you keep my bicycle till the weekend. (providing (that))
   ....

4 If you (not tell) anyone else, I'll tell you what happened. (so long as)
   ....

5 If it (be) a holiday on Monday, we can drive to the seaside. (assuming (that))
   ....

6 The children were never scolded if they (do) what they were told. (so long as)
   ....

14.4D   Context

Write: Put in the right conditionals.

THE SECRET OF A LONG LIFE
Grygori Pilikian recently celebrated his 114th birthday and reporters visited him in his mountain village in Georgia to find out the secret of a long life. 'The secret of a long life,' Grygori said, 'is happiness. If you (*be*) [1]........*are*........ happy, you will live a long time.' 'Are you married?' a reporter asked. 'Yes,' Grygori replied. 'I married my third wife when I was 102. If you are happily married, you (*live*) [2]........................ for ever. But for my third wife, I (*die*) [3]........................ years ago.' 'What about smoking and drinking?' a reporter asked. 'Yes, they are important,' Grygori said. 'Don't smoke at all and you (*feel*) [4]........................ well. Drink two glasses of wine a day and you (*be*) [5]........................ healthy and happy.' 'If you (*can/live*) [6]........................ your life again, what (*you/do*) [7]........................?' a reporter asked. 'I would do what I have done. If I had had more sense, I (*eat*) [8]........................ more yoghourt!' he chuckled. 'Supposing you (*can/change*) [9]........................ one thing in your life what (*you/change*) [10]........................?' another reporter asked. 'Not much,' Grygori replied. 'So you don't have any regrets?' 'Yes, I have one regret,' Grygori replied. 'If I (*know*) [11]........................ I was going to live so long, I (*look after*) [12]........................ myself better!'

The secret is ... happiness!

213

15 Direct and indirect speech

15.1 Direct speech

15.1A Quotation marks and other punctuation marks [> LEG 15.1-3]

Study:
★★

We use the term **direct speech** to describe the way we represent the spoken word in writing. We punctuate the four types of sentence [> 1.1B] by putting **quotation marks** (also called **inverted commas**) outside all other punctuation marks, such as commas (,), full stops (.), and exclamation marks (!). Quotation marks may be single ('...') or double ("..."). We put them at the beginning and end of each quotation, high above the base-line. We don't use dashes * – * or chevrons *< ... >* to punctuate direct speech. We use only one question mark or exclamation mark at the end of a question or exclamation:

statement:	'The shops close at 7 tonight.'	or:	"The shops close at 7 tonight."
question:	'Do the shops close at 7 tonight?'	or:	"Do the shops close at 7 tonight?"
command:	'Shut the window!'	or:	"Shut the window!"
exclamation:	'What a slow train this is!'	or:	''What a slow train this is!''

Write: Add correct punctuation marks to these examples of direct speech.

1 John's in a hurry
2 Have you been out
3 Where are my glasses
4 What a surprise
5 How are you
6 It's unbelievable
7 There's someone at the door

8 What a noise
9 When did you arrive
10 Tell me what happened
11 Don't shout at me
12 Have a cup of coffee
13 How do you like your coffee
14 Have you met Jean

15 Keep quiet
16 Stop
17 Are you all right
18 I'm waiting for a bus
19 Here's a letter for you
20 Haven't we met before

15.1B Quotation marks and 'reporting verbs' [> LEG 15.1-3]

Study:
★★

1 When we show direct speech in writing, we often use **reporting verbs** like *say, tell* and *ask*. What is said, plus reporting verb and its subject, is a whole unit of meaning.

2 When the subject + reporting verb comes at the beginning of a sentence, we put a comma after the reporting verb (sometimes a colon (:) in American English) and we begin the quotation with a capital letter:
John said, 'We're late.' (Not *John said, 'we're late.'*)

3 When the subject + reporting verb comes after what is said, we put a comma before the second quotation mark:
'We're late,' John said. or: *'We're late,' he said.* (Not *'We're late', John said.*)

4 If we end a quotation with a question mark or an exclamation mark, we do not use a comma as well:
'Where can I get a taxi?' John asked. (Not *taxi,?*) *'What a surprise!' John exclaimed.*

5 Subject + verb can come in the middle of a quotation-sentence:
'Where, in this wretched town,' John asked, 'can I get a taxi?' (Not *... asked, 'Can*)
The second part of the quotation does not begin with a capital letter because it is not a separate sentence.

Write: Add single quotation marks and other punctuation marks to these examples.

1 Where do you come from John asked
2 It's here Bill said
3 I've got a good idea Mark said
4 Is it something she asked that we all ought to know
5 As I was leaving he explained I heard someone shout
6 Don't shout at me he cried
7 John said We're late
8 We're late John said

9 What's the time Andrew asked
10 Bill said I'm hungry
11 What is it Jill asked
12 You are stupid sometimes she said
13 Where is he Tom asked
14 What a surprise she exclaimed
15 Is there anyone in she inquired
16 Which way did they go he asked
17 Tom said She's ill
18 She's ill Tom said

15.1C 'Quote within a quote' [> LEG 15.3ns.3,5]

Study:
★★★

1 If we are quoting someone else's words inside a quotation, we use a second set of quotation marks. If we have used single quotation marks on the 'outside', we use double ones on the 'inside' and vice-versa. The inside quotation has its own punctuation, distinct from the rest of the sentence:
   Ann said, 'Just as I was leaving, a voice shouted, "Stop!".'
   'What do you mean, "Are you all right?"?' Ann asked.

2 We can also use a second set of quotation marks when we mention the title of e.g. a book or a film: *'How long did it take you to read "War and Peace"?' I asked.*

3 We don't normally use quotation marks with verbs like *think* and *wonder*:
   So that was their little game, he thought.   Why hasn't she written, he wondered.

Write: Add correct punctuation marks to these examples of direct speech.

1 As I was leaving, he explained someone shouted Fire
2 Please don't keep asking me What's the time Jim said crossly
3 Have you read Who's Afraid of Virginia Woolf my teacher asked
4 What do you mean Have you lost your way the stranger asked me
5 Where are they now he wondered

15.1D Context

Write: In printed dialogue, each new speech begins on a new line in a new paragraph.
Punctuate the following.

The Roxy was closed ...

INSPECTOR WILEY INVESTIGATES
1 It's all lies Boyle cried
2 You think so Inspector Wiley asked mildly
3 Think so? I know it Boyle answered sharply
4 And no doubt the inspector continued you can prove it. Where were you on Saturday night, the night of the robbery
5 I was at the Roxy with my girlfriend Boyle replied. We saw Gone with the Wind. The film lasted four hours
6 But, cried the inspector the Roxy was closed all last weekend

15.2 'Say', 'tell' and 'ask'

15.2A 'Say', 'tell' and 'ask' [> LEG 15.5-9]

Study:
★★

1 The commonest reporting verbs in both direct and indirect speech are: *say, tell* and *ask*.

2 We must always use a personal indirect object after *tell* (*tell somebody ...*):
He told me he was tired. (Not *told to me*) **John told his mother** he was going out.
We can use *to me*, etc. after *say* if we want to, but we can't say *He said me* [> 1.3B]:
'You haven't got much time,' **he said (to me)**. or: *... he told me*. Not *he said me/he told*

3 We can use *me*, etc. after *ask* if we want to: *'Are you comfortable?'* **he asked (me)**.

Write: Choose the correct word from those in brackets to fill the blank in each sentence.

1 He often ......*says*...... things like that. (says/tells)
2 She always .... me her troubles. (says/tells)
3 The children always .... me if they can go out to play. (tell/ask)
4 They .... me to leave. (said/asked)
5 'Don't do that!' she .... to them. (said/told/asked)
6 'They've arrived,' she .... (said/told/asked)
7 'How are you both?' she .... (told/asked)
8 I .... that I didn't know what to do. (said/told/asked)
9 She .... me she didn't know what to do. (said/told/asked)
10 They .... if I knew what to do. (said/told/asked)
11 The nurse .... him whether he needed anything else. (said/told/asked)
12 Did he .... you where you came from? (say/ask)
13 Did she .... you where she had put my books? (say/tell)
14 The policeman .... us where we were going. (said/told/asked)
15 He didn't .... me how long the job would take. (say/tell)
16 'There's no match on Saturday.' – 'Who .... so?' (says/tells/asks)
17 'You were right. Those curtains look terrible!' – 'I .... you so!' (said/told/asked)
18 When I was introduced to the Princess, she .... a few words to me. (said/told)
19 That little boy's very bad. He .... a lot of lies. (says/tells)
20 'How much are those bananas?' – 'I've got no idea. Go and .... the price.' (say/tell/ask)

15.2B Fixed expressions with 'say', 'tell' and 'ask' [> LEG 15.7.2]

Study:
★★

There are many common expressions with *say, tell* and *ask*, for example:
say: *say a few words, say so, say no more, say nothing, say your prayers*
tell: *tell a lie, tell a story, tell you so, tell the time, tell the truth*
ask: *ask after someone, ask (for) a favour, ask a question, ask the price*

Write: Supply the missing phrases with *say, tell* and *ask*.

1 Don't say ......*'I told you so'*...... now that the worst has happened.
2 Don't offer to buy it. .... first.
3 You've told me more than I need to know.
....

4 If you need money, why don't you .... a loan?
5 Don't tell them anything. ....
6 'Who ....?' – 'I say so!'
7 When did your son learn to ....?
8 I did it. I cannot ....

15.2C Indirect statements with the reporting verb in the present [> LEG 15.10-11]

Study:
★★

1 If the reporting verb is in the present, the tenses that follow are usually the same as those used in the original spoken statement. This is often the case when we report words that have just been spoken. *That* is optional after *say* and *tell*:
Someone says *'I've eaten.'* and we report it as: *He says (that) he has eaten.*
Someone says *'I enjoyed it.'* and we report it as: *He says (that) he enjoyed it.*

2 The reporting verb is often in the present when:
– we are passing on messages: *'What does mother say?' 'She says you must come in now.'*
– reading aloud and reporting: *'The instructions say that you connect this plug to the set.'*
– reporting what someone often says: *'She's always telling me how rich she is.'*

Write: Report what these people are saying with the reporting verbs provided.

1 'She's going to America for six months.' They say *she's going to America for six months*.
2 'They went to Rhodes last year.' Peter tells me ....
3 A: 'I'm not feeling well.' B: 'Pardon?' C: 'She's not feeling well.'
   She says ....
4 A: 'I'll look at your work in a minute.' B: 'Pardon?' C: 'She'll look at your work in a minute.'
   She says ....
5 A: 'I've typed those letters.' B: 'What does she say?' C: 'She's typed those letters.'
   She says ....
6 'We must investigate this case.' The writer of this report says ....
7 'The last strike did no one any good.'
   The writer of this article says ....
8 'Turn off the electricity at the mains.' It says here ....
9 'You have to rub down the walls.' The instructions say ....
10 'I'm good at flower arranging.' She's always telling people ....

15.2D Context

Write: Put in appropriate forms of *ask, say* and *tell*.

WHO HAS THE LAST SAY?
Some people [1](*always*) *are always say* ....-ing that they don't build cars as they used to. What nonsense!
I walked round the beautiful new Ferrari again, admiring its lines, when my thoughts were rudely
interrupted. 'Will you be here long?' a voice [2].................. sharply. 'I haven't made up my mind yet,'
I [3].................., looking up at a sour-faced traffic warden. 'Well, you can't stop here,' he [4]..................
me. 'Who [5].................. so?' I [6].................. him cheekily. 'I [7].................. so,' he [8].................. to me. 'It
[9].................. here,' he added, 'in case you can't read, "No Waiting".' 'You read very well. Go to the top
of the class!' I [10].................. him, 'but I'll make my own decisions.' 'Oh, will you?' the traffic warden
[11].................. . 'Then so will I and I've decided to give you a ticket,' he [12].................. to me with relish
as he began filling out a form. 'Go ahead,' I [13].................. him. 'This car doesn't belong to me anyway.
I wish it did!'

I've decided to give you a ticket!

15.3 Indirect statements with tense changes

15.3A Common indirect speech forms [> LEG 15.12-13, 9.5]

Study:
★★

We tend to use past tenses in indirect speech because we are reporting past events, so we use the past tense of reporting verbs (*he said (that) ... he told me (that)*). How we report is a matter of common sense and we can mix tenses if we want to. We can say:
Jim says he's read *Tony's book and **didn't understand** it.* (= then, when he read it)
Jim said he'd read *Tony's book and **doesn't understand** it.* (= now), etc.
But what commonly happens is that present attracts present and past attracts past, so we would probably say: ***Jim said he'd read*** *Tony's book and **didn't understand** it.*
We move the reported clauses 'one tense back'. A useful general rule is:
'present becomes past and past becomes past perfect'.

Write: Report these statements with *said* (except 13) moving the clauses 'one tense back'.

DIRECT SPEECH STATEMENTS	INDIRECT SPEECH STATEMENTS
present becomes past	
1 MAC: I need a holiday.	*Mac said (that) he needed a holiday.*
2 SUE: I'm not wasting my time.	....
present perfect becomes past perfect	
3 TOM: I've had some good news.	....
4 PAM: I've been sleeping.	....
past becomes past or past perfect (past perfect is often optional)	
5 LOU: I went home early.	....
6 JAN: I was waiting for you.	....
past perfect does not change	
7 JOE: I had eaten earlier.	....
8 PAT: I had been waiting for you.	....
modal 'present' becomes 'conditional' or 'past'	
9 TIM: I will see you later.	....
10 DOT: I can speak French.	....
11 KIM: I may arrive later.	....
'shall' with a future reference becomes 'would'	
12 RON: I shall speak to him.	....
'shall' in offers and suggestions becomes 'should' [> 15.5B]	
13 MEG: Shall I speak to him?	Meg asked whether ....
'past' or 'conditional' modals do not change	
14 TED: I could help you.	....
15 ANN: I might see him.	....
16 JIM: I would enjoy that.	....
'perfect' modal forms do not change	
17 SAM: I must have fainted.	....
18 DON: I couldn't have said that.	....
19 NED: I needn't have gone there.	....
20 LYN: I ought to have helped her.	....
'should' (= 'it's advisable') doesn't change	
21 LEE: I should go to the dentist's.	....
'should' used in place of 'would' in conditionals becomes 'would'	
22 DAN: If I were you I should get legal advice.	....

'must' (= necessity in the past) does not change, or becomes 'had to'

23 PAUL: I must catch an early train. ....

24 JILL: I must speak to you. ....

'must' (= necessity in the future) does not change, or becomes 'would have to'

25 BILL: I must leave tomorrow. ....

26 JANE: I must work till late. ....

'must' (= deduction or possibility) does not change.

27 PHIL: John must be a fool. ....

'mustn't' (= prohibition) does not change, or becomes 'couldn't'

28 JEAN: I mustn't eat meat. ....

29 JEFF: They mustn't give up. ....

15.3B Pronoun and adverb changes in indirect speech [> LEG 15.12-13]

Study:
★★

1 Pronouns change (or not) depending on the view of the reporter:
'I'll send you a card, Sue.' (actual words spoken by Ann)
Ann told Sue she'd send her a card. (reported by someone else)
Ann said/told me she would send me a card. (reported by Sue)
I told Sue (that) I'd send her a card. (reported by Ann)

2 Time and place changes: Adverb changes depend on context, e.g.
now   →   immediately/then
today   →   that day
tonight →   that night, etc.
It is not always necessary to make these changes, especially in spoken indirect speech.
'I'll see you tonight,' he said.   →   *He said he would see me tonight.*

15.3C Context

Write: Turn each direct-speech statement into indirect speech with tense changes.

Nuts and water without the nuts

JUST WHAT THE DOCTOR ORDERED!
'I've conducted a number of tests,' Dr Grey said.
1 *Dr Grey said (that) she had conducted a number of tests.*

'I must put you on a very strict diet,' she told me.
2 ....

'You're putting on a lot of weight,' she said.
3 ....

'You have gained 5.5 kilos in six months,' she added.
4 ....

'You gained 10 kilos last year,' she reminded me.
5 ....

'You will get very fat if you go on like this,' she told me.
6 ....

'You should eat very little,' she said.
7 ....

'So I'll have to live on nuts and water,' I said nervously.
8 ....

'You can live on nuts and water without the nuts,' she said.
9 ....

15.4 Indirect questions with tense changes

15.4A Indirect Yes/No questions: 'He asked me if I was ready' [> LEG 15.17-18]

Study:
★★

1 We don't use quotation marks or question marks in indirect questions:
He asked me if (or whether) I was ready.

2 Tense changes: 'Present becomes past and past becomes past perfect', but [> 15.3A]:
'Are you ready?' → *He asked (me) if/whether **I was** ready.*
If we are reporting a question that has just been asked, we can say:
'Are you ready?' – 'What did John ask you?' – 'He asked me if/whether **I'm** ready.'

3 The inversion [> 13.1A] in the direct question changes to statement word order:
'Are you ready?' → *He asked (me) if/whether **I was** ready.*
A reported tag question [> 13.3] also changes to statement word order:
'You're ready, aren't you?' → *He asked (me) if/whether **I was** ready.*

4 We use *if* or *whether* after *ask, want to know, wonder, (not) know, didn't say/tell me.*

Write: Report these Yes/No questions moving the clauses 'one tense back'.

1 'Are you hungry?' She asked us ...*if/whether we were hungry*...
2 'Are you enjoying yourself?' He wanted to know ....
3 'Do you always go to church on Sunday?' He wondered ....
4 'Have you seen John recently?' She asked me ....
5 'Has Debbie been working here long?' He wanted to know ....
6 'Did you study hard for the exam?' She wondered ....
7 'Will Ted and Alice be at the party?' She asked us ....
8 'Will you be coming to the concert or not?' He wanted to know ....
9 'You like Italian food, don't you?' She asked me ....
10 'You don't like Italian food, do you?' She wanted to know ....

15.4B Indirect question-word questions: 'He asked me why I went there'
[> LEG 15.19-20]

Study:
★★

The inversion after a question-word in a direct question changes to statement word order in the reported question and, if necessary, the tense is changed at the same time:
*'Why **haven't you** finished?'* → *He asked (me) why **I hadn't** finished.*
*'When **did you go** there?'* → *He asked (me) when **I went** (or **had gone**) there.*

Write: Report these question-word questions moving the clauses 'one tense back'.

1 'What's the weather like?' She asked me ....*what the weather was like*...
2 'What does Frank do for a living?' I wanted to know ....
3 'Why is Maria crying?' She wondered ....
4 'What kind of holiday has Marco had?' You wanted to know ....
5 'How long have you both been living here?' They inquired ....
6 'Where did they go last week?' She wanted to know ....
7 'Who were you looking for?' He asked me ....
8 'When will lunch be ready?' You didn't tell me ....
9 'Which countries will John be visiting?' You didn't say ....
10 'How can I solve the problem?' I wanted to know ....

15.4C Indirect subject-questions [> LEG 15.21-22]

Study:
⭐⭐

A direct subject-question has the same word order as a statement [>13.8A]:
***John paid** the waiter.* → ***Who paid** the waiter? (Not *Who did pay the waiter?*)*
We keep the same word order when we report a subject-question, though, if necessary, we change the tense:
*'**John paid** the waiter.'* → *He asked (me) **who (had) paid** the waiter.*

Write: Report these subject-questions moving the clauses 'one tense back' only where necessary.

1 'Who's next please?' She wanted to know ....*who was next*...
2 'What makes a noise like that?' He wondered ....
3 'Which of you is waiting to see me next?' The doctor asked ....
4 'Whose composition haven't we heard yet?' The teacher asked us to tell her ....
5 'Who left this bag here?' Tell me ....
6 'What caused the accident?' Can you explain ....
7 'Which newspaper carried the article?' I'd like to know ....
8 'Whose painting will win the competition?' I haven't any idea ....
9 'Which firms have won prizes for exports?' This article doesn't say ....
10 'Which number can be divided by three?' The teacher asked ....

15.4D Context

Write: Put in the correct forms and tenses of the numbered verbs.

Burning the candle at both ends

BURNING THE CANDLE AT BOTH ENDS
The nurse asked me if I (*be*) [1] ......*was*.......... next and she led me into Dr Grey's surgery. Dr Grey smiled at me and asked (*what the problem be*) [2] .... I'm a young man and am not the sort of person she has to see very often! I told her I (*be*) [3] .... feeling rather run down. She asked me if I (*keep*) [4] .... regular hours and I said I (*have not*) [5] .... She wanted to know why I (*not/keep*) [6] .... regular hours and I said I (*be*) [7] .... out with friends almost every evening. Dr Grey then wanted to know how I (*spend*) [8] .... my time and I (*tell*) [9] .... her I (*go*) [10] .... to parties mostly. The doctor asked if I (*not/have*) [11] .... the chance to recover during weekends and I (*tell*) [12] .... her that my party-going (*be*) [13] .... even worse during the weekends! She asked me if I (*smoke*) [14] .... When I said I did, she asked how many cigarettes a day I (*smoke*) [15] .... She raised her eyebrows when I answered! Then she asked me if I (*take*) [16] .... any exercise and I answered that I (*not/have*) [17] .... time for that sort of thing. 'You're burning the candle at both ends, Mr Finley,' she told me. 'Rest is the only cure for you. You've really got to slow down.' She looked at me wistfully before I left her surgery and added, 'but I do envy you the life you've been living!'

Burning the candle at both ends

15.5 Uses of the *to*-infinitive in indirect speech

15.5A Reporting the imperative: 'He reminded me to post the letter' [> LEG 15.24]

Study:
★★

1 We report the imperative with suitable verbs + *to*-infinitive. The reporting verb matches the function of the imperative (*asking, telling, advising*, etc. [> 9.10A, 16.3C]), e.g.
'***Remember** to post the letter,*' he asked me. becomes: ***He reminded me** to post the letter.*

2 When we report a negative imperative, we put *not* or *never* before the *to*-infinitive:
'*Don't wait,*' he said. → *He asked me **not to** wait.* (Not *to not* or *to don't*)
'*Never do that again,*' he said. → *He told us **never to** do that again.* (Not *to never*)

Write: Report the following using the simple past of the verbs in brackets.

1 'Wait for me,' I said to him. (tell)
I told him to wait for me.
....

2 'Go on holiday when the weather gets warmer,' she told him. (advise)
....

3 'Keep out of this room at all times,' she said to them. (warn)
....

4 'Remember to post those letters,' he said to me. (remind)
....

5 'Don't go into my study,' he said to them. (ask)
....

6 'Don't wait for me,' I said to him. (tell)
....

7 'Don't go on holiday yet,' she told him. (advise)
....

8 'Don't ever enter this room,' she said to them. (warn)
....

15.5B Offers, suggestions, requests for advice: 'He asked if he should ...'
[> LEG 15.24.2]

Study:
★★

This is how we report offers and suggestions with *shall* or *should* [> 11.6E,F]:
– direct offer or suggestion: '***Shall I** phone her?*' '***Should I** phone her?*'
– reported with *if* or *whether*: *He wanted to know **if/whether he should** phone her.*
– reported with *whether to*: *He wanted to know **whether to** phone her.* (Not *if to*)

Write: Report each question in two ways.

1 'Shall I fax the information to them?' She asked *if/whether she should fax the information to them. She asked whether to fax the information to them.*

2 'Should I leave a message for her?' He asked ....
....

3 'Shall I heat the food for you?' She asked him ....
....

4 'Should I phone him now?' He wanted to know ....
....

5 'Shall I invite them to dinner?' She wanted to know ....
....

15.5C Requests for advice with question-words: 'He wanted to know how ...'
[> LEG 15.24.2, 16.24]

Study:
★★

> This is how we report requests for advice with question-words:
> – direct request for advice: ***How shall I*** repair it? ***How should I*** repair it?
> – reported with question-word + *should*:   He wanted to know ***how he should*** repair it.
> – reported with question-word + *to*-infinitive: He wanted to know ***how to*** repair it.
> We can use a *to*-infinitive after all question-words (*how to, when to,* etc.) except *why*:
> He wanted to know ***why he should*** wait. (Not **He wanted to know why to wait.**)

Write: Report each request in two ways, where possible.

1 'When should I be at the station?' She asked *when she should be at the station. She asked when to be at the station*.

2 'Where shall we have our meeting?' They asked ....
....

3 'Which should I choose?' He asked ....
....

4 'Who(m) shall I ask?' She wanted to know ....

5 'What should I do?' He asked me ....
....

6 'Why should I pay this bill?' She wanted to know ....

7 'Whose car should I borrow?' He wanted to know ....

8 'Why should I be punished?' She asked ....
....

15.5D Context

Write: Put in the correct forms.

'It's a welcome gift.'

A GIFT FROM CHICAGO
It had been a particularly bad winter in Chicago. Nearly forty inches of snow had fallen in a fortnight. Railway workers at Chicago station didn't know (*what/do*) [1] *what to do* with it. The foreman (*advise them/ shovel*) [2] .... it into huge mountains to keep the platforms clear. He (*tell/not leave*) [3] .... any snow on the platforms because it was dangerous for passengers. But it was an impossible task! Suddenly, one of the workers had a bright idea. 'I know (*how/get rid*) [4] .... of it,' he said. 'Let's load it onto this freight train. We can send it south to Mississippi and New Orleans. It'll just melt away.' The next day five tons of snow arrived in Memphis, Tennessee. 'It's a welcome gift,' a railway worker said. 'We know (*what/do*) [5] .... with it here. We'll send what we can to the children's playground. Some of us have never seen snow before!'

15.6 When we use indirect speech

15.6A Interpreting direct speech [> LEG 15.13n.2, 15.25, App 45]

Study:

1 Indirect speech commonly occurs in continuous paragraphs of reported language, not in unrelated sentences. To hold it together, we use phrases like: *she went on to say, he continued, he added that*. We also vary the reporting verbs: *he observed, she noted, they remarked*, etc. Yes/No answers or adverbs like *Well* are common in direct speech, but they disappear when we report them.

2 We don't apply 'rules' mechanically when we are reporting; we have to interpret what we hear or read, so we often use reporting verbs like *exclaim, insist, suggest*, etc.:
'You really must let me pay the bill,' Andrew said. can be 'interpreted' as:
Andrew insisted on paying the bill.

Write: Interpret these examples of direct speech, then re-express them as indirect speech.

1 'Why don't we go sailing?' Diana said.
.......*Diana suggested (that) we (should) go sailing*..

2 'You've just won a lottery!' Tom said.
'Really?' Jennifer exclaimed.
....
....

3 'More money should be spent on education,' Frank observed.
'Yes, I agree,' Gillian answered.
....
....

4 'I don't think you should take up wind-surfing at your age,' John said.
'I feel it's a sport that will suit all ages,' Jenny replied.
'But it requires great physical strength,' John said.
'And who told you I was short of that?' Jenny said.
....
....
....
....

5 'Don't go too near the lions' cage,' mother said.
'But I want to see the lions close up,' Billy answered.
'Isn't this close enough?' mother asked.
'No,' Billy replied.
'I'm sorry, Billy, but you can't go any closer than this.'
'But I want to,' Billy insisted.
'Well, you can't.'

No, you can't go any nearer...

....
....
....
....
....
....

6 'You really must keep to your diet, Mrs Flynn, if you're
serious about losing weight,' Dr Grey said.
'You have been keeping to it, haven't you?'
'Well, I ... er ...,' Mrs Flynn muttered.
'Have you or haven't you?'
'Well, I have occasionally had a bit extra.'
'What do you mean, "a bit extra"?'
'Oh – a cream cake or two.'

....
....
....
....
....
....
....

7 'You did enjoy the film, didn't you?' Sandra asked.
'I'm not sure,' Sam answered.
'I thought Gloria Gleam's performance was fantastic!'
'Well, I didn't like it at all,' Sam replied.
'Didn't you really?' Sandra replied.

....
....
....
....
....

15.6B   Context

Write: Put in the missing words.

The lady left in disgust

SECOND-HAND GOODS

It's a sad fact that people steal from hotels. Recently I interviewed Mr David
Wills, the manager of a large hotel, and he [1] ...*told*...... me that all kinds of
things, large and small, [2] .... constantly stolen. Mr Wills told
[3] .... that a check [4] .... made on a person's room as soon
as they (*leave*) [5] .... it, but unless someone had walked off with a
wardrobe, he (*advise*) [6] .... the staff (*not/make*) [7] .... a
fuss. 'What is even more surprising,' Mr Wills [8] .... 'is the things
people leave behind – anything from wooden legs to false teeth!' He then
[9] .... on to tell me a story about a snobbish lady who (*recently
check out*) [10] .... She (*object*) [11] .... that her bill (*be*)
[12] .... too high, but paid it nevertheless. Just as she (*leave*)
[13] ...., the phone rang and the cashier answered it. He then
[14] .... the lady that a hotel bathrobe was missing from her room.
The lady expressed great surprise and [15] .... that the hotel maid
must have packed it in by mistake. 'But the maid has just reported the
bathrobe missing,' the cashier [16] .... Handing over the bathrobe,
the lady left in disgust. 'Who wants a second-hand bathrobe, anyway?' she
said, as she made her way to a taxi complaining that hotel service (*be*)
[17] .... not what it used to be.

16 The infinitive and the '-ing' form

16.1 The bare infinitive and the *to*-infinitive

16.1A Forms of the infinitive [> LEG 16.1-3]

Study:
★★

1 We often use the base form of a verb (*go*) as an infinitive. We call this the **bare infinitive** because we use it without *to*. We must distinguish it from the ***to*-infinitive**, where we always use *to* in front of the base form of the verb (*to go*). The most common use of the bare infinitive is after modal verbs *He may/can* (etc.) *go* [> 11.1A-B].

2 Forms of the infinitive:

	active	passive
present infinitive	*(not) (to) ask*	*(not) (to) be asked*
present progressive infinitive	*(not) (to) be asking*	–
perfect or past infinitive	*(not) (to) have asked*	*(not) (to) have been asked*
perfect/past progressive infinitive	*(not) (to) have been asking*	–

Write: Using the verbs in brackets, supply the appropriate forms of the infinitive:
be doing, be done, do, have been doing, have been done, or *have done*.

1 We can ....*leave*........ soon. (leave)
2 I don't know what Mark's doing. He may .... in his room. (study)
3 She's a slow worker! I could .... the job twice in the time she's taken. (do)
4 Why were you waiting here? You should .... round the corner. (wait)
5 I promise you your order will .... today. (send)
6 'How was that table scratched?' – 'It must .... when it was being moved.' (do)

16.1B 'Let', 'make', 'would rather/sooner' and 'had better' [> LEG 16.4-5]

Study:
★★

1 We use the imperative form *Let's* (= Let us) + bare infinitive for making suggestions:
Let's take *a taxi!* ***Let's take*** *a taxi,* ***shall we?*** ***Do let's take*** *a taxi.* [> 11.6F]
The negative is: ***Let's not (take*** *a taxi).* Or: ***Don't let's (take*** *a taxi).*

2 *Let* as a full verb (= 'allow') is always followed by a noun or pronoun + bare infinitive:
I won't ***let you/him***, etc. ***go***. *Don't* ***let the children annoy*** *you. They won't* ***let us speak***.

3 *Make* (= compel) is followed by a bare infinitive in the active: *She* ***made them work*** *hard.*
It is followed by a *to*-infinitive in the passive: *They were* ***made to work*** *hard.*

4 We use the bare infinitive after *would rather (not), would sooner (not), had better (not)*:
*I'**d rather be** told the truth. You'**d better not go** near the edge.* [> 11.8A]

Write: Supply suitable infinitive forms for the verbs given in brackets.

1 Let's ....*go*... to the cinema. (go)
2 Let's .... out long. (not stay)
3 Let's .... , shall we? (go out)
4 Don't let's .... home yet. (go)
5 Let XYZ .... a triangle. (be)
6 Let me .... that letter for you. (post)
7 They didn't let her .... jeans. (wear)
8 He made me .... the mess. (clear up)
9 That T-shirt makes you .... younger. (look)
10 I was made .... floors. (scrub)

226

11 I'd rather .... for a walk in the rain than .... nothing at all. (go, do)

12 I'd rather .... anything if you don't mind. (not have)

13 I don't really want to see that play. I'd sooner .... at home. (stay)

14 You'd better .... what you think. (not say)

15 It's late. I think we'd better .... (go)

16.1C The infinitive with or without 'to' after 'help' and 'know' [> LEG 16.7]

Study: ★★

1 We may use a bare infinitive or a *to*-infinitive after a few verbs like *help* and *know*. The use of a *to*-infinitive is more formal:
*Mother **helped me (to) do** my homework.*
We do not usually omit *to* after *not*:
*How can I **help my children not to worry** about their exams?*

2 We sometimes use *help* without a noun or pronoun object:
*Everyone in the village **helped (to) build** the new Youth Centre.*

3 We have a noun or pronoun object after *know*:
*I've never **known her (to) be** late before. I've never **known her not (to) be** late.*
We use *to* in the passive: *He **was known to have/to have had** a quick temper as a boy.*

Write: Join or rewrite the sentences below using the words given.

1 I found this book. The librarian helped me.
The librarian ..... *helped (me) (to) find this book* ....

2 I have to fill in this job application form. Can you help me?
Can you ....?

3 You mustn't worry so much. I can help you.
I can help ....

4 People know him to be a very generous man.
He ....

5 He's a ruthless businessman. He is known for that.
He's known ....

6 She's never on time.
I've never known ....

16.1D Context

Write: Put in the correct forms of the verbs.

He had had a brilliant idea.

ONE CUBE OR TWO?
When we were at school as children we were (*make/wear*) [1] *made to wear* indoor shoes inside the school building. The teachers would never (*let us/wear*) [2] .... our outdoor shoes at all and they (*make us/change*) [3] .... in the changing rooms from the moment we entered the building. I'd never known teachers (*be*) [4] .... more strict about any other school rule. The trouble was that my indoor shoes really (*make me/suffer*) [5] .... because they were so tight. ('*Let/expand*) [6] .... our shoes!' a fellow sufferer suggested. He had had a brilliant idea. We put plastic bags inside our shoes and poured water into the bags. We sealed the bags carefully and put our shoes into the freezer. Of course the ice (*make the shoes/expand*) [7] .... and they were a pleasure to wear. This clever idea (*help me/get*) [8] .... through my schooldays with less discomfort and I have never forgotten it!

16.2   The bare infinitive or the '-ing' form; the *to*-infinitive

16.2A   Verbs of perception: 'Watch him draw/drawing' [> LEG 16.9.2-3]

Study:
★★

> **1** We can use a noun or pronoun object + the bare infinitive or *-ing* after these verbs:
> *feel, hear, listen to, look at, notice, observe, perceive, see, smell, watch* [compare > 16.6B].
>
> **2** The bare infinitive generally refers to the complete action:
> I **watched a pavement artist draw** a portrait in crayons. (i.e. from start to finish)
>
> **3** The *-ing* form generally refers to an action in progress:
> I **watched a pavement artist drawing** a portrait in crayons. (i.e. I saw part of the action)
>
> **4** We often use *hear, observe, perceive* and *see* in the passsive + *-ing* or a *to*-infinitive:
> They **were seen waiting**. They **were seen to climb** through the window.

Write: Join these pairs of sentences, deciding when to use a bare infinitive or *-ing*.

1   She crossed the road. I saw her.
I saw ...... *her cross the road.* ......
2   She was crossing the road. I caught sight of her.
I noticed ....
3   Something's burning. I can smell it.
I can smell ....
4   They sang a song. I listened to them.
I listened ....
5   She was shouting at the children. I heard her.
I heard ....
6   The robbers were waiting near the bank. They were seen.
The robbers were seen ....

16.2B   'Have' + object: 'Have the next patient come in' [> LEG 16.10.1-2]

Study:
★★

> **1** When we cause someone to do something for us, we use *have* + object + bare infinitive:
> **Have the next patient come** in, please. [compare > 12.3B]
> We may also use *have* + *know*, *have* +*believe*: I'll **have you know** I'm the company secretary.
>
> **2** We use *have* + object + *-ing* to refer to intended results, and unintended consequences:
> I'll **have you speaking** English in no time. You'll **have the neighbours complaining**.

Write: Use the bare infinitive or the *-ing* form after *have* in these sentences.

1   Have him ... *bring* .... his car round the back. (bring)
2   'I will not have students .... on the walls of this college,' the principal said. (draw)
3   I'll have you .... I'm a qualified accountant. (know)
4   He had her .... he was a millionaire. (believe)
5   We have people .... us up all hours of the day and night. (ring)
6   The film had them .... right from the first few minutes. (laugh)
7   He's an excellent piano teacher. He'll have you .... in about a year. (play)
8   I'll have the plumber .... the central heating boiler. (look at)
9   The sergeant had all the recruits .... like real soldiers inside a month. (march)
10   He had never had anything like that .... to him before. (happen)

16.2C '(Not) to', 'so as (not) to', 'in order (not) to' [> LEG 16.2, 16.12-18]

Study:
★★

1 We use *to, so as to* and *in order to* to express purpose [compare > 1.10A]:
*I went to France **to learn** French. I went to France **so as to/in order to learn** French.*
We can also use the *to*-infinitive (not **so as to* *in order to**) to express sequence:
*We came home after our holidays **to find** the house neat and tidy.* (= and found)

2 We use *not to* for alternatives:
*I went to France **not to learn** Spanish, **but to learn** French.*

3 We use *so as not to* and *in order not to* to express 'negative purpose' (Not **to not**):
*I shut the door quietly **so as not to/in order not to wake** the baby.*

4 We use the *to*-infinitive after many verbs like *appear, arrange, hope, 'd like*, and *want*:
*He **told me to phone** home. I **hope to see** you soon. I **want to travel** abroad.*
Note the difference in meaning between these negatives:
*He **didn't tell me** to phone home. He **told me not to phone** home.*

Write: Use *to, so as to, in order to* in these sentences. Alternatives are sometimes possible.

1 I went to town ......*to do/in order to do/so as to do*...... some shopping. (do)
2 He covered the floor with a sheet .... paint on it. (not splash)
3 I got out some more chairs for the other guests .... on. (sit)
4 Can you arrange for me .... the doctor tomorrow? (see)
5 We came home .... the house had been burgled. (find)
6 She left home .... (never return)
7 I'd like .... to the States for a holiday one year. (go)
8 We would like .... at your party. (have been)
9 Mr Smith wants .... you later. (see)
10 He appears .... all about our arrangement. (have forgotten)
11 The keeper told us .... the monkeys. (not feed)
12 She told us to feed the hens. She .... the horses. (not tell us/feed)

16.2D Context

Write: Put in the correct forms of the infinitive or *-ing*.

Go left! Go right!

THIS WAY! THAT WAY!
In a split second, when no one was paying attention, the two prisoners escaped from the back of the police van. They were handcuffed to each other. It was minutes before a policeman saw them (*run*) [1] ......*running*....... down the street. 'We'll follow,' two policemen said. 'Have the driver (*bring*) [2]........................... the van to the end of the road. Tell him (*not let*) [3]........................... them get away. If we're not careful, we'll have the whole neighbourhood (*complain*) [4]........................... that we've been careless.' The prisoners were still running side by side. The policemen saw them (*race*) [5]........................... up the hill and (*disappear*) [6]........................... round a corner. 'We'll never catch them now!' one of them said. 'I told you (*not leave*) [7]........................... them unattended.' The prisoners were running at top speed. Suddenly, they saw a lamp post in front of them 'Go left! Go right' they each shouted at the same time. They ran on either side of the lamp post. It just took time for the police (*find*) [8]........................... them, lying on the pavement, unhurt, dazed, and with silly grins on their faces.

16.3 Verb (+ noun/pronoun) + *to*-infinitive

16.3A 'He can't afford to buy it' [> LEG 16.19, App 46]

Study:
★★

> Some verbs are followed only by a *to*-infinitive, not by *-ing* or *that* ...:
> e.g. *can('t) afford, aim, apply, fail, hasten, hurry, manage, offer, prepare, refuse, seek*:
> **He can't afford to buy** a car. (Not *He can't afford buying/He can't afford that ...*).

Write: Rewrite these sentences to begin with the words in italics.

1 He'd like to buy a car. *He can't afford* it. ...... *He can't afford to buy a car.* ....
2 I didn't pass my driving test. *I failed.* ....
3 He'll pay for all of us. *He's offering.* ....
4 Can you move the desk on your own? *Can you manage* ....?
5 He wants to join the army. *He's just applied.* ....
6 Apologize to her? *I refuse.* ....

16.3B 'I want (you) to speak to him' [> LEG 16.20, App 46.1]

Study:
★★

> We use a *to*-infinitive after these verbs:
> *ask, beg, choose, expect, hate, help* [> 16.1C], *like, love, need, prefer, want, wish*:
> **I want to speak** to the manager. (= I will speak to the manager)
> Or we can use a noun or pronoun before the infinitive:
> **I want you to speak** to the manager. (= You will speak ...) Not (*I want that you ...*)

Write: Complete these sentences so that they refer to other people.

1 I don't want to speak to the manager. I want ... *you to speak to him* ....
2 She doesn't expect to pay. She expects ....
3 I don't want to write to them. I'd like ....
4 I don't want anyone to know about it. I'd hate ....
5 You won't listen to me. How many times do I have to ask ....?
6 I can't do the job myself. I need ....
7 We can't move it. Perhaps you can help .... [> 16.1C]

16.3C 'He advised me to take out a loan' [> LEG 16.21]

Study:
★★

> These verbs always have an object before the *to*-infinitive:
> *advise, allow, entitle, forbid, invite, order, remind, (it) takes, teach, tell, warn*:
> My bank manager **advised me to take** out a loan. [compare > 15.5A]

Write: Complete these sentences using an object + *to*-infinitive after the verbs.

1 Take out a loan. My bank manager advised .... *me to take out a loan.* ....
2 She didn't peel the potatoes. You didn't tell ....
3 We work hard. Our teacher taught ....
4 The soldiers fired. The officer ordered ....
5 You can apply for free travel. This certificate entitles ....
6 The public should not approach this man. The police have warned ....
7 My wife and I play tennis. My boss invited ....

16.3D 'I know him to be an honest man' [> LEG 16.22]

Study:
★★★

> We can use *that* or a *to*-infinitive after these verbs to refer to people or things:
> *believe, consider, discover, find, imagine, know, prove, suppose, think, understand.*
> Instead of: **People know (that) he is** an honest man.
> We can say: **People know him to be** an honest man.

Write: Rewrite these sentences using a *to*-infinitive instead of *that*.

1 People know that he is an honest man. *People know him to be an honest man.*
2 I imagine that he works very hard. ....
3 I believe that she is guilty. ....
4 I found that the job was too difficult. ....
5 We discovered the claim was false. ....
6 I know that she has an interest in the company. ....

16.3E 'I agreed to accept their offer' [> LEG 16.23]

Study:
★★

> We can use *that* or a *to*-infinitive after these verbs:
> *agree, arrange, claim, choose, decide, expect, hope, pretend, promise, swear, threaten, wish.*
> Instead of: **I agreed that I would accept** their offer.
> We can say: **I agreed to accept** their offer.

Write: Rewrite these sentences using a *to*-infinitive after the verbs.

1 I agreed that I would accept the offer. *I agreed to accept the offer.*
2 I hope that I will succeed. ....
3 I expect that I will hear from you ....
4 He claimed that he had met me. ....
5 I arranged that I should be there. ....
6 She pretended that she didn't know me. ....

16.3F Context

Write: Put in the correct forms of the verbs.

HOW TO GET RID OF RATS

When I was a young man, working in Malaya, my boss gave me a difficult job to do. The roof of his house had become infested with rats and he (*want/I get rid of*) [1] *wanted me to get rid of* them for him. I tried everything: rat poison, cats, even a mongoose, but I (*fail/move*) [2] .... them. Then a friend of mine (*advise/ I use*) [3] .... a python. I (*considered this/be*) [4] .... my last chance and (*agree/try*) [5] .... it. My friend brought me a box in which he had trapped a young python, about six feet long. We (*manage/get*) [6] .... the box into the roof and then released the python. The effect was amazing! The rats disappeared in no time! It (*prove/be*) [7] .... a wonderful solution. But then we didn't know (*what/do*) [8] .... with the python. I couldn't (*bear/shoot*) [9] .... this superb creature. It (*take/six of us an hour/ get*) [10] .... it into the box and then we returned it to the jungle.

GO-TO-YOUR-BOX!

... didn't know what to do with the python

16.4 Adjectives and nouns + *to*-infinitive

16.4A Adjective + 'to': 'It was kind (of him) to help us' [> LEG 16.26-31, App 44]

Study:
★★

We can use a *to*-infinitive after adjectives in a variety of ways, for example:

1 We use a personal subject (*he, she*, etc.), or we use *it* with adjectives like these:
   clever, foolish, generous, good, polite, right/wrong, rude, selfish, silly, wicked.
   Instead of: **He was kind (enough) to help us. She was silly not to buy** it.
   We can say: **It was kind** (of him) **to help us. It was silly** (of her) **not to buy** it.
   We can also say: **He was so good/kind** (etc.) **as to help** us.

2 We use only a personal subject (*he, she, it* or name) with these adjectives:
   afraid, anxious, ashamed, careful, curious, eager, fit, free, frightened, glad, keen, sorry:
   John is eager to please. (Not **It is eager to**) **I'm sorry to have troubled** you.

3 We use a personal subject or *it*, but not *of him*, etc. (> 1 above) with these adjectives:
   agreeable, amusing, boring, difficult, easy, hard, impossible:
   John is easy to please. It is easy to please John.

Write: Rewrite the sentence or join the pairs of sentences beginning with the word(s) given.

1 He was foolish. He left the firm.
   He was *foolish to leave the firm*. ....

2 You want to ask for more money. You would be stupid if you don't.
   You would be ....

3 Ring me later. Would you be so good?
   Would you ....?

4 Open the window. Would you be good enough?
   Would you ....?

5 He worked out the answer. It was clever of him.
   It was ....

6 They don't take any part in local life. It's silly of them.
   It's ....

7 We can't refuse their invitation. It would look rude.
   It would ....

8 She worked overtime. Wasn't it good of her?
   Wasn't it ....?

9 He's eager. He wants to help us in any way he can.
   He's ....

10 I was careful. I didn't offend them.
   I was ....

16.4B Adjectives with 'too/enough': 'too weak/not strong enough to' [> LEG 16.32]

Study:
★★

1 *Too* before an adjective means 'excessively' [> 7.6A, 7.7B]:
   *He **isn't strong**. He **can't lift** it.* → *He **is too weak to lift** it.* (Not **very weak to**)

2 *Enough* after an adjective means 'to the necessary degree'. It combines two ideas:
   *He **is strong**. He **can lift** it.* → *He's **strong enough to lift** it.*
   *He **is weak**. He **can't lift** it.* → *He **isn't strong enough to lift** it.*

Write: Join these pairs of sentences twice: **a** with *enough* **b** with *too*.

1 I'm not *strong*. I can't lift it.   a *I'm not strong enough to lift it.* b *I'm too weak to lift it.*
2 I'm not *rich*. I can't afford one.   a .... b ....
3 She's not *old*. She can't drive a car.   a .... b ....
4 I wasn't *interested*. I didn't watch the film.   a .... b ....
5 The pie is very *hot*. I can't eat it.   a .... b ....
6 The film was *boring*. I didn't watch it.   a .... b ....

16.4C   Noun + *to*-infinitive: 'My decision to wait was wise' [> LEG 16.33-37]

Study:
★★

> 1 Some nouns are related to verbs which are followed by a *to*-infinitive.
> They may have a different form from the verb: *I **decide** to* → *it's my **decision** to;*
> or they may have the same form as the verb: *I **wish** to* → *it's my **wish** to.*
>
> 2 Some nouns are related to adjectives which are followed by a *to*-infinitive.
> They usually have a different form from the adjective:
> *I am **determined** to* → *my **determination** to; I am **eager** to* → *my **eagerness** to.*

Write: Rewrite these sentences beginning with a noun phrase.

1 I *decided* to wait, which was wise. My ... *decision to wait was wise.* ....
2 He *refused* to help, which surprised us. His ....
3 She *failed* to get into college, which disappointed her parents. Her ....
4 I'm *pleased* to be with you. It's a ....
5 They were *eager* to help, which pleased me. Their ....
6 I was *determined* to pass the test and that helped me. My ....
7 I was *willing* to co-operate and this was appreciated. My ....

16.4D   Context

Write: Supply the correct *to*-infinitive combinations.

A most incompetent burglar!

THE BRAVE OLD LADY AND THE HOPELESS CROOK
Mrs Johns, a 75-year-old widow, woke up with a start. Peering into the darkness, she was astonished (*see*) [1] ... *to see* .... a man in her room. It was easy (*see*) [2] .... he was a burglar. At first, she was too afraid (*move*) [3] .... Then she plucked up her courage and said, 'We must talk about this over a cup of tea. Would you be so kind (*help me*) [4] .... downstairs?' To her surprise, the man meekly obeyed. He was eager (*help*) [5] .... and anxious (*please*) [6] .... the old lady. He prepared the tea and said he was sorry (*have disturbed*) [7] .... her. He was too frightened (*run away*) [8] .... After a cup of tea, he said he would be glad (*give*) [9] .... Mrs Johns his name and address and left empty-handed. Of course, Mrs Johns informed the police, who commended her for her bravery. Later, during the trial, the judge said it was his duty (*send*) [10] .... the man to prison, describing him as the most incompetent burglar he had ever met!

16.5 The '-ing' form

16.5A Basic information about the '-ing' form [> LEG 16.38-40, 2.16.5]

Study:
★★

> We use the *-ing* form in three ways:
>
> 1 We use it as a *verb* (called a **participle**): *He is **playing**. She is **writing**.* etc. [> 9.2B, 9.4B]
> **Walking** in the park yesterday, I saw a bird **building** a nest. [> 1.11-12]
> (= I was walking. + The bird was building a nest.)
>
> 2 We use the *-ing* form as an *adjective*:
> *I need some* $\begin{cases} hot \\ \textbf{boiling} \end{cases}$ *water.*   (= water which is hot)
>   (= water which is boiling) [> 2.2A]
>
> 3 We use the *-ing* form as a noun (called a **gerund**):
> *I like* $\begin{cases} coffee. \\ \textbf{swimming}. \end{cases}$ (i.e. 'the act of swimming')
> With a few exceptions, we use the *-ing* form (gerund) like any other noun.

Write: Supply gerund forms for the words in brackets. (For spelling, [> 9.2A])

A1 The gerund as an uncountable noun in general statements [> 3.5A]

1 .... *Dancing* .... is fun. (dance)
2 .... tall is an advantage. (be)
3 .... tall is an advantage. (not be)
4 What I like is .... (ride)
5 I enjoy .... (read)
6 .... makes me tired. (drive)
7 .... able to drive is a disadvantage. (not be)
8 .... keeps you fit. (run)
9 I like .... (cycle)
10 .... is a difficult profession. (act)

A2 The gerund as an uncountable noun with 'some', 'a lot of' 'a little', etc. [e.g. > 10.7A]

1 He does a lot of .... *reading* .... (read)
2 Did you do any ....? (iron)
3 I did some .... this morning. (shop)
4 I do very little .... these days. (swim)
5 There's no .... my decision (regret)
6 I heard a lot of .... last night. (shout)
7 There's more .... in the streets. (fight)
8 We all enjoy a bit of .... (sing)
9 We all need a little .... (encourage)
10 I've done enough .... for today. (garden)

A3 The gerund as an uncountable noun after prepositions [> 16.7D]

1 This is used for ..... *cutting* .... metal. (cut)
2 What can you do besides ....? (dig)
3 I'm against .... (box)
4 I'm always hungry after .... (sleep)
5 Try to work without .... a noise. (make)
6 What do you know about ....? (compute)
7 I'm not interested in .... (garden)
8 She's above .... (argue)
9 Since .... I've done nothing. (retire)
10 Taste it before .... (complain)

A4 The gerund as an uncountable noun after adjectives and possessives [compare >16.6C-D]

1 Quick ..... *thinking* .... saved us. (think)
2 Her quick .... saved us. (think)
3 Your .... to help hurt him. (refuse)
4 His .... doesn't matter. (not know)
5 I like your .... (violin play)
6 The meat will be fine with slow .... (cook)
7 We had some tough .... (train)
8 His .... woke us up. (shout)
9 Their .... delighted everyone. (sing)
10 Try deep .... (breathe)

A5 The gerund as an uncountable noun after 'no' in prohibitions [compare > 11.3B]

1 No ...*parking*... (park)
2 No .... (camp)
3 No .... (wait)
4 No .... (smoke)
5 No .... (trespass)
6 No .... (fish)

A6 The gerund as a countable noun in the singular and plural

1 He owns ..*a painting*.. by Hockney. (paint)
2 He owns several .... by Hockney. (paint)
3 .... is priceless.(Leonardo drawing)
4 Are there many ....? (Leonardo drawing)
5 I have .... of Tosca. (new recording)

6 There was .... on the door. (banging)
7 There was .... of bells. (ringing)
8 I have three .... of this. (recording)
9 There's .... on the left. (turning)
10 There are three .... to the right. (turning)

A7 The gerund after 'the', 'this' and 'these'

1 Who does the *cooking* in this house? (cook)
2 Have you done the ....? (shop)
3 The .... of rubbish is forbidden. (burn)
4 This .... is hard to read. (write)
5 These .... are expensive. (draw)

6 I've taken the wrong .... (turn)
7 The .... of wine is difficult. (make)
8 Have you heard this .... of Bach? (record)
9 The .... of Picasso are wonderful. (paint)
10 These .... are valuable. (record)

A8 The gerund followed by an object

1 He's good at .....*repairing*..... bikes. (repair)
2 .... fruit is good for you. (eat)
3 .... a car costs money. (run)
4 I hate .... the washing-up. (do)
5 He enjoys .... orders. (give)

6 .... holes is hard work. (dig)
7 Do you mind .... places? (change)
8 .... beds is boring. (make)
9 What do you know about .... maps? (make)
10 You should avoid .... rules. (make)

A9 Perfect gerund forms, active [> 16.6A]

1 I'm sorry for ....*having disturbed*....... you.
(have disturb)
2 I didn't take it. I deny .... it. (have take)
3 I'm annoyed about .... all that
money. (have lose)
4 I appreciate .... me (your have help)
5 I enjoy .... with you. (have work)

A10 Perfect gerund forms, passive [> 16.6A]

1 That explains *his having been fired* from his job.
(his have fire)
2 I don't mind .... above me.
(his have promote)
3 I resent .... (have dismissed)
4 He's surprised at .... (have find out)
5 She's angry at .... abroad. (have post)

16.5B Context

Write: Put in the correct forms.

IT TAKES YOUR BREATH AWAY!
The art of (*cook*) [1] ....*cooking*..... requires the use of garlic. Of course, the (*eat*) [2] .... of
garlic is not generally approved of. (*Work*) [3] .... beside someone who has eaten garlic is as
bad as (*sit*) [4] .... beside someone who smokes. But while (*smoke*) [5] .... is
definitely bad for you, there is no doubt that (*eat*) [6] .... garlic is good for the health. We are
likely to see more 'No (*smoke*) [7] .... signs, but we won't see any 'No (*breathe*)
[8] .... signs for garlic eaters! (*Cultivate*) [9] .... and (*export*) [10] .... garlic
has become big business now that so many people use it for (*flavour*) [11] .... meat and (*add*)
[12] .... to different dishes. People often buy it when they do the (*shop*) [13] ....
You don't have to deny (*use*) [14] .... it or (*have/eat*) [15] .... it. (*Be*) [16] ....
a garlic eater is something to be proud of and shows you enjoy good (*live*) [17] .... The story
of garlic is a breathtaking success!

A breathtaking success!

235

16.6 Verb + the '-ing' form

16.6A 'I deny taking it' [> 16.41-44]

Study:
⭐⭐

> **1** Some verbs are followed only by the *-ing* form, not by a *to*-infinitive: e.g.
> *admit, appreciate, avoid, consider, delay, deny, detest, dislike, enjoy, explain, fancy, feel like, finish, forgive, can't help, imagine, it involves, keep, mention, mind, miss, pardon, postpone, practise, prevent, recall, resent, resist, risk, stop* [> 16.8C] *suggest, understand.*
>
> | **verb + present '-ing' form** | **verb + perfect/past '-ing' form** |
> |---|---|
> | **active:** *I deny/denied taking* it. | *I deny/denied having taken* it. |
> | **passive:** *He resents/resented being accused.* | *He resents/resented having been accused.* |
>
> **2** After the verbs *come* and *go*, we often use the *-ing* form relating to outdoor activies: e.g.
> *climbing, driving, fishing, riding, sailing, shopping, skiing, walking, water-skiing:*
> *Why don't you* **come sailing** *with us? Let's* **go sailing***!* (Not **to sail/for sail(ing)**)
>
> **3** The *-ing* form can follow *need* and *want*:
> *He* **needs encouraging***. It* **wants mending***.*

Write: Supply any suitable verb in a suitable form.

1 Our neighbours are very considerate. They avoid .....*making*..... a lot of noise.
2 Just imagine .... in a country where it is always warm and sunny!
3 The police questioned me at some length and I didn't enjoy ....
4 What does the job involve? – It involves .... the engine apart.
5 I missed an interesting programme on TV last night. I really mind .... it.
6 We often go .... during the weekend. Would you like to come .... with us?
7 Look at the state of those windows! They really need ....!
8 Our front gate is falling to pieces. It really wants ....

16.6B 'Start him working' [>LEG 16.41-44]

Study:
⭐⭐

> **1** These verbs are followed by *-ing* [but compare > 16.2A]: *hear, keep, smell, start, stop, watch:*
> *When are you going to* **start working***?*
> But if we want to refer to someone else, we use a direct object after the verb:
> *When are you going to* **start him** *(John, etc.)* **working***?*
>
> **2** These verbs always have a direct object: *catch, find, leave, notice, observe, perceive, see:*
> *I'd better not* **catch you doing** *that again!*

Write: Match A and B.

A	B
1 It's difficult to keep them *f*	a) sheltering in the barn.
2 I think that's enough to start her __	b) coming from the forest.
3 I could smell smoke __	c) worrying again.
4 The police caught him __	d) opening the safe.
5 The searchers found the boy __	e) thinking about the problem.
6 They left us __	f) working all the time.
7 Will you please stop __	g) shouting in the distance.
8 I can hear someone __	h) changing TV channels.

16.6C 'We appreciate your helping us' [> LEG 16.45.2]

Study:
★★★

We can use a possessive (*my, John's*) + *-ing* after these verbs:
appreciate, avoid, consider, defer, delay, deny, enjoy, postpone, risk, suggest:
*We **appreciate your** (John's, etc.) **helping** us.* (Not **We appreciate you helping**)

Write: Match A and B.

A
1 We very much appreciate *f*
2 He strongly denied __
3 We enjoyed __
4 The chairman suggested __
5 I agreed to delay __
6 He should consider __

B
a) my leaving till the next day.
b) their meeting that afternoon.
c) her taking more responsibility.
d) the band's playing very much.
e) our postponing the question till later.
f) your helping us.

16.6D 'I can't imagine my mother('s) approving' [> LEG 16.45.3]

Study:
★★★

These verbs are followed by *-ing* on its own or by a direct object or possessive + *-ing*:
detest, dislike, escape, excuse, fancy, forgive, hate, imagine, it involves, like, love, mention, mind, miss, pardon, prevent, resent, resist, understand, can't bear, can't face, can't help:
a *I can't **imagine my mother approving**!* **c** *I can't **imagine my mother's approving**!*
b *They **resented me winning** the prize.* **d** *They **resented my winning** the prize.*

Write: Complete the following using either a direct object or a possessive + *-ing*.
    her not answering our invitation
1 I can't excuse ....
2 You must pardon ....
3 Would you mind ....?
4 I can't bear ....!
5 They can't prevent ....
6 Please forgive ....
7 I really miss ....
8 Fancy ....!

16.6E Context

Write: Put in the correct forms.

A FLYING START!
Gillian Forbes is only 17 and she has just got her pilot's licence. She is the country's youngest girl pilot. 'How do you feel, Gillian?' I asked her after her test. 'Wonderful!' Gillian cried. 'I enjoy (*fly*)
¹.....*flying*...... more than anything in the world. I can't imagine (*let*) ²....................... a week pass without spending some of my time in the air.' 'What started (*you/fly*) ³.......................?' I asked. 'I just love (*travel*) ⁴....................... in planes. I started (*learn*) ⁵....................... to fly when I was very young.' 'Would you consider (*fly*) ⁶....................... as a career?' 'I might, but I've got to pass my school exams now. There are some things you can't avoid (*do*) ⁷.......................!' 'Excuse (*me?/my?/ask*) ⁸.......................,' I said, 'but does everyone in your family approve of (*you?/your?/fly*) ⁹.......................?' 'Of course!,' Gillian exclaimed. 'I can't imagine (*anyone?/anyone's?/disapprove*) ¹⁰....................... . Can you?' 'Of course not!' I said. 'What's your greatest ambition now?' 'I want to learn to drive a car!' Gillian said with a big smile.

I want to learn to drive a car!

16.7 Adjectives, nouns and prepositions + '-ing'

16.7A Adjectives + '-ing' form (gerund) or *to*-infinitive [> LEG 16.47, 4.12-13]

Study:
★★

> We can use *-ing* or a *to*-infinitive after a great many adjectives and some nouns [> 4.3A]:
> **To lie** in the sun/**Lying** in the sun is **pleasant**. → It's **pleasant to lie/lying** in the sun.

Write: Use the *to*-infinitive and the *-ing* form in the following sentences.

1 It's difficult ......*finding / to find*.......... somewhere to live nowadays. (find)
2 It's awkward .... a friend that you don't like the way she dresses. (tell)
3 It isn't very nice .... you're useless. (be told)
4 It isn't easy .... work these days. (find)
5 It was kind of her .... you like that. (help)
6 It was fun .... to the north of Scotland. (drive)
7 It was just a piece of luck .... a restaurant open so late at night. (find)
8 It's a pleasure .... a surprise party for someone. (arrange)

16.7B Adjective + '-ing' form (participle) [> LEG 16.47]

Study:
★★

> We use some adjectives with a personal subject (Not *it*) + *-ing*:
> I am **busy**. + I am **working**. → I am **busy working**. (Not *to work*)

Write: Join the following sentences.

1 John gets bored. He watches TV all the time. *John gets bored watching TV all the time.*
2 Sylvia is frantic. She is getting ready for the wedding. ....
3 I got tired. I waited so long for an answer. ....
4 Jane's occupied. She's making lists. ....
5 We're busy. We're decorating our house. ....

16.7C Common expressions followed by '-ing' [> LEG 16.49]

Study:
★★

> We use *-ing* after common expressions like *It's no good* and *it's (not) worth*:
> It's **no good complaining** about it.

Write: Join the following sentences starting with the words in italics.

1 Don't complain about it. *It's no good.* ....*It's no good complaining.*...........
2 Don't worry about it. *It's just not worth* it. ....
3 Don't try to persuade him. *There's no point in* it. ....
4 Why apologize? *What's the use of* it? ....
5 I owe a lot of money. *There's nothing worse than* that. ....

16.7D Preposition + '-ing' [> LEG 16.50-54, Apps 27-30]

Study:
★★

> We use *-ing* after prepositions, not a *to*-infinitive [> 16.5A3]:
> He left the restaurant **without paying**. (Not *without to pay*)

Write: Complete these sentences with the correct forms of the verbs in brackets.

D1 Preposition + '-ing'

1 He left without ....*paying*........... (pay)
2 Don't punish him for .... (shout)
3 Open it by .... (pull)
4 She succeed after .... again. (try)

D2 Adjective + preposition + '-ing'

1 I'm interested in .....*acting*.................... (act)
2 We're bored with .... cards. (play)
3 I'm sorry for .... (complain)
4 He's fond of .... (sail)
5 We're keen on .... (ride)
6 I was afraid of .... you. (disturb)
7 She's clever at .... (sew)
8 I'm worried about .... the train. (miss)
9 I'm surprised at .... you in. (find)
10 You're very slow at .... (understand)

D3 Verb + preposition + '-ing' [compare > 8.6B-D]

1 I advise you against ...*doing*......... that. (do)
2 She believes in .... hard. (work)
3 They accuse him of .... (steal)
4 Excuse me for .... you. (disturb)
5 I must congratulate you on .... (pass)
6 You can't blame me for .... (try)
7 They insisted on .... (enter)
8 I prevented them from .... (enter)
9 Thank you for .... (help)
10 I apologize for .... (interrupt)
11 Who'll compensate me for .... time? (lose)
12 They charged him with .... money. (steal)
13 We aim at .... in this business. (succeed)
14 I often dream about .... you again. (see)
15 Everything depends on .... it right. (get)
16 Begin by .... nicely. (ask)

16.7E The '-ing' form after 'to' as a preposition [> LEG 16.56]

Study:
★★

> *To* is part of the infinitive in *I want **to go** home*, but it is a preposition in *object to, be used to*, etc. and we use a noun or *-ing* after it: *I object **to noise**, I object **to smoking**.*

Write: Join the following sentences.

1 I do all my own shopping. I'm used to it. ...*I'm used to doing all my own shopping*...
2 I live on my own. I'm accustomed to it. ....
3 I don't like to be kept waiting. I object to it. ....
4 I'll see you soon. I look forward to it. ....
5 He writes begging letters. He's resorted to it. ....
6 I'm criticized. I'm resigned to it. ....

16.7F Context

Write: Put in the correct forms.

... a loud burst on the drums!

A CASE OF THE SHAKES!

It's hard (*appreciate*) [1] *to appreciate* some of the problems of (*play*) [2] ....
in an orchestra, especially if you're not a musician. While the orchestra is busy
(*play*) [3] ...., all kinds of things are going on. Recently, my friend John, a
horn player, told me about his experiences (*play*) [4] .... with the
Philharmonic. One day, without even (*whisper*) [5] .... a word, he got up in
the middle of a performance of 'The Marriage of Figaro' and moved to another seat.
After the performance, the drummer, who played behind him, insisted on (*find*)
[6] .... out why John had moved. John said that he didn't object to (*sit*)
[7] .... in front of the drummer: he was used to (*sit*) [8] .... in this
position, but often, after a loud burst on the drums, he couldn't prevent his teeth
from (*rattle*) [9] .... and couldn't play the horn!

16.8 The *to*-infinitive or the '-ing' form?

16.8A Verb + *to*-infinitive or '-ing': no change in meaning: 'begin to read/reading' [> LEG 16.57]

Study:
★★★

> 1 We can use a *to*-infinitive or the *-ing* form without a change in meaning after:
> *attempt, begin, can't bear, cease, commence, continue, intend, omit, start* [> 16.6B]:
> *I **can't bear to see/seeing** people suffering.*
>
> 2 We do not use the *-ing* form after the progressive forms of *begin, cease, continue, start*:
> *I'm **beginning to realize** how difficult this is.* (Not *I'm beginning realizing*)
>
> 3 Stative verbs like *know* and *understand* cannot be used with an *-ing* form after *begin, cease, continue*: *I **began to understand** the problem.* (Not *began understanding*)

Write: Supply the correct forms. Give two forms where both are possible.

1 You must begin ....*to work / working*.... harder. (work)
2 I was beginning .... I was wrong. (think)
3 She continued .... all through the film. (talk)
4 I had just started .... when the waiter took my plate away! (eat)
5 We intended .... to the concert, but we were both ill. (go)
6 I'm intending .... him tomorrow. (see)
7 The conductor raised his baton and the orchestra commenced .... (play)
8 You omitted .... me about it. (tell)
9 I'll never begin .... how he thinks. (understand)

16.8B Verb + *to*- or '-ing': some changes in meaning: 'I love to read/reading'
[LEG > 16.58]

Study:
★★★

> We can use *to* or *-ing* after: *dread, hate, like, love* and *prefer*. Sometimes there is a difference in meaning and sometimes there isn't. Generally, the *-ing* form refers to a situation 'in general' and the *to*-infinitive refers to a future event:
>
> 1a *I **love/like watching** TV.* 1b *I **love/like to watch** TV.* (same meaning)
> 2a *I **hate disturbing** you.* (in general) 2b *I **hate to disturb** you.* (but I'm going to)
> 3a *I **dread visiting** the dentist.* (in general)
> 3b *I **dread to think** about what has happened.* (so I try not to) (Not *I dread thinking*)
> 4a *I **prefer walking** to cycling.* (in general) 4b *I **prefer to wait** here.* (now)
> 5a *I'd **love sailing** if I could afford it.* (in general)
> 5b *I'd **love to sail** if I could afford it.* (at some time in the future)

Write: Supply the correct forms. Give two forms where both are possible.

1 I love *watching / to watch* old films. (watch)
2 I hate .... for buses. (wait)
3 I hate .... you this, but your jacket's torn. (tell)
4 I dread .... for the telephone to ring. (wait)
5 I prefer .... at home to .... at restaurants. (eat, eat)
6 What will you have? – I'd prefer .... steak, please. (have)
7 Would you like .... to the beach with us tomorrow? (come)

16.8C Verb + *to-* or '-ing': different meanings: 'remember to post/posting'

[> LEG 16.59]

Study:
★★

The *to*-infinitive and *-ing* never mean the same when used after these verbs:
remember, forget, regret, try, stop, go on.

1 *To* refers to the present or future and *-ing* refers to the past in:
Remember to post my letter.   I **remember posting** your letter.
You mustn't **forget to** ask.   Have you **forgotten meeting** me years ago?
I **regret to** say I feel ill.   I **regret saying** what I said.
We can also refer to the 'future seen from the past': I **remembered to post** your letter.

2 *Try to* (= make an effort):   **Try to** understand.
Try + -ing (= experiment):   **Try holding** your breath for more a minute.

3 *Stop to* (= infinitive of purpose [> 16.2C]):   We **stopped to buy** a paper.
Stop + -ing [> 16.6]:   **Stop shouting**.

4 *Go on + to* (= do something different):   We **went on to** discuss finance.
Go on + -ing (= continue [> 16.7D3]):   **Go on talking**.

Write: Supply the correct forms (*to*-infinitive or *-ing*) of the verbs in brackets.

1a I remember ......*visiting*........ Paris when I was very young. (visit)
1b Please remember .... the door on your way out. (lock)
1c Did you remember .... Jim last night? (phone)
2a I shall never forget .... taken to see the Moscow State Circus. (be)
2b Don't forget .... how many are coming on Saturday. (find out)
2c I forgot .... to the chemist's on my way home. (go)
3a We all tried .... him, but he just wouldn't listen to any of us. (stop)
3b If you want to stop coughing, why don't you try .... some water? (drink)
4a She got annoyed because her husband stopped .... in every shop window. (look)
4b Just stop .... and listen for a moment. (talk)
5a If we hadn't turned the music off they'd have gone on .... till morning. (dance)
5b She got a degree in Physics and then went on .... a course in Applied Maths. (take)
6a I regret .... you that there's been an accident. (tell)
6b He regretted .... in the same job for so long. (stay)

16.8D Context

Write: Put in the correct forms.

Letterbox Finger

SNAP!
Postmen have stopped (*deliver*) [1] ....*delivering*... letters to the new houses in our area. They object to the letterboxes on the front doors. They hate (*push*) [2] .... letters through them, because the letterboxes snap shut. If you try (*push*) [3] .... a letter through, you can't get your fingers out! You try (*push*) [4] .... a letter into one of these boxes and see what happens! You quickly regret (*have*) [5] .... tried! They have been designed to stop burglars (*open*) [6] .... your front door from the outside, but postmen dread (*use*) [7] .... them as well. The painful condition known as Letterbox Finger is just as bad as Housemaid's Knee or Tennis Elbow!

Index

A

a/an: 3.1-2: general statements 3.1A;
the 'plural' of *a/an* 3.1B; with
countable nouns: *he's a doctor, it's a
Rembrandt* 2.3A, 3.1C; with
uncountables used as countables: *a
coffee*, etc. 2.3C-D; 'first mention'
3.2A; compared with *one*, with
numbers, etc. 3.2B; *twice a day* 3.2C;
illness (*a cold*) 3.2D; with
abbreviations (*an M.A.*) 3.3B; *no* in
place of *not a/an* 5.3C; *at a party*
8.2A; *a painting* 16.5A6
abbreviations: *the BBC*, etc. 3.3B
able to: and *can/could* 11.2, 11.3D
about: preposition/particle 8.1A; and *on,
around* 8.3A; *it's about time* 11.7D;
How/What about ...? 13.7E; + *-ing*
16.5A3, 16.7D3
about to: *be about to* 9.9B-C
above: preposition/particle 8.1A; and
over, on top of 8.5A; + *-ing* 16.5A3
abstract nouns: 3.5A
according to: and *by* 8.3A
accustomed to: + *-ing* 16.7E
across: preposition/particle 8.1A; and
over, through 8.3A
active voice: 12.1A; compared with the
passive and causative 12.3B; *sorry for
having disturbed you* 16.5A9
adjectival clauses: see **relative
pronouns and clauses**
adjectives: 6.1-5: formation 6.1A-C;
position 6.2; *a young man* and *the
young* 6.3A; *he looks good* 6.4A,
10.4A-B; word order 6.4B-D;
comparison of adjectives 6.5A-B; *-ing*
form (*boiling water*) 2.2A, 16.5A; *she's
American* or *she's an American* 3.1C;
the large one(s) 4.2B-C; *it's nice to
see you* 4.3A; compared with *-ly*
adverbs 7.1C; 'absolute adjectives'
7.5A; after *very* and *extremely*, etc.
7.6; after *be* 10.1-2; after *seem*, etc.
10.4A-B; after *get*, etc. 10.4C; *it's vital
that ... should* 11.13C; *How* +
adjective 13.7C; adjective + *to*-
infinitive 16.4A-B, 16.7A; adjective +
-ing 16.7A-B; adjective + preposition
16.7D; and see **demonstrative
adjectives/pronouns, -ed/-ing
forms, possessive adjectives, word
formation**
admit: *admit it to me* 1.3B; + *-ing* 16.6A
adverbial clauses: 1.8-10: introduction
1.8A; of time 1.8A-B; of place 1.8C; of
manner 1.8D; of reason 1.9A; contrast
1.9B-C; of purpose 1.10A-B; of result

1.10C; of comparison 1.10D; and
participle constructions 1.11B
adverb particles: words used as
prepositions or particles 8.1A-B;
particular particles and prepositions
8.3-5; after verbs 8.7-8
adverbs/adverbials: 7.1-8: of manner
7.1A-B; *friendly/in a friendly way* 7.1C;
time 7.2; adverbial phrases of duration
7.3; frequency 7.4; degree 7.5;
intensifiers 7.6; focus adverbs (*even*,
etc.) 7.7; viewpoint (*naturally*) 7.8A;
connecting (*however*) 7.8B; *little does
he realize* 7.8C *he plays well* 6.4A;
usual position in a sentence 1.1A,
7.2A, 7.4; with verb tenses: 9.2B,
9.3C, 9.4B, 9.5A-B, 9.6A-C, 9.7A-B,
9.8A-B; in indirect speech 15.3B
adverbs of degree: 7.5
adverbs of frequency: 7.4, 9.1B, 9.2B,
9.4B, 9.5A, 9.6A
adverbs of manner: 1.1A, 7.1
adverbs of place: 1.1A, 15.3B
adverbs of time: 1.1A, 7.2, 9.3C,
13.6A, 15.3B
advise: someone *about* 8.6C; + *that ...
should* 11.13B; *someone (not) to*
15.5A, 16.3C; *advise against* 16.7D3
afraid: *I'm afraid so* 4.3C; *(very) much
afraid* 7.6A; *seems to be afraid* 10.4B;
afraid to 16.4A; *afraid of* + *-ing* 16.7D2
after: preposition/particle 8.1A;
conjunction 8.1C; clauses of time:
1.5A, 1.8A-B, 9.6A; *after looking*
1.11B, 16.5A3, 16.7D; and *afterwards*
7.2C, 8.3A
again: connecting adverb 7.8B
against: preposition 8.1B; *fight against*
8.3A
ago: *ago, since* and *for* 7.3A; with
simple past 9.3C, 9.5D; *How long
ago?* 13.7D
agree: + *to/with* 8.6; *it is agreed* 12.2C;
agree to/that 16.3E
agreement: see **concord**
all: 5.1A; and *both* 5.5; and *a/the whole*
5.6A; and *everyone/everybody,
everything* 5.6B; *all day* 9.4B, 9.5B,
9.6B
allowed to: and *can/could/may/might*
11.3; *allow you to* 16.3C
almost: 7.4
along: preposition/particle 8.1A; *Come
along* 8.8A
a lot (of): 2.4B, 5.1-2; and *much/many*
5.4A-B; *a lot better* 7.5D; *do a lot of
reading* 16.5A2

already: and *yet* 7.2C; with the present
perfect 9.5A; with the past perfect
9.6A
also: *not only ... but ... also* 1.4; and *as
well* 7.7D
although: contrast clauses 1.9B
always: 7.4; with progressive tense
9.2B, 9.4B
among: preposition 8.1B; and *between*
8.4A
amount: *an amount of* 5.1A
and: in compound sentences 1.4; *go
and* 9.10D; *and I can, too* 13.4A; *Fail
to pay and ...* 14.1D
another: 5.7A, *another of* 5.7C-D
answers: questions, answers, negatives
13.1-9; and see **short answers**
any: with countable and uncountable
nouns 2.3C, 2.4B, 5.1-3; as the 'plural'
of *a/an* 3.1B, 5.3A; *not any* and *no*
5.3C, 13.2A; *I don't want any*
4.3B; *any of* 5.2A, 5.7C-D; *any good,
any better* 7.5D; *do any reading?*
16.5A2
anybody/anyone/anything: 4.6B-C,
13.2A; *anyone* and *you* 4.2A; with
imperatives 9.10B
any-compounds: 4.6B-C, 9.10B; 13.2A
any longer: and *any more* 11.11B
anywhere: conjunction, clauses of place
1.8C; and *nowhere* 13.2A
apostrophe s and s apostrophe: 2.2B,
2.8, 4.4B, 13.6C; *if I were in Jane's
position* 14.2B; and see **genitive**
appear: 9.1C, 10.3C, 10.4A-B, 16.2C
aren't I: 10.1B
around: and *about* 8.3A
arrange: *arrange to* 16.2C; *arrange to/
that* 16.3E
articles: 3.1-6; see *a/an*, **the**, **zero**
as: conjunction 8.1C; time 1.8A, 9.4B;
manner 1.8D; reason 1.9A; contrast
1.9B; comparison 1.10D, 4.1B;
preposition: 8.1C, and *like* 8.4A
as ... as: clauses of comparison: *as I
am/as me* 1.10D, 4.1B; *as (much) as
you like* 5.4B
as if: clauses of manner 1.8A,D
ask: + *for* 8.6B; + *that ... should* 11.13B;
in direct speech 15.1; and *say, tell*
15.2A-B; in indirect questions 1.5C,
15.4; *ask someone (not) to do
something* 15.5A, 16.3B; suggestions
15.5B-C
as soon as: clauses of time 1.5A,
1.8A-B, 9.6A
assuming (that): 14.4C

Key to exercises

1 The sentence

1.1 Sentence word order

1.1A The basic word order of an English sentence
Write 1:
1 **S** John Bailey **V** has set **O** a new high-jump record.
2 **S** The passport officer **V** examined **O** the passport.
3 **S** The dogs **V** don't like **O** these biscuits.
4 **S** The shop assistant **V** is wrapping **O** the parcel.
5 **S** The visitors **V** have seen **O** the new buildings.
6 **S** My father **V** didn't wash **O** the dishes.
7 **S** The plumber **V** is going to fix **O** the pipe.
8 **V** Will **S** the goalkeeper **V** catch **O** the ball?
9 **V** Has **S** the guest **V** enjoyed **O** the meal?
10 **S** John **V** can't play **O** the game.

Write 2:
1 **S** The children **V** slept **T** till 11 o'clock this morning.
2 **S** He **V** threw **O** the papers **P** into the bin.
3 **S** I **V** don't speak **O** English **M** well.
4 **S** Mrs Jones **V** hides **O** her money **P** under the bed.
5 **S** You **V** didn't pack **O** this suitcase **M** carefully.
6 **S** I **V** left **O** some money **P** on this shelf **T** this morning.
    (*or:* **T** This morning **S** I **V** left **O** some money **P** on this shelf.)
7 **S** You **V** 'll have to get **O** a loan **P** from the bank.
8 **S** The phone **V/O** woke me up **T** in the middle of the night.
    (*or:* **T** In the middle of the night **S** the phone **V/O** woke me up.)
9 **S** You **V** shouldn't walk **P** in the park **T** at night.
10 **S** You **V** should eat **O** your food **M** slowly.
11 **S** My term **V** begins **T** in October
12 **S** I **V** read **O** your article **M** quickly **P** in bed **T** last night
    (*or:* **T** Last night **S** I **V** read **O** your article **M** quickly **P** in bed.)

1.1B The forms of a sentence
1 Don't spill the coffee. (C)
2 Have you seen today's papers? (Q)
3 How nice to meet you! (E)
4 Where did you put my umbrella? (Q)
5 The train arrived fifteen minutes late. (S)
6 The plane won't arrive on time. (S)
7 I can't pay this electricity bill. (S)
8 Please open the door for me. (C)
9 'Where's the nearest hotel?' he asked. (Q)
10 'I can't pay the bill!' he cried. (E)

1.1C Context
1 I parked my car in the centre of the village.
2 I saw an old man near a bus stop.
3 'What a beautiful village!' I exclaimed.
4 'How many people live here?'
5 'There are seventeen people,' the old man said.
6 'How long have you lived here?'
7 'I have lived here all my life.'
8 'It's a quiet sort of place, isn't it?'
9 'We live a quiet life here.
10 We don't have a cinema or a theatre.
11 Our school was closed five years ago.
12 We have only one shop.
13 A bus calls once a day.
14 The Romans came here in 55 B.C.
15 Since then nothing has happened.'

1.2 The simple sentence: verbs with and without objects

1.2A What is a complete sentence?
The following need ticks:
2, 5, 8, 10, 11, 12, 13, 14, 15, 19, 20.

1.2B Verbs with and without objects
Possible answers for those verbs that need an object
1 contains pencils   4 ringing the doorbell
5 need a rest   7 hit him   8 beat the other team
9 opened the fridge
13 This sentence could be complete, or we could say e.g. I began my work.
16 enjoy the film?

1.2C Sentences with linking verbs like 'be' and 'seem'
Possible answers
1 tall (adjective)   **2** a teacher (noun)   **3** sour (adjective)   **4** in the garden (phrase of place)
5 at 6.30 (phrase of time)   **6** mine (possessive pronoun)   **7** like his grandfather (prepositional phrase)   **8** (too) loud (adjective)   **9** a nice person (adjective + noun)   **10** a lawyer (noun)

1.2D Context
1 My son Tim attends the local school.
2 My wife and I went to his school yesterday. (*or:* Yesterday, ...)
3 We spoke to his teachers.
4 We collected Tim's school report.
5 Tim's report wasn't very good.
6 His marks were low in every subject.
7 Tim was waiting anxiously for us outside.
8 'How was my report?' he asked eagerly.
9 'It wasn't very good,' I said.
10 'You must try harder.
11 That boy Ogilvy seems very clever.
12 He got good marks in all subjects.'
13 'Ogilvy has clever parents,' Tim said.

1.3 The simple sentence: direct and indirect objects

1.3A Subject + verb + indirect object + direct object: 'Show me that photo'
1 Please find them for me./Please find me them.
2 Please buy one for him./Please buy him one.
3 Please pass it to me./Please pass me it.
4 Please show it to her./Please show her it.
5 Please do it for me. (Not *Do me it*)
6 Please order one for me./Please order me one.

1.3B Verb + object + 'to' + noun or pronoun: 'Explain it to me'
1 this camera to the Customs   **2** me to your friend/your friend to me   **3** what you like to me   **4** this idea to you   **5** his crime to the police   **6** this to anyone
7 this man to me   **8** this to anyone   **9** this to the headmaster   **10** what I told you to anyone

1.3C The two meanings of 'for'
instead of: 2, 4, 6, 7, 9
for your/my benefit: 1, 3, 5, 8, 10

1.3D Context
The following need ticks: **1** buy me an expensive uniform   **5** write our parents a letter   **7** lend anyone anything   **8** give help to each other

1.4 The compound sentence

1.4A The form of a compound sentence
Write 1:
1 ... *and* complained about them.
2 ... *but* (she) didn't leave a message.
3 I can *either* leave now, *or* (I can) stay for another hour.
4 Jim *not only* built his own house, *but* (he) designed it himself *as well.*
5 I *neither* know *nor* care what happened to him.
6 ... very well, *but* (he) hasn't much experience ...

Write 2:
1 ... at the station *and* two men ...
2 *Either* you can give me some advice, *or* your colleague can.(*Either* you *or* your colleague can ...)
3 ... *but* it didn't stop.
4 ... when we called, *so* we left a message.
5 ... after the film, *so* we went straight back.
6 ... was nervous, *for* she wasn't used to strangers calling late at night.
7 ... in the country, *but* my parents ...
8 ... has been lost, *or* the postman has ...
9 ... was visible, *and then* a cloud covered it.
10 ... career woman, *yet* her mother ...

1.4B Context
1 and   **2** and   **3** and   **4** as well   **5** and   **6** but
7 yet   **8** either   **9** or   **10** for   **11** and   **12** and
13 but   **14** and

1.5 The complex sentence: noun clauses

1.5A Introduction to complex sentences
1 You can tell me all about the film ...
2 ... you can help me with the dishes.
3 You didn't tell me ...
4 I walk to work every morning ...
5 ... I left a message on the answer-phone.

1.5B Noun clauses derived from statements
1 (that) he feels angry.
2 (that) she has resigned from her job.
3 (that) you don't trust me.
4 (that) you are feeling better.
5 (that) she's upset.
6 (that) he didn't get the contract.
7 (that) it's a fair price.
8 (that) you're leaving.
9 (that) she's been a fool.

1.5C Noun clauses derived from questions
1 if/whether he has passed his exam.
2 if/whether you can (or could) type.
3 if/whether he will arrive tomorrow.
4 if/whether he likes ice-cream.
5 if/whether he was at home yesterday.
6 if/whether I should phone her.
7 if/whether she's ready.
8 when you met her.
9 how you will manage.
10 why he has left.
11 where you live.
12 which one she wants.
13 who's at the door.
14 what he wants.

1.5D Context
1 you know ...
2 you can turn into superwoman or superman ...
3 that her baby nearly slipped under the wheels of a car.
4 she lifted the car (to save her baby).
5 that he jumped nearly three metres into the air ...
6 if you can perform such feats.
7 that you can.
8 that we can find great reserves of strength ...
9 that adrenalin can turn us into superwomen or supermen!

1.6 The complex sentence: relative pronouns and clauses

1.6A 'Who', 'which' and 'that' as subjects of a relative clause
1 ... the accountant who does my accounts.
2 ... the nurse who looked after me.
3 ... the postcards which arrived yesterday.
4 ... the secretaries who work in our office.
5 ... the magazine which arrived this morning.
6 ... the workmen who repaired our roof.

1.6B 'Who(m)', 'which' and 'that' as objects of a relative clause
1 ... the accountant who(m) you recommended .../... the accountant you recommended ...
2 ... the nurse who(m) I saw at the hospital./... the nurse I saw ...
3 ... the postcards which I sent from Spain./... the postcards I sent ...
4 ... the secretaries who(m) Mr Pym employed./... the secretaries Mr Pym employed.
5 ... the magazine which I got .../... the magazine I got ...
6 ... the workmen who(m) I paid ... /... the workmen I paid ...

7 ... the dog which I saw .../... the dog I saw ...
8 ... the birds which I fed.../... the birds I fed ...

1.6C 'Who(m)', 'which' or 'that' as the objects of prepositions
1a He's the man to whom I sent the money.
 b He's the man who(m)/that I sent the money to.
 c He's the man I sent the money to.
2a She's the nurse to whom I gave the flowers.
 b She's the nurse who(m)/that I gave the flowers to.
 c She's the nurse I gave the flowers to.
3a That's the chair on which I sat.
 b That's the chair which/that I sat on.
 c That's the chair I sat on
4a He's the boy for whom I bought this toy.
 b He's the boy who(m)/that I bought this toy for.
 c He's the boy I bought this toy for.
5a That's the building by which I passed.
 b That's the building which/that I passed by.
 c That's the building I passed by.
6a They're the shops from which I got these.
 b They're the shops which/that I got these from.
 c They're the shops I got these from.

1.6D Context
1 who 2 (-) 3 who 4 (-)

1.7 The complex sentence: 'whose'; defining/non-defining clauses

1.7A 'Whose' + noun in relative clauses
1 ... the customer whose address I lost.
2 ... the novelist whose book won first prize.
3 ... the children whose team won the match.
4 ... the expert whose advice we want.
5 ... the witness whose evidence led to his arrest.
6 ... the woman whose house the film was made in./
 ... in whose house the film was made.

1.7B Defining and non-defining clauses
Commas are necessary in these sentences:
1 My husband, who is on a business trip to Rome all this week, ...
4 The author Barbara Branwell, whose latest novel has already sold over a million copies, ...
6 The play Cowards, which opens at the Globe soon, ...
9 The manager, whom I complained to about the service, ...
10 Sally West, whose work for the deaf made her famous, ...

1.7C Sentences with two meanings

1 Without commas: There were other test papers, which everyone didn't fail.
With commas: There was a single test paper and everybody failed it.
2 Without commas: I have another brother or other brothers somewhere else.
With commas: I have only one brother.

1.7D Context

1 who (no commas)   **2** which/that (no commas)
3 ..., which are commonly used, (commas)
4 ..., which are not so frequently used, (commas)
5 which/that (no commas)   **6** which/that (no commas)
7 who (no commas)   **8** No relative pronoun necessary; no commas   **9** ..., which is situated in a very rough area of London, (commas)
10 ..., which has a terrible lounge and a tiny dining room, (commas)   **11** which/that (no commas) (*or:* ..., which is fitted with a leaky shower. – one comma)
12 ..., which is expensive to run, (commas)
13 which/that (no commas) (*or:* ..., which is overgrown with weeds. – one comma)   **14** ..., who are generally unfriendly, ... (commas)   **15** ..., which is definitely not recommended, (commas)

1.8 The complex sentence: time, place, manner

1.8A Adverbial clauses of time (past reference)

1 ... weight *when I was ill.*
2 ... home *immediately after I arrived in the airport building.*
3 ... the letter *before she realized it wasn't addressed to her.*
4 ... burnt down *by the time the fire brigade arrived.*
5 ... gone wrong *as soon as we saw him run toward us.*

1.8B Adverbial clauses of time (future reference)

1 ... university *until I get my exam results.*
2 ... message *as soon as he phones.*
3 ... Duty Free Shop *before our flight is called.*
4 ... dead *by the time they find a cure for the common cold.*
5 ... surprise *the moment you open the door.*

1.8C Adverbial clauses of place

Possible answers
1 where the accident happened.
2 anywhere you like.
3 everywhere you go in the world.
4 wherever you can find a chair.
5 where everyone can see it.

1.8D Adverbial clauses of manner

Possible answers
1 as if it's raining.
2 as he likes it.
3 as though it was my fault.
4 in the way you wrote it last year.
5 the way I show you.

1.8E Context

1 when   **2** the way (that)   **3** as if   **4** before
5 which/that   **6** As   **7** As soon as   **8** that/which

1.9 The complex sentence: reason and contrast

1.9A Adverbial clauses of reason

Possible answers
1 Service in this hotel ought to improve *because there's been a change of management.*
2 *As the Air Traffic Controllers are on strike,* we have cancelled our holiday.
3 Could you sell your old computer to me, *seeing (that) you have no further use for it?*
4 *Since she's never in when I phone,* I'll have to write to her.
5 I've had to have the document translated, *since I can't read Russian.*

1.9B Contrast (1)

Possible answers
1 ... computer, *even though I haven't got much money.*
2 ... this morning, *even if it's raining.*
3 *Much as I'd like to help you,* I'm afraid ...
4 *While your design is excellent,* it isn't suitable ...
5 *Although I try hard to play the piano,* I don't ...
6 *Considering that Chinese is so difficult,* it's surprising ...
7 *Whereas the play was wonderful,* the film ...

1.9C Contrast (2)

Possible answers
1 *However expensive it is,* he's determined ...
2 *However hard I work,* I still ...
3 *However well you write,* it doesn't mean ...
4 *No matter how sorry she feels,* the damage ...
5 *No matter how much they pay us,* it will never ...
6 *No matter how many cards I send,* I always ...
7 *Whatever he tells you,* don't believe ...

1.9D Context

1 Even though/Though   **2** because/as, since
3 As/Because/Since   **4** even though   **5** though/as
6 while   **7** because   **8** because/as/since   **9** Because

1.10 The complex sentence: purpose, result and comparison

1.10A Adverbial clauses of purpose with 'so that' and 'in order that'
1 ... driving lessons *in order that/so that I might pass my driving test first time.*
2 ... the cinema early *in order that/so that I might not miss the beginning of the film.*
3 We stood up *in order that/so that we might get a better view* ...
4 ... a second car *in order that/so that his wife might learn to drive.*
5 ... and clearly *in order that/so that the audience might understand me.*

1.10B Adverbial clauses of purpose with 'in case'
1 ... immediately *in case you change* (or *should change*) *your mind.*
2 ... with you *in case you are not able* (or *should not be able*) *to get into the house.*
3 ... the kitchen *in case there is* (or *should be*) *a fire.*
4 ... train *in case there is* (or *should be*) *a lot of traffic on the roads.*
5 ... with me *in case I need* (or *should need*) *it.*

1.10C Adverbial clauses of result with 'so ... (that)' and 'such ... (that)'
1 We were *so late (that) we missed* ...
2 I was working *so hard (that) I forgot* ...
3 There was *such a delay (that) we missed* ...
4 We've had *such difficulties (that) we don't think* ...

1.10D Adverbial clauses of comparison with 'as ... as'
Possible answers
1 John works *as hard as Susan (does).*
2 John is *not so intelligent as Susan (is).*
3 This computer *does not hold as much information as that one (does).*
4 The film 'Superman 1' is *as enjoyable as 'Superman 2' (is).*

1.10E Context
1 in order that   2 which   3 so ... (that)   4 but
5 as ... as   6 in case   7 when   8 such ... (that)

1.11 The complex sentence: present participle constructions

1.11A Joining sentences with present participles ('-ing')
1 She got very worried, *thinking we had had an accident.*
2 He went to his room, *closing the door behind him.*

3 *Not hearing what he said*, I asked him to repeat it.
4 You didn't ask me for permission, *knowing I would refuse.*
5 *Not being a lawyer,* I can't give you the advice you are looking for.

1.11B The present participle in place of adverbial clauses
1 They broke this window *when trying to get into the house.*
2 *Though refusing to eat*, he admitted he was very hungry.
3 I damaged the car *while trying to park it.*
4 *While agreeing you may be right*, I still object to your argument.
5 *After looking at the map*, we tried to find the right street.
6 Don't get into any arguments *before checking your facts.*

1.11C The present participle in place of relative clauses
1 Delete *which is.*   2 Delete *who are.*
3 Delete *who is.*   4 Delete *which is.*
5 Change *which leave* to *leaving.*   6 Change *who complain* to *complaining.*   7 Change *who travel* to *travelling.*   8 Change *who work* to *working.*
9 Delete *who are.*   10 Delete *who is.*

1.11D Context
1 preparing   2 Feeling   3 As   4 commenting
5 after/when   6 hearing   7 who   8 When/After
9 knowing   10 announcing

1.12 The complex sentence: perfect/past participle constructions.

1.12A 'Being' and 'having been'
1 *Being out of work*, I spend a lot of my time at home.
2 *Being a scientist*, John hasn't read a lot of novels.
3 *Having been promised a reward*, he hopes he'll get one.
4 *Being near a newsagent's*, I went in and got a paper.
5 *Having been up all night*, they were in no mood for jokes.

1.12B 'It being' and 'there being'

1 *There being no questions*, the meeting ended quickly.
2 He kept helping himself to money *without it being noticed*.
3 He kept asking awkward questions *without there being a(ny) reason for it*.
4 *It being a holiday*, there were thousands of cars on the roads.
5 *There being no one in*, I left a message.

1.12C Agreement between present participle and subject

1 It wasn't the smell that was opening the door.
2 It wasn't the bus that was changing gear.
3 It wasn't the important papers that were burning the rubbish.

1.12D Past participle constructions

1 *Lost for many years*, the painting turned up at an auction.
2 *Although cooked for several hours,* the meat was still tough.
3 *If seen from this angle*, the picture looks rather good.
4 *The vegetables sold in this shop* are grown without chemicals.
5 *When read aloud*, the poem is very effective.

1.12E Context

1 When/Whenever/If 2 Looking 3 being
4 Opening 5 Although

2 Nouns

2.1 One-word nouns

2.1A Noun endings: people who do things/people who come from places

1 act*or* 2 beg*gar* 3 pian*ist* 4 driv*er* 5 Berlin*er*
6 Athen*ian* 7 assist*ant* 8 li*ar* 9 Texa*n*
10 histor*ian*

2.1B Nouns formed from verbs, adjectives, other nouns

1 deci*sion* 2 anxi*ety* 3 social*ism* 4 happ*iness*
5 agree*ment* 6 discover*y* 7 arriv*al*
8 child*hood* 9 abs*ence* 10 post*age* 11 try (no change) 12 effici*ency* 13 curi*osity* 14 address (no change) 15 refus*al* 16 warn*ing*
17 mouth*ful* 18 explan*ation* 19 tri*al* 20 argu*ment*

2.1C Nouns and verbs with the same spelling but different stress

1 p<u>er</u>mit 2 per<u>mit</u> 3 in<u>crease</u> 4 <u>increase</u>
5 <u>objects</u> 6 <u>object</u> 7 <u>conduct</u> 8 con<u>duct</u>
9 <u>entrance</u> 10 en<u>trance</u> 11 <u>record</u> 12 re<u>cord</u>
13 <u>present</u> 14 pre<u>sent</u> 15 pro<u>test</u> 16 <u>protest</u>
17 <u>accent</u> 18 ac<u>cent</u> 19 <u>exports</u> 20 ex<u>port</u>
21 es<u>cort</u> 22 <u>escort</u> 23 <u>imports</u> 24 im<u>port</u>

2.1D Context

1 boredom 2 communication 3 babble/babbling
4 knowledge 5 preparation 6 encouragement
7 recognition 8 solution 9 refusal 10 scientist
11 behaviour

2.2 Compound nouns

2.2A Nouns formed with gerund ('-ing') + noun: 'dancing-shoes'

The following need ticks: 1, 3, 5, 7

2.2B Apostrophe s ('s) or compound noun?

1 the car key 2 the doctor's surgery
3 the committee's idea 4 the pen nib
5 the computer keyboard 6 the desk top
7 King John's reign 8 Eliot's poetry 9 no one's responsibility 10 the suitcase handle 11 the front door knob 12 Scott's journey 13 the postman's bicycle 14 that cigarette stub 15 a new kitchen table 16 the horse's tail 17 the light switches
18 the boss's secretary 19 the new party policy
20 the book cover 21 Mr Jones's son
22 the factory gate 23 the garage door
24 the children's photos 25 the office phone
26 the film critic 27 a dancing teacher 28 the twins' mother 29 my brother's wife 30 a new reading lamp 31 the road surface 32 the President's secretary

2.2C Compound nouns which tell us about materials and substances

1 a plastic raincoat 2 a silk shirt 3 silky/silken hair
4 a glass table-top 5 glassy eyes 6 a leather wallet
7 a stainless steel spoon 8 steely/steel nerves
9 a woollen pullover 10 a cotton blouse 11 a silver teapot 12 a silvery voice 13 a stone wall
14 stony silence 15 a ceramic tile 16 a nylon nailbrush 17 a leathery tongue 18 a wooden spoon

2.2D Context

1 feather wings 2 a flying machine 3 flight path
4 a champion cyclist 5 pedal power 6 pilot's seat/ pilot-seat 7 carbon fibre machine 8 south wind

2.3 Countable and uncountable nouns (1)

2.3A Countable and uncountable nouns compared
1 painting C   **2** milk U   **3** photos C   **4** oil U
5 drawings C   **6** Hope U   **7** hope C   **8** flour U
9 shirts C   **10** coal U

2.3B Nouns which can be either countable or uncountable: 'an egg/egg'
1 onion U   **2** fish U   **3** eggs C   **4** cake U
5 motorway C   **6** ice C   **7** glasses C   **8** stones C
9 paper U   **10** iron C

2.3C Normally uncountable nouns used as countables (1): 'a coffee/(some) coffee'
1 I'd like (some) tea/(some) coffee, please.
2 I'd like a/one coffee and two teas, please.
3 I'd like a/one beer, a/one lemonade and a/one tomato juice, please.
4 I'd like two coffees, three teas and one milk/a glass of milk

2.3D Normally uncountable nouns used as countables (2): 'oil/a light oil'
1 a light oil   **2** an excellent wine   **3** a traditional cloth
4 a rare wood.

2.3E Context
1 (-)   **2** a/(-)   **3** a   **4** a   **5** a   **6** a   **7** a   **8** a   **9** a
10 (-)   **11** a   **12** a   **13** some   **14** a

2.4 Countable and uncountable nouns (2)

2.4A Singular equivalents of uncountable nouns: 'bread/a loaf'
1 coat/jacket/dress, etc.   **2** laugh
3 suitcase/bag/case, etc.   **4** job   **5** room/bed

2.4B Nouns not normally countable in English: 'information'

Write 1:
The following need ticks: 2, 4, 6, 7, 8, 12

Write 2:
1 some   **2** (-)   **3** any   **4** a   **5** the   **6** some/a lot of
7 some/a lot of   **8** a lot of/some/the
9 the/some/a lot of   **10** a   **11** a   **12** some/a lot of
13 some   **14** a lot of   **15** (-)   **16** any   **17** (-)
18 a lot of/some   **19** a lot of/some   **20** a

2.4C Partitives: 'a piece of', etc.
1 a cube of ice   **2** a bar of chocolate   **3** a slice of bread   **4** a sheet of paper   **5** a bar of soap
6 a bottle of milk   **7** a jar of jam   **8** a box of

matches   **9** a pot of tea   **10** a tube of toothpaste
11 a drop of water   **12** a pinch of salt   **13** a sip of tea
14 a splash of soda   **15** a wisp of smoke

2.4D Context
1 a   **2** (-)   **3** (-)   **4** (-)   **5** (-)   **6** (-)   **7** Some
8 a lot of   **9** (-)   **10** (-)

2.5 Number (singular and plural) (1)

2.5A Nouns with plurals ending in -s or -es: 'friends', 'matches'

/s/	/z/	/ɪz/
1 clocks	**7** bottles	**13** addresses
2 lakes	**8** cinemas	**14** beaches
3 lights	**9** guitars	**15** offices
4 months	**10** hotels	**16** pieces
5 parks	**11** islands	**17** spaces
6 tapes	**12** smiles	**18** villages

2.5B Nouns with plurals ending in -s or -es: 'countries' 'knives'
1 These cherries are very sweet.
2 I've lost my keys.
3 These knives are blunt.
4 The leaves are turning yellow.
5 The roofs have been damaged.
6 We have three Henrys in our family.

2.5C Nouns ending in -o and some irregular plural forms
1 Which videos do you like best?
2 Which volcanoes/volcanos are erupting?
3 These are John's pet mice.
4 These teeth are giving me trouble.
5 Can you see those geese?
6 Postmen are busy all the time.
7 We're going to sell those sheep.
8 I can see salmon/some salmon in the water.
9 Which aircraft have just landed?
10 The Swiss are used to mountains.

2.5D Context
1 food*s*   **2** cake*s*   **3** biscuit*s*   **4** tomato*es*
5 orange*s*   **6** *men*   **7** *women*   **8** li*ves*   **9** cuisine*s*
10 *Japanese*   **11** *Swiss*   **12** product*s*
13 strawberr*ies*   **14** peach*es*   **15** potato*es*
16 *spaghetti*

2.6 Number (singular and plural) (2)

2.6A Collective nouns followed by singular or plural verbs: 'government'
1 is/are   **2** is/are   **3** are   **4** is/are   **5** has/have
6 are   **7** have   **8** are   **9** is/are   **10** are   **11** is/are
12 have

2.6B Nouns with a plural form + singular or plural verbs: 'acoustics'

1 are **2** is **3** are **4** is **5** is **6** are **7** Are **8** are
9 Are **10** have **11** has **12** has **13** has **14** are

2.6C Nouns with a plural form + plural verbs: 'trousers'

1 have **2** are ... They **3** does **4** these/those ...
They **5** brains **6** Congratulations **7** are
8 haven't ... them **9** them **10** have
11 aren't ... are **12** don't

2.6D Context

1 is **2** are **3** show **4** is **5** is/are **6** own **7** are
8 is **9** is **10** are **11** are **12** spends/spend
13 are **14** are **15** favour/favours **16** make

2.7 Gender

2.7A Male and female word forms: 'waiter/waitress'

1 sister **2** uncle **3** nephew **4** bachelor, spinster
5 nuns **6** cows **7** hens **8** mares **9** sow **10** ram
11 actress **12** waitress **13** prince **14** lionesses
15 goddess **16** heiress **17** heroine **18** widower
19 saleswoman **20** female **21** queens
22 bridegroom **23** daughter **24** aunt **25** nieces

2.7B Identifying masculine and feminine through pronouns: 'He/She is a student'

1 she **2** She **3** he **4** his **5** She **6** her **7** his
8 He **9** she **10** her **11** she **12** her

2.7C Context

1 She **2** actors **3** She **4** Prince **5** she
6 princess **7** mother **8** Miss **9** she **10** Sisters

2.8 The genitive

2.8A How to show possession with 's, s' and the apostrophe (') on its own

1 This is a *child's* bicycle. **2** This is the *teacher's*
pen. **3** He described the *actress's* career.
4 That's a *stewardess's* job. **5** These are the
children's toys. **6** This is a *women's* club. **7** It's a
girls' school. **8** This is the *residents'* lounge.
9 This is *James's* umbrella. **10** That is *Doris's* hat.

2.8B Apostrophe s ('s/s'), compound noun or 'of'?

1 That's a *man's* voice. **2** (-) **3** That's *the
committee's* decision. **4** It's *no one's* fault.
5 This is a copy of *Keats'* poetry. **6** (-) **7** (-) **8** (-)

2.8C The use of 's and s' with non-living things: 'an hour's journey'

1 *an hour's* delay **2** *two days'* journey
7 *seven years'* work **8** the *earth's* surface
9 at *death's door* **10** a *year's* absence

2.8D Omission of the noun after 's

1 the hairdresser's **2** the chemist's **3** my aunt's
4 St Andrew's **5** Marks and Spencer's

2.8E Context

1 animal skins **2** a leopardskin coat **3** the earth's
wildlife **4** children's clothing **5** ladies' coats
6 an actress's fur coat **7** the crocodiles' revenge
8 customers' skins

3 Articles

3.1 The indefinite article: 'a/an' (1)

3.1A General statements with 'a/an' and zero (Ø)

1 *Small computers aren't* expensive.
2 *Quartz watches don't* last for ever.
3 I like *a play with a message*.
4 I admire *a politician who is* sincere.
5 *Big cities are* always fascinating.
6 Even *efficient systems* can break down.
7 *Road maps are always* out of date.
8 *Rules are* meant to be broken.
9 *A restaurant* shouldn't charge too much.
10 How much *does a car radio* cost?
11 *Buses leave* here every hour.
12 How long *do letters take* to get here?

3.1B The 'plural form' of 'a/an'

1 *They're architects*.
2 Do you want *any/some potatoes*?
3 *Doctors need* years of training.
4 How well can *cats* see in the dark?
5 Have you got *any cats* at home?
6 Why should *compact discs* be so dear?
7 I borrowed *some compact discs*.
8 Can you lend me *any/some compact discs*?
9 Why *are cars* so expensive?
10 There *aren't any cars* in the street.

3.1C Describing people and things with 'a/an' + noun: 'He's a doctor'
1 He's *a taxi-driver*.
2 She's *a Catholic*.
3 He's *an Englishman*.
4 It's *an ant*.
5 It's *a kind of insect*.
6 She's *a socialist*.
7 She's *a teacher*.
8 She's *an architect*.
9 It's *a Shakespeare sonnet*.
10 It's *a Picasso/a Picasso painting*.

3.1D Context
1 (-) 2 A 3 a 4 a 5 some 6 some 7 a 8 a/(-)
9 a/(-) 10 a/(-) 11 any 12 a 13 (-)

3.2 The indefinite article: 'a/an' (2)

3.2A the use of 'a/an' when something is mentioned for the first time
1 a 2 the 3 an 4 The 5 a/the [> LEG 3.20.4]
6 the 7 the 8 a 9 the 10 a

3.2B The difference between 'a/an' and 'one'
1 a 2 one 3 One 4 a 5 one 6 a 7 One
8 one ... a 9 a ... one 10 a/one 11 a 12 one

3.2C 'A/an' for price, distance and frequency: '80p a kilo'
1 They're 90p a kilo.
2 I take them once a day.
3 We're doing 100 km an hour.
4 I/We do 45 miles a (or to the) gallon.
5 It's collected twice a week.
6 It costs £3 a litre.

3.2D 'A/an' or zero with reference to illnesses: 'a cold'
1 a 2 a/(-) 3 (-) 4 (-) 5 a/(-) 6 (-) 7 a 8 a
9 a/(-) 10 (-)/a

3.2E Context
1 a 2 The 3 a 4 a 5 (-) 6 (-) 7 (-) 8 one
9 a 10 a 11 the 12 the 13 the 14 the

3.3 The definite article: 'the' (1)

3.3A Form and basic uses of 'the'
1 a 2 a 3 the 4 a 5 the 6 The 7 a 8 the

3.3B 'A/an', 'the' and zero in front of abbreviations: 'the BBC'
1 a 2 a 3 The 4 an 5 (-) 6 (-) 7 (-) 8 (-)

3.3C 'The' + nationality noun: 'the Chinese'
1 The Portuguese ... the Spanish/the Spaniards
2 The Americans ... the Russians 3 The Brazilians ... the Mexicans 4 The Germans ... the Japanese
5 The Greeks ... the Koreans 6 The British ... the Dutch

3.3D Context
1 a 2 a 3 the 4 the 5 The 6 the 7 a/the
8 a 9 a/the 10 a 11 the 12 the 13 The 14 the
15 the 16 the 17 a/the 18 The 19 a 20 The

3.4 The definite article: 'the' (2)

3.4A 'The' for specifying
1 We were looking for *a place* to spend *the/a night*. *The place* we found turned out to be in *a charming village*. *The village* was called (-) Lodsworth.
2 *An* (or *The*) *individual* has every right to expect personal freedom. *The freedom* of *the individual* is something worth fighting for.
3 Yes, my name is (-) *Simpson*, but I'm not *the Simpson* you're looking for.
4 Who's at *the door*? – It's *the postman*.
5 When you go out, would you please go to *the supermarket* and get some butter.
6 I've got *an appointment* this afternoon. I've got to go to *the doctor's*.
7 We went to *the theatre* last night and saw Flames. It's *a wonderful play*.
8 We prefer to spend our holidays in *the country, the mountains* or by *the sea*.
9 We have seen what *the earth* looks like from *the moon*.
10 This is the front room. *The ceiling* and *the/(-) walls* need decorating, but *the floor* is in good order. We'll probably cover it with *a /(-) carpet*.
11 You're imagining (-) *things*. All your fears are in *the mind*.
12 Look at this wonderful small computer. *The top* lifts up to form *the/a screen*; *the front* lifts off to form *the/a keyboard*, and *the whole thing* only weighs 5 kilos.
13 *The history* of *the world* is *the history* of (-) *war*.
14 Is there *a moon* round *the planet* Venus?
15 What's (-) *John* doing these days? – He's working as *a postman*.
16 (-) *Exercise* is good for *the body*.
17 Could you pass me *the salt*, please?
18 They're building *a new supermarket* in *the centre* of our town.
19 Where's your mother at *the moment*? – I think she's in *the kitchen*.
20 If you were a cook, you'd have to work in *a kitchen* all day long.

3.4B 'The' to refer to things that are unique (not place names)
1 *The Times* ... *The Washington Post*
2 *The Economist* ... *Time* magazine **3** *The New Yorker* ... *Punch* **4** the human race ... man ... the dinosaurs **5** *The Graduate* ... *Jaws* **6** the gods ... God **7** *(The) Odyssey* ... *Ulysses* **8** The United Nations ... Congress **9** the *Titanic* **10** the Navy ... the Army **11** the French Revolution
12 the President **13** President **14** the climate

3.4C Context
1 The **2** a **3** the **4** the **5** The **6** a **7** The **8** the **9** an **10** the **11** an **12** an **13** a **14** the **15** the

3.5 The zero article (1)

3.5A Basic uses of the zero article (Ø): 'Life is short'
1 (-) **2** The **3** (-) **4** the ... (-) **5** (-) **6** the **7** (-) **8** the ... (-) **9** (-) ... the **10** (-) ... the **11** (-) **12** the ... (-) **13** (-) **14** (-) **15** The **16** (-) ... (-) **17** (-) **18** (-) ... (-) **19** (-) **20** The ... (-) ... (-) **21** (-) ... (-) **22** (-) ... (-) **23** the **24** (-) ... (-)

3.5B The zero article with names and titles: 'Mr Pym'
The following need an X:
  1 We use nothing if we are addressing a stranger, or *Mr* + surname if we know it. In American English, we might use *Sir*.
  3 *Mrs* cannot be followed by a first name.
  6 Not normal use: old-fashioned.
  7 This use of *Mrs* is not generally considered polite.
  9 *Sir John Falstaff*. (Title + first name (+ surname) [> 3.5B, note 4])

3.5C Context
1 (-) **2** (-) **3** (-) **4** an **5** (-) **6** the **7** The **8** a **9** (-) **10** The **11** the **12** (-) **13** the **14** the **15** (-) **16** (-) **17** (-) **18** (-) **19** (-) **20** (-) **21** (-) **22** (-) **23** (-) **24** (-) **25** (-) **26** The **27** the

3.6 The zero article (2)

3.6A Zero article for parts of the day ('at dawn') and for meals ('for lunch')
1 (-) **2** (-) **3** (-) **4** (-) **5** The **6** (-) **7** (-) **8** (-) **9** the **10** a

3.6B Zero article for e.g. 'She's at school' and 'He's in hospital'
1 (-) **2** the **3** (-) **4** a **5** the **6** (-) **7** a **8** (-) **9** (-) **10** (-) **11** (-) **12** (-) **13** the **14** a **15** the **16** (-)

3.6C Zero article or 'the' with place names
1 the Dark Ages ... Medieval Europe **2** Central Asia ... the Arctic **3** Brazil ... Argentina ... the USA **4** London ... Paris ... Vienna **5** Montague Road **6** Brown's ... the Hilton **7** Bavaria ... Ohio **8** London ... Buckingham Palace **9** the Alps ... Mont Blanc **10** the Sahara **11** the Nile ... Luxor **12** Lake Geneva **13** Leoni's ... the Globe Theatre **14** Oxford Street ... Oxford Circus **15** London Bridge

3.6D Context
1 the **2** (-) **3** (-) **4** a/the **5** (-) **6** (-) **7** (-) **8** (-) **9** (-) **10** (-) **11** the **12** the **13** (-) **14** the **15** the **16** the **17** (-) **18** (-)

4 Pronouns

4.1 Personal pronouns

4.1A Subject and object pronouns
1 Your parcel ... *It* **2** Jane and I ... *We* **3** that? ... *It's* **4** Jane Wilson? ... *She's* **5** a baby! ... *it* **6** cat ... *It's* **7** John ... *him* **8** Catherine ... *her*

4.1B Subject or object pronoun?
1 me/him/her/us/them **2** Me/Him/Her/Us/Them **3** me/us **4** Me/Us **5** me/I **6** than me/I am ... I **7** I ... me/I am

4.1C Gender in relation to animals, things and countries
1 She **2** It **3** it/her **4** she/it **5** it/one **6** she/it **7** He/It **8** it **9** It **10** She **11** He **12** It/She

4.1D Context
1 you **2** it **3** who **4** him **5** they **6** me **7** I **8** he **9** He **10** he **11** you **12** They **13** you **14** him **15** them

4.2 'One'

4.2A 'One' and 'you'
The moment *you get* into the mountains, *you are* on *your* own. *You have* to rely on *yourself* for everything. This means *you have* to carry all *your* own food, though, of course, *you* can get pure drinking water from mountain streams. *You* won't see any local people for days at a time, so *you* can't get help if *you're* lost. *You have to* do *your* best to find sheltered places to spend the night.

4.2B 'One' and 'ones' in place of countable nouns: 'Use this clean one'
1 one 2 one 3 ones 4 ones 5 one 6 ones
7 water/(-) 8 one

4.2C 'Which one(s)?' – 'This/that (one)', etc.
1 ones 2 ones (tick) 3 one (tick) 4 ones (tick)
5 one (tick) 6 ones (tick) 7 one ... one (tick)
8 *These ones* or *those ones* are possible, but it would be best to omit *ones* (tick) 9 one 10 ones

4.2D Context
1 You/One 2 ones 3 you/one 4 ones 5 one
6 one 7 one 8 you 9 you/(-) 10 one/(-)
11 one/(-)

4.3 'It' and 'one/some/any/none'

4.3A 'It' as in 'it's hot' and 'it's nice to see you'
1 It's Monday, 13th June, today.
2 It's snowing (now). It snows a lot here.
3 It was 22° Celsius in London yesterday.
4 It's 100 kilometres from here to Paris.
5 It's important to get to the meeting.
6 It's difficult making such decisions.
7 It's a pleasure to welcome you all here.
8 It's a pity that they couldn't come.

4.3B 'It' and 'one' as subjects and objects: 'I like it'
1 one 2 it 3 none 4 some 5 it 6 them 7 any
8 some 9 them 10 one

4.3C 'I hope/believe/expect so'
1 Does the next train go to London? – I believe so.
2 The weather is going to improve. – I hope so.
3 Have the letters arrived yet? – I don't think so./I think not.
4 The rail strike hasn't ended. – It doesn't seem so./It seems not.
5 It's a holiday tomorrow. – Who says so?
6 There's been a terrible air disaster. – I fear so.
7 Will the democrats win the election? – I don't expect so./I expect not.

4.3D Context
1 It 2 they 3 It 4 one 5 them 6 them 7 any
8 them 9 it 10 so 11 It 12 it 13 it

4.4 Possessive adjectives and possessive pronouns ('my/mine')

4.4A Basic differences between 'my' and 'mine', etc.
1 her 2 His 3 mine 4 our 5 Yours 6 theirs
7 one's 8 his 9 her 10 its

4.4B The double genitive: 'He is a friend of mine'
1 That brother of yours 2 no friend of mine 3 a play of Shakespeare's 4 this/that problem of yours
5 a friend of ours 6 That loud music of hers
7 A friend of my sister's 8 Those neighbours of theirs 9 That radio of yours

4.4C 'My own' and 'of my own'
1 my own room/a room of my own 2 his own business/a business of his own 3 their own rooms/rooms of their own 4 its own kennel/a kennel of its own

4.4D 'The' in place of 'my', etc.: 'a pain in the neck'
1 the 2 my 3 the 4 the 5 my 6 My 7 My
8 the 9 the 10 the

4.4E Context
1 our 2 ours 3 its 4 your 5 our 6 Yours
7 your 8 hers 9 the 10 our 11 our 12 your

4.5 Reflexive pronouns ('myself')

4.5A Verbs commonly followed by reflexive pronouns: 'I enjoyed myself'
1 myself 2 yourself 3 himself 4 herself 5 itself/himself [> 4.1C] 6 oneself 7 ourselves
8 themselves 9 herself 10 himself

4.5B Verb + reflexive, or not?: 'I've dressed (myself)'
1 hide ourselves 2 washes itself 3 dress herself
4 sat ourselves down 5 got myself wet
6 woke myself up 7 got himself engaged
8 Get yourself/yourselves ready

4.5C Reflexive pronouns used after prepositions and for emphasis

Write 1:
1 himself 2 you 3 me 4 ourselves 5 herself
6 us/you/me, etc. 7 himself 8 himself

Write 2:
1 I didn't know about it *myself* till yesterday/till yesterday *myself*. (or: I *myself* didn't know about it ...)
2 The building *itself* is all right, I think./The building is all right *itself* ...
3 You can't do that *yourself/yourselves*!
4 I can't fetch it – (you) fetch it *yourself*.
5 Don't expect me to do it. Do it *yourself*!

4.5D Context
1 itself 2 ourselves 3 ourselves 4 ourselves
5 us 6 themselves 7 themselves 8 them 9 us
10 us 11 us 12 ourselves

4.6 Demonstrative adjectives/pronouns ('this', etc.)
'Some/any/no' compounds ('someone', etc.)

4.6A Different uses of 'this' and 'that'
1 Introducing someone.
2 On the phone.
3 Referring back to something that we mentioned earlier.
4 Referring to something we are talking about.
5 Meaning 'now' (*these days*) compared with the past.
6 Referring to someone we don't want to meet or don't like (*that man*).
7 Making comparisons. ('more than £50)'
8 Telling a story or an anecdote.
9 Making it clear who we mean.
10 Showing the size of something (usually with gestures).

4.6B Uses of 'some/any/no' compounds
1 nothing   2 anything   3 no one/nobody
4 something   5 anyone/anybody   6 something/anything   7 someone/somebody/no one/nobody
8 anything   9 anyone/anybody/no one/nobody
10 anyone/anybody/no one/nobody

4.6C 'Everyone', 'anyone', etc. with singular or plural pronouns
1 their ... them   2 they   3 their   4 they
5 don't they?   6 they   7 their   8 they are
9 they think ... they'll   10 they deserve ... they don't like ... they get

4.6D Context
1 they   2 No one   3 they   4 anyone   5 that
6 nothing   7 this (or that)   8 something   9 this
10 this (or that)   11 this (or that)

5 Quantity

5.1 Quantifiers + countable and uncountable nouns

5.1A Quantifiers + countable and uncountable nouns
1 fewer A   2 less B   3 a lot of C   4 a lot of C
5 much B   6 many A   7 most of the D   8 most C
9 most C   10 a little B   11 a few A
12 Several A   13 any C   14 any C   15 enough C
16 hardly any C   17 Neither D   18 Both A
19 no C   20 no D

5.1B Quantifiers that tell us roughly how much and how many
Possible answer

1a *too many* eggs	1b *too much* milk
2a *plenty of* eggs	2b *plenty of* milk
3a *a lot of* eggs	3b *a lot of* milk
4a *enough* eggs	4b *enough* milk
5a *a few* eggs	5b *a little* milk
6a *very few* eggs	6b *very little* milk
7a *not many* eggs	7b *not much* milk
8a *hardly any* eggs	8b *hardly any* milk
9a *no* eggs	9b *no* milk

Possible answers
1 There are *plenty of apples* in the bowl.
2 I've got *hardly any money*.
3 *A lot of people* turned up at the meeting.
4 You've put *too much salt* in the sauce.
5 We've got *enough time* for a drink.
6 We usually get a *few letters* every day.

5.1C Context
1 many   2 few   3 some   4 plenty of   5 hardly any
6 enough   7 very little   8 some   9 any   10 no
11 any   12 some

5.2 General and specific references to quantity

5.2A 'Of' after quantifiers ('a lot of', 'some of', etc.)
1 a lot of G   2 a small amount of G   3 a lot of S
4 – G   5 – G   6 any of S   7 a couple of G
8 plenty of G   9 plenty of G   10 plenty of S
11 – G   12 None of S   13 – G   14 Some of S
15 a bit of G

5.2B When to use quantifiers without 'of': 'I've got a lot'
Possible answers
1 Yes, there are a couple.   2 Yes, I bought a bit.
3 Yes, we've got a lot.   4 Yes, there's plenty.
5 Yes, there were lots.   6 Yes, there's a lot.

5.2C 'More' and 'less' after quantifiers: 'some more', 'a little less'
1 much less   2 any more   3 many more
4 much less   5 Lots more   6 some more
7 plenty more   8 a lot less   9 no fewer
10 much more   11 a lot more   12 much more

5.2D Context
1 many   2 plenty of   3 millions of   4 number
5 A lot of   6 Much   7 most   8 much   9 many
10 A lot of   11 bit of   12 number of

5.3 Uses of 'some', 'any', 'no' and 'none'

5.3A 'Some/any' or zero in relation to quantity
1 (-) 2 some 3 (-) 4 some 5 some 6 any 7 (-)
8 any 9 (-) 10 some 11 (-) 12 some or any
13 (-) Some could be used here to mean e.g. 'money that hasn't been given to you' [> 5.3B, note 4]
14 some 15 any 16 (-)

5.3B Four basic uses of 'some' and 'any'
1 some 2 some 3 some 4 Some 5 any 6 any
7 any 8 any

5.3C 'Not ... any', 'no' and 'none'
1 There *aren't any buses* after 12.30.
2 We've got *none*.
3 I'm *no accountant*, but these figures are wrong.
4 There's *no explanation* for this.

5.3D Other uses of 'some' and 'any'
1 f 2 e 3 b 4 g 5 d 6 c 7 a

5.3E Context
1 (-) 2 (-) 3 (-) 4 (-) 5 no 6 (-) 7 (-) 8 (-)
9 (-) 10 (-) 11 (-) 12 some (or any) 13 some
14 (-)

5.4 'Much', 'many', 'a lot of', '(a) few', '(a) little', 'fewer', 'less'

5.4A Basic uses of 'much', 'many' and 'a lot of'
1 a lot of 2 much 3 much 4 many 5 a lot of
6 many

5.4B Other common uses of 'much', 'many' and 'a lot of'
1 Much 2 Many 3 much 4 many 5 much
6 many 7 much 8 many

5.4C 'Few', 'a few', 'little', 'a little'
1 few 2 a little 3 little 4 a few 5 a few 6 a little
7 few 8 little

5.4D 'Fewer' and 'less'
1 less ... fewer (or *less*, informal) 2 fewer (or *less*, informal) 3 fewer (or *less*, informal) 4 less 5 less
6 less

5.4E Context
1 few 2 many 3 A lot of (*fewer* is also possible here, but not intended) 4 fewer 5 much 6 a little
7 a lot of (*a little* is also possible) 8 a few (*a lot of* is also possible)

5.5 'Both' and 'all'

5.5A 'Both/both the' and 'all/all the' with nouns
1 Both (the) 2 All 3 All the 4 All 5 All the
6 All the 7 Both (the) 8 All 9 Both (the)
10 Both (the)

5.5B 'Both' and 'all': word order with verbs
1 The customers *are all complaining*.
2 The patients *both had* appointments at 10.
3 The directors *have both retired*.
4 Our secretaries *can both speak* French.
5 The customers *should all have complained*.
6 The boys *both had* haircuts.
7 The pupils *may all leave* now.
8 The students *all wrote* good essays.
9 Our employees *all work* too hard.
10 The children *must all go home* early.
11 The children here *all learn* German.

5.5C 'Both' and 'all': word order with pronouns
1 *All of us* took 2 *Both of them* turned 3 I know *both of you* 4 She's interested in *both of them*
5 *All of it* went 6 She's concerned about *all of us*
7 *All of you* filled

5.5D 'None of' and 'neither of'
1 None of the passengers 2 Neither of us was/were [> 5.7C, note 2] 3 Neither of the tyres needed
4 None of us knew

5.5E Context
1 All 2 us 3 us 4 all the 5 all 6 All the 7 all
8 them 9 both/both the 10 both 11 Both
12 them 13 them 14 both 15 them

5.6 'All (the)', '(a/the) whole', 'each' and 'every'

5.6A 'All (the)' compared with '(a/the) whole'
1 all my hair 2 the whole situation 3 All the money
4 the whole truth 5 the whole story
6 a whole century

5.6B 'All' compared with 'everyone/everybody' and 'everything'
1 everyone 2 Everyone 3 Everything 4 All 5 All
6 Everyone 7 Everyone ... all 8 Everything 9 all
10 everything

5.6C 'Each' and 'every'
1 every 2 each 3 every 4 every 5 each
6 every 7 each/every 8 every/each 9 Each/every
10 each 11 each 12 every 13 each
14 every/each

5.6D Context
1 whole   2 Everyone   3 each   4 Each   5 each
6 all   7 whole   8 every   9 everything

5.7 'Another', '(the) other(s)', 'either', 'neither', 'each (one of)'

5.7A 'Another', 'other', 'others', 'the other', 'the others'
1 the other   2 the other   3 others   4 another
5 the next   6 another/the other ... the other
7 another   8 other   9 the others

5.7B 'Either' and 'neither' + singular nouns
1 Either   2 Neither   3 either   4 neither   5 either
6 neither

5.7C 'Each of', etc.
1 Another of the teaspoons   2 Neither of the
roadmaps is/are   3 Any of the roadmaps   4 Either of
the roads leads/lead   5 Each of the paintings
6 Neither of the boys is/are   7 either of the
secretaries   8 each of the porters.

5.7D 'One of'
One can be deleted in numbers: 2, 4, 5

5.7E Context
1 other   2 Some   3 others   4 Either   5 one   6 One
7 one   8 one   9 one   10 the other

6 Adjectives

6.1 Formation of adjectives

6.1A Adjectives formed with suffixes: 'enjoy/enjoyable'
1 attractive   2 manageable   3 hesitant   4 energetic
5 Victorian   6 reddish   7 boastful   8 permissible
9 humorous

6.1B Adjectives formed with prefixes: 'possible/impossible'
1 dishonest   2 illegal   3 irresponsible
4 unimaginable   5 incapable   6 uncooked
7 impractical   8 pre-war

6.1C Compound adjectives of measurement, etc.: 'a twenty-year-old man'
1 a two-million-pound office-block   2 a seventy-year-
old woman   3 a two-day conference   4 an eighty-
hectare farm   5 a three-day journey   6 a five-kilo
bag   7 a three-litre engine   8 a fifty-pound note
9 a twenty-mile fence   10 a fifty-kilometre tunnel

6.1D Context
1 illegal   2 17-year-old boy   3 impossible
4 an eight-hour lesson   5 careful   6 hesitant
7 wonderful   8 energetic   9 reddish   10 setting

6.2 Position of adjectives

6.2A Form and position of most adjectives
1 is big   2 are clever   3 is hardworking   4 are busy
5 are well-behaved

6.2B Adjectives that can change in meaning before a noun or after 'be'
Write 1: 1 an old friend   2 to me by my late uncle
3 a faint line   4 heavy   5 a heavy smoker

Write 2: 1 b (fine silk),   2 b (is fine),   3 e (I'm going
to be sick),   4 c (very ill)   5 d (in the early 1960s)
6 a (a sick woman)

6.2C Adjectives before and after nouns with a change of meaning
1 b   2 h   3 d   4 h   5 f   6 g   7 a   8 i   9 e   10 c

6.2D Context
1 beautiful/lovely   2 young   3 lovely
4 polished/shiny   5 pleased   6 shiny/polished
7 quick-drying   8 alive   9 asleep   10 complete
11 poor   12 big   13 fresh   14 tall   15 fast

6.3 Adjectives that behave like nouns; '-ed/ing' endings

6.3A 'The' (etc.) + adjective + noun: 'the blind'
Write 1: 1 a poor man   2 unemployed people
3 a young woman   4 an elderly man
5 a sick woman   6 healthy people

Write 2: 1 The rich ... the poor   2 the unemployed
3 the deaf   4 The old   5 the injured   6 the dead
7 the elderly   8 The healthy   9 the sick
10 The blind ... the sighted

6.3B Adjectives ending in '-ed' and '-ing': 'interested/interesting'
1 We were *amazed* by the coincidence.
2 The journey was *tiring*.
3 Sylvia was *upset* by the experience.
4 The experience was *upsetting* (for us).
5 Gloria was *enchanting*.
6 Gloria was *enchanted* (by me).
7 The children were *delightful*.
8 We were *delighted* by the children.
9 The new building is *impressive*.
10 Everybody is *impressed* by the new building.

6.3C Context

1 the rich   **2** the poor   **3** shocked   **4** embarrassed
5 the old   **6** The blind   **7** the sighted   **8** The deaf
9 The unemployed   **10** The healthy   **11** the sick
12 the young   **13** depressed   **14** distressed
15 distressing   **16** depressing   **17** the living
18 the dead

6.4 Adjectives after 'be', 'seem'; word order of adjectives

6.4A 'Look good' compared with 'play well'

1 nicely   **2** nice   **3** badly   **4** bad   **5** good   **6** well
7 smoothly   **8** smooth

6.4B Word order: two-word and three-word nouns: 'a teak kitchen cupboard'

1 a cotton shirt   **2** a cotton summer shirt   **3** a wire
rake   **4** a kitchen clock   **5** a plastic kitchen clock

6.4C Word order: past participle + noun: 'a handmade cupboard'

Possible answers:
1 a worn cotton shirt   **2** a handmade cotton
summer shirt   **3** a broken wire rake   **4** a damaged
kitchen clock   **5** an unused plastic kitchen clock

6.4D Word order: adjective + noun: 'a big round table'

1 a cheap white Taiwanese clock radio for my
bedside table.
2 a second-hand well-maintained sports car with a
low mileage.
or: a well-maintained second-hand sports car.
3 a beautiful antique English polished mahogany
dining-table.
or: a beautiful antique polished English mahogany
dining-table.
4 a pair of grey and red American canvas trainers
which I can use for jogging.
5 a small old stone-built country cottage.
6 a pink and white cotton summer dress for my
holiday.

6.4E Context

1 Expensive Italian handmade leather shoes (*or:*
Expensive handmade Italian leather shoes)
2 beautiful old pair   **3** back doorstep   **4** large friendly
dog (exceptionally, size comes before the general
adjective here)   **5** badly   **6** good   **7** good
8 remaining Italian shoe   **9** unchewed Italian shoe
10 red fur-lined slippers

6.5 The comparison of adjectives

6.5A Common comparative and superlative forms: 'cold – colder – coldest'

1 My room's *bigger* than yours. It's *the biggest* in the
house.
2 My room's *colder* than yours. It's *the coldest* in the
house.
3 My garden's *nicer* than yours. It's *the nicest* in the
street.
4 My desk's *tidier* than yours. It's *the tidiest* in the
office.

6.5B Adjectives with two or more syllables: 'clever', 'expensive'

1 She's *happier/more happy* than I am.
She's *the happiest/most happy* person I have ever
met.
2 His work was *more careless* than mine.
It was *the most careless* (work) in the class.
3 This problem is *simpler/more simple* than that one.
It's *the simplest/the most simple* (problem) in the
book.
4 This watch is *more expensive* than that one.
It's *the most expensive* (watch) in the shop.
5 This engine is *quieter/more quiet* than mine.
It's *the quietest/most quiet* (engine) ever built.

6.5C Comparative and superlative forms often confused: 'older/elder'

1 farther/further   **2** oldest   **3** worse   **4** lesser
5 latest   **6** further   **7** well   **8** last   **9** oldest
10 smaller   **11** less   **12** older   **13** most/more
14 better   **15** best   **16** farthest/furthest   **17** oldest
18 elder/older   **19** least   **20** most

6.5D Context

1 nearer/nearest (We can sometimes use superlatives
for 'only two' [> LEG 6.28].)   **2** biggest   **3** strongest
4 further/farther (*or:* furthest/farthest)   **5** smaller, i.e.
'of the two' (*or:* smallest, i.e. 'I have ever seen')
6 weaker, i.e. 'of the two' (*or:* weakest, i.e. 'I have
ever seen')   **7** the most violent   **8** smallest
9 biggest   **10** last   **11** best   **12** oldest

7 Adverbs

7.1 Adverbs of manner

7.1A Adverbs with and without '-ly': 'carefully', 'fast'
1 badly   2 hard   3 fast   4 better   5 airmail
6 suddenly   7 rudely   8 early   9 best   10 gladly
11 quickly   12 eagerly   13 last   14 high
15 carefully   16 late   17 bravely   18 near   19 wide
20 monthly

7.1B Two forms and different meanings: 'hard/hardly'
1 hard   2 hardly   3 last   4 lastly   5 lately   6 late
7 highly   8 high   9 justly   10 just   11 near
12 nearly

7.1C Adjectives which end in '-ly': 'friendly'
1 in a cowardly way/manner/fashion   2 quickly
3 loudly/loud   4 in a silly way/manner/fashion
5 in a lively way/manner/fashion   6 slowly   7 badly
8 in a motherly way/manner/fashion   9 in a lovely
way/manner/fashion   10 carefully   11 in a sickly
way/manner/fashion   12 in an unfriendly way/
manner/fashion

7.1D Context
1 Last   2 important   3 early   4 carefully   5 best
6 best   7 far   8 fast   9 past   10 beautiful
11 in a silly way/manner/fashion   12 quickly
13 rapidly   14 cheap/cheaply   15 full
16 hurriedly   17 new

7.2 Adverbs of time

7.2A Points of time: 'Monday', 'this morning'
Write 1:

1 *yesterday*	today	*tomorrow*
2 *yesterday morning*	this morning	*tomorrow morning*
3 *yesterday at noon*	at noon	*tomorrow at noon*
4 *yesterday afternoon*	this afternoon	*tomorrow afternoon*
5 *yesterday evening*	this evening	*tomorrow evening*
6 *last night*	tonight	*tomorrow night*
7 *last Monday*	this Monday	*next Monday*
8 *last January*	this January	*next January*
9 *last week*	this week	*next week*
10 *last year*	this year	*next year*

Write 2:
1 She is arriving *this morning*.
2 I can see him *today*.
3 She arrived *last night*.
4 I'm expecting her *tomorrow night*.
5 I'll be home *tonight*.
6 You can make an appointment *this afternoon*.
7 You can see me *the day after tomorrow*.
8 She left *yesterday evening*.
9 You can see me *the day after tomorrow in the morning*.
10 You can come to my office *at noon/at midday (today)*.
11 He left *yesterday morning*.
12 She'll phone *tomorrow afternoon*.

7.2B 'Still' and 'yet'
1 The children are *still* at the cinema.
2 I haven't met your brother *yet*./I *haven't yet* met your brother./I *still* haven't met your brother.
3 Jim *still* works for the same company.
4 Has she phoned you *yet*? No, not *yet*.
5 The new law hasn't come into force *yet*./The new law hasn't *yet* come into force./The new law *still* hasn't come into force.

7.2C 'Already' and other adverbs of time
1 I've *already* had it, thanks./I've had it *already*.
2 I haven't received an invitation to the party *yet*./I haven't *yet* received an invitation to the party.
3 I have *already* received an invitation to the party./I have received an invitation to the party *already*.
4 Have you finished eating *yet*?/Have you *already* finished eating/finished eating *already*?
5 Haven't you finished eating *yet*?

7.2D Context
1 This week   2 yet   3 still   4 already   5 Yesterday
6 immediately   7 Then

7.3 Adverbial phrases of duration

7.3A 'Since', 'for' and 'ago'
Write 1:
1 *Since* when have ...
2 ... a week *ago*.
3 ... seven months *ago*.
4 ... haven't seen her *since (last week)*.
5 ... been home *since* 1987.
6 How long *ago* did ...

Write 2:
1 ... *for* five years ...
2 ... here *since* 1984.
3 ... him *for* six years.
4 ... a letter *for* weeks.
5 ... a letter *since* last week.
6 ... jazz *since* I was a boy.

7.3B 'Till' (or 'until') and 'by'
1 till   2 till   3 by   4 till   5 by   6 by   7 till

7.3C 'During', 'in' and 'for'
1 during /in   2 during   3 during/in   4 during/in
5 during/in   6 for   7 during   8 during   9 during
10 during/in   11 during/in   12 for

7.3D Context
1 ago   2 For   3 since   4 during (or in)   5 since
6 till   7 by   8 till   9 by   10 during   11 for   12 till

7.4 Adverbs of frequency

7.4A Position of adverbs of frequency ('often') in affirmatives and questions
Possible answers
1 I *am generally* late.
2 I *was usually* late for work.
3 I *can always tell* the difference between the two.
4 I *would never have been able* to find a job like yours.
5 You *seldom tried* hard enough.
6 You *sometimes got* good marks at school.
7 *Are you often* late?
8 *Have you always lived* in this town?
9 *Did you ever get* good marks at school?

7.4B The position of adverbs of frequency in negative statements
1 Public transport *isn't always* reliable.
2 He *wasn't often* late when he worked here./*He often wasn't* ...
3 She *doesn't usually arrive* on time./*She usually doesn't* ...
4 *She sometimes doesn't arrive* on time.
5 We *don't normally worry* if the children are late. Or *We normally don't* ...
6 You *hardly ever phone.*
7 We *don't generally complain./We generally don't* ...
8 You're *sometimes not* at home when I phone./*You sometimes aren't* ...

7.4C Adverbs of frequency at the beginning of a sentence
1a) I *often* bring work home from the office.
 b *Often*, I bring work home from the office.
2a) John *normally* leaves home before his wife does.
 b) *Normally*, John leaves home before his wife does.
3a) I have *frequently* forgotten to lock the back door.
 b) *Frequently*, I have forgotten to lock the back door.
4a) I *usually* know when to wake up.
 b) *Usually*, I know when to wake up.
5a) I'm *generally* the one who pays the bills.
 b) *Generally*, I'm the one who pays the bills.
6a) The traffic is *often* heavy in the mornings.
 b) *Often*, the traffic is heavy in the mornings.
7a) We *sometimes* have power cuts.
 b) *Sometimes*, we have power cuts.
8a) There are *often* complaints about the service.
 b) *Often*, there are complaints about the service.

7.4D Context
1 Have you *ever forgotten* ...?
2 Don't say you *never have!*
3 We *can't always be* careful ...
4 ... most of us must *occasionally have left* something ...
5 ... who *never forgets* anything.
6 ... a year *are regularly dealt with* ...
7 People *don't normally carry/normally don't carry* .../*Normally, people don't carry* ...
8 The things people *most often lose/lose most often*
9 But *sometimes* there are items/there *are sometimes* ...
10 Can you *ever* imagine ... (*or:* ... and *not ever claiming* it?)
11 Prams and pushchairs *are often* lost./*Often*, prams and pushchairs ...
12 ... people *frequently forget* false teeth ...
13 Yet they *often do!/Yet often* they do!

7.5 Adverbs of degree

7.5A The two meanings of 'quite'
1 The film was *quite good* ('less than')
2 The exhibition was *quite amazing.* ('completely')
3 Pam's *quite wonderful!* ('completely')
4 The play was *quite awful.* ('completely')
5 I *quite enjoyed* my holiday. ('less than')
6 I *quite like* snails. ('less than')

7.5B 'Fairly'

1 quite ('complimentary')/fairly ('less complimentary')
2 quite ('completely')
3 quite ('completely')
4 quite ('complimentary')/fairly ('less complimentary')
5 quite ('completely')
6 quite ('completely')

7.5C 'Rather'

1 quite ('completely')/rather ('inclined to be')
2 quite ('completely')
3 quite ('completely')/rather ('inclined to be')
4 quite ('completely')
5 quite ('less than')/rather ('inclined to be')

7.5D 'Much', 'any', 'far' and 'a lot' as adverbs of degree

1 much/any   2 much/far/a lot   3 much/far/a lot
4 much/far   5 any/much   6 much/any   7 much
8 much/far   9 much/any   10 much/far/a lot

7.5E Context
Possible answers
1 quite late   2 rather tired   3 fairly middle-aged
4 rather a good meal   5 quite unaware   6 any more
7 any/much use   8 rather a good idea   9 quite dim

7.6 Intensifiers

7.6A 'Very', 'too' and 'very much'

Write 1:
1 very ill   2 very much faster   3 too fast for me
4 very (or too) good   5 too expensive   6 very (or very much) mistaken   7 very much interested
8 very much   9 very much admired   10 the very best
11 too intelligent   12 too cold   13 I very much like
14 very much faster   15 very late   16 too late
17 very much missed   18 too much pocket money
19 very much   20 very much alone

Write 2:
1 very much   2 too much   3 very   4 very much
5 very   6 very   7 too much   8 too much   9 too
10 too   11 very much   12 very or too

7.6B Adverbs in place of 'very': 'extremely happy', 'fast asleep'
Possible answers
1 awfully   2 terribly   3 greatly   4 extremely
5 terribly   6 wide   7 deeply   8 extremely   9 really
10 richly   11 painfully   12 awfully   13 terribly
14 awfully   15 terribly   16 extremely   17 extremely
18 fast   19 bitterly   20 terribly   21 badly
22 extremely   23 really   24 extremely

7.6C Context
Possible answers
1 too   2 very   3 fast   4 very much   5 painfully
6 too   7 really/very much   8 extremely
9 Much   10 richly

7.7 Focus adverbs

7.7A 'Even', 'only', 'just' and 'simply' for 'focusing'
Possible answers
1 I understood his lecture, but no one else did.
2 I listened, but I didn't take notes.
3 I didn't understand anyone else's lecture./I understood his lecture, but I didn't understand anything else.
4 Set the table in a simple manner.
5 I understood it, but with some difficulty./... but I didn't understand anything else.
6 I didn't understand anyone else's lecture./I understood his lecture, but I didn't understand anything else.
7 I understood it, but with some difficulty.

7.7B Two meanings of 'too'
1 It's too hot.
2 ... and it's hot, too.
3 ... and I went to the supermarket, too.
4 It was too far.
5 It was too expensive.
6 ... and expensive, too

7.7C 'Too' and 'not either'
1 too   2 too   3 either   4 too   5 either   6 either
7 either   8 too

7.7D 'Also' and 'as well'
1 she can also sing   2 I have also had a shower
3 he also writes TV scripts   4 he will also be tried
5 you should also have written   6 I also have to file some letters   7 I'd also like some sandwiches
8 he also owns the flat   9 we also export a lot
10 it's also too expensive

7.7E Context
1 ...she didn't leave any jewels, either   2 Even my mother was surprised   3 ... she had some rings and some lovely necklaces, too   4 I saw them only once/I only saw them once ...   5 ... in the bedrooms, in the bathroom, and in the attic as well   6 Millie was very careful and was also afraid of burglars   7 ... we'd better take all the food in the deep freeze, too
8 ... the goose was full of jewels and there were some gold coins, too!

7.8 Viewpoint adverbs, connecting adverbs and inversion

7.8A Viewpoint adverbs
1 d   2 c   3 b   4 e   5 a   6 f   7 h   8 g   9 i

7.8B Connecting adverbs
1 h   2 a   3 f   4 b   5 g   6 c   7 d   8 e

7.8C Inversion after 'negative adverbs', etc.
1 *Never has there been* such a display of strength by the workers.
2 *Only later did I realize* what had happened.
3 *On no account should you sign* the document.
4 *In no circumstances should you answer* the door when I'm out.
5 *So old was the papyrus*, we didn't dare to touch it.

7.8D Context
1 is   2 has there been   3 According to   4 However
5 agreeably   6 Moreover   7 In brief   8 Ultimately

8 Prepositions, adverb particles and phrasal verbs

8.1 Prepositions, adverb particles and conjunctions

8.1A Words we can use either as prepositions or as adverbs
1 Run across the road. Run across now.
2 Climb over the wall. Climb over now.
3 Come inside the house. Come inside now.
4 Go down the hill. Go down now.
5 Go up the ladder. Go up now.
6 Run past the window. Run past now.

8.1B Words we can use only as prepositions or only as adverbs
Possible answers
1 We waited at the station.
2 We went to the beach.
3 We jumped back. (no object possible)
4 We climbed out. (no object possible)
5 We drove away. (no object possible)
6 We ran into the building.
7 We ran out of the building.
8 We went upwards. (no object possible)

8.1C Words we can use either as prepositions or conjunctions
Possible answers
1 ... before breakfast/before I have had breakfast.
2 ... after work/after I have finished work.
3 ... till 4 o'clock/till you arrive.
4 ... since Monday/since I arrived on Monday.

8.1D Object pronouns after prepositions: 'between you and me'
1 me   2 us   3 them   4 us   5 us   6 me

8.1E Context
1 *in* one boot (preposition)   2 *in* the afternoon (preposition)   3 *for* the day (preposition)   4 *in* his police car (preposition)   5 go *by* (particle)
6 sat *up* (particle)   7 *in* a blue car (preposition)
8 drove *past* (particle)   9 *out of* the boot (preposition)
10 *round* the town (preposition)   11 *on top of* the police car (preposition)   12 no attention *to* it (preposition)   13 *in front* of her (preposition)
14 *in* the boot (preposition)   15 *from* the boot (prepostion)   16 *of* a strange noise (preposition)
17 *in* the back of this car (preposition)

8.2 Prepositions of movement and position Prepositions of time

8.2A 'At a point', 'in an area' and 'on a surface'
1 at   2 at   3 in   4 in   5 in   6 at   7 at   8 in   9 in
10 in   11 in   12 in   13 at   14 at   15 in   16 in
17 at   18 in

8.2B Prepositions of time: 'at', 'on' and 'in'
1 at... on   2 in   3 on   4 in   5 on   6 In   7 at... at
8 At   9 in   10 in   11 on   12 At   13 at   14 in
15 on

8.2C Context
1 in   2 in   3 In   4 in   5 in   6 to   7 to   8 at   9 from
10 in   11 in

8.3 Particular prepositions, particles: contrasts (1)

8.3A Prepositions, particles etc. often confused and misused
1 on/about   2 about   3 According to   4 According to
5 by/according to   6 across/over   7 across   8 over/
across   9 across   10 through   11 through/across
12 across/through   13 (far) away   14 away
15 because   16 because of   17 before   18 in front
of   19 before/in front of   20 after   21 afterwards
22 afterwards   23 (a)round/about   24 around/about
25 (a)round   26 (a)round   27 at   28 to   29 at
30 against   31 at   32 at   33 behind/at the back
34 back   35 at the back of/behind   36 back
37 back   38 back   39 back   40 behind   41 back

8.3B Context
1 across   2 According to   3 at   4 away   5 in front of
6 behind   7 because   8 after   9 about   10 before
11 on (or about)   12 at   13 about

8.4 Particular prepositions, particles: contrasts (2)

8.4A Prepositions, particles, etc. often confused and misused
1 beside   2 besides   3 Besides   4 between
5 between   6 among   7 but for/except for
8 except (for)/but (for)   9 Except for/But for
10 except (for)/but (for)   11 but   12 by/near
13 near/not far from   14 on/by   15 On   16 past/by
17 past/by   18 by   19 past/by   20 past   21 by
22 by   23 by   24 with/without   25 down/up
26 under   27 over/under   28 due to   29 owing to
30 owing to   31 like   32 As   33 as   34 like   35 like
36 As   37 As   38 like   39 as   40 like   41 like

8.4B Context
1 As   2 without   3 due   4 past/by   5 down/up
6 beside/by   7 among   8 between   9 by   10 like
11 except   12 without   13 by

8.5 Particular prepositions, particles: contrasts (3)

8.5A Prepositions, particles, etc. often confused and misused
1 of/out of   2 from   3 from   4 with   5 of   6 off
7 on   8 in   9 in   10 on   11 out of   12 out of
13 outside   14 outside   15 without   16 with
17 with   18 with   19 with/without   20 without
21 with   22 with   23 above/over   24 on top of
25 over/above   26 over/above   27 above   28 over
29 above   30 above   31 over   32 under   33 under

34 underneath/under/below   35 below   36 below/
under   37 below/under/underneath   38 under
39 with   40 without   41 with   42 in   43 in   44 with
45 of   46 of

8.5B Context
1 of   2 In   3 of/out of   4 of   5 off   6 over/above
7 out of   8 in   9 of   10 on top of   11 with
12 above   13 in   14 on top of   15 below   16 in/with

8.6 Phrasal verbs: Type 1, verb + preposition (transitive)

8.6B Type 1: Verb + preposition + object, non-idiomatic: 'look at the camera'
1 with/to   2 from   3 on   4 of   5 from   6 between
7 about   8 on   9 at   10 for   11 at   12 for   13 with
14 about   15 to   16 with   17 after   18 for   19 in
20 with   21 of   22 in   23 in   24 for

8.6C Type 1: Verb + object + preposition + object, non-idiomatic: 'tell me about it'
1 for   2 of   3 from   4 to   5 in   6 about   7 against
8 from/into   9 for   10 of   11 with   12 for   13 of
14 to   15 for   16 from

8.6D Type 1: Verb + preposition + object, idiomatic: 'get over an illness'
1 f   2 i   3 c   4 l   5 n   6 p   7 t   8 s   9 h   10 m
11 a   12 q   13 r   14 k   15 d   16 b   17 g   18 j
19 o   20 e

8.6E Context
1 at   2 out of/from   3 at   4 from   5 for   6 in   7 in
8 at   9 to   10 for   11 of   12 on   13 of   14 to
15 of

8.7 Phrasal verbs: Type 2, verb + particle (transitive)

8.7A Type 1 and Type 2 phrasal verbs compared
1 (-)   2 (-)   3 turn *off* the gas   4 (-)   5 given *out* the
papers   6 (-)   7 Write *down* the information   8 (-)
9 (-)   10 (-)

8.7B Type 2: Particles that extend the verb: 'write down'
1 f   2 b   3 k   4 n   5 j   6 p   7 h   8 s   9 c   10 q
11 t   12 r   13 e   14 o   15 d   16 i   17 m   18 l
19 g   20 a

8.7C Type 2: Verb + particle + object, idiomatic: 'bring about a change'
1 e   2 i   3 l   4 n   5 j   6 f   7 k   8 m   9 o   10 b
11 a   12 d   13 h   14 g   15 c

8.7D Context
1 (-) 2 (-) 3 puts a business suit *on* 4 (-)
5 put his shirt and tie *on* 6 picked the receiver *up*
7 (-) 8 (-) 9 check some figures *over* 10 (-)
11 cutting expenses *down* 12 put the meeting *off*
13 writing some notes *down* 14 (-) 15 put *down* the
receiver 16 (-) 17 (-) 18 (-) 19 (-) 20 had his
red shorts *on*

8.8 Phrasal verbs:
(Type 3, verb + particle (intransitive)
(Type 4, verb + particle (transitive)

8.8A Type 3: Verb + particle, intransitive, non-idiomatic: 'hurry up'
Possible answers
1 Come along. 2 Come away. 3 Come in.
4 Come up. 5 Go away. 6 Go in. 7 Go up.
8 Hurry along. 9 Hurry up. 10 Hurry away.
11 Sit down. 12 Sit up. 13 Stand up.
14 Come down. 15 Hurry in. 16 Go down.

8.8B Type 3: Verb + particle, intrasitive, idiomatic: 'break down'
1 b 2 h 3 j 4 e 5 m 6 f 7 q 8 o 9 c/d 10 p
11 i 12 n 13 a 14 l 15 k 16 c/d 17 g

8.8C Type 4: Verb + particle + preposition + object, non-idiomatic: 'walk up to the top'
Possible answers
1 The lift takes a long time to *come down from* the
top floor.
2 We'd better try to *drive on to* Calcutta before
sunset.
3 I *hurried over to* Tom's as soon as I heard the
news.
4 *Run along to* the shop for me and get a loaf of
bread.
5 It's best to *stay away from* the town centre on
Friday nights.

8.8D Verb + particle + preposition + object, idiomatic: 'put up with it'
1 e 2 l 3 b 4 t 5 i 6 n 7 g 8 k 9 q 10 s
11 p 12 j 13 o 14 a 15 r 16 d 17 f 18 h
19 m 20 c

8.8E Context
1 put *up with* 2 lie *down* 3 stay *up* 4 come *about*
5 lie *in* 6 catch *up on* 7 looks *down on* 8 face *up
to* 9 let me *in on* 10 coughed *up* 11 cheer *up*
12 look forward *to*

9 Verbs, verb tenses, imperatives

9.1 The simple present and present progressive tenses (1)

9.1A Pronunciation and spelling of the 3rd person, simple present
1 He *laughs*	/s/		8 She *rushes*	/ɪz/
2 She *drops*	/s/		9 She *saws*	/z/
3 She *drinks*	/s/		10 He *wears*	/z/
4 She *forgets*	/s/		11 She *loves*	/z/
5 He *loses*	/ɪz/		12 He *sees*	/z/
6 She *manages*	/ɪz/		13 He *pays*	/z/
7 He *passes*	/ɪz/		14 She *cries*	/z/

9.1B Uses of the simple present tense: 'I work/he works'
1 boils 2 rises 3 works 4 wear 5 eat 6 works
7 go 8 drives 9 gets 10 eat 11 leaves
12 starts 13 see 14 know ... agree 15 hope
16 says

9.1C Stative and dynamic verbs
The following need ticks: 1a, 2a, 3b, 4b, 5a, 6a, 6b,
7a, 7b, 8a, 8b
1b I envy 2b I understand 3a You know 4a Does
he seem 5b I prefer

9.1D Context
1 Are you sitting 2 hope 3 are studying 4 have
5 does not include 6 try 7 regard 8 want

9.2 The simple present and present progressive tenses (2)

9.2A Spelling: how to add '-ing' to a verb: 'wait/waiting'
1 making 2 eating 3 writing 4 forgetting
5 putting 6 travelling 7 catching 8 dying
9 carrying

9.2B Uses of the present progressive tense: 'I am working/he is working'
1 I am working (1) 2 are you drinking? (1) 3 is still
waiting (1) 4 is hurrying (1) 5 are constantly
panicking (4) 6 are becoming (2) 7 is John doing ...
is riding (2) 8 are enjoying (1) 9 is always upsetting
(4) 10 is he arriving (3) 11 is forever forgetting (4)
12 am having (2) 13 is always lying (4)
14 is running (3)

9.2C The simple present and the present progressive tenses in typical contexts

1 you take ... and sort ... you file
(Spoken or written explanation or demonstration)
2 We hope you are enjoying ... We sunbathe and go ... Next week we're going
(Letter or postcard from someone who is on holiday)
3 The action takes place ... goes up ... are sitting ... They are arguing
(Review of a play in a newspaper or on the radio)
4 The plumber is putting ... are rewiring ... is building
(Letter to, or telephone conversation with a friend)
5 I think ... you are doing ... I doubt ... knows ... you tell me
(Letter to a friend or relation in reply to a phone call or a letter)
6 Pym passes ... runs ... shoots ... pushes
(Spoken commentary on a football match on TV or radio)

9.2D Context

1 am studying   2 am working   3 don't have to
4 opens   5 closes   6 are always coming in
7 asking   8 am learning   9 enjoy/am enjoying
10 find/am finding   11 use   12 are   13 are   14 are always finding   15 think   16 love
17 miss/am missing

9.3 The simple past tense

9.3A The past form and pronunciation of regular verbs

1 waited /ɪd/   2 cleaned /d/   3 played /d/
4 posted /ɪd/   5 smiled /d/   6 stopped /t/
7 dreamt /t/, or dreamed /d/   8 burnt /t/, or burned /d/
9 cried /d/   10 watched /t/   11 laughed /t/
12 obeyed /d/   13 hurried /d/   14 lied /d/
15 finished /t/   16 included /ɪd/   17 locked /t/
18 travelled /d/

9.3B Irregular past forms

1 saw   2 understood   3 knew   4 met   5 found
6 left   7 wrote   8 sold   9 was   10 had   11 kept
12 ate

9.3C Uses of the simple past tense: 'I worked/he worked'

1 I *worked* as a civil servant *five years ago*.
2 I last *played* football *when I was 14*.
3 The Carters *left* for their summer holiday *last night*.
4 John *arrived at 4*.
5 I last *saw* 'Gone with the Wind' *recently*.
6 I/We *waited* at the airport *till they arrived*.
7 Sally *told* me/us about her engagement *when she was here*.

9.3D Context

1 claimed   2 attacked   3 was   4 had   5 chased
6 jumped   7 believed   8 called   9 set out
10 offered   11 captured   12 visited

9.4 The simple past and past progressive tenses

9.4A Irregular verbs with the same form in the present as in the past: 'put/put'

1 past   2 present   3 past   4 past   5 present
6 present or past   7 past   8 past   9 past   10 past
11 present or past   12 past   13 present   14 past

9.4B Uses of the past progressive tense: 'I was working'

1 was not listening   2 were enjoying   3 Were they playing   4 was gardening   5 Were you watching
6 was raining   7 was wondering   8 Were you still working   9 were living   10 was always doing
11 were constantly improving   12 Were you reading   13 was getting

9.4C The simple past and the past progressive in story-telling

1 It *was* just before
2 Tom *was* only 20
3 (he) *was living* with his mother (1)
4 He *was working* and *travelling* (1)
5 He *received* a mysterious letter
6 It *was addressed*
7 ... *was signed* ... *asked*
8 as he *was dealing* ... Tom *was wondering* (3)
9 he *decided*
10 It *was* full
11 He *was just wondering* ... when a stranger *introduced* himself (2)
12 (The stranger) *said* ... when Tom *was* a baby
13 The stranger *explained* ... Bill *was*
14 Tom *was* recruited ...
15 *was already working* ... when the war *began* (2)

9.4D Context

1 was driving   2 was driving   3 saw   4 stopped
5 got out   6 was   7 looked   8 was crossing/crossed
9 went   10 noticed   11 told   12 pulled   13 pulled
14 pulled   15 thought   16 looked/was looking
17 noticed   18 gave   19 seized   20 put
21 continued

9.5 The simple present perfect and present perfect progressive

9.5A Uses of the simple present perfect tense: 'I have eaten/he has eaten'
1 have/'ve visited   2 has/'s typed   3 Have you ever eaten   4 have/'ve never quarrelled   5 haven't written   6 haven't been   7 haven't seen   8 has/'s driven   9 have/'ve known   10 has/'s been   11 have/'ve bought   12 has/'s travelled   13 Have you forgotten   14 have/'ve ridden   15 has/'s just flown   16 has/'s recently become   17 have/'ve already spoken   18 haven't drunk   19 hasn't answered   20 have/'ve met

9.5B The present perfect progressive tense: 'I have been eating'
1 have/'ve been digging   2 have you been waiting   3 have/'ve been standing   4 have you been learning   5 has/'s been studying   6 Have you been running?   7 have/'ve been living   8 have/'ve been crying   9 have the children been sleeping   10 have you been doing

9.5C The simple present perfect and the present perfect progressive compared
1a I've typed   1b I've been typing   2a She has/'s been cooking   2b I've cooked   3a We have/'ve built   3b We have/'ve been building

9.5D The simple past and the simple present perfect compared
1a never read   1b has never read   2a had   2b have just had   3a Has he gone   3b Did he go

9.5E Context
1 visited   2 told   3 asked   4 said   5 arrived   6 have been staying   7 have never visited   8 have been swimming   9 arrived   10 suggested   11 agreed   12 noticed   13 were   14 was (or informally were)   15 remembered   16 came   17 asked   18 waved

9.6 The simple past perfect and past perfect progressive tenses

9.6A Uses of the simple past perfect tense: 'I had worked'
1 locked/had locked ... got   2 arrived ... had finished   3 rang ... checked/had checked   4 discussed/had discussed ... wrote   5 had ... had all left   6 rang ... had already gone out   7 took ... had never seen   8 had just cleaned ... came ... shook   9 promised/had promised ... hadn't finished

9.6B Uses of the present and past perfect progressive: 'I have/had been working'
1 had been digging   2 have been waiting (or had been waiting if the context is the past)   3 have/had you been waiting   4 had been standing   5 had been studying   6 has been raining   7 had been writing   8 have/had been ringing   9 had been painting   10 Had you been running?

9.6C The simple past perfect and past perfect progressive compared
1 had been cooking   2 had prepared   3 had been doing   4 had done   5 had done   6 had been doing

9.6D Context
1 had spent   2 had looked/had been looking   3 had not been able   4 had been   5 had been cooking   6 had prepared   7 had made   8 had baked   9 had always enjoyed/always enjoyed   10 had to   11 had lost   12 said   13 found   14 put   15 smiled   16 fished

9.7 The simple future tense

9.7A Some uses of 'will' and 'shall'
1 d   2 f   3 g   4 b   5 k   6 l   7 j   8 a   9 h   10 i   11 e   12 c

9.7B 'Will' and 'shall' to refer to the future
1 they'll/they will   2 They'll/They will   3 You'll/You will   4 I'll/I will/I shall   5 I will/I shall   6 you will   7 won't   8 I'll/I will/I shall   9 everything'll/everything will   10 When'll/When will/When shall   11 They'll/They will   12 You'll/You will

9.7C Context
1 shall/will/'ll   2 shan't/won't/will not/shall not   3 shan't/won't/will not/shall not   4 will   5 shan't/won't/will not/shall not   6 will (we shall, but not *My wife and I shall*)   7 shall/will/'ll   8 shall/will/'ll   9 will   10 will/shall/'ll   11 will not/won't/shan't   12 will/shall/'ll   13 will/'ll/shall   14 will/'ll/shall   15 will/'ll/shall   16 will/'ll/shall   17 will/shall

9.8 The simple future, the future progressive, the future perfect

9.8A Simple future 'I will work' and progressive 'I will be working' compared

Write 1:

1 *will be taking off* ('more polite') or *will take off* (arrangement [> 9.7B])
2 *will you be going* (referring to future time) or *will you go* (intention)
3 *you will still be working* here ('imagining')
4 They *will be sailing* (planned action) or *will sail* (more definite)
5 The President *will be meeting* (planned action) or *will meet* (more definite)
6 *will you be staying* (planned action) or *will you stay* (more definite)
7 We *will be driving* (planned action) or *will drive* (intention)
8 *will be writing* (imagining)
9 *will be circling* (imagining)
10 *will be seeing* (referring to future time) or *will see* (intention)

Write 2:

1 will you be leaving   2 we'll be leaving
3 you'll arrive   4 we'll check in   5 we'll have
6 you'll be lying   7 I'll be doing   8 we won't be sitting around

9.8B The future perfect simple and the future perfect progressive tenses

1 will have completed   2 will/shall have been waiting
3 will/shall have been living/have lived   4 will/shall have finished   5 will have left   6 will/shall have been flying   7 will have completed   8 will have been travelling/will have travelled

9.8C Context

1 will have built/will be building   2 will be circling/will circle   3 (will) probably be circling/will probably circle
4 will have established/will be establishing
5 will have increased/will be increasing   6 will be orbiting   7 will have   8 will stay/will be staying
9 will not be clearing up   10 will just be watching

9.9 'Going to' and other ways of expressing the future

9.9A Uses of the 'going to'-future compared with 'will'

1 are we going to spend   2 We're going to run out of
3 I'll stop   4 We're going to get stuck   5 We'll (or We're going to) have to walk   6 someone'll
7 It's going to rain   8 I'll wave   9 He's going to stop

9.9B 'am/is/are to', 'be about to', 'be due to'

1 are to   2 are to   3 are not to   4 is (just) about to
5 I'm (just) about to   6 is due to   7 not due to/isn't due to

9.9C The future-in-the-past

Possible answers

1 was to   2 was going to   3 would   4 was about to
5 was due to

9.9D Context

Possible answers

1 are we to do   2 We are going to/are to deliver
3 I'll just check/'m just going to check   4 will be/is
5 are taking off/take off/are going to take off/will be taking off   6 would be/was to be/was going to be
7 would/was going to break loose   8 I'll take over

9.10 The imperative

9.10A Some uses of the imperative to express different functions

1 Do have   2 Do make   3 Do stop   4 Do hurry
5 Do try   6 Do help

9.10B The imperative to address particular people

Possible answers

1 Enjoy yourself/yourselves   2 You try   3 You make/Make ... Meg/Meg, you make   4 Somebody turn off/Turn off ... somebody   5 Nobody turn/Don't ... anybody/Don't anybody turn   6 You carry/Carry ... John!   7 Everybody sit down/Sit down, everybody
8 Everybody have/Have ... everybody   9 Don't move anybody/Nobody move!/Don't anybody move!
10 John, you/John, post/You ... John
11 Don't anybody listen/Don't listen to her, anybody!/Nobody listen to her!   12 Enjoy yourselves, children!

9.10C The imperative with question tags

Possible answers

1 Stop whistling, will you?   2 Do something useful, can't you?   3 Stop asking questions, won't you?
4 Post this letter, could you?   5 Hold this bag, would you?   6 Get me some stamps, can you?   7 Come in, won't you?   8 Take a seat, will you?

9.10D Double imperatives joined by 'and'

Possible answers

1 Come and see us soon.
2 Try and lift it./Try to lift it.
3 Sit here and wait until the doctor is ready.
4 Wait and see what will happen.

9.10E Context

1 DO   2 KEEP   3 MIND   4 ASK   5 AVOID
6 COME AND ASK   7 DON'T WASTE   8 THINK!

10 Be, Have, Do

10.1 'Be' as a full verb (1)

10.1A Some uses of the imperative of 'be': 'Be careful'

Write 1:

1 *Be* an angel!   2 *Don't be* a silly idiot!   3 *Be* the proud owner ...   4 *Don't be* a writer.   5 You *be* Batman and I'll *be* Robin.

Write 2:

1 (Do) be quiet!   Don't be noisy!
2 (Do) be careful!   Don't be careless!
3 (Do) be generous!   Don't be mean!
4 (Do) be friendly!   Don't be critical!
5 (Do) be brave!   Don't be afraid!

10.1B The use of 'aren't'

1 aren't   2 aren't   3 aren't   4 isn't   5 aren't
6 aren't   7 wasn't   8 weren't

10.1C 'Be' in the simple present and simple past

1 was   2 was ... is   3 am   4 is   5 is ... was   6 is
7 is ... was   8 are ... were   9 are ...were ... are
10 is ... is   11 are ... are   12 is   13 Is ... was... is
14 Were ... weren't ... are   15 is ... was   16 is ... was
17 was   18 is (or was)

10.1D Context

1 *was*   2 you*'re*   3 *aren't*   4 I*'m*   5 *aren't*   6 You*'re*
7 You*'re*   8 I*'m*   9 I*'m*   10 *be*   11 *Be*   12 What*'s*
13 I*'m*   14 Don*'s*   15 *be*   16 *Be*   17 *Are*   18 I*'m*

10.2 'Be' as a full verb (2)

10.2A Progressive forms of 'be' for 'temporary behaviour'

The following sentences need ticks: 1, 3, 5

10.2B 'Has been', 'have been', 'had been' + adjectives and nouns

1 has/Your brother's   2 have/long've   3 have/I've
4 had/she'd   5 has/It's   6 has/She's ... has/She's
7 had/you'd   8 have/I've

10.2C 'Have been' and 'have gone'

1 has gone/he's gone   2 have been/I've been
3 have been   4 have gone   5 have been/you've
been   6 has gone/He's gone   7 has gone/He's gone
8 has been/He's been

10.2D 'Have been' with 'since' and 'for'

1 She has been waiting ...
2 I have worked/I have been working ...
3 We have lived/We have been living ...
4 How long have we been waiting ...?
5 How long has Silvia worked/been working ...?
6 How long has your brother lived/been living ...

10.2E Context

1 have gone   2 have been/They've been   3 have been/I've been   4 have ever been/I've ever been
5 is being/She's being   6 were   7 were   8 have not been/haven't been   9 has been/She's been   10 has been/She's been   11 has been/It's been

10.3 'There' + 'be'

10.3A 'There + 'be' as a 'natural choice'

The following sentences need ticks: 1, 3, 6

2 *There is a good clothes shop* not far from here.
4 *There was a photograph of that girl* in last week's magazine.
5 *There will be a new security system* in operation ...
7 *There is a public holiday* on May 1st.
8 *There will be a meeting* between the two world leaders ...

10.3B 'There is', etc. compared with 'it is', etc.

1 There ... they   2 There's ... She's   3 There's ... it's
4 There'll ... He's   5 There ... It   6 There ... They
7 There's ... It's   8 There's ... It's   9 there ... it
10 there ... they

10.3C Combinations with 'there' + 'be'

1 There was   2 There are   3 Are there/Have there been ... there are/there've been – There are
4 Is there ... there is   5 There are/There will be
6 There has been/There's   7 There will be
8 There's   9 there had/has been   10 ... isn't there?   11 There seem   12 There seems/There seemed

10.3D Context

1 There had been   2 it was first opened
3 There was   4 there were   5 there were
6 They were   7 There were   8 There was   9 It was
10 There has never been   11 there never will be

10.4 Verbs related in meaning to 'be'

10.4A Certainty and uncertainty with 'be', 'seem', etc.
1 They *seem (to be)* very happy.
2 He *seemed (to be)* a genius at maths.
3 She *seems to be* finding the job difficult.
4 They *seemed to be* looking for something.
5 He *seems to have been* knocked out.
6 It *seems (to be)* very dark outside.
7 It *seems to be* raining very hard outside.
8 My watch *seems to have* stopped.

10.4B 'To be' or not 'to be'?
1 (to be)   2 (to be)   3 to be   4 (-)   5 (-)   6 (-)   7 (-)
8 (to be)

10.4C 'Process verbs' related to 'be' and 'become'
Possible answers
1 grow   2 get   3 has turned/is turning   4 goes
5 has run/is running   6 becoming   7 has come/
came   8 fell   9 are wearing/have worn   10 get
11 become   12 make

10.4D Context
1 seemed/appeared   2 looked   3 smelt
4 got/became   5 seemed/appeared   6 became/got
7 seems/looks   8 feel   9 proves   10 seems

10.5 'Have' as a full verb = 'possess'; 'have got' = 'possess'

10.5A 'Have got' = 'own' and 'have got' = 'obtain'
1 have received   2 possess/own   3 possess/own
4 have obtained   5 possess/own   6 have obtained

10.5B Uses of 'have' and 'have got' to mean 'possess'
1 They have/They've got   2 I don't have/haven't got
3 Do you have/Have you got (*Have you* is possible,
but less common)   4 My uncle had   5 I've had
6 We'll have   7 I will have had   8 she had had
9 I must have   10 he should have   11 Does your
brother have/Has your brother got (*Has your brother*
is possible but less common)   12 Will you have
13 Have you had   14 Do you have/Have you got
(*Have you* is possible but less common)

10.5C Common uses of 'have' and 'have got'
1 Have you got/Do you have   2 have (got)   3 Have
you got/Do you have   4 Have you got/Do you have
5 She has (got)   6 He has (got)   7 He has (got)
8 has (got)   9 haven't (got)/don't have
10 hasn't (got)/doesn't have   11 have you (got)/do
you have   12 have (got)   13 have (got)
14 have (got)   15 has (got) on   16 had she got/did

she have   17 I have (got)   18 did you last have
19 have (got)   20 has (got)   21 have (got)
22 Have you (got)/Do you have   23 have (got)
24 has (got). Note that *have you* is also possible, but
less common, in **1**, **3**, **4** and **22**.

10.5D Context
1 to have   2 doesn't have/hasn't (got)   3 has
4 has (got)   5 has (got)   6 haven't (got)/don't have
7 has (got)   8 had (got)   9 had   10 had   11 had
12 haven't (got)/don't have

10.6 'Have' as a full verb meaning 'eat', 'enjoy', etc.

10.6A 'Have' (= 'eat', 'enjoy', etc.) compared with 'have (= 'possess')
Write 1:
1 Do you have   2 They have (got)   3 We have (got)
4 She has   5 I've just had   6 We had   7 She has
(got)   8 I have   9 I don't often have   10 Have you
(got) (or Do you have)   11 they had had
12 did you have

Write 2:
1 Have   2 has   3 is having   4 had   5 were having
6 have had/have been having   7 has been having (or
has had)   8 had ... had   9 had had/had been having
or had   10 will be having   11 will have had
12 will have had

10.6B Common 'have' + noun combinations
Write 1:
Possible answers
1 We *had an awful meal* at the Station Hotel.
2 I *had a bad dream* last night.
3 When are you going to *have a haircut*?
4 I *have an appointment* to see Mr Jay at 10.
5 *Have a good trip* to America!
6 We *had a lovely day* for the wedding.
7 You'll *have a pain* if you eat any more apples.
8 Our teacher *has* a wonderful *sense of humour*.

Write 2:
1 are always having fights   2 Have a look at
3 have a rest   4 have a ride   5 I had a talk to/with
Jim   6 have a swim   7 have a wash
8 Have a sleep

10.6C Context
1 has (got)   2 has had   3 has (got)   4 has (got)
5 'Has Worzel had?   6 having   7 has/is having
8 have   9 has (got)   10 has (got)   11 aren't having
12 have (got)

10.7 'Do' as a full verb

10.7A Forms and uses of 'do' as an auxiliary and as a full verb

Write 1:
1l   2g   3j   4h   5k   6d   7a   8f   9m   10c   11e
12b   13i

Write 2:
1 What are you doing?   2 ... she never does the washing up   3 No, don't do that   4 What is that flowerpot doing ...?   5 do the/their washing
6 ... when you've done that   7 How does he do it?
8 he doesn't do any reading   9 What have you done?
10 What are those suitcases doing ...?   11 I've been doing a bit of gardening   12 What's that car doing ...?
13 I've already done so.

10.7B 'Do' and 'make' compared
do: one's best, business with someone, an experiment, research, one's hair, something for a living, an impression (= imitate), somebody a service.
make: an appointment, an arrangement, an attempt, a noise, something for a living, progress, an impression (= impress), a journey, a fortune, war.

Possible answers
1 You should always try to *do your best*.
2 I must *make an appointment* to see the dentist.
3 We *do a lot of business* with your firm.
4 We *did a very interesting experiment* in chemistry today.
5 I*'ve made an arrangement* to meet him on Thursday.
6 Mary *does research* into the causes of acid rain.
7 Mr Stuart *does my hair* once a fortnight.
8 I *made several attempts* to start the car before I phoned the garage.
9 Don't *make a noise*! We don't want to wake the children.
10 What does Tom *do for a living*? – Tom *makes toys for a living*.
11 Janet *has made excellent progress* this term.
12 He *does very funny impressions* of famous people. She *has made a good impression* in her new job.
13 Will you *do me a service* and take this to the post office?
14 He *has just made a journey* to the village where he was born.
15 You can *make a fortune* in the antiques business these days.
16 The Persians *were always making war* against the Greeks.

10.7C Context
1 did   2 don't   3 do   4 do   5 done   6 made
7 doing   8 do   9 make   10 do

11 Modal auxiliaries and related verbs

11.1 The two uses of modal verbs

11.1A The first use of modal verbs (1)
1c   2f   3d   4a   5b   6e

11.1B The first use of modal verbs (2)
Must is not possible in the following:
2 have had to   4 had had to   5 had to
6 haven't had to   7 having to

11.1C The second use of modal verbs
1 certain   2 very uncertain   3 fairly certain
4 almost certain   5 fairly certain   6 almost certain
7 fairly certain   8 very uncertain   9 almost certain

11.1D Context
1 May/Can   2 must be   3 am   4 must have
5 couldn't   6 can't   7 must/can   8 have had to
9 haven't been able to   10 can/may

11.2 Uses of modals (etc.) to express ability and inability

11.2A Expressing present and past ability: 'can' and 'be able to'
1 can   2 can't   3 can   4 could/was able to ... can
5 Can ... can't   6 couldn't   7 could/was able to/ managed to   8 was able to/managed to   9 couldn't/ wasn't able to   10 were able to/managed to

11.2B 'Can/could' with verbs of perception: 'I can see'
1 *Can* you see   2 I *can* smell   3 I *could* understand
4 *Could you* understand   5 I *can't* see   6 I *couldn't* understand

11.2C Ability in tenses other than the present and the past
1 will be able to   2 haven't been able to
3 would have been able to   4 had been able to
5 will be able to   6 being able to   7 be able to
8 had been able to

11.2D 'Can/could' in place of 'is often' and 'was often'
1 The sea *can be*   2 She *can be*   3 She *could be*
4 It *can be*   5 He *could be*

11.2E Context

1 had not been able to/had been unable to
2 could only/had only been able to   3 could
4 were able to/managed to   5 could/would be able to/
would manage to   6 could/was able to/were able to
7 Can/Do

11.3 Uses of modals (etc.) to express permission and prohibition

11.3A Asking for permission with 'can', 'could', 'may' and 'might'
Possible answers
1 Can I make myself some coffee (please)?
2 Could/May I use your/the lavatory, please?
3 I wonder if I might (possibly) see your garden?
4 Could I (possibly) make a phone call (please)?
5 Do you think I could (possibly) borrow your car?

11.3B Giving and refusing permission/Expressing prohibition
Possible answers
1 *You may not* smoke. (This notice is trying to sound polite.)
2 *You are not allowed to* camp or picnic here.
3 *You are forbidden to* fish here.
4 *You may* camp here.
5 This is private (property). *You are not permitted to* enter.
6 *You mustn't* lean out of the window.
7 *You can* leave your litter here.
8 *You can't* stop here.

11.3C Permission/prohibition in tenses other than present and future
1 were allowed to   2 was never allowed to   3 has only been allowed to   4 has just been allowed to
5 have not been allowed to   6 had not allowed him to

11.3D 'Can' (= ability) and 'can/could' (= have permission, be free to)
Can is possible in the following:
2 We *can* go   3 She *can* drive   5 I *can* play
6 You *can* use

11.3E Context
Possible answers
1 Am I allowed to   2 can   3 can't   4 mustn't
5 will be allowed to   6 can't   7 could

11.4 Uses of modals (etc.) to express certainty and possibility

11.4A Certainty and possibility

Write 1:
1C 2P 3C 4P 5C 6P 7C 8P 9C 10P
11C 12P 13C 14P

Write 2:
1 He *may/might/could* be at home now.
2 He *may/might/could* be at home tomorrow.
3 He *may/might/could have been* at home yesterday.
4 She *may/might/could* leave at 9.
5 She *may/might/could* leave tomorrow.
6 She *may/might/could have* left.
7 She *may/might/could have* left last night.
8 She *may/might/could have* left by 9.
9 He *may/might/could be* working today.
10 He *may/might/could be* working today.
11 He *may/might/could have been* working today.
12 He *may/might/could have been* working all day.

Write 3:
Possible answers
1 He *may/might/could* be at home.
2 He *may/might/could* have been at home.
3 He *may/might/could* be at home.
4 It *may/might/could* leave at 10.
5 It *may/might/could* have left at 10.
6 She *may/might/could* be working.
7 She *may/might/could* have been working.
8 She *may/might/could* be working.
9 She *may/might/could* have been working.
10 He *may/might/could* have had tea and toast.
11 She *may/might/could* have parked in the car park.
12 It *may/might/could* have cost £15,000.

11.4B Certain and uncertain answers to questions
Possible answers
1 (Yes,) she *may (do)*.
2 She *might live* in London.
3 (Yes,) he *could have (done)*.
4 He *might have caught* the 8.30.
5 (Yes,) they *might be*.
6 They *might be living* abroad.
7 (Yes,) he *may have (done)*.
8 He *could have finished* work at 4.30.
9 (Yes,) I *could (do)*.
10 I *may leave* tomorrow.

11.4C Context
Possible answers
1 can   2 may   3 may   4 might   5 might   6 could
7 could   8 might   9 might   10 could

11.5 Uses of modals to express deduction

11.5A Certainty or deduction?
1C 2C 3C 4C 5C 6D 7D 8D 9D 10D
11D 12D

11.5B Two kinds of 'must be'
1 mustn't be (O)   2 must be (O)   3 can't be (D)
4 must be (D)   5 must be (D)   6 can't be (D)
7 must be (O)   8 mustn't be (O)   9 can't be (D)
10 mustn't be (O)

11.5C 'Must have been', 'can't/couldn't have been'; 'had to be/didn't have to be'
1 must have been   2 can't/couldn't have been
3 had to be   4 did she have to be   5 didn't have to
6 didn't have to   7 must have been   8 must have
been   9 can't have been   10 had to be
11 must have been   12 had to be

11.5D Context
1 didn't have to be   2 must be/must have been
3 can't be/can't have been   4 must be   5 must be
6 had to be   7 must have been imported
8 must have laid

11.6 Uses of modals for offers, requests and suggestions

11.6A Offering things and substances
Possible answers
1 *Would you like* a sandwich?
2 *Wouldn't you like* some coffee?
3 *Would you like* a slice of toast?
4 *Would you like* some potatoes?
5 *Wouldn't you like* an orange?
6 *Would you like* some fruit?

11.6B Requests for things and substances
Possible answers
1 *Can I have* a sandwich, please?
2 *May I have* some coffee, please?
3 *Could I have* a slice of toast, please?
4 *May I have* some potatoes, please?
5 *Might I have* an orange, please?
6 *Could I have* some fruit, please?

11.6C Making suggestions, inviting actions
Possible answers
1 *Would you like to* stay with me?
2 *Would you like to* join us for a meal?
3 *Wouldn't you like to* come on an excursion?
4 *Would you like to* have a holiday with us?

11.6D Requesting others to do things for you
Possible answers
1 *Will/Would you* hold the door open for me, please?
2 Please *will/would you* dial a/this number for me?
3 *Will/Would you* please translate a/this letter for me?
4 *Will/Would you* deliver some/these flowers for me, please?

11.6E Offering to do things for others
Possible answers
1 *Shall I* put your suitcase on the rack (for you)?
2 *Shall I* close the window (for you)?
3 *Shall I* pick those up (for you)?

11.6F Making suggestions that include the speaker
1 *Shall we* drive to the coast?
2 *Shall we* have a meal out this evening?
3 *Shall we* travel first class?
4 *Shall we* have a holiday in Bahia?

11.6G Context
1 Would you   2 Shall I   3 Will/Would you
4 Would you   5 Can I/Could I (etc.)   6 Shall we
7 Shall I   8 Will/Would you   9 Would you

11.7 Expressing wishes, etc.: 'I wish', 'if only', 'it's (high) time'

11.7A Present and past reference with 'I wish', 'if only' and 'it's (high) time'
1 present   2 present   3 present   4 past   5 past

11.7B Expressing wishes and regrets with 'I wish' and 'if only'
Possible answers
1 I wish/If only I *was/were* fit/fitter!
2 I wish/If only it *was/were* cooler!
3 I wish/If only it *wasn't/weren't* raining!
4 I wish/If only I *had been* less impatient/more patient!
5 I wish/If only I *hadn't wasted* a lot of/so much time watching TV!
6 I wish/If only they *had* more friends!
7 I wish/If only we *had locked* the back door!
8 I wish/If only he *wasn't/weren't* abroad!
9 I wish/If only she *hadn't read* it!
10 I wish/If only he *had taken* it!

11.7C 'Would' and 'could' after 'I wish' and 'if only'
1 would   2 wouldn't   3 could   4 could   5 would
6 could

11.7D 'It's (high) time' and 'It's (about) time'
Possible answers
1 It's high time they got married!
2 It's about time we went to the theatre!
3 It's high time you both left!
4 It's about time they tidied it!

11.7E Context
1 was/were   2 contained   3 opened   4 was/were
5 could be   6 had/could have

11.8 Expressing preferences: 'would rather' and 'would sooner'

11.8A Expressing personal preference with 'I'd rather'/'I'd sooner'
Write 1:
1 be   2 have been   3 have been   4 have lived
5 make   6 not have to   7 not have had to

Write 2:
1 I'd rather/sooner not.   2 I'd rather/sooner not
(have been).   3 I'd rather/sooner not.   4 I'd rather/
sooner not (have done).

11.8B Expressing preferences about other people's actions
1 caught   2 didn't wait up   3 hadn't done
4 asked/had asked   5 was/were   6 had been/were

11.8C 'I'd rather he didn't', etc.
1 I'd rather/sooner she *didn't*.   2 I'd rather/sooner you
hadn't.   3 I'd rather/sooner she *hadn't*.   4 I'd rather/
sooner he *didn't*.   5 I'd rather/sooner you *didn't*.
6 I'd rather/sooner he *hadn't*.   7 I'd rather/sooner
they *didn't*.   8 I'd rather/sooner they *hadn't*.   9 ... I'd
rather/sooner you *hadn't*.   10 ... I'd rather/sooner she
didn't.   11 ... I'd rather/sooner he *hadn't*.

11.8D Context
1 would rather/sooner their children didn't decide
2 would rather/sooner their children chose
3 would rather/sooner do   4 would rather/sooner be
5 would rather/sooner talk, walk and behave
6 would rather/sooner be called   7 would rather/
sooner have been called   8 would rather/sooner have
lived   9 would rather/sooner be

11.9 'It's advisable ...'/'It's necessary ...'

11.9A 'It's advisable' —> 'It's necessary': 'a scale of choice'
1 advisable   2 necessary   3 advisable   4 advisable
5 necessary   6 advisable

11.9B 'Must', 'have to' and 'have got to'
1 must   2 have (got) to/must   3 must   4 have (got)
to/must   5 have to/must always   6 MUST   7 Must
8 must

11.9C Expressing necessity in other tenses
1 He will have to   2 They have had to   3 she has
been having to   4 We had already had to   5 I would
have had to   6 We are having to/We have been
having to

11.9D Context
1 have to/must   2 must/have to   3 has to/will have to
4 MUST   5 having to   6 should have   7 must/have
to/should   8 will have to/must/should/has to
9 have to/must   10 should   11 had to

11.10 'It isn't advisable ...'/'It isn't necessary ...'/'It's forbidden ...'

11.10A 'It isn't advisable' —> 'It's forbidden': 'a scale of choice'
1b   2c   3d   4a

11.10B 'Mustn't', 'needn't', 'don't have to', 'haven't got to'
1 don't have to/needn't/haven't got to
2 needn't/don't have to/haven't got to
3 doesn't have to/needn't/hasn't got to   4 mustn't
5 mustn't   6 needn't always/don't always have to
7 needn't/don't have to/haven't got to
8 needn't/doesn't have to/hasn't got to
9 needn't/don't have to/haven't got to   10 mustn't
11 mustn't   12 needn't/don't have to/haven't go to
13 mustn't   14 needn't/don't have to/haven't got to
15 mustn't   16 needn't

11.10C 'Needn't have', 'didn't have to', 'didn't need to'
1 I needn't have phoned   2 I didn't have to phone
3 You needn't have brought   4 I didn't have to bring
5 I needn't have washed   6 I needn't have cooked

11.10D 'Shouldn't have' and 'oughtn't to have'
1 You shouldn't have done that.   2 He shouldn't have
done that.   3 They shouldn't have done that.
4 She shouldn't have done that.   5 You shouldn't
have done that
Note: in all these *oughtn't to have done that* can also
be used.

11.10E Context
1 must not   2 didn't need to   3 shouldn't have
4 should have

11.11 Modals to express habit: 'used to', 'will' and 'would'

11.11A The form of 'used to'
1 didn't   2 did   3 didn't use to/never used to
4 Did you use to   5 did   6 did   7 did you use to
8 didn't use to/never used to

11.11B Uses of 'used to'
1 used to go   2 didn't use to (or never used to) like
3 Did you use to like   4 used to have to   5 I never
used to enjoy   6 was having   7 used to be
8 used to be   9 were working   10 Was it raining?

11.11C 'Would' in place of 'used to' and in place of the simple past
The first *used to* (*Gerald used to spend*) sets the
scene. After that, the following should be underlined:
used to get up (would get up), caught (would catch),
put (would put), took ((would) take), always used to
go, (would always go) was often (would often be)

11.11D 'Will/would' to describe 'usual behaviour'
1 would always tell   2 will still tell   3 would only
discuss   4 will play   5 would work
6 won't always tell

11.11E Context
Possible answers
1 was   2 was   3 used to/would   4 loved/used
to love   5 never accepted/would never accept/never
used to accept   6 will always find   7 would/used to
say   8 used to/would say   9 would always be/was
always/always used to be   10 often used to visit/
often visited   11 never used to tire/never tired
12 would say/said

11.12 'Need' and 'dare' as modals and as full verbs

11.12A 'Need' as a modal and as a full verb
modal	full verb
1 Need you go ...?	Do you need to go ...?
2 Need I wait ...?	Do I need to wait ...?
3 They needn't wait ...	They don't need to wait ...
4 You needn't have said ...	You didn't need to say ...
5 I hardly need explain ...	I hardly need to explain ...
6 He needn't learn ...	He doesn't need to learn ...
7 All that you need do ...	All that you need to do ...
8 I don't think you need explain	I don't think you need to explain

11.12B The form of 'dare' as a modal and as a full verb
1 daren't/don't dare/don't dare to   2 daren't/didn't
dare/didn't dare to/dare(d) not   3 dare/dare to
4 Dare we/Do we dare/Do we dare to   5 didn't dare/
didn't dare to/dare(d) not/daren't   6 dare   7 daren't/
doesn't dare/doesn't dare to   8 daren't have
9 daren't/didn't dare to/dared not

11.12C Uses of 'dare'
1d 2c 3d 4a 5b 6c 7b 8a 9d 10b
11b 12d

11.12D Context
1 dared not/did not dare (to) *move*   2 need not
have worried   3 dared (to) *breathe*   4 didn't dare to /
dare not /dared not *open*   5 need (to) *tell*

11.13 'Would/wouldn't'; 'that ... should'; 'there' + modal

11.13A 'Would' and 'wouldn't' in place of the simple present tense or 'will' future
1 would be   2 wouldn't be   3 would think
4 wouldn't seem   5 would be   6 wouldn't imagine
7 Would that seem

11.13B 'That ... should' after verbs like 'suggest'
Possible answers
1 we should buy (a)   2 we should avoid (a)   3 he not
raise (c)   4 they do not break (b)   5 she should
do? (a)   6 we improve (b/c)   7 you take (b/c)
8 not delay (c)   9 we take (b/c)   10 he should be
allowed (a)

11.13C 'That ... should' after adjectives like 'essential'
1 we should send (a)   2 she return (c)   3 he is
informed (b)   4 she be (c)

11.13D 'There' + modal auxiliaries
Possible answers
1 could be   2 must be   3 will never be
4 Couldn't there be   5 Might there be
6 should there be   7 can't there be

11.13E Context
Possible answers
1 you (should) take   2 you (should) get   3 you begin
4 could be   5 you (should) follow   6 will be
7 may be   8 would seem

12 The passive and the causative

12.1 General information about form

12.1A Basic forms of the passive

Write 1:
The following should have been marked P: 1, 3, 6, 9.

Write 2:
1 A lot of money is owed to the bank.
2 It has been proved that there is no life on the moon.
3 Videos like this one can be bought anywhere.
4 The history of the European Community has to be written one day.
5 The history of the European Community may already have been written.
6 When we arrived home, we found that one of our windows had been broken.
7 Their car has been sold to pay their debts.
8 A meeting is held in the village hall once a week.

12.1B The passive with progressive forms: 'She is being interviewed'

1 New employees *are always welcomed* by the manager.
2 A new supermarket *is being built* near the church.
3 The battle *was fought* in 1623.
4 The windows *were being cleaned* while I was there.
5 My desk *has been moved*!
6 The refugees *are being taken* to a camp outside the village.
7 All the documents *had been signed* before I arrived.
8 We *were being questioned* and our vehicle *was being searched* at the same time.
9 Our letters *will be posted* when the ship arrives at the next port of call.
10 The case *is being opened* again because they're not satisfied with the verdict.

12.1C Context

1 died 2 was given 3 was attended 4 be held
5 lined 6 was drawn 7 followed 8 was given
9 watched 10 could be heard 11 turned
12 whispered

12.2 Uses of the passive

12.2A Uses of the passive
Possible answers
1 has been damaged ... has widened/is widening ... has been investigated
2 are visited ... can be arranged

3 English Spoken ... Shoes Repaired ... are translated
4 are constantly reminded ... is becoming ... are flashed
5 are involved ... is hurt ... have to ... are damaged

12.2B The use of 'by' + agent (= 'doer') after a passive

1 was sold ... was shown by the general public.
2 was composed by Beethoven ... was written
3 are being replaced by modern ones ... is not controlled

12.2C The passive with verbs of 'saying' and 'believing': 'It is said (that) ...'

1 It is expected 2 It was feared
3 (Joyce) is supposed 4 (Jack Smith) is thought
5 It is thought 6 There is thought
7 (Jim) is considered 8 There are said 9 It is said
10 There is/was supposed

12.2D Context

1 have been seen 2 is supposed 3 to be shown
4 was bought 5 was eventually sold
6 was exhibited 7 is/was said 8 must have been disappointed 9 was/had been cleverly made
10 was/had been delicately sewn 11 was/had been so skilfully done 12 must have been required

12.3 Form and use of the causative

12.3A Form of the causative: 'have something done'

1 decorated 2 looked at 3 tested 4 cut
5 photocopied 6 written

12.3B The causative compared with the active and passive

Write 1:
1 I'm cleaning 2 It's being cleaned 3 I have it cleaned 4 we had it decorated
5 It's being decorated 6 must have your shoes repaired 7 have just been repaired
8 I repaired 9 (to have this film) developed and printed 10 to photocopy 11 mends
12 It's being photocopied

Write 2:

1a She had her best skirt cleaned yesterday.
b She's having her eyes tested today.
c She's going to have a tooth extracted tomorrow.
2a She had two trees planted yesterday.
b She's having a film developed today.
c She's going to have two teeth filled tomorrow.
3a She had her car serviced yesterday.
b She's having some furniture delivered today.
c She's going to have her hair done tomorrow.

12.3C 'Get' in the causative: 'get something done'
1 get   **2** getting   **3** getting   **4** get   **5** Get

12.3D Context
1 have/get it repaired   **2** have/get a new washing machine installed   **3** have/get it serviced
4 having/getting films developed and printed
5 have/get our eyes tested   **6** (have/get) our teeth filled   **7** (have/get) our chests X-rayed
8 have/get my hair cut   **9** have/get any jobs done

13 Questions, answers, negatives

13.1 Yes/No questions, negative statements, Yes/No answers

13.1A Yes/No questions (expecting 'Yes' or 'No' in the answer)
 1 Am I late?
 2 Is this the London train?
 3 Are my photos ready?
 4 Is John working in the garden?
 5 Are the children studying?
 6 Does Jane give piano lessons?
 7 Was Tony enjoying himself?
 8 Do they live in the south?
 9 Should she be here?
10 Could she ask a question?
11 Will it be fine tomorrow?
12 Will your friend be staying?
13 Would they like an invitation?
14 Do they often argue like that?
15 Do you run a mile every morning?
16 Did Sheila go to the lecture?

13.1B Negative statements
 1 No, I'm not ready.
 2 No, she isn't (she's not) right.
 3 No, they aren't (they're not) late.
 4 No, I'm not being silly.
 5 No, he isn't (he's not) working in London.
 6 No, they aren't (they're not) playing tennis.
 7 No, you aren't (you're not) going to fail.

 8 No, she wasn't waiting for me.
 9 No, he can't speak Russian.
10 No, he won't (he'll not) be leaving soon.
11 No, it wouldn't be a very good idea.
12 No, it doesn't look like rain.
13 No, they don't always win.
14 No, they didn't miss the last lesson.
15 No, she hasn't (she's not) always been good at sport.
16 No, I haven't (I've not) met her.

13.1C Yes/No short answers
Possible answers
1 Yes, I am.   **2** No, she isn't (she's not).   **3** No, they aren't (they're not).   **4** Yes, I am.   **5** No, she isn't (she's not).   **6** Yes, we are.   **7** Yes, I am.
8 No, she wasn't.   **9** Yes, they were.
10 Yes, you should.   **11** No, I won't.
12 No, I wouldn't.   **13** Yes, she (still) does.
14 Yes, I do.   **15** No, he didn't.   **16** Yes, he has.
17 No, I haven't.   **18** No, she hasn't.

13.1D Context
1 Did we turn off/Have we turned off   **2** Yes, we did/ Yes, we have   **3** Are all the taps off?
4 Yes, they are   **5** haven't remembered/ didn't remember   **6** Yes, we have/Yes, we did
7 Are there any windows open?   **8** No, there aren't
9 Are the front and back doors locked?
10 Yes, they are   **11** haven't got

13.2 Alternative negative forms and negative questions

13.2A Negative statements with 'negative adverbs': 'never', etc.
 1 I *never go* to the cinema.
 2 She *hardly ever watches* TV.
 3 I *can seldom get* him on the phone.
 4 They *barely greeted* me.
 5 We *scarcely ever go out*.
 6 We *can hardly wait* till tomorrow.
 7 We *rarely see* our neighbours.
 8 It's *scarcely worth* the trouble.
 9 I*'ve bought no* eggs.
10 I *spoke to no one*.
11 I *want none* of them.
12 She *said nothing*.
13 We *went nowhere*.
14 Please *tell nobody*.
15 She *hardly understands* English.

13.2B Cancelling what has just been said: 'No, not Wednesday'
Possible answers
1 (No,) not Diana, Josephine.
2 (No,) not 5, 5.30.
3 (No,) not London, Luton.
4 (No,) not today, tomorrow.
5 (No,) not coffee, tea.
6 (No,) not the salt, the pepper.

13.2C Negative questions: 'Can't you ...?'
1 Aren't I   2 Isn't she   3 Aren't those   4 Isn't he
5 Aren't they   6 Wasn't she   7 Weren't you
8 Aren't you   9 Can't you   10 Couldn't you
11 Don't you   12 Doesn't she   13 Didn't he
14 Haven't you   15 Hasn't he   16 Haven't I
17 Shouldn't you   18 Aren't I

13.2D Context
1 everyone   2 no one   3 hardly ever   4 no
5 anywhere   6 anything   7 nothing

13.3 Tag questions and echo tags

13.3A Tag questions 1: 'It is ..., isn't it?'/'It isn't ..., is it?'
1 isn't she?   2 aren't they?   3 aren't I?
4 wasn't she?   5 weren't we?   6 haven't you?
7 hasn't he?   8 don't I?   9 doesn't she?   10 is she?
11 are they?   12 am I?   13 was she?   14 were we?
15 have you?   16 has he?   17 do I?   18 does she?

13.3B Tag questions 2: 'You painted it yourself, did you?'
1 e   2 c   3 g   4 f   5 b   6 d   7 a

13.3C Echo tags: 'Is he?'/'He is?'
Possible answers
1 Is he? (rising tone: interest)
2 They aren't, are they? (falling tone: confirmation)
3 She wasn't was she? (rising tone: surprise, disbelief)
4 Weren't you? (rising tone: interest, sympathy)
5 He does, doesn't he? (falling tone: confirmation)
6 Don't they? (rising tone: interest)
7 I shouldn't, should I? (falling tone: confirmation)
8 You can, can you? (falling tone: disbelief)
9 Can't we? (rising tone: asks for more information)
10 There will, won't there? (falling tone: confirmation)

13.3D Context
Possible answers
1 do we?   2 has?   3 did you?   4 didn't you? or
did you?   5 haven't I   6 shouldn't you?
7 don't you?

13.4 Additions and responses

13.4A Additions and contrasts: 'John can ... and I can, too/but I can't'
Possible answers
1 Rudi can speak English, and Roxanne can, too.
2 Rudi can't speak Italian, but Roxanne can.
3 Rudi plays tennis, and so does Roxanne.
4 Rudi goes skiing, but Roxanne doesn't.
5 Rudi doesn't like classical music, and neither does Roxanne.
6 Rudi visited London last year, but Roxanne didn't.
7 Rudi doesn't speak Italian, but Roxanne does.
8 Rudi didn't visit Rome last year, but Roxanne did.
9 Rudi can speak English, and so can Roxanne.
10 Rudi plays tennis, and Roxanne does, too.
11 Rudi doesn't like classical music, and Roxanne doesn't, either.
12 Rudi speaks English, and Roxanne does, too.

13.4B Parallel responses: 'John can ...'/'I can, too/So can I'
1 I can, too./So can I.
2 I can't, either./Neither (Nor) can I.
3 So should I./I should, too.
4 I won't, either./Neither (Nor) will I.
5 I do, too./So do I.
6 I don't, either./Neither (Nor) do I.
7 So did I./I did, too.
8 I didn't, either./Neither (Nor) did I.
9 I was, too./So was I.
10 So have I./I have, too.
11 Neither (Nor) have I./I haven't, either.
12 I did, too./So did I.

13.4C 'So have you' and 'So you have!'
1 confirmation/surprise   2 addition   3 addition
4 confirmation/surprise   5 confirmation/surprise
6 addition
Possible answers
7 Jane's got flu. – So have I. (addition)
8 She's got egg on her blouse! – So she has! (confirmation/surprise)
9 Jack's spoken to the boss. – So has Diana. (addition)
10 I've been to Russia. – So have I. (addition)
11 Sam's had a haircut at last. – So he has! (confirmation/surprise)
12 Jenny's new coat is exactly the same as yours! – So it is! (confirmation/surprise)

13.4D Context
Possible answers
1 'i'm not, either' or 'Neither/Nor am I'   2 'I will, too' or 'So will I'   3 '... so would I' or '... I would, too'
4 'So there is!'   5 'Neither/Nor can I' or 'I can't, either'

13.5 Question-word questions (1): 'Who(m) ...?', 'What ...?'

13.5A Form of question-word questions (except subject questions)

1a Is she arriving today? **b** When is she arriving?
2a Has he written a letter? **b** Why has he written a letter?
3a Can she help us? **b** How can she help us?
4a Do they live in Jamaica? **b** Where do they live?
5a Does he arrive at 10? **b** What time does he arrive?
6a Can't you tell us? **b** What can't you tell us?

13.5B 'Who(m) ...?' as a question-word

1 Who(m) did you invite to your house?
2 Who(m) did Jane see this morning?
3 Who(m) did you speak to?
4 Who(m) did they employ?
5 Who(m) did she buy this present for?
6 Who(m) did John phone?
7 Who(m) did you complain to?
8 Who(m) did she write to?

13.5C 'What ...?' as a question-word
Possible answers
1 What are you doing?/What are you looking at?
2 What do you do (for a living)?
3 What (kind/make/sort of) shampoo do you use?
4 What's your boss like?
5 What was the weather like?
6 What's this (called) in English?
7 What (make/kind/sort of) car is that?
8 What nationality is Ibrahim?
9 What time are they leaving?
10 What date is it?/What's the date?
11 What's that (thing) (for)?

13.5D Context
1 What's his name? 2 What's he done this time?/What did he do? 3 Who(m) did he steal it from?
4 What date was it? 5 What did you do that for?
6 What are the chances ... 7 What do you say ...?

13.6 Question-word questions (2): 'When?', 'Where?', 'Which?', 'Whose?'

13.6A 'When ...?' and 'Where ...?' as question-words
Possible answers
1 When is (or When's) Jim's birthday?
2 Where did you get that T-shirt, Alice?
3 When does the coach leave, Mary?
4 Where's Kyzyl?

13.6B 'Which ...?' as a question-word
Possible answers
1 film did you go to?
2 books do you prefer?
3 soap does Amy use?
4 girls did you meet at the party?
5 is the longest river in the world?
6 desk is the cheapest?
7 of these three briefcases do you prefer?
8 year will you always remember?
9 month is the hottest in Italy?
10 way did the boys go?

13.6C 'Whose?'
1 Who 2 Whose 3 Who 4 Whose 5 Whose
6 Whose 7 Whose 8 Whose 9 Who
10 Whose (or Who)

13.6D Context
1 When 2 Who 3 which 4 Whose 5 Where
6 when 7 Where 8 Which 9 who 10 When

13.7 Question-word questions (3): 'Why?', 'How?'

13.7A 'Why ...?' as a question-word
Possible answers
1 are you still downstairs?
2 don't we have a party?
3 didn't you ask me to help?
4 did you ring Jack just now?
5 have you bought me these flowers?
6 have you got to ring Tony?
7 are you in such a hurry?
8 don't you leave the job till tomorrow?/Why not leave ...?
9 did you go round the back?

13.7B 'How ...?' as a question-word; 'How much?/How many?'
1 How much 2 How much 3 How many
4 How much 5 How many 6 How many

13.7C 'How ' + adjective or adverb: 'How far?'
1 How old 2 How deep 3 How far 4 How big
5 How long 6 How high

13.7D 'How long ... (for)?' and 'How long ago?'
1 How long ... (for)? 2 How long ago
3 How long ago 4 How long ... (for)?

13.7E Social uses of 'How ...?'
1 d 2 g 3 c 4 h 5 f 6 e 7 b 8 a

13.7F Context

1 'What do you charge?' or 'What (price) do you charge/are you charging?'   2 'How much space do you want?'   3 'How long do you want it (for)?'
4 'Do you want a box ...?'   5 'Do you want ...?'
6 'How much have you made ...?'   7 'How's your leg ...?'   8 'Why do you ask?' or 'Why are you asking?'

13.8 Subject-questions: 'Who?', 'What?', 'Which', 'Whose?'

13.8A Subject or object?

Write 1:

1 S   2 O   3 O   4 S   5 S   6 O   7 O   8 S
9 O   10 S   11 O   12 S

Write 2:
Possible answers
 1 *Who* can play chess? – Mary can.
 2 *Who* wants to have a day off? – We all do.
 3 *Who* broke the big glass vase? – I didn't.
 4 *Who*'ll help tomorrow? – I will.
 5 *What* made this mark on the table? – A knife (made it)./A knife did.
 6 *What* will make you happy? – A new car (will make me happy)./A new car will.
 7 *Which/What* teacher took you for maths? – Mr Johnson (took us)./Mr Johnson did.
 8 *Which/What* tie goes best with this shirt? – Your blue one (goes best)./Your blue one does.
 9 Whose dog bit you? – My neighbour's (dog)./My neighbour's dog did.
 10 *Which/What* dog bit you? – The dog which lives next door (did).
 11 *Whose* suitcase got lost on the journey? – Janet's (suitcase) (did).

Write 3:
Possible answers
 1 Who can play the guitar?/Which of you can ...?
 2 Who would like some more coffee?
 3 What happens in the film?
 4 Who's coming? Which of you are coming? How many of you are coming?
 5 Which actor impressed you the most?
 6 Whose chair is squeaking? Which chair is squeaking?
 7 Whose car is the blue Fiat?
 8 Who's coming/Which of you are coming on an excursion with me?

13.8B Context
Possible answers
1 Who composed ...?   2 What songs did he compose?   3 Which party will/would win ...?
4 Who will/would be ...?   5 What are/were the papers saying?   6 Which papers are/were ... ?
7 Which country has/had ...?   8 Whose system does/did ...?   9 What does/did Mr Berlin think ...?

13.9 Questions about alternatives; emphatic questions with 'ever'

13.9A Questions about alternatives (1): 'Did you laugh, or cry?'
 1 Did they listen to records, or go for a walk?
 2 Can she dance, (or) sing, or play the piano?
 3 Do you buy clothes when you need them, or wait for the summer sales?
 4 Has she gone to church, or stayed at home?
 5 Will you phone her, or wait till she rings back?

13.9B Questions about alternatives (2): 'Did you take it, or didn't you?'
1a Do you like fish, or don't you?
 b Do you or don't you like fish?
 c Do you like fish, or not?
2a Can you help me, or can't you?
 b Can you or can't you help me?
 c Can you help me, or not?
3a Have you sent a card, or haven't you?
 b Have you or haven't you sent a card?
 c Have you sent a card, or not?
4a Will you phone the plumber, or won't you?
 b Will you or won't you phone the plumber?
 c Will you phone the plumber, or not?

13.9C Emphatic questions with 'ever', etc.
1 Who ever   2 Why ever   3 When ever
4 What ever   5 Where ever   6 How ever
7 How ever
These answers could also be expressed with *Who on earth*, etc.

13.9D Context
Possible answers
1 What ever   2 What ever/on earth   3 whenever
4 'Have you broken down, or run out of petrol?'
5 'Have you tried to start it, or not?'   6 have you or haven't you?

14 Conditional sentences

14.1 Type 1 conditionals

14.1A Type 1 conditionals, basic uses: 'If the weather clears, we'll go for a walk'
1 is ... will go/will be going   2 have ... will finish
3 rains ... will not (won't) be able to   4 is leaving ...
will ask   5 has driven ... will be   6 have been
working ... will probably need   7 can't finish ... will try
8 is picked ... will be boasting   9 have forgotten ... will
have gone   10 stay ... will have been living

14.1B 'If' + present + modal: 'If it's fine tomorrow, we may go for a swim'
Possible answers
1 are ... ought to   2 finish ... could   3 has ... must
4 is not coming ... might   5 has only just
arrived ... may   6 have been waiting ... must
7 can't go ... should

14.1C 'If + should' instead of 'if + present'
1 If you *should see* him ...   2 If she *should ask* you ...
3 If he *should phone* ...   4 If the temperature
should fall ... 5 If you *should receive* ...   6 If you
should go out ...

14.1D Imperative + 'and/or' + clause: 'Fail to pay and ... '
1 *Ask me* nicely *and* I'll ...
2 *Crash* my car *and* I'll ...
3 *Work* late tonight *and* ...
4 *Hurry, or* you'll ...
5 *Take* a taxi, *or* you'll ...
6 *Stop* shouting, *or* I'll ...

14.1E Context
1 is   2 should be   3 might be   4 must be   5 Go

14.2 Type 2 conditionals

14.2A Type 2 conditionals, basic uses: 'If you went by train, you would ...'
1 If I *had* a spare ticket, I *could/would take* you to the
   concert.
2 If she *didn't drink* too/so much coffee, she *would
   feel* calm(er).
3 If he *could type*, he *would be able* to operate a
   computer.
4 If they *understood* (or *they could understand*) the
   problem, they *would find* a solution.
5 If he *didn't sit around* too/so much, he *would be*
   fit(ter).

14.2B 'If + were/was' + 'would': 'If I were you, I would ...'
Possible answers
1 *If she were in your position*, she *would be able to*
   advise you.
2 If I *wasn't/weren't* in a hurry, I *would stay* to dinner.
3 If he *were* a millionaire, he *would(n't)* buy you a
   palace.
4 If the weather *was/were* sunny, we *wouldn't* stay
   indoors.
5 If I *was/were* fit, I *would* go climbing.
   Or: If I *wasn't/weren't* fit, I *wouldn't go* climbing.

14.2C 'If' + past + modal: 'If he knew the facts, he might ...'
Possible answers
1 were (or was) ... could give   2 failed ... ought
to think   3 could play ... could help   4 had ... might
be able to   5 could have ... might improve
6 ran ... could be   7 went ... ought to visit
8 borrowed ... ought to return   9 wanted ... could ask

14.2D Context
1 would we be doing   2 was/were not shining
3 we wouldn't be lying   4 would we do/would
we be doing   5 we were   6 we were rich   7 could
travel   8 we had   9 could drive   10 we were
11 We would return   12 would put out/would be
putting out   13 would prepare/would be preparing
14 would   15 we owned   16 we would also have
17 we had   18 we could swim   19 we were   20 we
could lie/we could be lying

14.3 Type 3 conditionals

14.3A Type 3 conditionals, basic uses: 'If you had gone by train, ...'
Possible answers
1 If John *hadn't eaten* too/so much birthday cake, he
   wouldn't have been sick.
2 If we *hadn't run out of* money, we *wouldn't have
   come home* from our holiday early.
3 If the fire brigade *hadn't come* immediately, the
   house *would have burnt down*.
4 If the men *hadn't been wearing* protective clothing,
   they *wouldn't have all been* safe.
5 If I *had been watching* the road, I *wouldn't have
   had* an accident.
6 If it *hadn't been* so hot, I *wouldn't have been
   sweating*.
7 If my father *had earned more* money, life *would
   have been* easy/easier for us.
8 If I *had enjoyed* school, I *would have done better*.

14.3B 'If I had been you/If I had been in your position'
Possible answers
1 *If I had been* Marie, I *wouldn't have paid* £200 for a/that dress.
2 *If I had been* Franz, I *would have taken* that job.
3 *If I had been in Ali's position,* I *would have* studied more.
4 *If I had been* Sandra, I *wouldn't have walked* to work in the rain.

14.3C 'If' + past perfect + modal: 'If he had known the facts, he might have ...'
Possible answers
1 had managed ... could have driven   2 had known ... could have visited   3 had not wanted ... might have missed   4 had asked ... might have helped
5 had been ... could have stayed   6 might have been ... hadn't known   7 might have made ... had not read
8 could have had ... had not been   9 had fastened ... mightn't have been   10 mightn't have heard ... hadn't turned on   11 could have seen ... might have laughed   12 had told ... could have lent
13 could have saved ... had known   14 might have played ... had had

14.3D Context
1 had been   2 would/could/might have killed
3 had been driving   4 wouldn't have been
5 had known   6 would have kept   7 had known
8 wouldn't have been driving   9 hadn't been
10 would/might/could be (*or:* would/might/could have been)

14.4 Mixed conditionals; 'unless/if ... not', etc.

14.4A Mixed tenses in conditional sentences
Possible answers
1 If I were you ... I would have checked   2 If you are so hungry, you shouldn't have missed   3 If he didn't catch ... he won't arrive   4 He will be feeling ... if he played   5 If the snake bite had been poisonous, you'd feel   6 If I were ... I would have answered

14.4B 'If not' and 'unless'

Write 1:
The following sentences need ticks: 1, 2 and 5.

Write 2:
1 Unless you tell me/If you don't tell me   2 if he didn't have   3 – unless we had broken
4 Unless management and unions become/If union and management do not become   5 unless I get held up/if I don't get held up   6 Unless we have/If we

don't have   7 If you hadn't warned

14.4C Conjunctions we can sometimes use in place of 'if'
1 *Even if you gave me $10,000*, I still wouldn't go down a coal mine.
2 I'll lend you my book *on (the) condition (that) you let* me *have it back by Monday*.
3 *Providing (that) you look after it,* I'll let you keep my bicycle till the weekend.
4 *So long as you don't tell anyone else,* I'll tell you what happened.
5 *Assuming (that) it's a holiday on Monday*, we can drive to the seaside.
6 The children were never scolded, *so long as they did what they were told*.

14.4D Context
1 are   2 (will) live   3 would/should have died
(*or:* might/could have died)   4 will feel   5 will be
6 could live   7 would you do   8 would have eaten
9 could change/could have changed   10 would you change/would you have changed   11 had known
12 would have looked after

15 Direct and indirect speech

15.1 Direct speech

15.1A Quotation marks and other punctuation marks
1 'John's in a hurry.'
2 'Have you been out?'
3 'Where are my glasses?'
4 'What a surprise!'
5 'How are you?'
6 'It's unbelievable!'
7 'There's someone at the door.'
8 'What a noise!'
9 'When did you arrive?'
10 'Tell me what happened.'
11 'Don't shout at me!'
12 'Have a cup of coffee.'
13 'How do you like your coffee?'
14 'Have you met Jean?'
15 'Keep quiet!'
16 'Stop!'
17 'Are you all right?'
18 'I'm waiting for a bus.'
19 'Here's a letter for you.'
20 'Haven't we met before?'
Note: double quotation marks (" ... ") can, of course, also be used.

15.1B Quotation marks and 'reporting verbs'

1 'Where do you come from?' John asked.
2 'It's here,' Bill said.
3 'I've got a good idea, (or !)' Mark said.
4 'Is it something,' she asked, 'that we all ought to know?'
5 'As I was leaving,' he explained, 'I heard someone shout.'
6 'Don't shout at me!' he cried.
7 John said, 'We're late.'
8 'We're late,' John said.
9 'What's the time?' Andrew asked.
10 Bill said, 'I'm hungry.'
11 'What is it?' Jill asked.
12 'You are stupid sometimes!' she said.
13 'Where is he?' Tom asked.
14 'What a surprise!' she exclaimed.
15 'Is there anyone in?' she inquired.
16 'Which way did they go?' he asked.
17 Tom said, 'She's ill.'
18 'She's ill,' Tom said.
Note: double quotation marks can also be used.

15.1C 'Quote within a quote'

1 'As I was leaving,' he explained, 'someone shouted, "Fire!".'
2 'Please don't keep asking me, "What's the time?"!' Jim said crossly.
3 'Have you read "Who's Afraid of Virginia Woolf?"?' my teacher asked.
4 'What do you mean, "Have you lost your way?"?' the stranger asked me.
5 Where are they now, he wondered.
Note: double quotation marks can also be used for single and vice versa.

15.1D Context

1 'It's all lies!' Boyle cried.
2 'You think so?' Inspector Wiley asked mildly.
3 'Think so? I know it!' Boyle answered sharply.
4 'And no doubt,' the inspector continued, 'you can prove it. Where were you on Saturday night, the night of the robbery?'
5 'I was at the Roxy with my girlfriend,' Boyle replied. 'We saw "Gone with the Wind". The film lasted four hours.'
6 'But,' cried the inspector, 'the Roxy was closed all last weekend!'
Note: Double quotation marks can also be used for single and vice versa.

15.2 'Say', 'tell' and 'ask'

15.2A 'Say', 'tell' and 'ask'

1 says 2 tells 3 ask 4 asked 5 said 6 said
7 asked 8 said 9 told 10 asked 11 asked
12 ask 13 tell 14 asked 15 tell 16 says 17 told
18 said 19 tells 20 ask

15.2B Fixed expressions with 'say', 'tell' and 'ask'

1 'I told you so' 2 Ask the price 3 Say no more
4 ask for 5 Say nothing 6 says so 7 tell the time
8 tell a lie

15.2C Indirect statements with the reporting verb in the present

1 she's going to America for six months.
2 they went to Rhodes last year.
3 she's not (or she isn't) feeling well.
4 she'll look at your work in a minute.
5 she's typed those letters.
6 we must investigate this case.
7 the last strike did no one any good.
8 turn off the electricity at the mains.
9 you have to rub down the walls.
10 she's good at flower arranging.

15.2D Context

1 are always saying 2 asked 3 said 4 told
5 says 6 asked 7 say 8 said 9 says 10 told
11 asked (or said) 12 said 13 told

15.3 Indirect statements with tense changes

15.3A Common indirect speech forms

1 Mac said *(that) he needed a holiday.*
2 Sue said *(that) she wasn't wasting her time.*
3 Tom said *(that) he had had* (or *he'd had*) *some good news.*
4 Pam said *(that) she had* (or *she'd*) *been sleeping.*
5 Lou said *(that) (s)he went* (or *had gone*) *home early.*
6 Jan said *(that) (s)he was* (or *had been*) *waiting for me/us.*
7 Joe said *(that) he had* (or *he'd*) *eaten earlier.*
8 Pat said *(that) (s)he had* (or *(s)he'd*) *been waiting for me/us.*
9 Tim said *(that) he would* (or *he'd*) *see me/us later.*
10 Dot said *(that) she could speak French.*
11 Kim said *(that) (s)he might arrive later.*
12 Ron said *(that) he would* (or *he'd*) *speak to him.*
13 Meg asked whether *she should speak to him.*
14 Ted said *(that) he could help me/us.*
15 Ann said *(that) she might see him.*
16 Jim said *(that) he would* (or *he'd*) *enjoy that.*
17 Sam said *(that) he must have fainted.*

15.3A (continued)

18 Don said *(that) he couldn't have said that.*
19 Ned said *(that) he needn't have gone there.*
20 Lyn said *(that) she ought to have helped her.*
21 Lee said *(that) (s)he should go to the dentist's.*
22 Dan said *(that) if he were me he would get legal advice.*
23 Paul said *(that) he must* (or *had to*) *catch an early train.*
24 Jill said *(that) she must* (or *had to*) *speak to me/us.*
25 Bill said *(that) he must* (or *would have to*) *leave tomorrow.*
26 Jane said *(that) she must* (or *would have to*) *work till late.*
27 Phil said *(that) John must be a fool.*
28 Jean said *(that) she mustn't* (or *couldn't*) *eat meat.*
29 Jeff said *(that) they mustn't* (or *couldn't*) *give up.*

15.3B Pronoun and adverb changes in indirect speech
No exercise here.

15.3C Context
1 Dr Grey said *(that) she had conducted a number of tests.*
2 She told me *(that) she must* (or *had to/would have to*) *put me on a very strict diet.*
3 She said *(that) I was putting on a lot of weight.*
4 She added *(that) I had gained 5.5 kilos in six months.*
5 She reminded me *(that) I (had) gained 10 kilos last year/the year before.*
6 She told me *(that) I would get very fat if I went on like this/that.*
7 She said *(that) I should eat very little.*
8 I said nervously *(that) I would have to live on nuts and water.*
9 She said *(that) I could live on nuts and water without the nuts.*

15.4 Indirect questions with tense changes

15.4A Indirect Yes/No questions: 'He asked me if I was ready'
1 if/whether we were hungry.
2 if/whether I was enjoying myself.
3 if/whether I (or we) always went to church on Sunday.
4 if/whether I had seen John recently.
5 if/whether Debbie had been working (t)here long.
6 if/whether I (or we) had studied hard for the exam.
7 if/whether Ted and Alice would be at the party.
8 if/whether I (or we) would be coming to the concert or not.
9 if/whether I liked Italian food.
10 if/whether I liked (or we liked) Italian food.

15.4B Indirect question-word questions: 'He asked me why I went there'
1 what the weather was like.
2 what Frank did for a living.
3 why Maria was crying.
4 what kind of holiday Marco had had.
5 how long we had both been living (t)here.
6 where they had gone last week (or the week before).
7 who I had been looking for.
8 when lunch would be ready.
9 which countries John would be visiting.
10 how I could solve the problem.

15.4C Indirect subject-questions
1 who was next.
2 what made (or makes) a noise like that.
3 which of us was waiting to see him next.
4 whose composition we hadn't heard yet.
5 who left this bag here.
6 what caused the accident?
7 which newspaper carried the article.
8 whose painting will win the competition.
9 which firms have won prizes for exports.
10 which number could/can be divided by three.

15.4D Context
1 was   2 what the problem was   3 was/had been
4 kept/had kept/had been keeping
5 hadn't/hadn't been   6 didn't keep/hadn't kept/hadn't been keeping   7 was/had been   8 I spent/had spent/had been spending   9 told   10 went/had gone/had been going   11 did not have/had not had   12 told
13 was/had been   14 smoked   15 smoked
16 took/had taken/had been taking   17 did not have/hadn't had

15.5 Uses of the *to*-infinitive in indirect speech

15.5A Reporting the imperative: 'He reminded me to post the letter'
1 I *told him to wait for me.*
2 She *advised him to go on holiday when the weather got* (or *gets*) *warmer.*
3 She *warned them to keep out of this* (or *that*) *room at all times.*
4 He *reminded me to post those letters.*
5 He *asked them not to go into his study.*
6 I *told him not to wait for me.*
7 She *advised him not to go on holiday yet.*
8 She *warned them never to enter this* (or *that*) *room.*

15.5B Offers, suggestions, requests for advice: 'He asked if he should ...'
1 ... *if/whether she should fax* the information to them.
 ... *whether to fax* the information to them.
2 ... *if/whether he should leave* a message for her.
 ... *whether to leave* a message for her.
3 ... *if/whether she should heat* the food for him.
 ... *whether to heat* the food for him.
4 ... *if/whether he should phone* him now.
 ... *whether to phone* him now
5 ... *if/whether she should invite* them to dinner.
 ... *whether to invite* them to dinner.

15.5C Requests for advice with question-words: 'He wanted to know how ...'
1 ... *when she should be* at the station.
 ... *when to be* at the station.
2 ... *where they should have their* meeting.
 ... *where to have* their meeting.
3 ... *which he should choose.*
 ... *which to choose.*
4 ... *who(m) she should ask.*
 ... *who(m) to ask.*
5 ... *what he should do.*
 ... *what to do.*
6 ... *why she should pay* this bill.
7 ... *whose car he should borrow.*
 ... *whose car to borrow.*
8 ... *why she should be* punished.

15.5D Context
1 what to do/what they should do   2 advised them to shovel   3 told them not to leave   4 how to get rid/ how we should get rid   5 what to do/what we should do

15.6 When we use indirect speech

15.6A Interpreting direct speech
Possible answers
1 Diana suggested (that) we (should) go sailing.
2 Tom told Jennifer (that) she had just won a lottery. She was amazed.
3 Gillian agreed with Frank when he observed that more money should be spent on education.
4 John told Jenny (that) he didn't think she should take up wind-surfing at her age. She disagreed, and said (that) she felt it was (*or* is) a sport that would suit all ages. When John pointed out that it required (*or* requires) great physical strength, Jenny asked, rather indignantly, who (had) told him she was short of that.

5 Billy's mother warned him not to go too near the lions' cage, but Billy protested that he wanted to see the lions close up. When his mother asked him if this wasn't close enough, he replied that it wasn't. She told him that she was sorry, but ordered him not to go any closer. When he continued to insist that he wanted to, she repeated the order.
6 Dr Grey told Mrs Flynn that she really must keep to her diet if she was serious about losing weight. When Dr Grey asked her if she had been keeping to it, she hesitated and muttered something in reply. After Dr Grey had repeated her question, Mrs Flynn confessed that she had occasionally had a bit extra. When asked to explain what she meant, she reluctantly admitted that she meant 'a cream cake or two'.
7 When Sandra asked Sam if/whether he (had) enjoyed the film, he replied that he wasn't sure. Sandra said she thought Gloria Gleam's performance had been fantastic, but Sam hadn't liked it at all. Sandra was surprised to hear this.

15.6B Context
1 told   2 ... are/were   3 me   4 is/was   5 leave/left
6 advised   7 not to make   8 said   9 went
10 (had) recently checked out   11 (had) objected
12 was   13 was leaving   14 told
15 said/protested, etc.   16 said/pointed out, etc.
17 was/is

16 The infinitive and the '-ing' form

16.1 The bare infinitive and the *to*-infinitive

16.1A Forms of the infinitive
1 leave   2 be studying   3 have done
4 have been waiting   5 be sent   6 have been done

16.1B 'Let', 'make', 'would rather/sooner' and 'had better'
1 go   2 not stay/Don't let's stay   3 go out
4 go/Let's not go   5 be   6 post   7 wear
8 clear up   9 look   10 to scrub   11 go ... do
12 not have   13 stay   14 not say   15 go

16.1C The infinitive with or without 'to' after 'help' and 'know'
1 *helped (me) (to) find* this book.
2 *(me) (to) fill in* this job application form?
3 *help you not to worry* so much.
4 *is known to be* a very generous man.
5 *to be* a ruthless businessman.
6 *known her (to) be* on time.

16.1D Context

1 made to wear   2 let us wear   3 made us change
4 (to) be   5 made me suffer   6 'Let's expand
7 made the shoes expand   8 helped me (to) get

16.2 The bare infinitive or the '-ing' form; the to-infinitive

16.2A Verbs of perception: 'Watch him draw/drawing'

1 *her cross* the road.
2 *her crossing* the road.
3 *something burning*.
4 *sing* a song.
5 *her shouting* at the children.
6 *waiting* near the bank.

16.2B 'Have' + object: 'Have the next patient come in'

1 bring   2 drawing   3 know   4 believe   5 ringing
6 laughing   7 playing   8 look at   9 marching
10 happen (or happening)

16.2C '(Not) to', 'so as (not) to', 'in order (not) to'

1 to do/in order to do/so as to do   2 so as not to/in
order not to splash   3 to sit   4 to see   5 to find
6 never to return   7 to go   8 to have been   9 to see
10 to have forgotten   11 not to feed   12 didn't tell us
to feed

16.2D Context

1 running   2 bring   3 not to let   4 complaining
5 race/racing   6 disappear/disappearing
7 not to leave   8 to find

16.3 Verb (+ noun/pronoun) + to-infinitive

16.3A 'He can't afford to buy it'

1 He *can't afford to buy* a car.
2 I *failed to pass* my driving test.
3 He's *offering to pay for* all of us.
4 Can you *manage to move* the desk on your own?
5 He's just *applied to join* the army.
6 I *refuse to apologize* to her.

16.3B 'I want (you) to speak to him'

Possible answers
1 you to speak to him.
2 her parents to pay.
3 you to write to them.
4 anyone to know about it.
5 you to listen to me?
6 two people to help me.
7 help (us) (to) move it.

16.3C 'He advised me to take out a loan'

1 me to take out a loan.
2 her to peel the potatoes.
3 us to work hard.
4 the soldiers to fire.
5 you to apply for free travel.
6 the public not to approach this man.
7 my wife and me to play tennis.

16.3D 'I know him to be an honest man'

1 People *know him to be* an honest man.
2 I *imagine him to work* very hard.
3 I *believe her to be* guilty.
4 I *found the job to be* too difficult.
5 We *discovered the claim to be* false.
6 I *know her to have* an interest in the company.

16.3E 'I agreed to accept their offer'

1 I *agreed to accept* the offer.
2 I *hope to succeed*.
3 I *expect to hear* from you.
4 He *claimed to have met* me.
5 I *arranged to be* there.
6 She *pretended not to know* me.

16.3F Context

1 wanted me to get rid of   2 failed to move
3 advised me to use   4 considered this to be
5 agreed to try   6 managed to get   7 proved to be
8 what to do   9 couldn't bear to shoot   10 took six of
us an hour to get

16.4 Adjectives and nouns + to-infinitive

16.4A Adjective + 'to': 'It was kind (of him) to help us'

1 He was *foolish to leave* the firm.
2 You would be *stupid not to ask for* more money.
3 Would *you be so good as to ring* me later?
4 Would you *be good enough to open* the window?
5 It was *clever of him to work out* (or *to have worked out*) the answer.
6 It's *silly of them not to take any part in local life*.
7 It would *look rude to refuse* their invitation.
8 Wasn't it *good of her to work* overtime?
9 He's eager *to help us in any way he can*.
10 I was *careful not to offend* them.

16.4B Adjectives with 'too/enough': 'too weak/not strong enough to'

1a I'm *not strong enough to* lift it.
 b I'm *too weak to* lift it.
2a I'm *not rich enough to afford* one.
 b I'm *too poor to afford* one.
3a She *isn't old enough to drive* a car.
 b She's *too young to drive* a car.
4a I *wasn't interested enough to watch* the film.
 b I was *too bored* (or e.g. *uninterested*) *to watch* the film.
5a The pie *isn't cool enough to eat.*
 b The pie is *too hot to eat.*
6a The film *wasn't interesting* (or e.g. *exciting*) *enough to watch.*
 b The film was *too boring to watch.*

16.4C Noun + *to*-infinitive: 'My decision to wait was wise'

1 My *decision to wait* was wise.
2 His *refusal to help* surprised us.
3 Her *failure to get into college* disappointed her parents.
4 It's a *pleasure to be* with you.
5 Their *eagerness to help* pleased me.
6 My *determination to pass the test* helped me.
7 My *willingness to co-operate* was appreciated.

16.4D Context

1 to see   **2** to see   **3** to move   **4** as to help me
5 to help   **6** to please   **7** to have disturbed
8 to run away   **9** to give   **10** to send

16.5 The '-ing' form

16.5A Basic information about the '-ing' form

A1 The gerund as an uncountable noun in general statements

1 Dancing   **2** Being   **3** Not being   **4** riding
5 reading   **6** Driving   **7** Not being   **8** Running
9 cycling   **10** Acting

A2 The gerund as an uncountable noun with 'some', 'a lot of', 'a little', etc.

1 reading   **2** ironing   **3** shopping   **4** swimming
5 regretting   **6** shouting   **7** fighting   **8** singing
9 encouraging   **10** gardening

A3 The gerund as an uncountable noun after prepositions

1 cutting   **2** digging   **3** boxing   **4** sleeping
5 making   **6** computing   **7** gardening   **8** arguing
9 retiring   **10** complaining

A4 The gerund as an uncountable noun after adjectives and possessives

1 thinking   **2** thinking   **3** refusing   **4** not knowing
5 violin playing   **6** cooking   **7** training   **8** shouting
9 singing   **10** breathing

A5 The gerund as an uncountable noun after 'no' in prohibitions

1 parking   **2** camping   **3** waiting   **4** smoking
5 trespassing   **6** fishing

A6 The gerund as a countable noun in the singular and plural

1 a painting   **2** paintings   **3** A Leonardo drawing
4 Leonardo drawings   **5** a new recording
6 a banging   **7** a ringing   **8** recordings   **9** a turning
10 turnings

A7 The gerund after 'the', 'this' and 'these'

1 cooking   **2** shopping   **3** burning   **4** writing
5 drawings   **6** turning   **7** making   **8** recording
9 paintings   **10** recordings

A8 The gerund followed by an object

1 repairing   **2** Eating   **3** Running   **4** doing   **5** giving
6 Digging   **7** changing   **8** Making   **9** making
10 making

A9 Perfect gerund forms, active

1 having disturbed   **2** having taken   **3** having lost
4 your having helped   **5** having worked

A10 Perfect gerund forms, passive

1 his having been fired   **2** his having been promoted
3 having been dismissed   **4** having been found out
5 having been posted

16.5B Context

1 cooking   **2** eating   **3** Working   **4** sitting
5 smoking   **6** eating   **7** smoking   **8** breathing
9 Cultivating   **10** exporting   **11** flavouring
12 adding   **13** shopping   **14** using   **15** having eaten
16 Being   **17** living

16.6 Verb + the '-ing' form

16.6A 'I deny taking it'

Possible answers
1 making   **2** living   **3** being questioned   **4** taking
5 having missed   **6** fishing ... fishing   **7** cleaning
8 mending

16.6B 'Start him working'

1f   **2**c   **3**b   **4**d   **5**a   **6**e   **7**h   **8**g

16.6C 'We appreciate your helping us'
1 f **2** b **3** d **4** e **5** a **6** c

16.6D 'I can't imagine my mother('s) approving'
Possible answers
1 I can't excuse *her not answering* our invitation.
2 You must pardon *my/me not getting up.*
3 Would you mind *Jane/Jane's practising* in the room next to yours?
4 I can't bear *him/his whistling* when I'm trying to concentrate.
5 They can't prevent *us/our escaping.*
6 Please forgive *Jim/Jim's arriving* so late.
7 I really miss *you/your bringing* me breakfast in bed.
8 Fancy *you/your meeting* Miss Smithers!

16.6E Context
1 flying **2** letting **3** you flying **4** travelling
5 learning **6** flying **7** doing **8** me (or my) asking
9 your (or you) flying? **10** anyone (or anyone's) disapproving

16.7 Adjectives, nouns and prepositions + '-ing'

16.7A Adjectives + '-ing' form (gerund) or *to*-infinitive
We can use *-ing* or the *to*-infinitive in all these sentences:
1 finding/to find **2** telling/to tell **3** being told/ to be told **4** finding/to find **5** helping/to help
6 driving/to drive **7** finding/to find **8** arranging/ to arrange

16.7B Adjective + '-ing' form (participle)
1 John gets *bored watching* TV all the time.
2 Sylvia is *frantic getting* ready for the wedding.
3 I got *tired waiting* so long for an answer.
4 Jane's *occupied making* lists.
5 We're *busy decorating* our house.

16.7C Common expressions followed by '-ing'
1 It's no good complaining **2** It's just not worth worrying **3** There's no point in trying
4 What's the use of apologizing? **5** There's nothing worse than owing

16.7D Preposition + '-ing'

D1 Preposition + '-ing'
1 paying **2** shouting **3** pulling **4** trying

D2 Adjective + preposition + '-ing'
1 acting **2** playing **3** complaining **4** sailing
5 riding **6** disturbing **7** sewing **8** missing
9 finding **10** understanding

D3 Verb + preposition + '-ing'
1 doing **2** working **3** stealing **4** disturbing
5 passing **6** trying **7** entering **8** entering
9 helping **10** interrupting **11** losing **12** stealing
13 succeeding **14** seeing **15** getting **16** asking

16.7E The '-ing' form after 'to' as a preposition
1 I'm *used to doing* all my own shopping.
2 I'm *accustomed to living* on my own.
3 I *object to being kept* waiting.
4 I *look forward to seeing* you soon.
5 He's *resorted to writing* begging letters.
6 I'm *resigned to being criticized.*

16.7F Context
1 to appreciate/appreciating **2** playing
3 playing **4** playing **5** whispering **6** finding
7 sitting **8** sitting **9** rattling

16.8 The *to*-infinitive or the '-ing' form?

16.8A Verb + *to*-infinitive or '-ing': no change in meaning: 'begin to read/reading'
1 to work/working **2** to think **3** to talk/talking
4 to eat/eating **5** to go/going **6** to see/seeing
7 to play/playing **8** to tell/telling **9** to understand

16.8B Verb + *to*- or '-ing': some changes in meaning: 'I love to read/reading'
1 watching/to watch (same meaning)
2 waiting (in general) is preferable **3** to tell
4 waiting **5** eating ... eating **6** to have **7** to come

16.8C Verb + *to*- or '-ing': different meanings: 'remember to post/posting'
1a visiting **1b** to lock **1c** to phone **2a** being
2b to find out **2c** to go **3a** to stop **3b** drinking
4a to look **4b** talking **5a** dancing **5b** to take
6a to tell **6b** staying

16.8D Context
1 delivering **2** pushing **3** to push **4** pushing
5 having **6** opening **7** using